Mark Bando

Vanguard of the Crusade

The 101st Airborne Division in World War II

HEIMDAL

Texts: Mark Bando

Conception et realisation: Heimdal

Layout: Harald Mourreau

Follow-up of realization: Georges Bernage

Follow-up of fabrication : Ghislain Cheguillaume

DEDICATION
To the Memory of Albert A. Krochka
501st Regimental and later 101st Divisional Photographer

Editions Heimdal
Damigny - BP 61350 - 14406 BAYEUX Cedex
Tél. : 02.31.51.68.68 - Fax : 02.31.51.68.60 - E-mail : editions.heimdal@wanadoo.fr
Site internet : *www.editionsheimdal.fr*

ISBN 978-2-84048-338-0

Foreword

It is a privilege for me to publish this new edition of *Vanguard of the Crusade*. As a Norman publisher, I feel it is very important to bring again to the readers this impressive work of Mark Bando. This work was accomplished by interviewing a thousand veterans from the 101st Airborne Division.

I am also happy to publish a French edition of the book, for the first time.

Georges Bernage, Historian and Publisher
Damigny, Normandy, 23 May 2012

Contents

Vanguard of the Crusade
The 101st Airborne Division in World War II

Shortly before D-day, orders originated at division level forbidding the invading troopers from keeping a diary, taking souvenirs, or using a camera. There may be some written evidence of these orders, but they were passed down the ranks verbally, until every private in the division was advised. There were, no doubt, several reasons 'behind this order, and some are obvious. The diary ban was, no doubt, an attempt to prevent the enemy from gaining information through captured written records. The ban on souvenirs was obviously to protect any captured trooper from retaliation, should he be found in possession of German items. The ban on cameras must have been also partially inspired by the same reason as the diary ban to deprive the enemy of potentially useful information that could contribute to intelligence.

There must have been other reasons as well. Any combat NCO or officer must have feared a diminished battle potential should any of the men in his command have been snapping photos instead of firing their weapons during actual combat. This fear was largely unfounded. As you will see, the troopers who snapped the pictures in this work did it during lulls in the action or immediately after the shooting subsided. The instinct to survive is strong enough to make common sense prevail.

Today, many years later, it is easy to state that the camera ban was unnecessary, but we are looking from a different perspective than the Allied leaders possessed in June 1944 when there was still the possibility that the invasion would fail and that the armada would be flung back into the Channel, leaving the survivors abandoned to their fate on the continent. There was even the remote chance of an eventual Axis victory, in which case the Allied minions would find themselves under scrutiny as possible war criminals. After all, the victorious powers ultimately define and decide what constitutes a war crime and who the guilty parties are.

After interviewing over 900 former World War II Screaming Eagles, I encountered only one who is still vociferously in favor of the rule against cameras in combat. He is former Lieutenant William J. Russo, leader of the Heavy Mortar Platoon, 2nd Battalion, 501st Parachute Infantry Regiment (501st) in Normandy. Russo said, "Somebody with *damn good reason* made that rule... It wasn't just pulled out of a hat. Everyone knows that a soldier with a camera is going to take pictures of dead enemy soldiers if he doesn't take pictures of anything else." As Russo thumbed through my album of Normandy photos, he remarked, "I wouldn't want to be any one of these guys if we lost the war... especially when the Germans start figuring out which units they got tangled up with..."

"You mean, they might use your photo as evidence that you are a war criminal?" I asked.

"You'd better believe it," he answered. "You bet!"

In his book, *The Last Battle,* Cornelius Ryan described an American officer who, in the last weeks of WWII, had a price on his head. German forces had deemed that this officer was a "war criminal." His crime was that he had killed too many German soldiers in open combat.

The point is that war crimes can be defined in a number of ways, and the vindictiveness of whatever regime reigns victorious at the end of hostilities will determine the question of who is culpable. Certainly—even beyond the normal carnage of combat—there were acts of brutality by both sides. These episodes are explained, if not justified, by the stress and confusion of the time, yet some troopers are haunted to the end by memories of a few spontaneous seconds of action.

We can be grateful now that a few individuals made the remarkable effort to lug a camera into Normandy, along with all their other equipment, somehow managing to record a small part of what they saw. The camera ban was difficult to enforce, once in the chaos of the invasion, and despite all the factors working against the amateur cameramen, some evidence of their efforts is preserved in this book.

A Letter from Lieutenant Morton

When World War II ended in 1945, Lieutenant James Morton of the 506th Parachute Infantry Regiment (506th) wrote a letter to his friend, Lieutenant Bill Reed, who had been taken prisoner earlier in the conflict. Part of the letter is a grim recitation of casualties in the Normandy campaign:

Dear Bill,

I am happy to know that you are alive... Since D-day, we have spoken of you and wondered... We were notified that you had been taken prisoner, but feared you might have been killed later in air raids or perhaps died in a horror camp. So many of our comrades have been killed. Have you heard the tragic story? Our 3rd Battalion officers were slaughtered during that fateful night when we invaded Normandy...

Lieutenant Colonel Wolverton was riddled by machine-gun fire shortly after he landed. His body was found near St. Come du Mont. Major Grant was killed, too. "Jeb" Holstun was shot dead as he ran atop the dike along the Douve River, picked off like a duck in a shooting gallery. All our company commanders were killed or missing. Van Antwerp dead in his harness, McKnight, Harwick, and you taken prisoner. Harwick escaped three days later...

Some of our paratroopers descended into a bivouac area of Russian cavalry, mercenaries in the employ of the Nazis. Our men never had a chance. They were butchered by knives, bayonets, and machine pistols as they struggled in their harnesses. Subsequently, I saw the scene of this carnage. It was terrible dead horses, Russians, and paratroopers sprawled everywhere. Several hundred of our troops died in this area...

Headquarters Company, 3rd Battalion suffered appalling losses. Littell was killed by a machine pistol on D-day morning as he tried vainly to hide from a German patrol. "Pop" Machen's body was found. I understand Dilburn was killed while trying to do the Pathfinders' job. Wedeking was shot through the wrist, and Barr got a bad face wound from grenade fragments...

The battalion enlisted staff was virtually wiped out. Sgt. Simmerall, Ross, and others were killed before daybreak. 1st Sgt. Shirley was killed. The company lost 101 of 176 men. Sgt. Robinson and most of the bazooka platoon met an unkind fate. There were only six survivors, two of whom were killed by a direct hit from a 105mm gun several weeks later…

Gerry Howard's plane was shot down; all were lost. Tom Meehan's plane exploded in midair, and K. A. Beatty was killed when his plane became a flaming torch…

Turner Chambliss was one of the first persons I encountered. I had broken my foot on an anti-parachute obstacle and couldn't get around very well. About four o'clock, Chambliss reached our objective. At daylight, he peered over the dike. A German sniper shot him through the throat and Chambliss died…

During our attack on St. Come du Mont, Lieutenant Colonel Turner studied the terrain from a vantage point atop a Sherman tank. A sniper shot him through the head. Captain Peters, "Eggie" Knott, Colt, Gross, Gunther, Lavenson, Mr. Hill, were among those killed in Normandy…

"Dixie" Howell had an eye shot out. M. O. Davis was badly hit. Windish was wounded in the ankle. Major Foster and Holmes were shot up…

During an attack southwest of Carentan…Christianson's shoulder was shattered by a rifle bullet and a slug from a machine pistol put Santarsiero out of action. We suffered heavy casualties that day, when our precipitous attack collided with an attack by *SS* troops. They called the scene "Bloody Gully." There were dead and wounded on every hand, blood-smeared men staggering and crawling out of the gully to our aid set-up. Raudstein, too, was hit here…

Cox, Ferebee, Rogers, McDowell [and] Tom Kennedy were among the wounded… We were withdrawn from Normandy in July… our battalion strength was reduced from 690 to 268 officers and men. Company I could muster only 49 men…

The above letter tells only part of the story. As the *506th Scrapbook* tells it:

You fought through Pouppeville, Vierville, Angoville au Plein, Saint-Come-du-Mont, and Carentan; and you piled up enemy dead until you gave up trying to figure ratios because an attacking force was supposed to lose more than the defenders, the Book said, yet there were the gray dead stacked like cord wood and only an occasional body dressed in tan.

As Ben "Chief" McIntosh of the 502nd Parachute Infantry Regiment (502nd) put it, "We went on sort of a rampage." Read on.

Airborne Photographers

Mike Musura *(left)* and Albert A. Krochka pose with their Speedgraphic camera in front of a European Eastman Kodak store. Musura started as regimental photographer of the 502nd PIR, and Krochka likewise for the 501st Unfortunately, the 506th PIR and 327th GIR were without designated regimental photographers. Because of the valuable photos they took in Normandy, they were elevated to the status of official divisional photographers and transferred to HQ/101st for the duration of the war. The author knew each of these men personally; Musura died in the early 1980s after working as a photographer for the *San Francisco Examiner*. Krochka died in early 1993. Where known, individual photos are credited to one or the other; many others, simply credited to US Army or Signal Corps, were actually shot by the above duo. We are deeply indebted to them both.

Origins

The 82nd Infantry Division was divided into two separate airborne divisions on 16 August 1942 at Camp Claiborne, Louisiana. General W. C. Lee, the first commanding general (CG) of the 101st Airborne Division, issued an order beginning with these words: "The 101st Airborne Division has no history, but it has a rendezvous with destiny. Like the early American pioneers whose invincible courage was the foundation stone of this nation, we have broken with the past and its traditions in order to establish our claim to the future."

Thus, the new 82nd and 101st briefly shared the premises at Camp Claiborne before being shipped to Fort Benning, Georgia, for parachute and glider training. From there they moved on to Fort Bragg, North Carolina, which would be their assigned station before departure for combat in the European Theatre.

The two new divisions, born of the same parent organization, were to become arch-rivals. Members at the time of the split were given the option of refusing parachute training. The Army, however, could order a soldier into any vehicle, so the glider troops were coerced into glider training without a refusal option. This was to remain a sore spot with the glider troops as the paratroopers received $50 extra per month as hazardous duty pay; the often-injured glider men did not. Although para and glider troops wore the same shoulder insignia, with the word "airborne" on a tab above, the paratroopers considered themselves a cut above. They jealously guarded their unique status symbols: brown jump boots and silver jump wings on their chests.

The 101st Airborne that arrived at Fort Bragg consisted of the 327th Glider Infantry Regiment (GIR); the 326th Airborne Engineer Battalion (AEB); Division Artillery and other artillery battalions, including the 81st Airborne Antiaircraft Battalion (AAAB), 321st Glider Field Artillery Battalion (GFAB), and 377th Parachute Field Artillery Battalion (PFAB); plus headquarters (HQ) personnel; Military Police (MPs); the 326th Medical Company; and assorted supply and support troops. Shortly thereafter, the 502nd was added as an official Table of Organization and Equipment (TO&E) element of the division. The 502nd under Colonel G. V. H. Moseley, had been activated as a battalion in 1941 and recently expanded to regimental stature. In July 1942, the 506th was added (by attachment) at Fort Bragg, under the leadership of Colonel Robert Sink.

Much later, the 501st under Colonel Howard R. "Jumpy" Johnson was attached to the division to bring it up to strength for the Normandy invasion. Each attached parachute infantry regiment had an approximate strength of 2,200 men. The 506th eventually became an integral element of the 101st Airborne Division. The 501st was a member by attachment only until its deactivation.

It is likely that the members of the 501st and 506th were in the best physical condition of any US troops because of torturous runs up and down the three-mile Currahee Mountain at Camp Toccoa and grueling encounters with its obstacle course. (Currahee is a Native American word that translates to "stands alone." The mountain and its name were adopted as

"Father of the Airborne"

General William C. Lee, of Dunn, North Carolina, was first commanding general of the 101st Airborne Division and known as the *"Father of the Airborne."* Lee was forced to relinquish his command when he suffered a heart attack before D-Day. *US Army Photo*

the official insignia and slogan of the 506th.) After basic training at Toccoa, 2nd Battalion of the 506th (2nd/506th) marched 118 miles, from Toccoa to Atlanta, Georgia, enroute to jump school at Fort Benning. The 3rd Battalion of the 506th (3rd/506th) went 132 miles from Atlanta to Benning. The 1st Battalion was allowed to ride to Benning by train.

The 501st followed the 506th in training at Toccoa, under the dynamic leadership of firebreathing Annapolis dropout Colonel Howard R. Johnson, whose mass pep rallies incited his "Geronimo" troopers into a peak of homicidal enthusiasm. There is no dispute that Johnson was one of the great motivators of all American troop leaders in WWII; even General Patton's "Blood and Guts" speeches were sometimes outdone by those of "Jumpy" Johnson.

The merciless training of the 501st and 506th continued in North Carolina on the sun-scorched sands of Camp Mackall and Fort Bragg. The 1943 war games were conducted here, and the games and training forged the survivors into veritable supermen. Morale was high in these units and men on forced marches carried extra equipment out of team spirit. Many saw black spots in front of their eyes and passed out due to heat prostration.

Mount Currahee

Mount Currahee at Camp Toccoa, Georgia, summer of 1942. This three-mile mountain was the forging ground for the earliest members of the 501st and 506th. Jim "Pee Wee" Martin of the 506th momentarily dropped out from the run to snap this photo of Company G heading back down as another company comes up. The 506th wore blue swimming trunks with a Currahee patch sewn to the front on morning runs. *Jim Martin.*

The obstacle course

Prospective paratroopers of the 506th PIR negotiate an obstacle on the course they designed at Camp Toccoa, Georgia, in 1942. An infiltration (confidence) course negotiated by some companies of the 506th required the men to crawl through hog innards while machineguns fired barely over their heads. *Bob Martin.*

250-Foot tower

"C" stage involved a drop from the 250 foot free tower; the chute canopy was held open by hoops. *Signal Corps*

The 101st Airborne shared Fort Bragg with the 82nd Airborne until the latter unit set sail for north Africa in April 1943. The 82nd would be the first US airborne division to see action (participating in the invasions of Sicily and Italy at Salerno) well before the 101st's combat debut at Normandy. Even before the 82nd's drop into Sicily, the 509th Parachute Battalion had made a combat jump into North Africa. This unit had been redesignated three times.

Ocean Voyage to the British Isles, 1943

Most of the 101st Airborne set sail in September 1943 aboard two ships, the *SS Strathnaver* and the *SS Samaria.* The troops sailed from Camp Shanks, New York. The *Strathnaver* broke down at St. Johns, Newfoundland, and was replaced by the *SS John Erickson,* which finished the job of transporting the 502nd, 377th PFAB, the 907th GFAB, the 326th AEB, and other miscellaneous units. The several weeks spent in Newfoundland qualified these troops for the American Theatre Campaign Medal.

"Trainasium"

The *"Trainasium"* or *"Plumber's nitemare"* was copied from a device in the German parachute school. By crawling through a prescribed course, it worked most muscles of the body to the fullest extent. The trainasium was eliminated as a training device before the war ended. *US Army.*

H/506th Troopers

When 2nd/506th marched from Toccoa to Atlanta, Georgia, they made it in 72 hours, beating the world's marching record previously held by a Japanese Army battalion. The Company H, 3rd Battalion men, shown above, marched 14 miles farther than 1st Battalion. Troopers shown, left to right, include John Purdie, Lou Vecchi, and Staff Sergeant Gerald McCullough. *Bob Martin.*

"Look out hitler! here we come!"

A gruesome-looking member of G/501st menaces an effigy of *Der Führer* on the streets of Schicklegruberburg in 1943. This training camp was a mock German city built near Camp Mackall, North Carolina, for combat maneuver exercises. *Urbank.*

Old Abe

An important aspect to the story of the WWII 101st Airborne is its shoulder insignia, a tribute to the Civil War mascot of the 8th Wisconsin Infantry Regiment, a real bald eagle named Old Abe. According to legend, Old Abe was tethered close to the 8th's colors and was carried into battle, during which it would fly forward from its perch, screaming defiance at the enemy and inspiring Union troops. Old Abe was wounded several times, and the Confederate General Price offered a reward for the killing of the bird.

The 101st Airborne now wore a bald eagle upon their shoulder patches and also obtained a new eagle mascot which they named "Young Abe." It is doubtful that any highranking member of a rival Airborne organization put a price on Young Abe's head, but the bird was discovered dead of unknown causes at Fort Bragg on 8 July 1943.

The division was on maneuvers in Tennessee when Young Abe died, and although there were accusations of skullduggery or poisoning by members of rival organizations (the prime suspects would have been members of the 82nd Airborne, but they had sailed for England several months prior to Abe's demise), there may be another explanation for the eagle's untimely passing. Winfield McCraw, a member of the 101st's Division Recon Platoon, sometimes cared for the bird, and thinks that Young Abe may have died due to an allergic reaction to some salt pork he was fed.

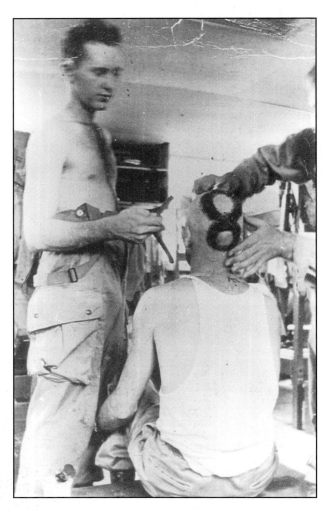

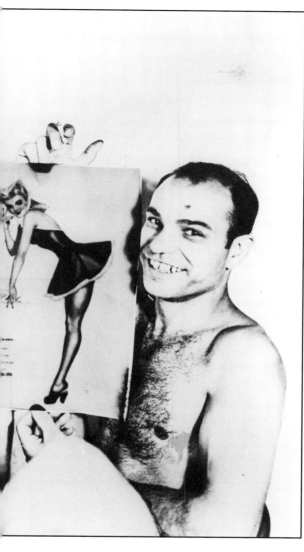

Colonel Howard R. "Jumpy" Johnson
The hard-bitten CO of the 501st PIR embodied and personified the very soul and spirit of his regiment. At unit assemblies, he would shout, "Who's the BEST?" "We are!" the troops would scream in reply. *Krochka*

Above: **What are we fighting for?**

Sergeant Frank Anness, D/506th, offers his answer to the famous question in this 1944 photo. Publications like the 506th Para Dice magazine followed this theme by printing photos of the sweet hearts and wives of Currahee troopers. Frank's example is less specific, but the general idea is the same. *Anness.*

Previous page, at the top: **Airborne Haircuts**

What began as a form of punishment for misconduct in the States, continued overseas as a form of pride. Left, the "8 Ball" haircut. This chronic offender had his hair styled by Claude Langston, D/501st. *Ritzler.*

Right, a trooper was given a Native American scalplock haircut as punishment for going AWOL, Camp Mackall, 1943. *Author's Photo.*

Previous page, below: **Playful Fellows**

Members of the 501st PIR at Camp Mackall, North Carolina, practice knife fighting with the trusty M-3 trench knife, commonly worn on the ankle by paratroopers. *Krochka.*

Previous page, opposite : **Strongman**

In an impressive strongman feat, Private James McHugh, B/501st (from Pennsylvania), hoists an unidentified buddy overhead at Camp Mackall in 1943. McHugh was noted as the strongest member of Company B and later proved to be one of the best combat men in the outfit as well. *Rich Harper.*

The 501st followed in January and sailed aboard the USAT (US Army Transport) George W. Goethals. They arrived in Glasgow, Scotland, and were attached to the 101st in England, an assignment that would last until after V-E Day.

L. Allen Hurd of Headquarters, 2nd Battalion, 501st, (HQ/2nd/501st) wrote a V-Mail letter to his parents during the *Goethals* voyage. Part of it reads:

"My sea voyage is almost over. The waves on this man's ocean are something to see. Huge, rolling mountains of water. We enlisted men are packed like sardines in the hold of the ship. Good place to store cargo… if the cargo isn't too fragile. To kill time I'm forced to read 10-year-old *National Geographic* magazines, which is just about rock bottom in the sphere of human activities."

Sea sickness and gastrointestinal disorders kept the medics and chaplains busy, dispensing bismuth and paregoric as cures. Craps games flourished and Father Sampson, the 501st's Catholic chaplain, later recalled the men often gambled while waiting in line to go to confession.

2 England

Despite complications on the ocean voyage, most of the division arrived in England in the fall of 1943. The 502nd was stationed in assorted types of tents and buildings, including Nissen huts, stables, and M34 pyramidal tents. Officers usually acquired manor houses or similar billets. Most of the 502nd was situated in and around Hungerford, at Chilton Foliat, and Denford.

The 509th Parachute Infantry Battalion had been stationed in the Chilton Foliat area before the 101st Airborne arrived and had established good relations with the locals. The 101st's Rigger Sections moved into the area and remained there until after the Battle of the Bulge.

Most of the 506th was stationed close by. The 2nd Battalion with HQ/1st Battalion and Companies A and B, were some distance away, at Aldbourne, with some troops living in horse stables. The regimental HQ was at Littlecote, Company C at Manor Park, and Service Company at Chilton Foliat. The 3rd Battalion was close by at Ramsbury. The billets overlapped into Wiltshire and Berkshire, two British counties.

Most of the other assorted divisional units were scattered around Berkshire County. The 907th GFAB with their 105mm howitzers were at Benham-Valence Park. The 326th Airborne Medical Company was at Donnington. The 101st Airborne HQ was located at Greenham Common. The 377th PFAB was at Wickham. The 327th GIR's glider troops were near Reading. The 81st AAAB was at Basildon Park, as was the 326th AEB.

In January 1944, the 501st landed in Glasgow, Scotland, and traveled by train south to Newbury. Arriving in the middle of the night, they were assigned one squad to each pyramidal tent, which the Corps of Engineers had set up before they arrived. Thick mud was everywhere and large concrete slabs had been laid as floors for each tent. The troops later devised a method of digging secret compartments for hiding swiped food, live ammo, and contraband under certain slabs.

The HQ/501st and 2nd/501st were at Newbury. The 1st/501st and 3rd/501st were stationed many miles away at Lambourne. Some of the troops lived in Nissen Huts. Other lived in brick stables.

There were a number of brawls and other mischief, mainly with the Air Corps, and many fines were assessed for poaching deer and blowing up of English trout with hand grenades in the local streams.

Above: **Louis Frey**
Frey, from New Orleans, Louisiana, a member of the 2/501st's S-2 Section, studies a map during training exercises in pre-D-day England. *Frey*

Opposite: **Major General Maxwell Davenport Taylor**
General Bill Lee, who had commanded the 101st Airborne from the start, suffered a heart attack in England on 5 February 1944. For a brief time, General Don Pratt, Lee's assistant, took command. Lee was retired after being sent back to the States on 9 April 1944. On 14 March, General Max Taylor, former artillery commander of the 82nd Airborne, took command of the 101st. A West Pointer, Taylor had already become legendary for his exploits in Italy, most notably a daring mission behind the lines in Rome. There, Taylor met with Marshal Badoglio to arrange the Italian capitulation. Before D-day, Taylor addressed his 101st troopers and told them to shout "Bill Lee!" instead of "Geronimo!" in honor of their former commander, on their first combat jump. *US Army*

Machismo in England

In a letter to the author dated 19 January 1991, Ray Hood, HQ/2nd/502nd, wrote:

We stood in line for meals, for movies, and for everything else. We had a sergeant whose pet hate was people who bucked the line and got in ahead of others.

On one occasion on a weekend, the battalion was standing in line waiting to see a show, and a corporal from one of the other companies got in ahead of the sergeant. He didn't say a word. He Sunday Punched the guy, floored him, then went to work with his boots. Nobody really blamed him for knocking the man on his ass, because bucking the line wasn't popular. But kicking the guy was too strong, and the sergeant was pulled off.

He was berserk, raving, and literally frothing at the mouth and he challenged the whole battalion. He meant it, too he wasn't blowing smoke.

Another corporal, a friend of the man the sergeant had kicked, stepped out of the crowd, and I still remember what he said, "I think I'll try you out sergeant, and see how you do against somebody who's ready for you." The sergeant started toward the corporal. The corporal raised his hand and he said, "Get your breath back before you start believe me, you don't want to start from behind."

As it was, everybody wanted to see the sergeant lose, but we were all disappointed when the O.D. [officer of the day] showed up and stopped it before it started.

Just Another Jump

Captain Cecil Simmons wrote the following short story, describing a late-afternoon practice jump in England. Due to typical adverse circumstances, including a pilot flying too fast and high winds on the drop zone, the jump became a hazardous event.

"Go."

With that command, the captain jumped out into the darkening cold of the prop wash. He knew when he jumped that the plane was going at least 20 mph too fast. He had the green light. He had his orders, jump on the green light. During the first three seconds, all

VIP visit
British Prime Minister Winston Churchill with Major General Maxwell Taylor troop the line with the colors of the 327th GIR.

of the ugly cuss words he could think of were hurled at the pilot of the ship that he had just left. There was a fierce blast of cold air tearing at his clothes. It almost threw his feet up over his head. Just as he began to wonder whether he better count, he got a jerk that nearly cut him in two. Almost at the same time, something hit him in the back of the head that made a "bong" on his helmet. Suddenly he saw all of the prettiest stars whirling around each other and he

Demonstration Jump, 23 March 1944

The 506th PIR, minus 1st Battalion, makes a demonstration jump for Churchill. He had reviewed 1st Battalion in a ground inspection that day.

Many have hailed British Prime Minister Winston S. Churchill as "The Man of the Century," although many revisionist historians disagree. Jack Womer of the Filthy 13 might be inclined to agree with them. *Krochka*

"Should I Have Shot Him?"

On a practice jump before D-day, two battalions of the 506th landed and assembled to impress a delegation of VIPs, including Prime Minister Winston Churchill, Supreme Commander Dwight D. Eisenhower, and Major General Maxwell D. Taylor.

Among those jumping was Jack Womer, a member of the 506th Demolitions Platoon. "I hated that jump," Womer later said, "because… what the hell are we jumping for?"

At the pre-jump briefing, the troops were instructed to camouflage themselves on the drop zone immediately after landing. The officers wanted a first class job to impress the Brass.

Womer landed in a large field, devoid of any possible cover, except for the large haystack at the edge of a road. He and another trooper decided to get in the hay to take shelter from a light rain that had started to fall.

The duo completely covered themselves with hay so they could not be seen and could barely see out. Not long afterwards, a staff car came up the road and stopped alongside them. In the staff car were Churchill, Eisenhower, and Taylor.

As Womer recalls, "Churchill gets out, walks over to the hay pile, and starts pissin' all over my boots. That's why I ask, do you think I should have shot him? I don't care if he's a prime minister or not, I don't want him pissin' on me! Well, I figured I can't drown, cause they only come up to my ankles, but they never did find out we were in that hay pile. Because with two generals behind him… you don't interfere with the Brass. And I tell everyone who hears this story, I was so close that I know Churchill needed to be circumcised… only me and his wife knew that."

British Paras

Two British paras from a battlaion of The Parachute Regiment assigned to the 6th Airborne Division in front of a brick stable, visiting B/501st. During February and March 1944, an exchange program sent several hundred American paras to trade places for two weeks with British paras. There was an exchange of ideas and training with weapons, jump equipment, and tactics. *Mishler*

thought, "How nice it would be to get some sleep, I'm sooo tired. Fight. Fight What? You're jumping. Oh, God, yes, open your eyes you damn fool."

He opened his eyes and shook his head as much as he could with a heavy helmet down over his face, pushed the helmet back on his head and looked up. Yes, there it was… outlined against the sky was the heavy silk that was holding him up. All in one piece, too… good deal. He had a headache, but knew that because of a poor body position, the connector links had hit him in the back of the head on the opening shock. He checked the ground and saw that he was drifting like the devil. Looking back and up, he saw the rest of his stick [planeload of paratroopers] drifting father apart. He checked the ground again and saw that he was going to hit pretty hard. He made a body turn so that he would come in frontwards, and saw that he was headed right for a cement crossroads. To hell with that. He let go of the risers and snapped himself back to his original position. He grabbed the two front risers that would slip him into

the wind and tend to make him slow up his drift towards the crossroads. But, at the same time, it would increase his rate of descent because of the partially-collapsed canopy. Between the devil and the deep blue sea, and only a matter of split seconds to decide… he took the rapid descent.

The ground came up and hit him with a crash and, with a grunt, he gave a backward tumble. The wind, which had increased to 22 mph, caught his chute and started to drag the skipper to the barbed-wire fence which surrounded the field and bordered the road. He got to his feet and ran around to the windward side of the chute to find the fence between him and the top of the chute. He cleared the fence in a leap, and slid into the ditch between it and the road. Part of the suspension lines were fouled on the barbed wire, and despite the wind, they kept the chute from dragging the officer any farther. He got up and collapsed the chute, and was taking his harness off when he heard a shout from above. He saw one of his men, who had jumped in one of the planes following his, headed for the same spot on the crossroads.

"Slip, boy, slip," he shouted. But the man was coming in so fast that he either didn't hear the skipper or was too occupied trying to rock his chute to prevent a ground oscillation, that he hit almost the exact

Soft Landing

A soft landing for a change. Pictured is William Baird of Waco, Texas. About 60 percent of the parachutes used on the Normandy drop had canopies of multishade green camouflage, as shown in this photo. The remainder were white. *Musura*

center of the crossroads. He hit with a dull thud and the wind started to take him off up the road. The Skipper ran over and collapsed the chute and took a look at the man who had not even tried to get up from the ground. He could see from the crazy angle of the man's left leg that it was broken… evidently a compound fracture, from the way the trousers tried to stick out in the wrong place.

Training Jump, 1944

Members of 3rd/502nd on a training problem in England, 1944. The trooper in the center wears a parachutist's first aid kit, which consisted of a cloth bag with tie strings containing sulfa powder, compress bandage, cloth tourniquet, and disposable oneshot morphine syrette. *Musura*

He removed the harness from the man, handed him his own weapon and ammunition and told him he would send the first aid man as soon as he saw one. "Meanwhile, take care of yourself." With that, the Skipper got his own gun out of the holster (an M-1 carbine in leg scabbard), adjusted his musette bag and harness, and took off for the assembly area where he would meet his men and prepare for the night attack. *En route* to the assembly area, he met a medic and told him where to find the man with the broken leg. When he arrived in his unit area, he was reminded of the crack on the back of his head by a headache. One of his officers asked how his jump was. "I landed just like a sad sack, as usual, but oh, that opening shock," he said, as he felt for the first time where the connector links had hit him. There

Swiped Tommy gun

Sergeant Ed Benecke took many of the photos in this book. Here he displays a Tommy gun swiped from a troop carrier plane. "We needed them more than they did," he said. *Benecke*

Healy and Spear
F/502nd members in the plane before a practice jump in England. Front, Healy and George Spear (KIA, Holland). Rear (left to right), Beszouska, Chiccoine, Floerchinger (KIA), Sergeant Manuel (standing), Tiedeman, Bennett, Sapinski. *D. Tiedeman*

was a large lump on the back of his head and he knew that the skin had been broken a little by the streak of blood on his fingers as he drew his hand across the wound.

As he received the reports from the jump casualties, he was surprised that there were not more men hurt in the high wind they had jumped in. The men were really getting rugged and they showed that, despite the difficulties they encountered, they could cope with the situation.

As they gathered in the assembly area, the captain gave the word that every man was to have his face blackened with cork, mud, or anything that would prevent his being seen. It had started to rain right after the jump, and now it was dark. The officers who commanded the platoons were with the Skipper when he issued the order, and promptly began to smear mud on their faces.

It was getting colder and darker by the minute, and every minute that passed, it seemed like the rain beat down that much faster.

"Ah, I found a good place," said one of his officers as he continued putting mud all over his face... he reached into a small place that looked like a particularly juicy puddle and began to smear it on his face. "Judas! This stuff stinks!" he snorted.

"Why, you damn fool, don't you know that even in England there are cows?" as he went a little closer to the place to get mud for his own face.

"So help me if it ain't SO," he said as he started to spit and snort. "What a hell of a life."

Unrepentant Patriot

The following are excerpts from a V-Mail letter written by Captain Cecil L. Simmons to his parents, 23 February 1944. Simmons commanded H/502nd.

Dear Folks,

Sorry I haven't had the time to write you... but then we never have all the time we would like to have for ourselves...I have been quite busy out in the field.

I have had a hundred wild experiences that I'd like to tell you about, but can't on account of the censorship. I got a letter telling of the work that Madge is doing, and although I don't approve of it, I guess there is nothing I can do about it from this distance. By rights, I guess I should be there like a good hus-

Unrepentant Patriot
Captain Cecil L. Simmons scales a tall hill of baled hay, England, 1944.

Officers of the 502nd

England, Spring 1944. The training time before the great invasion is becoming short. (Left to right) Captain Cecil L. Simmons, H/502nd; Lieutenant Colonel Robert Cole, CO 3rd/502nd; Captain Carl Trimble, D/502nd; Major John P. Stopka, executive officer, 3rd/502nd; and Captain Cleveland R. Fitzgerald, B/502nd. Fitzgerald survived a bullet wound to the chest at Foucarville on D-day, only to die in a car crash in France after V-E Day. *Simmons*

band instead of some of the dizzy things I am doing here in a foreign country, with so many men depending on me for their lives… to tell you the truth, I am not so repentant as I should be, for when I get back to my home I will know that I have every right to it because I have fought for it… If I don't get back, I will go down knowing that I have made it safe for my kids to grow up to be free people…When the history of this war is written, those of us in the Paratroops will have our place in it… I believe we will go down as fearless and competent fighters who don't know when to give up and who, after fighting a good fight, have accomplished our mission what more can a man ask of life? I enjoy your letters so write when you all get the chance.

Love,

CEC

Pathfinders

Specially-trained teams of parachutist Pathfinders would jump about one hour ahead of the main serials to land on each of the designated drop zones (DZs). These men would set up special Halifane lights and Eureka radar sets, using the British GEE system and 717-C screen. The BUPS beacon was also used, with signals sent from the Rebecca device in each plane triggering the Eureka set on the ground. The whole program's accuracy could be rendered useless if the ground teams were dropped in the wrong place to begin with, or neutralized by enemy fire, as happened in some instances. Pathfinder teams were comprised of nine to fourteen signaling specialists with two Eureka sets and nine Halifane lights, plus a five-man security detachment to protect them while they performed their signaling functions.

Off to Pathfinder school

Pathfinder volunteers of 2nd/501st posed at Newbury, England, before going to Lillyman's school at Nottingham. Russ Waller, top left, was KIA in Holland. To his right are Bob Sechrist, E/501st; and Bob Howard, D/501st. At bottom left is T. K."Red" Larsen, F/501st. To Larsen's right is Harold "Gene" Sellers, F/501st. Laying down, with pipe and hatchet is Leonard Newcomb, F/501st. Sellers was KIA on landing in Normandy. Newcomb was captured. *Alice Larsen*

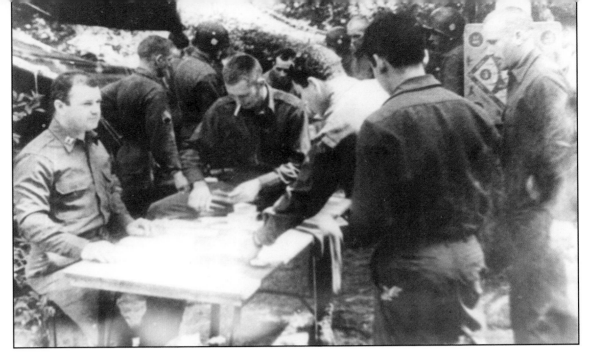

Invasion Currency

Captain William G. Burd, CO of HQ/501st, distributed invasion currency. Invasion currency was used by the troopers to pay French civilians for food and other necessities. Burd was killed at Heeswijk, Holland, during Operation *Market-Garden*. *Krochka*

Early in 1944, a handful of volunteers from each company in the division left their parent units to train at the new Pathfinder School in Nottingham, England. There was no TO&E or precedent for such training, but over 350 American and British signaling technicians were trained as Pathfinders here before D-day. In requesting volunteers, preference was given to those with communications school training as they were familiar with radio equipment and the Morse code.

As the first men to land in enemy-occupied France, the Pathfinders were viewed as a potential "suicide squad," and in the years since the war, a definite mystique has attached itself to the men who served in that capacity. It is interesting to see how the actual selection was done.

Below: **Base stick, 502nd Pir, 5 June 1944**

Most of the personnel in this photo, taken at North Witham Airfield, have been identified as follows. (Standing, left to right) 1st Lieutenant Samuel McCarter, Lieutenant Robert "Buck" Dickson (S-2), Private John McFarlen, Private August Mangoni, Private Bluford Williams, Private John S. Zamanakos, T/5 Owen R. Council, unknown, T/5 Thomas G. Walton, Private First Class Delbert Jones. *(Kneeling, left to right)* 2nd Lieutenant Reed Pelfrey, Private Francis Rocca, Private Raymond Smith (medic), Private First Class Fred A. Wilhelm, Private John G. Ott (S-2), Private Jarris C. Clark (S-2), unknown.

Also listed on the manifest for this stick were Private James Bement, Private Paul O. Davis, and Private John H. Funk (KIA), all of whom were security personnel. Two of these three men are probably the unknowns in the photo. Although Captain Frank Lillyman himself jumped with this stick, he is not pictured. Dickson, Ott, and Clark of the S-2 Section were along to recon a route to the 502nd's primary objective, the 122mm guns near Saint-Martin-de-Varreville. Lieutenant Colonel Joel Crouch, CO of the 9th Troop Carrier Pathfinder Group, piloted Lillyman's lead plane. Incidentally Air Corps troop carrier personnel who flew Pathfinders also wore the Pathfinder wing.

Joseph Haller's company commander requested that he volunteer. "We'd like to have you in the Pathfinders because you can speak German," Captain Simmons told him.

"If it's my time to die, I'm going to die no matter where I am," Haller said. "If you want me in the Pathfinders, I'll join the Pathfinders." There was more to it, however. Haller often talked pro-German around his buddies to entertain himself and to provoke them. "Today Germany Tomorrow the World… then I shall rule in this district!" Haller would loudly proclaim.

Joe's best buddies were Joe Dejanovich, a Serbian trooper, and David Hadley. "The Three Kings," Haller called them. All were from the communications platoon and worked together as a team through training. Captain Simmons, however, suspected that Dejanovich was a Communist he had been heard threatening to go over the hill once he landed on the continent so he could join Tito and fight with the partisans.

Lieutenant Albert Watson, known as "The Gremlin," was the battalion mess officer and not popular with the top officers in 1st/501st. Somehow he wound up volunteering for the Pathfinders, along with "The Three Kings."

Many members of the division were never given the opportunity to volunteer for Pathfinder duty as the slots were filled before they even heard about the outfit.

Around February 1944, Leonard Newcomb of F/501st was in his tent at Hamstead Marshall, minding his own business, when Lieutenant Hugh Hendrickson, the executive officer of his company, walked in and stated that volunteers were needed for a special outfit to jump in ahead of everyone else in the invasion to signal the other planes. In a letter to the author dated 16 April 1973, Newcomb wrote:

I asked him if he was going in it and he said yes so Joe Bass and I both said okay. Red Larsen, who had the first bed in the tent, said he wanted to be in it, so Lieutenant Hendrickson said yes. Harold Sellers came in the tent to get mail at this time, and he said he wanted to join for we were all in the same squad.

Thus were all the available slots for F/501st filled. Only one other slot was available and Ralph "Pinky" Newton of F/501st's 2nd Platoon got it. No one in the 3rd Platoon even had a chance to volunteer before the slots were filled. Also, as Leo Gillis of that company points out, certain NCOs who were considered essential to the functioning of a company wouldn't have been allowed to go.

The 2nd/501st group of volunteers had little idea at the time that they would land on Drop Zone D, the hottest of all on D-day. Sellers was killed upon landing, becoming the first fatality of F/501st in the war. Newcomb was captured on D-day afternoon and spent the duration as a prisoner of war (POW).

Lieutenant Hendrickson was struck by a laundry truck while crossing the street in Nottingham. His leg was badly broken before D-day and he never got into combat until the Korean War.

Captain Frank Lillyman, who had previously commanded I/502nd in training, organized and ran the Pathfinder School. Lillyman was a flamboyant, publicity conscious, and controversial officer. He was a diminutive man, filled with determination, who wanted to be sure his Pathfinders received their due recognition for being the first to land in enemy territory. Lillyman's ego must have rubbed someone the wrong way as he was a captain going into Normandy and was still a captain when the war ended in 1945. He was then given command of the division's MP platoon, an additional slap in the face. Members of

Captain Frank Lillyman, 1943
Lillyman in a photo taken at Fort Bragg, North Carolina. He commanded I/502nd before forming the division's Pathfinder School. *Koskimaki*

Pathfinder wing
An original British-made Pathfinder sleeve wing, worn by Hilary McKenna, E/501st, who served on the security detail of the 501st's Base Stick on DZ D. Security personnel who had served in that capacity on an actual combat mission were also eligible to wear the wing.

that platoon at the time were forbidden to wear the Airborne tab above their eagle shoulder patch.

One of Lillyman's passions was photography, and not being satisfied with still photos, he carried a 16mm movie camera with which he recorded most every aspect of training. His most famous stunt in pre-D-day England was a jump he made with his movie camera attached to his chest and aimed at his own face as he jumped from a plane. This camera recorded his facial expressions (he had a cigar clenched in his teeth), and showed the blossoming open of his canopy and landing on the ground.

As S. L. A. Marshall pointed out in *Night Drop* (Battery Press, Nashville, TN, 1962), Frank Lillyman was a pioneering soul who was born years before his time. He would have been more at home in the era of space exploration.

Certain pilots and crews from the Ninth Air Force's Troop Carrier Command worked in cooperation with the parachutists and were also considered part of the Pathfinder teams. A special insignia was designed before D-day to indicate Pathfinder training, but in most cases, it was not issued until after the Normandy campaign. It could be worn on the lower left sleeve above hash marks and overseas bars by any parachutist who had completed Pathfinder training and by Air Corps personnel who had completed the corresponding training. The patch depicts a flaming golden torch and the earliest examples are of typical British construction, with the design sewn in cotton thread on a blue flannel base.

The photos of Pathfinder sticks were taken by Air Corps personnel and appear thanks to the Pathfinder Association. A few sticks are missing, but ironically, there are more photos of Pathfinder sticks avai-

Louis Frey, Louisiana; Fred Baynes, New York; and Sergeant Alfred "Pop" Dornick, Indiana, S-2 Section, 2nd/501st, admire the work they did in constructing sand tables for briefing the battalion on its objectives. Using maps and aerial photos as references, the features of terrain such as hills, roads, and rivers were reconstructed to scale. Sand, small sticks, pieces of carved soap, and coloring were used to create the dioramas. Reference grids were laid over the top using pieces of string. Officers were briefed, followed by each platoon of each company. The purpose was to acquaint the troops not only with the location of their objective but also to familiarize them with the general vicinity they were to land in. This proved valuable for those fortunate enough to drop in the correct area. Private First Class Donald Zahn, H/506th, later said that as he floated down on DZ D, "I felt like I was looking down on a giant sand table of the DZ – everything looked just as I had expected from the briefing."

violent opening shocks.

On the approach to the Cotentin Peninsula across the Channel, the planes bearing Pathfinders flew at extremely low altitudes to avoid German radar detection. Some of the Pathfinders recall the tops of the waves on the Channel splashing into the open door of their plane.

Joe Haller had consumed a lot of coffee at the North Witham Airfield before taking off on D-day night. As a result, he had to urinate during the flight across. He stood in the open door of the C-47, unzipped, and let go. The wind from the propellers blew the urine back into the plane, spraying his mortified buddies. Naturally, there was a lot of cursing and protesting.

"You guys are gonna have a lot more to worry about than a little pee!" Haller told them. Like many of the others aboard, Haller was smoking a cigarette. He began to sing a song he had heard in a western movie:

I'm smoking my last cig-a-rette,

sing that cowboy song

I ne-ver will for-get…

I'm smokin' my last cig-a-rette.

"Shut up, you bastard!" the men shouted; they didn't want to hear that.

Joe wasn't too scared, even when violent flak began to rock the plane. Over DZ D, the plane banked and the first three jumpers fell out the door; they didn't even have to jump. Haller was one of them. As he fell, his Tommy gun flew down in front of his chest but he caught it. Shrapnel burst open his chest reserve chute and he grasped that desperately in his arms. He soon hit the ground and could see tracer bullets passing over him as he struggled to get out of his harness.

"The Germans must have been scared, too," he later said. "They weren't far away they could have rushed me."

Haller began to walk, went through a gap in the hedgerow and crossed a dark road.

A German voice yelled, "Halte!"

Haller answered in fluent German, "There's more of them over here be careful!"

Haller could hear a commotion as the Germans were capturing another member of his stick. He was able to escape and rejoin his regiment after signaling in concert with Russell Waller, of the 2nd Battalion stick, whom he encountered in a large ditch. This was near Saint-Come-du-Mont.

Lillyman's Landing
These 16mm movie sequences filmed by a camera attached to Lillyman's chest shows his chute blossoming; Lillyman's face with a cigar clenched in his teeth; and his landing on the ground. *US Army*

lable than there are of regular rifle company sticks.

On D-day, Pathfinders jumped carrying their lights and radar sets. Other than that, their equipment was similar to that used by regular paratroopers. Notably in the 101st, the Pathfinders' helmets were devoid of the regimental playing card symbols used by other units as assembly aids. Although they would rejoin their original companies on the ground in France after performing their initial signaling missions, they had left their parent units before the stencils were applied. Unlike the regular troopers, the Pathfinders were not issued crickets for ground recognition. (Some of the security personnel received them, according to Larry McKenna of the 501st.) Instead they had a password and countersign: "Boise" and "Idaho." Other troopers of the division were to use "Flash" and "Thunder" as an alternative to cricket challenges.

Unlike the regular serials, the planes carrying the Pathfinders would fly a constant speed of 150 mph for the entire course, instead of slowing down during the drop. As a result, many of the jumpers had their weapons and equipment torn off by especially

501st Pathfinders, D-1

There only seems to be one Air Corps photo in existence of 501st Pathfinders on the eve of Dday and this is it, taken at North Witham Airfield. Like the other regiments, the 501st used three sticks of Pathfinders, and it seems that men of all three battalions mingled together to make this photo. Of course, most are missing, but there seems to also be a mixture of trained Pathfinders and security people. The man bending forward at far left may be Mileski, of Company E, who went along as part of the security detachment. It is only via the diamond stencil on his helmet that we can even speculate that this group is of the 501st. Trained Pathfinders didn't have regimental unit stencils on their helmet as they were a divisional organization and had left their parent units to train in isolation in Nottingham some time before the stencils were applied. The security people were assigned less than two weeks before the invasion and thus brought stenciled helmets with them. In any case, it is possible that Red Larsen is at upper left, standing beside Joe Dejanovich (HQ/1st; POW), Michael Rofar (I/501st; KIA) stands right in the center. The trooper beside him is possibly Lary McKenna (E/501st security). Of the three sticks, the Base stick (2/501st men) and Primary Stick (1/501st) landed on DZ D and took the highest casualties of any of the Pathfinder sticks killed and missing. The alternate (3/501st) stick landed closer to Hiesville to light the DZ C area.

Captain Lillyman's Team A was the first to land in the DZ A area. The team was scheduled to land at 1220, but the plane arrived over the area 10 minutes early. The pilot passed the DZ, circled back, and dropped the stick flying from northeast to southwest. The last three members of the stick were members of the 502nd's S-2 Section, Lieutenant Buck Dickson, Jack Ott, and Jim Clark. They were supposed to recon a route to the Saint-Martin-de-Varreville coastal gun battery, but landed so far west (near Beuzeville au Plain), that they never got to that objective on D-day. Lieutenant Colonel Crouch's plane, with Lillyman's crucial stick aboard, ended up being misdropped several miles northeast of the intended DZ A, which was closer to Loutres. Lillyman realized he didn't have time to move his signaling teams before the main serials began to fly over, so he directed his radar and lights to be set up where they were, at St. Germain de Varreville. As a result, only two (misdropped) sticks landed on the originally designated DZ A. Many of the rest dropped accurately on Lillyman's signal.

After assembling near the church at Saint-Germain-de-Varreville, Lillyman set up a Eureka set and signaled the large flock of planes that came over some time later. The fog and cloud bank encountered over the west coast of the Cotentin, however, had already badly dispersed the formations. As a result, many sticks intended for DZ A were misdropped, ranging from areas north of Montebourg to the north, and the vicinity of Sainte-Marie-du-Mont in the south. Conversely, many planes of 2nd/506th intended for DZ C dropped their men on Lillyman's signal far to the north of the intended landing area. Like an omen of the fouled-up misdrops to come, the Pathfinder stick of Lieutenant Rothwell (506th) was shot down and ditched in the Channel.

326th AEB Pathfinders

These three men were the only members of the 326th AEB to serve as Pathfinders in Normandy. They are *(from left to right)* Private First Class Louis DiGaetano (KIA, Bastogne), Private Albert Kouba, and Corporal Calvin Jackson. All belonged to C/326th. *Kouba*

21

501st Demolitions Platoon

Part of the Regimental Demolitions Platoon, 501st, just prior to going to the marshaling area. *(Standing left to right)* Sergeant Leon "Pappy" Brown, California; Private First Class Edward Case, Arizona: Private First Class King J. Bogie, Minnesota; Corporal Thomas Arrey, New Mexico; Private First Class Lafayette Hillman, Pennsylvania: Private Marvin Johnson, Minnesota; Private Clement Henwood, California; Lieutenant Jess Tidwell, Tennessee. *(Bottom row left to right)* Private First Class Irvin Lloyd, Virginia; Private Howard Finch, California: Private First Class Richard Wisniewski, New York: Private Louis Sorace, New York; Private First Class Nae Paugh, Michigan: and Private John Kildare, Nebraska.

It is evident in this photo that most of the troopers have shaved their heads. In his book, Look Out Below!, Father Francis Sampson wrote, In addition to head shaving, men allowed their whiskers to grow out before a jump. "We always wore them [beards] into combat – supposed to make you look tough, I guess."

Some troopers cut Indian scalplocks on their domes, but simple cropping had a practical purpose. It would be much easier to keep short hair clean under field conditions. Most troopers wouldn't enjoy a shower for the first two weeks in Normandy.

501st Regimental S-2 Platoon

Staff Sergeant John F. Tiller, S-2/501st, reads the mission before a practice jump, England, 1944. Also visible are Gerald Beckerman *(far left)*, Waldo Brown *(fourth from left)*, Ken Collier, Jimmy Ganter, and Irby H. Palmer. Colonel Howard Johnson considered his hand-picked S-2 platoon as the elite of his regiment. *Krochka*

1st/327th GIR, Dartmouth-Brixham, England
Members of the 1st/327th GIR were transported to Normandy by ship, rather than by air, due to a limited number of gliders and tow aircraft. This photo was taken in the Dartmouth-Brixham area near Slapton Sands. *US Army*

Departure Airfields

Aldermaston Airfield

The "Chicago Mission" was to land important surgeons, medical supplies, and antitank guns a few hours after the paratroopers were on the ground. They flew the same route as the parachutists, as opposed to the evening "Keokuk Mission" in British-made Horsa gliders, which came in across Utah Beach at 2130.

The anticipated counterthrust by German armor didn't materialize until a week later, and then in the form of the *17th SS-Panzer-Grenadier Division.* This unit was understrength and arrived too late to push the invaders back into the Channel. The only armor the Germans had behind Utah Beach were a handful of Renault light tanks of pre-war design belonging to *Panzer Battalion 100.* Nevertheless, elements of the 81st AAAB with 57mm guns were brought in to repel tanks in the morning, and the Antitank Platoon of the 327th GIR landed with their 37mm pieces in the evening lift. (Unique among US Army divisions, airborne divisions possessed organic, not attached, antiaircraft battalions. These included an antitank company in each one, as there were no antitank guns in the parachute infantry regiments at all.)

The Chicago Mission departed Aldermaston airfield at 0221 with gliders arriving in France between 0400 and 0600. The mission was flown by 434th Troop Carrier Group (TCG), which consisted of the 71st Troop Carrier Squadron (TCS; planes marked CJ), 72nd TCS (CU markings), 73rd TCS (CN markings), and 74th TCS (ID markings).

A similar "Detroit Mission" took off and landed around the same time to resupply the 82nd Airborne.

Many of the gliders struck Rommel's Asparagus poles or collided with hedgerows in fields that were too small.

It is well known that Colonel Mike Murphy of the 434th Troop Carrier Group (TCG) piloted a CG-4A named "Fighting Falcon" into Normandy with Brigadier General Don Pratt aboard. General Pratt became the first American general to die in the invasion when Fighting Falcon collided with a hedgerow outside Hiesville. The general had a parachute underneath him while seated in a jeep inside the glider. The parachute raised Pratt's head just high enough to cause it to strike an overhead beam, breaking his neck upon impact.

Few people know that there were two Fighting Falcons Pratt died in Fighting Falcon No. 2. The original Fighting Falcon was replaced by a newer model at the last minute. This newer ship became Glider No. 1 in Murphy's 72nd Troop Carrier Squadron (TCS). The newer model was equipped with a "Griswold Nose," to help insulate against frontal impacts, a feature that the original Falcon didn't have. The original Fighting Falcon reverted to Glider No. 45 in the 52-glider serial and was piloted to Normandy by Robert Butler and Everard Hohmann. Lieutenant Lawrence Hensley's Pathfinders had set up a green lighted T on LZ E, but the second glider to land smashed into the string of lights as it slid over the grass, forcing the rest of the serial to land by moonlight.

Glider pilots and copilots were to fight as infantry and make their way to the 101st's command post. A number of pilots and copilots were lost on landing or *en route* to the assembly area. These included Jack Willoughby, pilot of Glider No. 3; Thomas Ahmad, copilot of Glider No. 42, who landed seven miles southeast of Carentan and was KIA at Graignes; and Clinton Griffin, copilot of Glider No. 40, listed as killed in action (KIA). Four other pilots were listed as missing in action (MIA).

Greenham Common Airfield

Serial 1 consisted of 36 planes, carrying troops of the 2nd and 3rd Battalions of the 502nd. Serial 2 consisted of 45 planes, carrying half of the 377th PFAB. The two serials combined were supposed to land a total of 1,430 troops on the amber marking lights arranged in a "T" on DZ A. The Air Corps claims an accuracy of 80 percent on the drop.

In reality, many jumpers in Serial 1 landed far south near DZ C, outside Sainte-Marie-du-Mont. Others landed west of the DZ near Sainte-Mère-Eglise and much of the 377th PFAB was scattered far north, near Montebourg, Valognes, Sain-Vaast-la-Hocque, and so on.

These serials departed England from Greenham Common before 2330. The mission was flown by the 438th TCG, which included the 87th TCS (3X markings), 88th TCS (M2 markings), 89th TCS (4U markings), and 90th TCS (Q7 markings). Those planes from Serial 1 that found the DZ dropped troopers between 0048 and 0050 on 6 June. These earlier serials received less ground fire from the surprised Germans.

377th PFAB and 326th AEB

This plane included stick 2, 377th Lieutenant L. J. Hensley jumpmaster and part of Team E for DZ E. Team E was supposed to drop on DZ C at 0027, northeast of Hiesville. Instead, they landed west of Angoville, about 3,000 yards off target. Paratroopers aboard included: Private First Class John J. Hosta, Private Saul Sancedo, Private First Class Louis DiGaetano, Private Arthur L. Brooks, Private Albert Kouba, T/5 Donald N. Green, Private Norman D. Gannon, T/5 Jerold J. Quinn, Corporal Vincent L. Cart, and 1st Lieutenant Lawrence Hensley. The last five troopers to exit, including DiGaetano and Kouba, landed in the flooded wastelands east of Angoville and were missing for the first two days. The Air Corps crew was 1st Lieutenant Paul Egan (pilot), 1st Lieutenant Richard Young (copilot), 1st Lieutenant Fern Murphy (navigator), Staff Sergeant Marvin Rosenblatt (radio operator), and Sergeant Jack Buchanan (crew chief). (Information on this stick was researched and provided by Frank DiGaetano, Louis's brother.)

A sizable group under Lieutenant Colonel Robert Cole, 3rd/502nd, joined forces with a group from 2nd/506th (intended for DZ C), which had also landed near Sainte-Mère-Eglise.

Near dusk on 5 June, General Dwight Eisenhower, the supreme commander of OVERLORD, personally visited troops of the 101st Airborne at two departure fields. We have photographic evidence that he saw the 2nd/502nd at Greenham and the 3rd/501st at Welford. The car trip from Portsmouth to the Newbury area took 90 minutes of winding through troop convoys and checkpoints. Eisenhower arrived unannounced to avoid disrupting the loading schedule. He was a popular figure and was quickly recognized, despite the covered stars on his staff car. Ike was troubled by the predictions of British Air Chief Marshal Sir Trafford Leigh-Mallory, who had estimated 80 percent casualties among the paratroopers of the 82nd and 101st Airborne Divisions, some 13,000 of which would make the initial landings.

Eisenhower continued through the admiring ranks, asking some individuals what state they were from, what their job was in the Army, and what they had done in civilian life. The visit seemed to do more to lift the general's morale than it did to bolster the paratroopers' morale; they were ready.

Membury Airfield (Serials 3 and 4)

Planes of the 436th TCG which consisted of the 79th TCS (S6 markings), 80th TCS (7D markings), 81st TCS (U5 markings), and 82nd TCS (3D markings) departed from Membury Airfield, which was situated north of Greenham Common, for DZ A (marked by amber lights). One serial of the 436th TCG flew 1st/502nd (Lieutenant Colonel Cassidy's troops) in 36 planes, delivering them to the vicinity of DZ A, where they jumped between 0055 and 0102 on 6 June. Elements flown by the 85th Squadron of the 437th TCG misdropped their passengers of the 377th PFAB, far to the north and west of DZ A. As a result, only one of the 377th's 12 75mm howitzers was recovered by members of Battery C.

The artillerymen dropped between 0055 and 0108 on 6 June. Misdrops among them were the rule rather than the exception, with many landing in the Montebourg-Valognes area and others between Saint-Marcouf and Ravenoville (see Chapter 28). In the two above serials, a total of 1,084 paratroopers were dropped into France.

All DZ A units were to concentrate on the Saint-Martin-de-Varreville area and the four captured Soviet 122mm howitzers situated southwest of town.

Lieutenant Colonel Cassidy's 1st/502nd was to eradicate the German artillerymen stationed in the "XYZ complex" at Mesiéres. (See page 53) The 2nd/502nd (Chappuis) was to team up with the 377th's howitzers to knock out the actual emplacements, using combined artillery and demolitions.

Lieutenant Jim Keane, of HQ/502nd, was assigned to investigate why parts of two A/502nd sticks were misdropped in the Channel, resulting in numerous drownings. During his probe, he learned that the serial carrying 1st/502nd was the only one of those carrying 101st Airborne troops that suffered no losses.

It is fortunate that Sergeant Edward Benecke, A/377th PFAB, was at Membury with his camera. Thanks to his photos, some 436th TCG's nose art has been preserved for posterity. Few paratroopers remember the name of the plane they rode in, and even a few pilots no longer recall the name of their own plane after all these years.

Cherbourg Choo-Choo
A C-47 of the 74th TCS. *Krochka*

CG-4A Waco Glider
Typical shot of a C-47 towing the US-made CG-4A Waco glider. The towplane would cut the glider loose over the LZ and the glider pilot would glide the engineless craft to the ground. The CG-4A could carry a 3,750 pound payload; that is, 13 infantrymen, a jeep with trailer, or a 57mm anti-tank gun and crew. *Musura*

Load Up
This photo snapped by Eddie Sapinski's camera at Greenham Common shows his F/502nd stick preparing to load. The C-47 belonged to the 438th TCG. The trooper with coiled jump rope, second from the left is Eddie Sapinski. *Sapinski*

British Horsa Glider
The unique profile of the larger British-made Horsa Glider, used in the evening Keokuk Mission. The 327th PIR's Antitank Platoon with 37mm guns landed in Horsas. The British Horsa could carry a 6,700 pound payload; it could carry 32 infantrymen or a jeep with attached howitzer. *Musura*

"Ma Petite Jeanne"
This C-47 belong to the 80th TCS, on departure of Membury. *Benecke*

Nookie Wagon
The crew of this C-47 first touched down on English soil at a place called New Quay, which the Brits pronounce Nookie. The crew decided to use this as the nose art name of their plane because of the double (also naughty) meaning. *Benecke*

Uppottery Airfield (Serials 5 and 6)

The 439th TCG which consisted of the 91st TCS (L4 markings), 92nd TCS (J8 markings), 93rd TCS (3B markings), and 94th TCS (D8 markings) flew from Uppottery with 1st/506th, 2nd/506th, and HQ/506th to attack DZ C (marked by green lights). These troops had numerous missions, including the capture of beach exits 1 and 2 at Pouppeville and Sainte-Marie-du-Mont. The 1st Battalion, as well most of the regimental headquarters, had a fairly concentrated drop near Holdy, although many troops from Companies A and C landed way up near Ravenoville. We know that Captain Brown's HQ/506th stick also landed near Montebourg, far to the northwest.

Most of Lieutenant Colonel Strayer's 2nd/506th landed in a concentrated area near DZ A at Foucarville and headed south after assembling. Some 2nd/506th sticks landed in or near Saint-Mère-Eglise, nearly an hour before elements of the 82nd Airborne arrived. It is small wonder that elements of the 505th dropped into an aroused hornet's nest around 0200.

Serial 5 departed Uppottery around 2350 on 5 June, dropping its paratroopers over France at 0114 on 6 June. Serial 6 departed Uppottery around 2356 on 5 June, dropped its paratroopers over France between 0114 and 0120 on 6 June. A total of some 1,357 troops of the 506th, minus 3rd Battalion, were carried in these two serials.

Colonel Robert Sink's regimental command group established a command post at a cluster of farmhouses known as Culoville; Major Kent, the 506th surgeon, established his aid station in the Culoville farm complex.

A week later

Tom Beszouska in France. Beszouska was misdropped near Sainte-Mère-Eglise and fought for a week with the 82nd Airborne. Note that he is wearing German paratrooper gloves – a favorite souvenir with the 101st troopers. *Sapinski*

"Don't worry General…"

The troopers quickly put Eisenhower at ease with wise-cracks, "Don't worry General, we've got it under control!" Note that a censor has obliterated the eagle patches, and the troopers have switched their musette bags to their backs for this impromptu inspection. On the jump, they would wear them in front of their bodies, just below the reserve parachute chest packs. The trooper with his back to the camera is Tom Beszouska, F/502nd. Eisenhower's aide de camp, Navy Commander Harry C. Butcher, is highly visible at Eisenhower's rear in the blue uniform. Butcher was a close friend and nearly constant companion to Eisenhower. The trooper at far left clearly has a gas-detection brassard on his right shoulder, and the paratrooper second from left is Lieutenant Colonel Mike Michaelis, who assumed command of the entire 502nd PIR after Colonel Moseley broke his leg on the D-day jump. *Sapinski*

Welford Airfield (Serial 7)

Serial 7 of the 435th TCG which consisted of aircraft from the 75th TCS (SH markings), 76th TCS (CW markings), 77th TCS (1B markings), and 78th TCS (CM markings) carried the jump element, mainly medical and communications personnel from HQ/101st under General Maxwell Taylor, as well as Lieutenant Colonel Julian Ewell's 3rd/501st, which was considered in "reserve." This battalion's mission was to provide security for the divisional HQ at Hiesville. The 677 troopers dropped from 45 planes in the vicinity of DZ C (marked by green lights) between 0120 and 0126 on 6 June 1944. Much of this serial landed reasonably closely to Hiesville, but some planes bearing troops from HQ/101st and 3rd/501st strayed far south, dropping men west of Carentan, near Baupte, and also far south of Carentan.

Merryfield Airfield (Serials 8 and 9)

One serial of 45 planes of the 441st TCG – which consisted of the 99th TCS (3J markings), 100th TCS (8C markings), 301st TCS (Z4 markings), and 302nd TCS (2L markings) – from Merryfield Airfield carried HQ/501st, Service Company, and 1st/501st to DZ D, where they landed between 0126 and 0131. Another serial of 45 planes carried 2nd/501st and elements of C/326th AEB to DZ D (marked by red lights), where they jumped between 0134 and 0137. These combined serials dropped a total of 1,475 paratroopers in the area east of Saint-Come-du-Mont.

Sink's message

Most history buffs have seen Eisenhower's Great Crusade invasion message, but the above memo from Colonel Robert Sink to all his 506th troopers is much more obscure. This specimen was preserved by Sergeant WilliamKnight, C/506th. *Knight*

A message from Colonel Sink

First Lieutenant Carl McDowell reads Colonel Robert Sink's invasion message to his stick. (Left to right) Don Emelander, Tom Alley, McDowell; trooper at right is possibly Bill Green. These men belonged to Headquarters Section, F/506th. The white scarves worn at their necks are cloth maps of France from the escape and evasion kits. *Young*

Colonel Howard Johnson's stick

The pilot of the C-47 that carried the stick was Colonel Kershaw. Among others, the passengers included Private First Class Leo Runge (center front, with eyes closed), who distinguished himself at Hell's Corner. Beside him is Major Francis Carrell, the regimental surgeon of the 501st, wearing a Red Cross brassard. *US Army*

"Total victory—nothing less!"

Press captions for this photo throughout the Western World claimed that Eisenhower was demanding, "Total Victory—nothing less!" as he talked to Lieutenant Wallace Strobel of Saginaw, Michigan. Strobel, an American of Irish-German origin, says that when Eisenhower learned he was from Michigan, he said, "I've been there and liked it … good fishing there!" This is probably the most famous invasion photo from D-day and certainly ranks as one of the great photos of WWII. There has always been a great debate over the names of the troopers pictured, Without engaging in that controversy, it can be stated that Schuyler "Sky" Jackson is closest to Eisenhower's nose. Jackson was a member of regimental demolitions, assigned to 2nd/502nd for his Dday mission. Most of the other troopers belonged to D/502nd and E/502nd. Enough said. We can state with some certainty that the lieutenant facing Eisenhower is Wallace Strobel, E/502nd, of Saginaw, Michigan. For those who follow astrology, this is a classic pairing of two compatibles, Eisenhower (Libra) and Strobel (Gemini). In fact, the photo was taken on Strobel's birthday, 5 June. Strobel passed away in 1999; Sky Jackson, one of the most popular members of the 101st Airborne Association, passed away in early 1993. *US Army*

The objectives of the 501st were to capture Saint-Come-du-Mont, the Douve River Bridge on the Carentan Causeway (N-13), and the La Barquette lock. The 1st/501st, which landed farther south than 2nd/501st, dropped close to the lock, in the same area as 3rd/506th. The casualties of 1st/501st were very high. Lieutenant Colonel Robert A. Ballard was one of the few field grade officers in the night drop to recognize where he was from terrain features, immediately upon landing. His 2nd/501st troops came down in and near the flooded area southeast of Angoville-au-Plein, concentrated in a reasonably small area.

Exeter Airfield (Serial 10)

The ill-fated 3rd/506th had as its mission the capture of the two wooden bridges near Brévands. Only 130 men managed to find and assemble at that objective the following afternoon. Many had been killed, captured, or were wandering around lost.

This serial departed Exeter at 0020, dropping its 723 troopers between 0140 and 0143 on 6 June. Demolition saboteurs from the Filthy 13 were also along, in case the bridges needed to be blown.

The 3rd/506th was flown from Exeter to DZ D (marked by red lights) by the 440th TCG – which consisted of the 95th TCS (9X markings), 96th TCS (6Z markings), 97th TCS (W6 markings), and 98th TCS (8Y markings).

Drop Zone Maps

DZ maps like this were issued to some of the troopers who landed on DZ C and a similar map exists for DZ A near Saint-Martin-de-Varreville. The maps are about 20 inches square and printed in black and white. Although the center section is a reproduced to scale aerial photo of the DZ, it is done with tiny dots similar to newsprint photos in a newspaper. This map shows the Sainte-Marie-du-Mont zone C, which was the intended target of the troops who departed from Uppottery and Welford airfields. *Hood*

Shack rabbit
This aircraft carried one of at least three nose art designs all having the same flying woman, but with varying names, including Shoo-Shoo Baby and Dark Beauty. All were painted by glider pilot Adelore Chevalier, of Urbana, Illinois. *Benecke*

Last-minute Preparation
Albert A. Krochka, HQ/501st, sews an eagle patch to his M-42 jump jacket shortly before D-day. *Krochka*

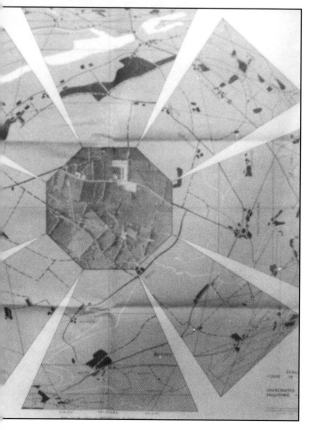

Johnson's "Knife Speech"

It was at Merryfield that Colonel Howard R. Johnson, the fire-breathing CO of the 501st, made his famous blood thirsty "knife speech" to his troops before boarding the planes. Johnson exhorted his men to give their all in the invasion. Standing before them he yelled, "We've worked together, sweated together, trained together… but what we do tonight will be written in history!" The carefully calculated climax to the colonel's speech called for him to raise a trench knife over his head for the dramatic final line. He stooped to release the weapon from his ankle, but for a few embarrassing moments, the knife would not yield from the scabbard. Turning redfaced at this unseemly interruption, Johnson removed his trusty Randall Bowie knife from his waist and raised it on high.

"'Ere another dawn… I hope this knife is buried in the back of the foulest, black-hearted Nazi bastard in France! Are you with me?"

His faithful minions replied with a bloodcurdling roar. "Then let's go get 'em! Good hunting!"

This serial had a fairly accurate drop south and east of Saint-Come-du-Mont, but this was not necessarily fortunate. The Germans had anticipated that this was an ideal area for an airborne landing and had prepared a hot reception. A barn at the edge of the landing fields had been doused with gas and set alight, making many of the troopers clay pigeons as they floated down. Add to this the fact that all the other 101st serials had already landed, giving the Germans more time to react and prepare for this one. Many of these men were hit before they reached the ground, or pounced upon and killed or captured while still in their harnesses. Some landed on a bivouac area of *Ost* volunteers from Russia and a wholesale slaughter ensued. Other groups were ambushed while *en route* to the bridges. The survivors of Serial 10 were indeed fortunate.

The Filthy 13

Jake McNiece, a Native American from Ponca City, Oklahoma, conceived this group of demolitions saboteurs from HQ/506th. The group, which always seemed to number more than a dozen men, changed members from time to time. Their basic premise was to take solemn Indian vows not to wash or shave until they had returned from battle. This vow was taken

War Paint
Joe Oleskewicz, a demolitions specialist of the Filthy 13 (RH 506th), stands in the door at Exeter airfield before departure. Joe section was attached to 3rd Battalion, 506th along with membe of the 326th Airborne Engineer battalion, for the mission at t wooden bridges. *US Army*

"I Let the Order Stand"

When asked at a High School Press Club meeting in Chicago in 1947 what his toughest decision of WWII was, Dwight Eisenhower told about the decision to send paratroopers ahead of the seaborne landings on D-day. He explained about the four causeways, elevated roads leading inland from Utah Beach across otherwise impassable salt marshes. He told how crucial to the landings it was for the causeways to be secured and the German defenders to be neutralized. Eisenhower also told of Air Chief Marshal Leigh-Mallory's prediction that 80 percent of the paratroopers would be killed and wounded and that 90 percent of the gliders would be casualties before reaching the ground.

Eisenhower admitted he had agonized many hours over the decision, but realized that the plan had been scrutinized by other top leaders and approved. He also thought about what the beach landings would be like without the prior air drop.

After a dramatic pause, with voice low, Eisenhower spoke these five words "I let the order stand."

The next edition of the Chicago Daily News carried the story "Ike's Greatest War Decision." This Keen Teen Press Club meeting was the first time Eisenhower had publicly revealed that decision and it made headlines across the country.

A high school teacher in Illinois told writer Val Lauder that she had been a Red Cross worker in England, passing out coffee and doughnuts to paratroopers at the airfield on the eve of D-day. When Eisenhower drove up, she handed him a cup of coffee, but noticed his hand was shaking so badly the hot coffee was in danger of splashing out and burning him. She gently eased the cup from his hand, and understood the incident better when she learned what he said after the war.

At Welford, General Eisenhower arrived as it was getting dark, and some troopers there saw him peek in the door of their plane and wave just before takeoff.

From Al Krochka's album:

"General Eisenhower spent several hours circulating among us. As usual, his visit was well received by all. This time, his visit was particularly welcome. His cheerfulness and ever-ready wit, his display of confidence in our ability in choosing us to strike the first blow at the enemy… all of this was very heartening. He displayed all this cheerfulness even though his own problems were many. His heart was heavy because he was very down to earth and very human in his dealings with troops under his command. As he waved at the troops who were boarding the planes, it must have hurt him to know many of his sky fighters would be dead before morning, for tears were rolling down his face, yet he made no attempt to wipe them away. He just kept smiling through the tears and waving, until the last transport cleared the field."

The Filthy 13

A famous photo taken at Exeter that came to symbolize not only the Filthy 13, but also the entire 101st Airborne Division in Normandy. Two demolition saboteurs of the Filthy 13 apply war paint before boarding for D-day, Clarence C. Ware (left), from San Pedro, California, and Charles R. Plaudo, from Minneapolis, Minnesota. *US Army*

around December 1943, and the men were pretty ripe by D-day, living apart from the others in their company by mutual agreement.

Frank Palys, a one-time member of the 13, suggests that nobody stationed in the area took many baths, as water was not readily available. He says the group first started in Camp Toccoa in 1942 as "The Warsaw Seven" a group of Polish boys that included himself, Martin Majewski, Eddie Malas, Joe Oleskiewicz, and others, including Jake McNiece, who was made an "Honorary Polack" at the time.

Later in England, McNiece started his own group and there were Poles and many other ethnic groups represented in it, contrary to articles in the *Stars and Stripes,* which stated the group was composed entirely of Native Americans, with a Caucasian lieutenant who could whip them all in command.

"No reflection on Lieutenant Mellen," says McNiece, "but any one of our group could have whipped him without working up a sweat." Mellen was found dead in Normandy, with his arm and leg bandaged. "The first bullets didn't stop him."

Largely due to highly sensationalized articles in *Stars and Stripes* and also a famous photo showing two members of the group wearing Indian scalplocks and war paint, the Filthy 13 gained great notoriety. They were certainly the real-life inspiration for the later novel and movie *The Dirty Dozen,* although none of them were criminals. Although the roster of Filthy 13 members changed from time to time, the basic original group consisted of: Jake McNiece, Jack Womer, John Agnew, Lieutenant Charles Mellen, Joseph Oleskiewicz, John Hale, James T. Green, George Radeka, Clarence Ware, Robert S. Cone, Roland R. Baribeau, James E. Leach, and Andrew Rasmussen. Others, including Frank Palys and Chuck Plaudo, were sometimes members of the group.

Airborne Switchblade, M-2

These spring-activated switchblade knives were carried in special dual zippered pockets below the front collar of M-42 coats (jump jackets), and many troopers used them to cut their way out of overly-tight T-5 harnesses. This specimen was carried in Normandy by T/4 Dick Rowles, E/501st. *Author's Photo*

Cricket

Toy cricket noise-making device (British made). This was the standard design for the infamous signaling device, made of brass with a spring-steel snapping plate attached to the bottom. As was common practice, a nail hole has been punched through this specimen to affix it to a cord and prevent loss. This one was carried by Sergeant Bill Knight, C/506th, who landed near Ravenoville. Contrary to what they told us in *The Longest Day,* few, if any, 82nd Airborne troopers were issued crickets. General James Gavin of the 82nd later wrote, "There was a lot of gadgetry around, and a lot of it didn't make any sense. In Normandy, we used an oral password. That was enough." *Author's Photo*

The dirty 13

The group known as the Dirty 13 started out as the Dirty Dozen. It was comprised of men from the Headquarters Section and 1st Platoon, F/501st. The first 12 members had the identical tattoo of a skull, bones, and 13 on their left forearm. The thirteenth member, John Zeilmeier, had his on the right arm. Glen Haley and Rudy Korvas reveal their matching tattoos at a 501st reunion in Columbus, Georgia, 1990. After the war, Haley became fire chief in Seymour, Indiana. Korvas drove a delivery truck in Chicago. The preoccupation of many paratroopers with fate, chance, and good versus bad luck helps explain their choice of the number 13 in a number of situations. By embracing that unlucky number, they were thumbing their noses at fate. *SMR and Author's Photo*

The Flight to France

Men on both sides of the aisle; (left) Sergeant Frank and Blanchette. Standing at the end of the aisle is Lieutenant Beamsley, then Tiller and Dick Thorne, facing camera. Beamsley seems to have a large map case hung under his musette bag. *Krochka*

All Aboard for France

Shortly before Lieutenant Colonel Robert Wolverton's men of 3rd/506th boarded their planes at Exeter, he led them in a prayer. As they knelt, he told them to look not down, but up at God, as he asked, "That if die we must, that we die as men would die, without complaining, without pleading, and safe in the feeling that we have done our best for what we believed was right." His request proved to be tragically appropriate because of the many casualties his battalion suffered on DZ D.

The men had spent the last hours being briefed at sand tables and there were plenty of dice and poker games day and night. A great variety of last minute haircuts had proliferated, and Ed Benecke, A/377th PFAB, recalls seeing a group of 502nd troopers at Membury, who stood in a row, bowed their heads, and displayed the word V-I-C-T-O-R-Y. Each trooper had one large letter of the word cut from the hair on the dome of his head.

Joe Taylor, A/501st, was at Merryfield and heard Colonel Howard Johnson's famous knife speech. He also recalls Johnson raising a clenched fist and shouting, "Blood!" His men screamed "Guts!" in reply.

Taylor and another friend were concerned about the depressed and haunted look of one of their fellow jumpers. They discussed his look and demeanor and agreed that they didn't think he would survive the mission. Their guess later proved to be correct.

Many men who survived Normandy to jump again into Holland have stated that they really didn't realize how terrible combat was going to be, and approached the Normandy drop with a far more casual attitude than they did future missions.

Harry T. Mole, a radioman with HQ/2nd/501st, later wrote of the pre-jump period:

You want to know how I felt before the invasion? Just as apprehensive as before any other jump. I think paratroops have an advantage over other types of troops because we are as concerned with our equipment as we are with the coming battles. In other words, our thoughts are projected into so many different directions that we cannot allow ourselves to overly worry about being killed. I never gave the enemy a thought. I always felt I could handle that situation when it arose. My concern was if the plane

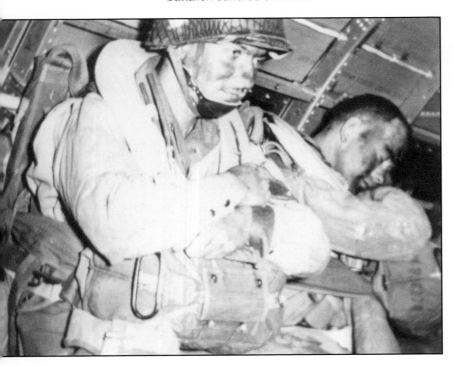

Master Sergeant Peter Frank

The trooper in the foreground is Master Sergeant Peter Frank, a native of Belgium, who served as interpreter. Frank later distinguished himself on the famous "Incredible Patrol" in Holland, earning the Silver Star. At right is Norman Blanchette, who died in an ambush near Neffe, Belgium, in December 1944 during the siege of Bastogne. Peter Frank reportedly returned to Belgium after the war. *Krochka*

should crash, if I should break a leg on the jump… I worried about landing in water and drowning. I became airsick and worried about smelling of vomit.

Sergeant Leo Gillis, F/501st, says, "We felt very powerful as a group," and his lieutenant, Clair Hess later wrote, "The feeling was like we were going to play in the Super Bowl, and we would win."

Not all the troopers were so upbeat, and David Webster of Headquarters Company of the 2nd/506th wrote of his buddies as they marched toward the planes, "Nobody sang, nobody cheered – it was like a death march."

The ominous significance of what they were about to undertake was sinking in, and Joe Taylor wrote:

When the planes started taking off, we flew over England for almost two hours; it took this much time for the hundreds of planes to form the planned formation. A thousand different thoughts went through my mind during the o-so-short 21-mile Channel crossing. Everyone was unusually quiet. Absent was the usual bantering, shouting, and kidding that had always taken place before the many Stateside and England training jumps.

The Flight Across

The photos in this section were snapped in the blacked-out interior of one plane by Albert Krochka of HQ/501st. Krochka was probably the only man in the airborne invasion to take photos in the plane while actually en route to Normandy. Most of the shots are candid in that the men were not posing or prepared when Krochka's flashbulbs popped in the darkness. Thus, the men are shown napping, meditating, and simply enjoying the ride. In addition to identifying some of the faces, Krochka's original written narrative, which he penned in his personal album, accompany the shots.

These unique photos give a rare peek at the men and their equipment as they prepared to open the greatest invasion of modern history. Krochka wrote:

The eagle soldiers were thoughtful in that two-hour ride and some perhaps lived a lifetime in those two

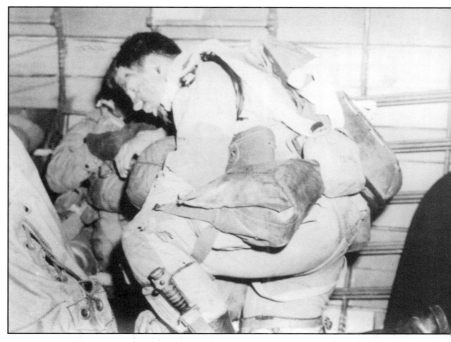

A Prayer
This 506th PIR trooper, with blackened face and helmet removed, appears to be kneeling in prayer. Visible on his ankle is an M-3 knife in an M-8 plastic scabbard.

hours. All of us were a little tired because of the heavy equipment which was strapped very tightly to our bodies. Some of us attempted to snooze. Others just closed their eyes and relaxed as well as possible. Long, hard days lay ahead, and strength would be needed. It would be difficult to even guess what went through each man's mind as the transports roared over the countryside and out to the English Channel. On this and the following pages I attempted to catch various men's expressions while they were not aware of my actions, since the interior of the plane was dark. My own mind was occupied with cameras, flash-

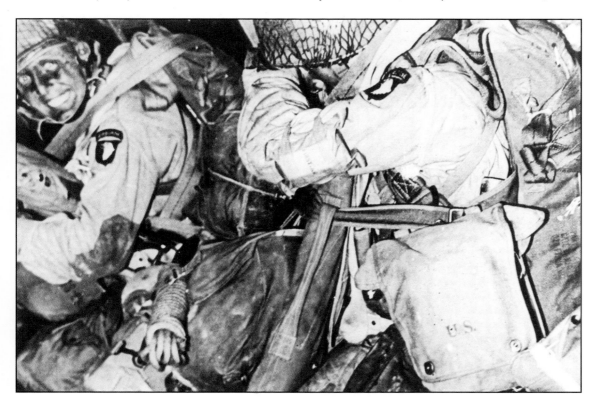

A Famous smile
This famous shot has found its way into several publications. Flak hasn't started to greet them yet and Thorne gives a confident smile. As of this writing, Thorne lives in Garland, Texas, while Sayers passed away in the early 1980s. *Krochka*

The 506th Parachute Infantry Prayer
(written by Lieutenant James G. Morton)

Almighty God, we kneel to Thee and ask to be the instrument of Thy fury in smiting the evil forces that have vis ited death, misery, and debasement on the people of the earth. We humbly face Thee with true penitence for all our sins for which we do most earnestly seek Thy forgiveness. Help us to dedicate ourselves completely to Thee. Be with us, God, when we leap from our planes into the dread abyss and descend in parachutes into the midst of enemy fire. Give us iron will and stark courage as we spring from the harnesses of our parachutes to seize arms for battle. The legions of evil are many, Father. Grace our arms to meet and defeat them in Thy name and in the name of freedom and dignity of man. Keep us firm in our faith and resolution, and guide us that we may not dishonor our high mission or fail in our sacred duties. Let our enemies who have lived by the sword turn from their violence lest they perish by the sword. Help us to serve Thee gallantly and to be humble in victory. Amen.

Frank Sayers

Sayers was known as "Chief," like hundreds of other Native Americans in the service. Sayers was from Ballpark, Minnesota, and worked as a hunting guide. Note his gas-detector arm brassard, Griswold Bag, jump rope, Mae West, reserve chute, and other equipment. As the C-47 bucked and shimmied its way across the Channel, the photographer caught Sayers in his lens at this cockeyed angle. *Krochka*

bulbs, exposures, etc., trying to keep on my feet and at the same time hold the camera…

My own mission upon reaching the ground gave me cause for concern, for I memorized both it, and a course of action. As all the rest, I had too much time, since the ride was so long, to dwell on what was in store for us. And I wondered how in the hell I ever got mixed-up in this novel way of ending an interesting life. I kept wishing that the fellas back home could see me then… back home!

Prayer

Last-minute prayers, murmured or thought on the flight across the Channel, were a highly personal matter, indulged not only by the religious and thoughtful, but even by some who didn't usually talk to God.

Many of the callow youths, however, were oblivious to the gravity of the situation. This, combined with the paratroopers' necessary ability to blot out negative thoughts, gave some individuals a sense of well being. Many troopers fell asleep on the flight across. Others prayed continually, throughout the operation.

In his book, *Currahee,* Private First Class Don Burgett, A/506th, wrote:

We had so much equipment on and were so uncomfortable that the best way to ride was to kneel on the floor and rest the weight of the gear and chutes on the seat itself. Later I read an account by a reporter who didn't jump, but who did make the round trip in one of our planes. He wrote that we were knelt in prayer. Actually, it was just a comfortable way to ride.

Although Burgett later stated that he never attended church in his life and didn't know how to pray, his serene attitude indicates that he probably wouldn't have prayed anyway. He further wrote, "After taking the [airsickness] pills, I felt a happy glow on and at peace with the world and even managed to sleep a little during the flight."

Art "Jumbo" DiMarzio, D/506th, later recalled:

I remember it was almost like daylight in our plane, because the moon was out real bright. Lipinski got over and got on his knees. He was praying, but not out loud. He was my age, and what he was thinking about or what he thought he knew about combat was beyond me. I couldn't realize or fathom what was ahead of us. It was a… nothing to me… like a ball game or something… really not understanding it. Yet, being so naive, coming out of high school not a year earlier, going into a situation like that… *awesome… devastating* experience…

Landing

3

The Troop Carrier pilots were supposed to hold their course and formation and avoid evasive action, speeding up, sudden altitude changes, and so on. But the neat formations suddenly went into dense fog and cloud banks when crossing the west coast of the Cotentin Peninsula. The pilots spread out to avoid bumping other planes in the "zero visibility" sky. By the time they emerged into clear moonlight again, they had dispersed like the spokes of a bicycle wheel. Some began trying to readjust their course, but the flight over the peninsula took only about 10 minutes. Lots of 20mm cannon fire and flak began to come up at the planes, and many pilots did take evasive action. Often, the lighted "T's" of the Pathfinder teams were not visible on the ground, so pilots sometimes failed to turn on the green light to signal the start of the jump.

On an HQ/3rd/501st plane, the pilot executed a sudden, sharp climb, pointing the nose of the plane straight up. This caused men in the plane to slide to the tail and a few, slipping in vomit, were unable to make the jump.

Several planes went back over the Channel with paratroopers still aboard—they had crossed the entire peninsula without getting a green light from the pilot. Two pilots in the DZ A serial turned the green light on while over the Channel, resulting in the drowning of one entire stick of A/502nd and most of the men in another stick of the same company. These troops drowned off the coast of Ravenoville Plage and the dead included Captain Richard L. Davidson, the commander of A/502nd.

A few paratroop officers successfully talked their pilots into making a U-turn and taking them back over land. Some pilots made a second run of their own volition.

Sergeant Roy Berger of HQ/3rd/506th was on such a plane and went up to converse with the pilot about going back. The pilot initially refused, and battalion legend has it that Roy had to show him his .45 automatic to persuade him. Roy denies this, but admits he "convinced" the pilot to make another run over France.

The pilots were supposed to slow down as the jumpers exited their plane. At least some of them did. Sergeant Joe Kenney of E/501st noticed that his pilot slowed down and lifted the tail of the plane in textbook fashion as he and his men jumped out. Other troopers, such as Sergeant Arthur Parker and his group of the 377th PFAB, were forced to jump from aircraft that were flying too low, too fast, and were taking violent evasive action. Said Parker:

As we came out of the fog and clouds from the west, we were supposed to be flying at 1500 feet, but we could see that we were much lower than that. Anti-aircraft fire, every color in the rainbow, started to come up and the pilots began to take evasive action. My pilot dove down, banked to the left, and picked up speed. I didn't think a C-47 could move that fast. Our plane did suffer a few hits as we could feel the old bird shudder and hear bullets and shrapnel like stones on a tin roof find the plane. No one was hit in the cabin and the red light came on. The men stood and hooked up.

We moved three heavy equipment bundles to the door and hooked their static lines under difficult conditions. We were being bounced around by the evasive action of the pilot and the shell bursts rocking the plane. We managed a quick equipment check – I was third man in the stick. Our plane never did slow down to the proper jump speed. As we waited, it seemed that the sky was full of planes going in all directions at different heights, and I just knew there was going to be a midair collision or if we did jump now, we would be chewed up by the planes around us.

The green light came on and out went the equipment bundles and away we went, ass over elbows. Everything we had tied to us was blown off by the prop blast. My chute opened with such a jerk that I thought I broke my neck and cut my balls off at the same time. All the planes that were around us a minute ago were gone and I was hanging in the sky, all alone. Just before I hit the ground, I looked around and didn't see one parachute in the sky or on the ground. I landed with a bounce and laid there for a few seconds, listening. The straps had tightened up and the long struggle to get out of my chute seemed like half an hour. I got my folding stock carbine out of its holster, loaded it, and laid it beside me. All this time, planes were crossing the sky in all directions, but no jumpers were leaving the planes…[I] gave my trusty cricket a few chirps and waited for an answer. No luck.

Lieutenant Bill Sefton of HQ/2nd/501st was convinced that he was about to jump over the Channel. He could look down and see moonlight glinting on the shallows of the flooded fields east of Angoville. He knew that returning to England with the plane was out of the question. He did not exit dramatically, shouting "Bill Lee!" as prescribed. Instead, Sefton said, "Oh shit!" then "tumbled out the door like a drunk falling off a ledge."

Upon landing, he was pleasantly surprised to hit solid ground, and he had a long hike to reach the 2nd/501st assembly area.

Air and Sea Routes of 101st Airborne Division in Operation Neptune 6-8 June 1944. (Original map courtesy of Ivan Worrell and 101st ABD Association.)

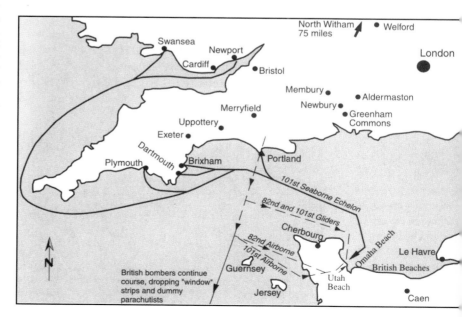

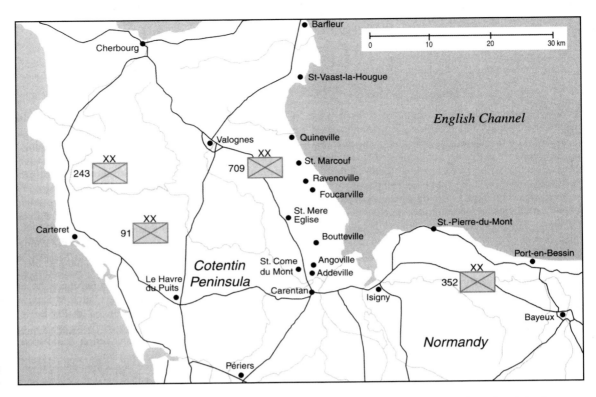

Sergeant Howard Colley, 3rd/502nd, came down through the branches of an apple tree. The impact knocked him unconscious. He later told his friend, Gordon Deramus, "The moon was shining. I heard nightingales singing like mockingbirds…I awoke smelling blossoms and hearing birds singing. I thought I'd died and gone to heaven."

An unknown paratrooper who landed in and hung up in a tree near Boutteville was aided by a French teenager, Paul Mauger, who came into his backyard and found the trooper struggling to get out of his harness. Mauger stood below the trooper, who handed him a knife and asked him to help. Mauger took the knife and cut the trooper's harness straps. Before

Paul Mauger

French civilian Paul Mauger lived at Boutteville, France, in 1944. In this 1989 photo, he displays the sheath knife given to him as a pres ent on D-day by a grateful American paratrooper who Mauger cut down from a tree. *Author's Photo*

the grateful trooper vanished into the night, he gave Mauger the knife as a present. At this writing Mauger, who lives on the N13 near Dead Man's Corner, still has it.

Many troopers, especially in the 506th, dropped heavy equipment attached to their leg in a British "leg bag." After their chute opened, they were supposed to lower the bag on a 20-foot rope to dangle below them so the weight of the equipment therein would hit the ground before they did. A number of planes in the DZ D area flew over so fast that the opening shock ripped the bags and even some other equipment clean off each jumper. Pee Wee Martin of G/506th managed to retain his, but couldn't release it on the way down, so he had to land with it attached to his leg. Miraculously, his leg wasn't broken.

Various colored lanterns, bells, whistles, bugles, and other signaling devices were brought to Normandy to aid in night assembly on the ground, but few troopers saw or heard them. The typical troopers landed in isolation in a dark field, with nobody in sight, except perhaps some cows or horses. On DZ D, however, the Germans had ignited a large barn doused with benzine. This gave an eerie brightness to the scene and the first troopers to land there could see following men actually coming out the door of their transports, clearly visible from the gasround. It was a dramatic scene as some of the planes were on fire and losing altitude as the paras bailed out.

Most feared of all were water landings. The shock of hitting cold water after a brief descent in darkness had a terrible effect. With many pounds of dead-weight equipment strapped on, a number of troopers drowned in even the shallow water created by the flooding from the La Barquette Lock. The fields south of Angoville were inundated and symmetrical deep ditches (some as deep as eight feet) crossed at intervals. Many troopers far west in the 82nd Airborne's area also drowned in floods from the Merderet River.

Flooded ditches and fields became trying obstacles for the survivors as well. To cross the shallow flooded fields, they had to wade across the ditches, some of which had barbed wire on the bottom, under the water.

The Air Corps pilots in many cases also dropped their sticks at a low altitude, allowing barely enough time for the chute fully deploy before landing. T-5 Hugh Pritchard of D/506th landed in chest-deep water with a heavy radio strapped to his leg. He had only about eight seconds to prepare for landing after his chute opened. He wrenched his back from the opening shock and could not release the bag from his leg before landing. The wind caught his canopy and dragged him, repeatedly. His account in George Koskimaki's book, *D-day with the Screaming Eagles* (Vantage Press, 1970), says:

… just as I started to unhook my harness, the chute jerked me down and I was dragged face down in the water. Fortunately, when I thought I could hold my breath no longer, the chute stopped and I scrambled to my feet and was able to gulp a few breaths before being jerked down again. This was repeated several times before the canopy collapsed in the water. I know I am not the bravest man in the world, nor do I think of myself as a coward, but the stark terror I saw and lived through in the Normandy campaign, and especially the first night, remains so vivid even today, that sometimes I wake up in a cold sweat and nearly jump out of bed.

Father Francis L. Sampson, the Catholic chaplain of the 501st, landed in a flooded area east of DZ D. He lost his government-issued mass (communion) kit in waist-deep water, then was dragged some distance away from it by his chute. When he returned to the approximate spot where he had dropped the kit, he retrieved it by diving under the murky water a number of times. He got it on the sixth try. This incident was depicted in the movie *The Longest Day,* but for some reason a British "Padre" was shown performing the dives instead of Father Sam.

A number of daring troopers jumped with a fully-assembled bazooka in addition to a rifle or submachine gun and all the other usual equipment. These landings were tricky to say the least. Dick Knudson of F/506th did it and broke his pelvis on landing. His days in the paratroops were over and he laid in no-man's land outside St. Mere Eglise for several days before being evacuated.

Gus Liapes of HQ/1st/506th belonged to a special squad of bazookamen known as the "Ha-Ha Squad" or the "8-Ball Squad." This group was led by Lieutenant Wayne "Bull" Winans (KIA in Holland). Liapes landed with a fully-assembled bazooka in the V of land formed by the roads north of Dead Man's Corner. He succeeded in landing without breaking any bones and killed a German who rushed him before he could get out of his harness. Gus had been in the 29th Division's rangers before transferring to the paratroops.

Some troopers landed on barbed-wire fences and got hung up. Joe "Pappy" Walkowski, G/502nd, landed on such a fence and got twisted around in it. He was injured and trapped and unable to get loose for two days, whereupon he was evacuated to England. A member of F/502nd was killed by his own M-1 rifle when he leaned it against another barbed-wire fence with the safety off and climbed over. A twig caught the trigger and fired the weapon as he was going over.

One of the most memorable stories about D-day night comes from H/502nd commander Captain Cecil Simmons. When he was growing up, Simmons and his twin brother took many belt thrashings from their father, a hard-nosed disciplinarian. He would take the boys in the bathroom, bend them over the toilet, and lash away with a belt. Simmons' brother would cry and yell, but Cecil practiced being silent, despite the pain. He later told his wife, Madge, that this training proved useful on D-day.

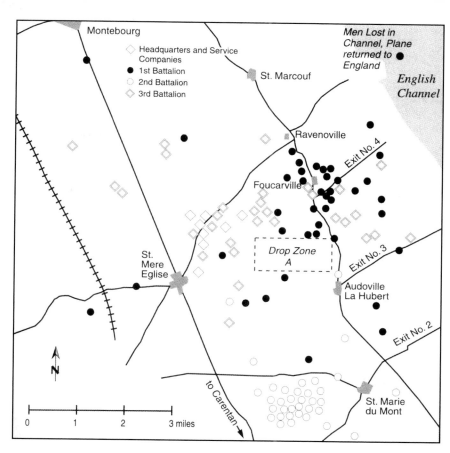

Men Lost in Channel, Plane returned to England ●

Montebourg
St. Marcouf
Ravenoville
Exit No. 4
Foucarville
Exit No. 3
St. Mere Eglise
Drop Zone A
Audoville La Hubert
Exit No. 2
to Carentan
St. Marie du Mont
English Channel

◇ Headquarters and Service Companies
● 1st Battalion
○ 2nd Battalion
◇ 3rd Battalion

N

0   1   2   3 miles

Drop Pattern 502nd Parachute Infantry Regiment.
(Original map courtesy of Ivan Worrell and 101st ABD Association.)

Simmons had barely gotten out of his chute when he became aware of many German troops running in his direction. He jumped off the road and concealed himself in the gorse in the ditch near the shoulder, but Simmons left one hand out, lying flat on the shoulder. A German soldier ran up, stood right on Simmons's hand with his hobnailed boot, and spun around, looking for American parachutists. Seeing no one, he darted off to continue searching. Germans were running everywhere in this area, but Big Cecil stayed quiet, which saved his life.

Not far from there, Sergeant Gordon Little of S-2/502nd was moving along a ditch east of St. Mere Eglise with a medic named Rogge. They spotted a road sign and Rogge walked up to try and read it. As he stood there in the moonlight, a German dispatch rider pulled up on a motorcycle. Little was only a few yards away in the ditch—he blew the startled German right out of his seat with a burst from his Tommy gun.

The men soon learned there were many, many Germans in the area. They began moving quickly eastward, evading large enemy groups for most of the night. A slug went through the crown of Little's helmet before dawn.

This may be an apocryphal story, but Glen Bartlett of HQ/3rd/501st swears it's true. Moving in the area east of St. Marie du Mont in the morning darkness, Bartlett's group came upon an American MP who was soaking wet. The man said he had joined the army to fight and had jumped into the Channel from a boat in the invasion fleet several miles off shore. He had swum to shore and was allowed to join the 101st in fighting behind Utah Beach.

Captain Frank L. Brown, Pathfinders, told of his men's experiences upon landing. One of the best ones reads:

The Pathfinders, having accomplished their mission, were attempting to infiltrate through the German defenses and reach the 101st Division Command Post. A group of one officer and five men were moving away from the DZ. A sergeant requested permission to return to the DZ and attempt to locate

"Rommel's Asparagus"

"Rommel's Asparagus" were simply tree trunks transplanted into open fields by the Germans and were intended to smash gliders upon landing or impale descending paratroopers. Some had barbed wire running from the top to the ground like Maypoles. Others had wire from top to top. Most were not completed by D-day. Many French civilians had been pressed into work gangs to help install these poles. At first light on D-day, many US paras were dismayed to see French civilians busily installing them as usual. The area near St. Marie du Mont was heavily planted with such poles, and some were reported on DZ D. Due to the shortage of wood in Normandy, the French used all of them for other purposes after the war.

Prior to being briefly captured, Lieutenant Jim Haslam, a 501st officer who had landed on DZ D with the Pathfinders, hid for almost a whole day in a large hole that had been dug for one of the poles. Jim and several others were captured by a small squad of Germans who used them as point men, forcing them to walk in the vanguard each time they moved. While double-timing past a church with an aid station inside, the Germans pointed at the entrance and kept running as the POWs trotted right into the entrance. Haslam and his companions were free and continued to serve in future battles.

Evidence that the Germans had plans to make the pole obstacles even more deadly was presented by former 101st Division Chief of Staff Colonel Gerald Higgins. Writing in George Koskimaki's consummate history, D-Day with the Screaming Eagles, Higgins recalled:

"One captured German officer, who had been in charge of planting the poles in the fields, told us that the Germans calculated the earliest date the Allies could make the drop and the invasion proper, would be the 21st of June. Accordingly, they had their sights set on finishing the job by 15 June, with the real pressure to be put on in the last ten days. In fact, in order to keep the mines which were attached to the barbed wire strung from pole to pole from being detonated by grazing cows, the mines were not to be activated until the 18th of June, After that, the French were to keep their cattle out of those fields, under penalty of their cows being shot. As you know, this never came to pass as the invasion took place some two weeks earlier than their calculations."

"Rommel's Asparagus" in a Norman field. *Krochka*

See map p. 260.

more of the men and lead them to the CP. Permission was granted and *en route* the NCO saw a group of seven men moving along a road. A low wall separated him from the group. Taking cover behind the wall, he challenged the group, thinking possibly that they were friendly. One of the group came forward and at a distance of about four feet, answered the challenge in German. The sergeant immediately opened fire and emptied a thirty-round clip into the nearest of the enemy. Dropping behind the wall, he threw two fragmentation grenades over the wall and reloaded his weapon. Rising, he again opened fire. Two of the group escaped. In relating the incident, the sergeant cursed fervently and blamed the escape to poor light and lack of guts on the part of the Germans. Although the American was fired upon, he apparently so surprised the enemy that their fire was inaccurate and he was unhurt.

Lieutenant Colonel Robert Cole, commanding 3rd/ 502nd, landed in a huge rosebush and struggled helplessly to get out for 15 minutes, the thorns tormenting his face and hands. He was finally able to reach his trench knife and cut his way out. In the process, he lost his cricket and the first man he encountered was Captain George Buker, the regimental intelligence officer. Buker recalls clicking his cricket at a silhouetted trooper in the darkness. He heard a voice say "Who is that?" in an irritated tone. It turned out to be Cole, who explained he had lost his cricket. (This contradicts the account in the book *Night Drop,* based on what Cole told S. L. A. Marshall.)

Cole moved west for some time, gathering more men, until they knocked at a door and a French-speaking 82nd trooper determined that they were on the edge of Sainte-Mère-Eglise. Cole reversed directions and met a group under Lieutenant Richard Winters, of E/506th. They marched east for some time, ambushing a convoy of German soldiers and horse-drawn wagons. The Germans were decimated by combined fire from both sides of the road, but Major J. W. Vaughan, S-4 of the 502nd, was killed in this action.

When the force reached the D-14, Winters struck off to the south with his men, and Cole dispersed the 502nd personnel to cover exits 3 and 4, where they were able to ambush retreating Germans later in the morning.

We shall never hear the stories of troopers who were killed before they could get out of their harnesses, but some, like Cecil Hutt, G/506th, went down shooting and survived to tell about it. Hutt found himself in a sizable group on D-day night, but they didn't want to move. Impatient to get on to his objective at Brévands, Hutt found a kindred spirit in Corporal Stanley Zebrosky of I/506th. They set off down the road together and were ambushed *en route* to the bridges. A fusillade of bullets came from Germans concealed in bushes. Zebrosky fell dead and Hutt heaved a grenade and sprayed the bushes with his weapon before going down with multiple wounds. He managed to kill one German and wound two others before being captured. Hutt spent the duration as a POW.

Some troopers actually experienced a peaceful landing – Major Hank Hannah, S-3 of the 506th, had jumped armed only with his rechambered .38-caliber Colt Peacemaker and a trench knife. He set off to find Culoville with a grenade in one hand, a pistol in the other, and his trench knife in his teeth. He wrote in his journal:

The night was clear and cool, the air was fragrant, the grass long and green, the fields small. There were many dairy cattle and horses roaming in the fields like shadows. Nearly all fence rows and roadsides had high banks and trees. I was thrilled beyond words.

Major J. W. Vaughn

Major J. W. Vaughan, a policeman in Indianapolis before WWII, was later killed when Cole's group ambushed a German convoy on D-day night.

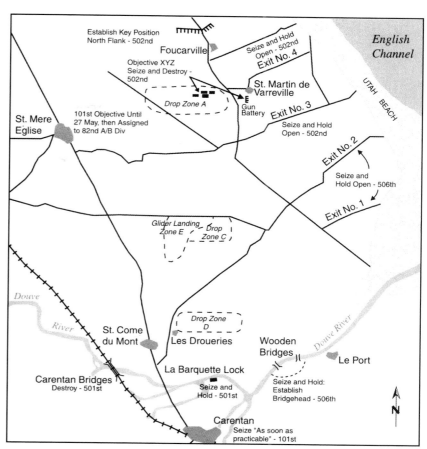

Main Objectives 101st Airborne Division.

(Original map courtacy of Ivan Worrell and 101st ABD Association.)

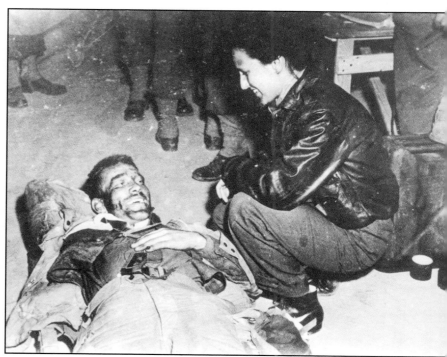

Wounded trooper

Back in England, a trooper who was seriously hurt by ground fire while standing up in his plane, returned to his airfield. Historian Bill Brown has identified this trooper as Roy Cobb, E/506th, in plane #68 of the 439th TCG. Cobb was wounded in the plane and Sergeant Mike Ranney cut his static line to prevent him from jumping. Cobb counted 250 holes in the plane. An alternate identification was given by Helen Briggs, who believed the wounded trooper to be John Androsky (KIA, Holland), G/506th.

***Opposite:* Corporal Stan Zebrosky**

Zebrosky (left), I/506th, teamed up with Cecil Hutt (not shown), G/506th, on D-day night. A German ambush killed Zebrosky and made Hutt a POW. In this 1943 photo, Jerry Beam, I/506th, stands at right. *Beam*

4

Saint-Marcouf

The northern boundary of the consolidated 101st Airborne drop was in the Crisbec-Saint-Marcouf area. Most of the troopers who landed north of there were either killed or captured. Dozens of troopers landed in the northern areas of Montebourg, Valognes, Quineville, and Saint-Vaast-la-Hocque. Most of the men who landed south of Crisbec managed to fight their way south to rejoin their units, although too late to arrive at their objectives on D-day.

Troopers who landed in the St. Marcouf area were six to 10 miles north of their assigned DZs near Saint-Martin-de-Varreville and Saint-Marie-du-Mont. The Crisbec gun battery area was the scene of some early encounters between American parachutists and German naval infantrymen on D-day night. Troopers who came down in the area southwest of Saint-Marcouf found a number of coastal gun emplacements in concrete casements. Several hundred over-aged German naval reservists under command of a Leutnant Ohmsen manned them. The average age of Ohmsen's troops was 38, but the canny older men would fight with distinction. At the position were four 210mm guns, one 150mm gun, and six antiaircraft guns. In the months before D-day, Allied bombers had dumped some 600 tons of bombs on the concrete fortifications, but failed to destroy them. Indeed, half a century later, they are still a major tourist attraction, although the guns have been removed for salvage.

German historian Paul Carrell, in his book, *Invasion – They're Coming* (Bantam Books and E. P. Dutton), described early encounters between men of the 377th PFAB and 502nd, misdropped near Crisbec, with

some of Ohmsen's garrison. Around 0100 on 6 June 1944, Ohmsen's men were alerted to Allied parachutists landing in their area. Some of the Germans conducted a patrol in the darkness and heard strange clicking sounds coming from the bushes. They butt-stroked a paratrooper who tried to signal them with his cricket device. As they continued walking in the area, more soldiers challenged them with the clicking device. According to Carrell, Ohmsen's men soon realized that the cricket was a recognition signal and proceeded to equip themselves with more and more captured crickets, with which they were able to capture or kill a number of other troopers.

Some of the troopers who were taken prisoner in this manner were later liberated and told media reporters that an intelligence leak before D-day had given the Germans information on the crickets. They were under the impression that the German Army had supplied its troops in Normandy with crickets of their own.

The cricket signaling device got mixed reviews. Private First Class Charles O'Neill of F/501st says, "The first thing I did was throw mine away." Major Allen W. "Pinky" Ginder of the 502nd, however, felt the person who conceived the cricket idea deserved a medal. If Carrell's story is true, we can realize in retrospect what actually occurred.

Ohmsen, who later became an admiral in the Federal German Navy, had quite a saga of his own. His reservists waged a private war of their own with the US fleet sitting off the coast near Utah Beach. For seven days, the battered garrison held out, claiming

Guns of Crisbec
One of the huge guns at Crisbec was photographed by Lieutenant Jim Haslam, a Mormon from Utah, who jumped as Pathfinder security on D-day. Haslam spent a brief period as a POW then mistakenly headed north in search of his regiment. He got as far as Saint-Marcouf before changing directions. *Haslam*

Saint-Marcouf

One of the most famous invasion photos was taken near the wall of the church in Saint-Marcouf. The US government's official history, *Utah Beach to Cherbourg*, gives the information that the men pictured are from the 4th Infantry Division, but blackened faces, bloused trousers, gauze armflags, and trench knives on ankles all point to them being paratroopers. A few sticks of the 508th PIR were misdropped in this area. Their men wore these gauze arm flags. The stairway is blown down to rubble by one of the 8 inch guns of the cruiser *USS Quincy. US Army*

one US destroyer sunk (the US Navy claims the destroyer hit a mine in the Channel) and repulsing numerous ground assaults by elements of the 4th Infantry Division, as well as heavy counterbattery fire from the US Navy. In one assault, American engineers actually succeeded in surmounting the casements to plant demolitions charges, but were killed by artillery fragments before they could set them. Ohmsen had called for artillery on his position from neighboring German guns at Azeville. When an assault group from the 9th Infantry Division was brought in, they were relieved to find that Ohmsen's garrison had withdrawn to the north. He had received orders to fall back to Cherbourg with his survivors.

Ravenoville And Saint-Marcouf

On D-day morning, Sergeant Benecke and his group from Battery A, 377th PFAB, were on the loose between Ravenoville and Saint-Marcouf, as this photo proves. *Benecke*

Ravenoville

So many troopers of the 101st Airborne and even the 82nd Airborne landed in the vicinity of Ravenoville that it became a hub of activity on D-day. Men of the 502nd, 506th, and 377th PFAB assembled on the outskirts and eventually wrested the town from a strong German garrison of at least a company in strength. The photos that appear in this section suggest the confusion that reigned as troopers came into the town from the north and east, but departed headed east or south.

To add to the confusion, there is another group of dwellings known as Ravenoville Plage (Beach), situated on the coast. The actual town of Ravenoville proper is several kilometers inland from the Channel. Don Burgett's A/506th stick landed near Ravenoville Plage and worked their way west, eventually attacking the German garrison in Ravenoville proper in a spontaneous attack led by Lieutenant William Muir, a former policeman from Bay City, Michigan. Although Burgett credits Muir with leading the attack, an enlisted man of the same company was decorated with the Silver Star for leading the attack that resulted in the capture of Ravenoville. Private (soon to be sergeant) Donald Brinninstool, of Jackson, Michigan, was credited with aggressive leadership in the citation for his Silver Star. It states that Brinninstool's aggressiveness resulted in 10 enemy dead, 30 captured, and the capture of an ammo dump, two recon cars, and a staff car.

It is unknown if Burgett and Brinninstool fought in the same group on D-day, but in any case, the German garrison was driven from the heavy stone houses in Ravenoville by a relatively small force of troopers. There was some fighting in and near the town church, and a Renault light tank was captured in the area.

Charles "Red" Knight, an A/506th man from Speed-way, Indiana, was in a small band of troopers who were captured early on D-day. When the Germans searched him, they found a canned chicken which had been sent by Brinninstool's mother before the invasion. Not wanting the Germans to enjoy the chicken, Knight lied and told them the can contained explosives. The Germans made him dig a hole and bury it. "We would have liked to mark that grave," he said later. The troopers never did get back to dig up the chicken, although shortly afterward, Knight and his group escaped and went on to fight through the war with the 506th. Contrary to previous reports, Brinninstool says he was not in the captured group and was at no time a POW.

Being captured and then escaping was to become a common experience within the 101st Airborne. Many troopers were captured while in the midst of the enemy, only to be liberated a matter of minutes or hours later when the circumstances changed.

Sergeant Bill Knight of C/506th met a small group from his company. They joined members of other units in assembling at the ancient Marmion farm, at the south edge of Ravenoville. This became a hub of activity for members of many units.

Most of the troops who left Ravenoville headed directly south on the D-14, toward Foucarville. Burgett's group did so early on 7 June, after spending the night in Ravenoville. The Company A group of the 506th repulsed a German counterattack that night, during which a concussion grenade landed in Lieutenant Muir's foxhole, exploding between the dirt wall of the hole and the gas mask in the rubberized invasion bag attached to Muir's leg. The concussion of the blast broke Muir's femur. He tried to walk south with the group that departed the next morning, but couldn't keep up. He stayed behind and was evacuated to England.

En route to Foucarville early on 7 June, Burgett's group walked through an area along the D-14 that had been totally desolated by naval or aerial bombardment. The area was spooky looking as Burgett reported in his book, *Currahee:*

On the march, we passed through a section that had been blasted to rubble. I don't know whether it was from bombing or shelling from one of the large battleships. The trees were shredded stumps with wisps of smoke or ground fog laced through them. The ground was plowed into loose dirt with large craters scattered all over. The whole scene reminded me of some oil paintings I had seen that were reputed to have been done by some demented artist. Not a single bird flew in the area nor did I see an insect on the ground. A deadly silence hung over the area like a suffocating blanket. The shuffling of our boots, along with an occasional pebble being kicked across the hard surface of the blacktop sounded loud. I thought to myself that this must be the home of death itself. We kept walking and soon left the desolate place behind. The fields on either side of the road became greener and more peaceful as we moved along.

On a lighter note, as Sergeant Ed Benecke of the 377th PFAB was walking out of Ravenoville with other stray troops, he noticed that snipers seemed to be singling him out. More enemy fire seemed to come in Benecke's direction. He eventually figured out it was caused by the squirrel's tail he had attached to the back of his helmet, so he took it off.

French Family At Ravenoville, D-day

This remarkable photo was taken on D-day morning about 200 yards south of Dodainville. Sergeant Benecke, A/377th PFAB, encountered this French family sheltering from the naval and aerial bombardment of their and other coastal villages. It is possible that they heard the BBC radio broadcast on 6 June after midnight, warning French coast dwellers to move inland and take cover. *Benecke*

Ed Benecke of A/377th photographed members of 1st Bn 506th marching toward Ste-Mère-Eglise, from the Marmion Farm, along the D-15 road.

Foucarville

Pre-invasion planners had decided that Foucarville was to be the far north flank of their airborne bridge-head. There was a known strongpoint on a fortified hill near the north edge of the town. A barrage from the 377th PFAB was to eradicate it; and the 1st/502nd was to establish roadblocks to prevent German rein-forcements from attacking Utah Beach from the north or west.

Shortly after 0100 on D-day, a small group under Captain Cleveland Fitzgerald, CO of B/502nd assem-bled and attacked the town. In *Night Drop*, S. L. A. Marshall wrote that this was the first French town to be brought under attack by American forces on D-day.

In the courtyard of one house, Fitzgerald killed a Ger-man at point-blank range, but received a bullet through his chest in return. He told his men he was dying and wanted them to leave him. He was saved, however, only to die a year later in a car crash in Reims, France, after V-E Day.

A number of 502nd troopers dropped almost on top of the fortified strongpoint and were immediately cap-tured. Lieutenant Joseph Smith was one of them. He was shot and captured after giving the Germans quite a battle. Other POWs on the fortified hill included Sergeant Charlie Ryan, and Hewitt Tippins, both of A/502nd.

Throughout D-day, Ryan and his buddies plotted a way to escape. They acted apprehensively and told

Lieutenant Wallace Swanson

Swanson assumed command of A/502nd after the com-pany CO, Captain Richard Davidson, drowned in the Chan-nel. Swanson set up a roadblock west of Foucarville that was instrumental in preventing German reinforcements from reaching the coast. This Stateside photo shows Swanson wearing his prized leather A-2 flight jacket with chest insi-gnia of the 502nd PIR. *Swanson*

1st/502nd Company Commanders

Shown before D-day are Richard L. Davidson (top left), Cleveland Fitzgerald (top right), Warner Broughman (bottom left), and Fred Hancock (bottom right). *Smit*

their captors that the planned artillery barrage was going to wipe the hill off the map in the evening. The Germans became restless and unsure of their situation. In the evening, part of the German force broke and ran from the position, leaving others behind who wished to surrender. Troops outside opened fire on the fleeing Germans and they were killed. Ryan killed the German major who had commanded the strongpoint, and acquired his pistol.

There was shooting in all parts of the town throughout D-day, with persistent sniping from the church steeple. Private John T. Lyell was among those killed, and A/502nd characters like Asay, Zweibel, and Nicolai kept the Germans busy.

A stray trooper from the 82nd Airborne had stayed in the bushes near the church all day. Late in the day, he saw several Germans coming out the church door a few feet away and shot them all.

Captain Jim Hatch was in town late in the evening and was too tired to guard his prisoners. He placed them in a wooden farm shed, told them to throw their boots outside, sprinkled thumbtacks outside the door, and slept soundly.

502nd Machine gunners

Troopers of the 502nd pose with their M-1919A4 light machine gun in Normandy. *Musura*

Survivors

Surviving officers of 1st/502nd posed in France near the end of the campaign. (Standing, left to right) Hancock, Choy, Hatch, Michaelis, Schmidt, Smit, Cassidy, Sutliffe, Dr. William Best. (Below, left) Emzy W. Gaydon. (Below, right) Sid Clary and Wally Swanson. *Choy*

Saint-Germain-de-Varreville, 1990s

Part of the small village of Saint-Germain-de-Varreville as seen looking south on the D-14, in the early 1990s. Lieutenant Colonel Patrick Cassidy's parachute landing put him down in the cross-roads at left. He came under immediate machine-gun fire, but escaped to make his way to Objective W.

Although Captain Frank Lillyman's Pathfinder team had made a rendezvous at the small church in Saint-Germain, that village continued to be a passing point for troops moving north as well as south on D-day. Lieutenant Colonel Pat Cassidy, the CO of 1st/502nd, landed right on the main crossroads of the D-14 and came under machine-gun fire immediately. Like Lillyman, Cassidy moved south toward the gun batteries of St. Martin de Varreville. Cassidy's main focus was to set up a battalion CP at Objective W *(see Chapter 9)*.

As stated previously, Captain Lillyman's Pathfinder plane had arrived too early. The pilot passed the pre-designated DZ A area near Loutres, eventually circling back. As a result, Lillyman and his radar man, Gus Mangoni, were dropped at Saint-Germain, several miles NE of the predesignated DZ. They did not have time to run cross crountry with their signalling equipment before the serials of aircraft began coming over, so the radar and lights were established in an orchard behind the church in Saint-Germain. Many 438th TCG planes dropped on those signals, although the entire 2nd/502nd was deposited on the wrong DZ (DZ C). This explains, though, why only one plane dropped on the pre-planned DZ near Loutres. That stick actually strayed from Lillyman's signals. The bulk of 2nd/506th (Strayer's battalion) also dropped on Lillyman's signals and landed above DZ A east of Foucarville, many miles north of their intended DZ C. Strayer's battalion marched south along the D-14 road, encountering resistance which slowed, but did not stop, them near Audoville-la-Hubert. At le Grand Chemin, they tied in with Lieutenant Dick Winters's small force from E/506th and attacked the Brecourt Battery to help open Exit 2.

Lieutenant Colonel Cassidy was a man of many roles on D-day and figured in the events at a number of locations. He made important decisions during the "XYZ" fight, and in the afternoon was personally reconning a route toward Company C's fight near Haut Fornel.

Cassidy's battalion was hailed by S. L. A. Marshall as the unit that did the one best job for America on D-day, but Cassidy had his human foibles as well.

In a letter dated 1991 from C. E. "Jack" Applegate of 2nd/502nd to his wartime buddy, Ray Hood, Applegate recalled spending the first five days in Normandy with Cassidy's group. In the brief story that follows, Applegate recalls Cassidy with typically rough GI humor:

Me and my buddy had been through Demolitions School; I was skinny then, so I carried a lot of explosives. Every time we got near Cassidy, he yelled at us to get the Hell away from him! He seemed to have a spring in him. Every time anyone saluted him, he'd scream "You son of a bitch" and hit the ground!!! You suppose he was afraid of snipers???? I guess he'd heard they like to shoot at officers.

Lieutenant Wally Swanson, who assumed command of A/502nd, had landed in the salt marshes near the coast, close to Exit 4. He led his assembled group to the gun batteries, then north through Saint-Germain to establish roadblocks near Foucarville.

Of course, the usual hedgerow hide-and-seek and defense against German probes went on in the area throughout D-day.

Haut Fornel
The Legend of Smit's Pond

D-day afternoon saw elements of C/502nd probing toward Beuzeville in the confusing maze of hamlets west of Foucarville. Lieutenant Morton J. Smit and Private Harold Boone found themselves on point, entering the courtyard of a sizable chateau in Haut Fornel. This chateau had been used as a German barracks (in a 1992 correspondence to the author, Smit said he felt that the chateau was more likely used as a CP rather than a barracks). The compound was filled with enemy equipment, although it was presently devoid of troops. When a truckful of Germans pulled up in front of the stone gate, Smit and Boone sprayed the debarking soldiers with their weapons, inflicting about 10 casualties.

Like hornets from an aroused nest, the surviving Germans began swarming into the courtyard in search of the Americans. Smit and Boone ran through the chateau then out the back door (in that same later correspondence, Smit also indicated he ran around the back of the building after firing at the Germans, rather than through the inside). The two Americans found the back wall too high to surmount with their weapons and equipment. Encountering an algae-covered pond in one corner of the courtyard, they slid into the water and submerged until hidden from view of the searching Germans.

In *Night Drop,* S.L.A. Marshall depicts a carbine-equipped Smit breathing with just his lips and nose protruding through the algae. Smit's own account in Koskimaki's D-day says he disassembled his M-3 "Grease Gun" submachine gun, and breathed through the barrel, while submerged. Smit says the idea was derived from watching a Western movie shortly before the invasion.

The troopers succeeded in hiding this way for nearly an hour, until attacking Americans drove the Germans out. A trooper named Lesinski saw Smit emerging from the water and nearly ran him through with his bayonet. He couldn't recognize the muck-covered officer until Smit shouted to identify himself, just in time.

As the story goes, the Germans counterattacked at that moment, causing all three troopers to enter the pond for another extended period of hiding.

Sergeant Charles Tinsley was also in the area and is credited in Smit's written account as being the man who almost ran him through with the bayonet, but Tinsley himself, interviewed in 1992, did not recall the incident.

The chateau had remained mostly unchanged until the present owners bought it in the early 1980s. Much work has been done to repair the roof, heighten and expand the wall, renovate the pond, and terrace the yard.

Lieutenant Morton J. smit, C/502nd
Smit and Private Harold Boone were trapped in a walled courtyard and saved themselves by submerging themselves in a pond.

Captain Fred Hancock
Hancock commanded C/502nd. He and his men sprung an ambush east of Haut Fornel that stopped German reinforcements from reaching the coast. *Hancock*

Lieutenant colonel Patrick Cassidy
A fine study of Cassidy, CO of 1st/502nd. S.L.A. Marshall wrote of the battalion saying it "did the one best job for America on D-day." *Buker*

Saint-Martin-de-Varreville

9

Allied planners considered the Saint-Martin-de-Varreville area of high military importance because of the four concrete-emplaced captured Soviet 122mm howitzers situated in a field southwest of the village and the series of stone houses west of the village (at Mesiéres), which housed their crews. The large guns were captured on the Russian Front and integrated into the defenses of the Atlantic Wall.

Because of the high trajectory of these large-caliber guns, they were sited some two to three miles behind the coast, to cover Exits 3 and 4. The guns were manned by the *1st Battalion* of *Army Coastal Artillery Regiment 1261.*

The RAF had bombed the field where the guns were situated on 29 May. The field was bombed again on the night of 5 June, just before the paratroopers dropped. On 29 May, one bunker caved in (possibly from the sheer weight of 500-pound bombs landing on the roof, as the other three bunkers were undamaged), and the 122mm howitzer at this collapsed bunker was trapped out in front of it. The Germans, realizing that the position had been pinpointed, hastily moved the other three guns away from that site to an unknown location.

The final bombing had torn up the field and tossed crates full of German munitions and equipment all over the field. A small Renault light tank had been flipped over by the bombing. When Captain Lillyman's small group scouted the location near dawn on D-day, they located the field and found it was deserted, with the guns removed. Leaving part of his force behind, Lillyman went back up the D-14, where he met Lieutenant Colonel Cassidy and reported what he had found. The absence of the guns was a major relief as they had been considered a serious threat to the D-day beach landings. Lieutenant Colonel Steve Chappuis, CO of 2nd/502nd, arrived and stayed at the bombed field to intercept his troops as they arrived and to reorganize them for another assignment.

It is interesting to note that at least one trooper landed right in the field where the gun battery was situated. He was Lieutenant Gordon Deramus, of HQ/3 502nd.

Captain LeGrand "Legs" Johnson commanded F/502nd. He later recalled that Company F had won a competition during training in England and was designated as the assault company of 2nd/502nd. They had envisioned storming the de Varreville battery bunkers with artillery support from the 377th PFAB. The plan, if all else failed, was to use ropes and grappling hooks to surmount the bunkers individually and plant explosive charges. Legs recalls scouring English hardware stores before D-day to find the ropes and grappling hooks, which were dropped in an equipment bundle but never recovered by his men. He later said, "No doubt some French farmer found that bundle and wondered how we hoped to defeat the enemy with grappling hooks."

In the years since WWII, the field housing the gun bunkers has not been a tourist attraction because of its obscure location. Accessible only via a two-track cart path, even many history-minded residents of the Cotentin Peninsula don't know the location. Also, the farmer who owns the field doesn't want tourists

Pows digging trenches, D-day

This photo has appeared in print before, with the erroneous information that the German POWs are digging graves near Hiesville. It was actually taken D-day afternoon, behind Objective W. The POWs are digging trenches to repulse the anticipated German counterattacks from the west, which might threaten the CP. Shortly after the photo was taken, the guard with the Tommy gun shot a German who walked over to the bushes at the side of the field without permission. Hearing the shots, Lieutenant Pangerl and Sergeant Patheiger rushed out and talked to the wounded POW. He stated he wasn't trying to escape, but only wanted to urinate, and was too shy to ask permission. Another photo, which does show POWs digging graves, was taken by Sergeant Benecke, 377th PFAB *(see Chapter 15). Musura*

Objective W, 1990s

In June 1944, this house was known as Objective W. It actually lies west of the town of Saint-Martin-de-Varreville northwest of the intersection of the D-14 with the Mesières Road. Pre-invasion planners had earmarked it for Lieutenant Colonel Pat Cassidy's 1st/502nd CP. When Colonel George Moseley broke his leg on the drop and failed to show up at the designated regimental CP at Loutres, France, Lieutenant Colonel Mike Michaelis assumed command of the 502nd, moving his assembled group into the house at Objective W and establishing it as the new regimental CP. From here, Staff Sergeant Harrison Summers, B/502nd, jumped off on his epic assault on the group of houses along the Mesières road, known as Objective XYZ.

During D-day afternoon, Lieutenant Joseph Pangerl, the IPOW officer of the 502nd, began interrogating German prisoners in the kitchen of Objective W. As he spoke to a prisoner, two fully-armed and equipped German soldiers emerged from the root cellar of the house, acting surprised that there were Americans in the house. They surrendered to Pangerl without incident. This house was largely destroyed and has been rebuilt in mostly the same configuration as it was in 1944.

About one kilometer east of Objective W lies the small village of Saint-Martin-de-Varreville. Not much fighting took place there, although a patrol drove some Germans out of the church and captured a radio transmitter and an arms cache. These items were placed in the street and blown up with explosives. *Author's Photo.)*

47

The bunkers, 1990s
One of the bunkers photographed in the 1990s – the farmer has disguised them with rose and raspberry bushes. *Author's Photo*

Staff Sergeant Harrison Summers at the XYZ Complex

Although this section is being included with the Saint-Martin-de-Varreville chapter, the series of stone houses that housed the German artillerymen were actually in the hamlet of Mesiéres, just west of Saint-Martin. Starting from Cassidy's CP at Objective W near the D-14–Mesiéres crossroads, Staff Sergeant Harrison Summers led the attack on the complex.

After visiting the area, one realizes that the term "barracks complex," which has been applied to the area in previous writing, is misleading. The term "barracks" conjures up rectangular buildings all of a relatively uniform shape, size, and type of construction. This XYZ complex is nothing but a series of old, stone-constructed French farmhouses of varying shapes and sizes, which straddle both sides of the Mesiéres road west of the D-14. The 122mm howitzer battery that was situated several hundred yards away, across the D-14, was manned by troops who had simply commandeered this group of houses for use as billets.

When Summers started out on D-day morning to drive German troops from this series of houses, he had only an understrength platoon, most of whom were strays from other companies and didn't know him or each other. This made them reluctant to follow orders and reticent about joining the fight. Many were no doubt preoccupied with thoughts of their own assigned objectives.

As a result, Summers became a one-man army, attacking each house in the complex singlehandedly, although he was occasionally joined by other individuals. By the time he had reached Building 11 in mid-afternoon, Summers had personally killed several dozen enemy soldiers and routed a unit over 100 men.

tramping around it (he has even covered the bunkers with rose and raspberry bushes). Three of the four bunkers are intact, however, with subterranean tunnels connecting them. The fact that two heavy bombing raids, concentrated on four bunkers in an area about the size of a football field, failed to destroy three of the four bunkers is instructive. Like the bunkers at Crisbec, it is evidence of the ineffectiveness of aerial bombardment on steel-reinforced concrete fortifications.

502nd Troopers Guard Prisoners
On 7 June 1944, Sergeant Benecke, A/377th PFAB, passed through the Saint-Martin-de-Varreville area and snapped this photo of 502nd troopers guarding German prisoners. *Benecke*

After clearing Building 11, Summers sat down for a smoke. When asked about his behavior, he later said, "I have no idea why I did what I did that day. I know now that it was a crazy thing to do and I wouldn't do it again under the same circumstances. The other men were hanging back – they didn't seem to want to fight."

If the 101st ever had a "Sergeant York" in WWII, it was Summers, a mild-mannered and soft-spoken man who became a coal-mine inspector after leaving the Army. S. L. A. Marshall called him "laughing boy in uniform." He campaigned to get Summers the Medal of Honor for his feats on D-day, but as mentioned elsewhere, higher authorities seemed to feel that one per campaign for the division would suffice. Colonel Cole earned the honor for Normandy, but Summers survived until the 1980s to bask in his accomplishment, if not fame.

The name of Harrison Summers and others like him should be known to students in all American schools. This has not come to pass, however, and his D-day triumphs were only recognized with the Distinguished Service Cross (DSC). Half a century later, a walk through the XYZ complex reveals that the houses themselves have changed little, except for the addition of TV antennas on the roofs. Some houses had firing ports cut in the stone walls, but the French people closed them after reclaiming their homes.

Eyes of a hero

Staff Sergeant Harrison Summers, B/502nd, with a Hawaiian girl taken before WWII while he was stationed at Schofield Barracks. Summers was a veritable one-man army at the XYZ complex. *via Rick Summers*

A well-Zarned medal, D+1

A group of 502nd officers make a meal in front of a house in les Mesieres. *(Left to right)* Captain Ivan Phillips (regimental communications officer), Lieutenant Gordon Johnson (platoon leader), Lieutenant Jim Kean, Lieutenant Joe Pangerl (IPW officer), Lieutenant Bill Geddes (assistant communications officer), and an unknown platoon leader. Phillips had assembled a large force in the area north of Saint-Martin and just behind the coast on D-day morning. He found the camouflaged Ford in the photo in his travels en route to the Objective W area. It was marked "Assembled in England." Lieutenant Kean was sent by General Anthony McAuliffe to investigate what happened to Captain R. L. Davidson and his men, who had been misdropped in the Channel on D-day night. He learned that the Navy had recovered their bodies from the waters off the coast and that every plane of the serial that dropped them had made it back to England – the only serial carrying 101st men that could make that claim. *Pangerl*

See map p. 260.

49

Buildings 2, 3, And 4, Summers's charge

Sergeant Harrison Summers, armed with a Tommy gun, attacked Building 1 alone. He kicked in the door, shot four Germans and others escaped, running west on the Mesieres road toward the next buildings. These three buildings are clustered in a group. In Building 2, Summers found only a sick child. Approaching Building 3, Summers got covering machinegun fire from Private William Burt. Summers burst in and shot six more Germans. Building 4 was empty.

Building 5, Summers's charge

Crossing to the north side of the road, Summers attacked building 5, which sat back some distance from the road. On the approach, Summers was joined by an unidentified captain from the 82nd Airborne. They attacked the house together, but the captain fell dead from a rifle bullet. This is a large house, which required a room-to-room search. Summers entered alone and gunned down six more Germans in the various rooms.

Building 8, Summers's charge

While attacking Buildings 6, 7, and 8, Summers was joined by Private John Camien, who had a carbine. They took turns on these three houses, trading weapons. One would kick the door and cover with the carbine, as the other jumped inside and sprayed with the Thompson. Together, they killed another 15 Germans combined in these three houses.

Building 9, Summers's charge

From Building 8, it is about a quarter of a mile walk down the road to the driveway north of the road, which gave access to the last three buildings of the complex. Building 9 is a large, impressive chateau that the German artillerymen used as their messhall. Summers entered and found 15 Germans seated at a long table, eating. They were either oblivious to the fight outside or, as Summers put it, "The biggest chowhounds in the German Army." At any rate, as they rose to get weapons, Summers swept the lot of them with his Tommy gun.

Building 11, Summers's charge

Building 10, a sizable wooden shed that contained munitions, once stood beside this building. It was set afire by tracers from William Burt's machine gun and the ammo started exploding. Thirty Germans were flushed from the building and shot by Summers and others who had joined the fight. Lieutenant Colonel Cassidy had sent more troops up to join the fight and now Summers had help, although seven of the others were killed and four wounded in taking the last two buildings. Building 11 was a large, two story farm building that was used as a barracks to house a company of German troops. They were firing out of the windows at two different levels. Staff Sergeant Roy Nickrent, the battalion operations sergeant for 1st/502nd, arrived, kicked one foot into the dirt embankment of the road, and fired a number of bazooka rounds at the roof of Building 11. This finally started the building on fire. More than 80 Germans came pouring out of the building, some running north across the open field at the rear. They were caught in a crossfire from three sides, including fire from Michaelis's group and a group in the van guard of the 4th Infantry Division. About 50 Germans were killed and the rest surrendered

Para-Cavalry, D+4
Two paratroopers patrol the town on horses captured from the 795th Ost Battalion (Georgian), which had been stationed in nearby Turqueville. The entrance to the town square and approaches to the famous church (Eglise), can be seen at the upper-right rear. *US Army*

Sainte-Mère-Eglise is one of the few sizable cities on the N-13 between Carentan and Cherbourg and lies somewhat in the center of the Cotentin Peninsula. It was originally to be the drop area for the 101st Airborne, but their DZs were moved east when the German *91st Air Landing/ Infantry Division* moved into the region less than a month before D-day.

The 82nd Airborne, which was originally slated to land near St. Saveur le Vicomte, shifted its area east, putting Sainte-Mère in the center of its area of operations. Because John Steele of F/505th landed atop the town church and dangled from the steeple, feigning death, the town has been closely identified with the legend of the 82nd Airborne. Yet it also has a place in the annals of the 101st. Stray sticks from the 506th and 502nd landed in or near the town by mistake as much as 45 minutes before 505th PIR troopers began to arrive, inciting the defending garrison into a frenzy of activity. There were some headquarters elements of the *91st Division* in the town, and, according to German historian Paul Carrell, a *Luftwaffe* flak battalion. The 3rd Battalion of the 505th, under Lieutenant Colonel "Cannonball" Krause, is credited with seizing St. mere before 0400 on 6 June.

Lieutenant Turner Turnbull of the 505th led his platoon in a fierce battle on D-day afternoon, stopping a battalion-sized German attack that was driving toward St. Mere Eglise from the north. Turnbull, who was killed shortly thereafter, has become a legend in the rich lore of the 82nd Airborne Airborne Division.

The *91st Division* was an anomaly in the German Army – its members had started as *Luftwaffe* ground troops, but in 1943 were converted to a regular army unit. A former member of their headquarters returns to the town from Germany each year in June. Sergeant Rudi Escher was one of those who removed John Steele from the roof of the church. Steele was soon liberated when the town was captured and Rudi Escher went into American captivity.

The legends of Sainte-Mère-Eglise have been repeated many times over, so here are a couple of lesser-known stories.

Glenn Dempsey, E/502nd, landed on the tiled rooftop of a house in Sainte-Mère-Eglise. He could hear Germans inside, talking. Still in his chute, he feared they might have heard some of the tiles that dislodged, so he tossed a grenade in the window and killed them. He squirmed out of his harness and got to relative safety outside the town. He was seriously wounded near Carentan on 11 June.

A young French girl who had a German soldier for a lover lived in an upper-story apartment in town. When the alarm came of Allied parachutists landing, the German soldier grabbed his helmet and ran outside to help in the fighting. A 505th trooper came under sniper fire from an upstairs window. He ran up the stairs and shot the *mademoiselle,* who had picked up her boyfriend's rifle and fired it at the invaders. Today, she is listed among the names on the town honor roll as one of those who died in the 1944 liberation of her community. Many people in the town know this, but no one speaks about it.

Fifty years later
The same spot in the early 1990s. The storefronts have changed, but the location is still recognizable. Phil Juttras, curator of the Airborne Museum, chats with a citizen in the doorway. *Author's Photo*

Left: Wounded Paratrooper

Who is he? Eddie Sapinski and a handful of others from F/502nd were misdropped west of Sainte-Mère-Eglise and fought with a group from the 82nd for the first six days. Sapinski took this photo of a wounded paratrooper in that area. John Cucinotta, also of Company F, claims this man was a 508th pathfinder and that he died of wounds about two days after this photo was taken. Howard Matthews of Company F claims the man is Willard L. Davis, a Company F man from Texas. Sapinski can no longer remember, but we are indebted to him for a most dramatic photo. *Sapinski*

Combat Condom

Two 82nd Airborne troopers dug in at the base of a hedgerow. One has fitted a condom over the muzzle of his folding stock carbine to keep out rain. *Sapinski*

German Sergeant Rudi Escher

Portrait of Sergeant Rudi Escher in the early 1940s – before the 91st Air Landing Division was converted to an army division. He wears a Luftwaffe noncom's uniform. Escher survived the fighting and still makes annual pilgrimages to Sainte-Mère-Eglise. *Escher*

Right: Foxhole living

Sapinski recorded these two 82nd Airborne Division troopers (note small mesh helmet nets), in their hole west of Sainte-Mère-Eglise. *Sapinski*

Audouville and Le Grand Chemin | 11

Shaub's charge, D+1

Somewhere in the vicinity of Audoville la Hubert. (Left to right) Joe Pistone, Floyd Baker (medic), and Sergeant Mike Milenczenko (a.k.a. "Mike the Cat") with German artillerymen killed in Benjamin Shaub's one-man charge. Pistone

Shaub's charge at Audoville certainly ranks with the actions at Holdy and le Grand Chemin for valor, yet little is known about it. To set the stage for the action, it must be explained that Joe Pistone of F/502nd was the man with the camera. Pistone was supposed to land on DZ A to attack the Saint-Martin 122mm howitzer battery. He was misdropped miles south of there on the DZ C area near Sainte-Marie-du-Mont. He saw Colonel Robert Sink of the 506th on D-day, which means he was even farther south, near Culoville. After getting his bearings, Pistone set off to the north to try to reach his objective. Others he met from his company joined him *en route (see Chapter 12)*.

Rendezvous with Destiny, the divisional history of the 101st Airborne, written by Leonard Rapport and Arthur Norwood (Infantry Journal Press, Washington, DC, 1947), has mentioned that twelve 105mm howitzers of the *91st Division's Artillery Regiment 191* were stationed in the area behind Utah Beach. We know that the four covering Exit 1 at Pouppeville were destroyed at Holdy. Another four, covering Exit 2 at Sainte-Marie-du-Mont, were destroyed by Lieutenant Richard Winters and company at the Brécourt Farm near le Grand Chemin. It has been suggested by the official US government history, *Utah Beach to Cherbourg,* that the remaining guns and their crews escaped from the invasion area. It is possible that the battery shown wiped out in this series of Pistone's photos depicts the missing battery. Since Pistone and friends were making their way north toward de Varreville, it is logical that they would have passed through the Audoville area *en route*. It also seems logical that the Germans would have had an artillery battery somewhere in that vicinity to cover Exit 3. Exit 4 was presumably covered by the 122mm howitzers at Saint-Martin-de-Varreville until they were removed between 29 May and 5 June.

No better way of pinpointing the location has yet become available unless some local French people recognize the locale from the photos. Joe Pistone cannot tell us where he took the photos because he didn't know where he was at the time.

When a small group of F/502nd strays – including Pistone, Benjamin Shaub, Floyd Baker, Mike Milenczenko, and William Carberry – came upon the German artillery battery quite by chance, Shaub challenged them with walking fire, shooting his M-1 from the hip. Steadily advancing and firing, Shaub broke into a run and jumped into a long ditch where the Germans had taken cover. Stopping only once to insert a fresh clip in his rifle, Shaub ran along the ditch, spraying the occupants with his fire. When he was finished, the Germans were all dead. Shaub's

Spoils for the victors

Mike Milenczenko and Bill Carberry (facing camera) examine the living quarters of the late German artillerymen. Looting and pilfering of enemy equipment and possessions was a favorite pastime of the troopers. Carberry died in the fierce fighting at Bastogne, Belgium

Battlefield Promotion

Dick Winters, E/506th, was a lieutenant on D-day, but was soon to become a captain. He posed for this photo in his A-2 jacket with 506th pocket patch in place before leaving the States in 1943. *Winters*

Le Grand Chemin: The Battery at the Brécourt Farm

The small group led by Lieutenant Richard Winters hit the D-14 on D-day morning and joined the bulk of Lieutenant Colonel Strayer's 2nd/506th, moving south from Audoville. Winters was soon to inherit E/506th, as the unit's CO was MIA.

To this day, the spot where the D-14 joins the D-913 seems inconspicuous, but it was a pivotal turn for 101st troops headed south on D-day and D+1. On the morning of 6 June, a four-gun battery of German 105mm artillery pieces were situated at intervals along a long treeline in a field southwest of the D-14 road. The guns were supported by German infantry, manning machine guns with mutually-supporting fire. The action took place on the grounds across from Brécourt Manor, below le Grand Chemin, France. Three of the four 105s were zeroed-in on Utah Beach Exit 2, and taking them quickly would save the lives of many men landing on that beach.

This was no simple task for Easy Company, so Lieutenant Winters led his intrepid band personally. They had to approach the guns one at a time, which was difficult because of the stubborn German infantry who defended the approach with machine gun and rifle fire.

With Winters in the lead, his dozen brave men cleaned out the gun positions one by one. Guarnere, Malarkey, Toye, Wynn, Ranney, Lipton, and Lieutenant Compton of E/506th were instrumental in the action. Private John D. Hall and Private First Class Gerald Loraine of Service Company/506th also joined them. After taking the first three guns, the exhausted group paused to rest. At that time, Lieutenant Ronald Speirs, that deadly killing machine from D/506th, came up with Jumbo DiMarzio, Ray Taylor, Rusty Houch, and a handful of others from Dog Company.

As soon as the final gun emplacement was pointed out to Speirs, he made a spontaneous one-man charge across a long open area, spraying the German gun pit with his Tommy gun as he ran. Ray Taylor heard the men comment, "Look at that crazy mother – Go!!"

The German artillerymen were scarcely a match for the unmitigated fury of a warrior like Speirs, and they knew it. They jumped out of their emplacement and ran, just as Speirs came sailing in feet first. He sprayed them in the back as they ran, and narrowly survived the blast of a concussion grenade the Germans left behind before vacating their position.

During this action, the 506th lost four men killed and two wounded, including Houch from Company D, who was KIA. The troops counted 15 German dead, many wounded, and 12 prisoners.

After the action was over, four Sherman tanks that had come up from the beach through Exit 2 joined with Winters and his men. It has been a continual source of irritation to Winters that ever since *Night Drop* appeared, these tanks have wrongly been credited with knocking out the German artillery positions just described. This myth was repeated as late as 1993 in another book as well.

European Theatre of Operations (ETO) historian S. L. A. Marshall had written that E/506th had 195 men of 2nd Battalion available to take the battery. "With that many E Company men, I could have taken Berlin" Winters says (see *Band of Brothers,* by Stephen Ambrose, Simon & Schuster, 1992, for a complete history of E/506th).

A final incident, which took place after the action, should be mentioned. While in the courtyard of his family's home, Michel, a teen-aged boy who was a

companions had given him covering fire, but it was basically a one-man feat and all over in less than a minute.

A strange silence and isolation hung over the area as the men paused to rest and posed for Pistone's photos. In a field in front of the German position were some dead paratroopers who had landed there on D-day.

Ben Shaub, the intrepid hero of the incident, lost his life in the fighting in Holland in October 1944. Shaub stepped on a land mine, which blew off his foot. As his buddy, Andrew Hemrock, was dragging the wounded man out, he stepped on another mine, which inflicted mortal wounds to Shaub's head and upper body.

The Silver Star was awarded to Shaub, thanks to the witnesses to this one-man charge, but he didn't live long enough to wear it. Mike Milenczenko, who changed his name to Mike Miller after the war, died in the 1970s. Floyd Baker had his nose shot off in subsequent fighting and his current whereabouts, if living, are unknown. William Carberry, the other witness to this incident, was killed at Bastogne.

See map p. 260.

member of the DeVallavielle family at Brécourt, was shot numerous times by two American paratroopers, but he survived. He later became mayor of Sainte-Marie-du-Mont. The French were not happy about the incident and claimed that the men who shot him were laughing when they did it. Michel himself never held a grudge and, in the years following WWII, became great friends with American veterans of Normandy landings. Stephen Ambrose writes that Michel was mixed in with a group of Germans when shot. This has been a touchy subject with the French locals until quite recently.

With Exit 2 cleared, 4th Infantry Division infantrymen and attached tanks began pouring inland, and paratroopers who landed between Saint-Marcouf and Audoville were able to move south to the D-913, make a sharp right, and proceed to Sainte-Marie-du-Mont, or other points south.

Richard Winters was among those considered for the Medal of Honor, but the award was reduced to a DSC. After the war, as an executive with the Hershey Chocolate Company, he developed a system for utilizing the waste products of candy making in a mixture for cattle feed.

Brécourt manor

The entrance to Brecourt Manor on the south edge of le Grand Chemin. The action of Lieutenant Richard Winters's group took place in a large field across the road to the left of this photo. Michel DeVallavielle, the future mayor of Sainte-Marie-du-Mont, was shot here on D-day in a case of mistaken identity. He was the first French civilian to be evacuated to England for medical treatment. *Author's Photo*

Sainte-Marie-du-Mont 12

Sainte-Marie-du-Mont on D-day was definitely 101st country. It was near the center of the 101st's area of operations and a hive of activity. The village with the domed church steeple is to the 101st what St. Mere Eglise is to the 82nd Airborne. The round steeple enabled General Maxwell Taylor, the 101st CG, to figure out where he was at first light. In reading the town's rich D-day history, one detects a feeling of tragedy and regret. The French observers had sympathy for the fate of those lost on both sides.

The Legend of Ambrose Allie

A humble private from Two Rivers, Wisconsin, Ambrose Allie of 3rd/501st will long be a folk hero in Sainte-Marie-du-Mont. Ambrose had come to earth in a field north of there. Near first light, he walked into town with another trooper.

As they entered the town square at the north bend of the D-913, the duo was cut down by German machine-gun bullets. Ambrose was wounded in the arm, and his companion severely hit in the head. German troops immediately pounced on, disarmed, and searched them. The wounded captives were dragged into the nearest house in a hurry. The town was being hotly contested and the outcome was still in question. For an hour or two, the frantic Germans rushed their wounded prisoners from house to house, glancing out windows and occasionally firing their weapons.

Eventually, the Germans became too concerned about their precarious situation and became tired of dragging their prisoners around. They marched Ambrose and friend into a nearby yard, stood them against the wall of a house, then backed up to shoot them, firing-squad style. A fusillade of bullets struck them down, though, fired by American paratroopers who had come upon the scene in the nick of time.

Private First class Ambrose Allie, 1943

Ambrose Allie's German captors were about to execute him and a gravely wounded companion when they were rescued by American paratroopers.

On left: **Sainte-Marie-du-Mont steeple, D+1**
Ed Benecke's 7 June photo shows clearly where the bore-sighted shell from Holdy went through the steeple. *Benecke*

On right: **Sainte-Marie-du-Mont, D+1**
American troops march past the front of the church on 7 June 1944. *Musura*

The Hunter in the Town Pump

This story comes from the town's history records.

At first light on D-day morning, an American paratrooper was seen to hide in the recess of the town pump. He was "stocky, obviously older than his fellows, his face wrinkled with fine furrows, pale eyes without expression, and bow-legged, like a rider." Holding his rifle in the bend of his elbow like a hunter, he looked out from the recess and began to fire on the German garrison, who were "stricken by fear." He is credited with 10 kills, of whom two were shot at a range of less than 50 meters.

A hero among heroes

Circa 7 June 1944 in a field near Sainte-Marie-du-Mont. Sergeant Joe Pistone and Private First Class Ben Shaub pose for this photo, taken with Pistone's camera, soon after they joined forces on D+1. Shaub, from Pennsylvania, almost single-handedly wiped out a four-gun German 105mm artillery battery, for which he received the Silver Star. In this fine study, note that Shaub wears the Air Corps issue ammo pouches and, for some reason, has discarded his jump trousers, wearing OD trousers instead. He wears his M-3 trench knife on his waist. Pistone's paper gas-detection brassard shows the wear resulting from crawling through hedgerows under fire and would soon be discarded. His gas-impregnated, reinforced M-42 trousers are complete with rigger-applied leg tie-downs. *Pistone*

Western Style Shoot-Out with an Ironic Outcome

Also in the morning, the town saddler witnessed a duel that happened a short distance from the pump, in front of the town's WWI monument. An American and a German suddenly met in front of the monument and simultaneously raised their weapons to shoot. Each man fell wounded by the other's fire. The American died of his wound. The German, seriously wounded, was carried into the nearby *boucherie* (butcher shop or meat market), where an American doctor saved his life.

Meeting the Mademoiselles

This famous invasion photo shows paratroopers trying to fraternize with French girls near the town pump in St. Marie du Mont. They are believed to be from 1st/506th. The girl at far left is Andree Desselier, who later married Frank Polosky, a 101st trooper from Chicago. Her wedding gown was sewn from the reserve parachute worn by Polosky on the night drop. Polosky, who belonged to HQ/1st/506th, has since passed away. Also identified in the photo are Leon F. Jackson of A/506th (tall man in center rear), and Ralph Spearman of C/506th second from far right. *US Army*

The Quick...

Joseph A. Pistone and Benjamin C. Shaub, F/502nd, round a bend in the maze of hedgerows near Sainte-Marie-du-Mont. Minutes earlier, the duo had surprised a lone German sentry, who was guarding this corner. It was early morning on D+2 and the startled German awakened, stumbled to his feet, and raised his rifle. He tripped in his blanket and was shot by the troopers. Pistone then gave his camera to another member of their group, who snapped the photo as they again rounded the bend, reenacting the scene.

Shaub, who won the Silver Star for his one-man attack on a German artillery battery, died in Holland on 5 November 1944. Pistone, who took many of the photos in this book, survived all the campaigns of the 101st in WWII. This photo has appeared in at least two post-war books, with erroneous information, stating that Shaub was killed shortly after the picture was taken. These works also misspelled Pistone's name as Pastore, and Shaub's name as Schaub. *Pistone*

...And the dead

Joe Pistone examines the dead sentry's steel helmet. Pistone cannot pinpoint the location where this took place. He had landed in the area above Culoville, where he saw Colonel Robert Sink of the 506th on D-day. He had worked his way north toward his objective at Saint-Martin-de-Varreville, where he met familiar faces. The F/502nd men were probably heading south again when this incident happened. *Pistone*

Three Troopers, Twenty-Eight German Casualties

The missing commander of the 502nd, Colonel George Van Horn Moseley, had never showed up at the planned CP in Loutres. His leg was badly broken on the night drop and he had landed far south of the intended area on DZ C. Found in the afternoon by several troopers, including Fasanella, Sky Jackson, Vic Nelson (all of Moseley's regimental Headquarters Company), Moseley was eventually hauled to the Division CP at Hiesville in a wheelbarrow.

About 1600 on D-day, Sky Jackson chased two Germans behind a hedgerow and fired into it. This story has appeared in print in at least four different books and magazine articles—each account contradicts the other in details.

Sky himself wrote a short story called "My Part in The Invasion of France." His comments on this action:

Three of us ran into an enemy patrol of 28 men. We each had M-1 rifles, the best damn rifle in the world! We emptied clip after clip at them, killing 10 and capturing 18—8 of whom were severely wounded. They were mostly kids of around 17 (one of them could not have been over 15). We then took them to our makeshift POW enclosure in an old monastery.

Moseley reportedly stayed in action with his regiment until 8 June, barking out orders from his wheelbarrow. General Anthony McAuliffe saw him along the N-13 and ordered Moseley's evacuation. Lieutenant Colonel John H. "Mike" Michaelis was now in command.

3rd/502nd Troopers, D+2

Elements of 3rd/502nd move south from their D-day positions near Exit 3 and head west toward les Forges at the N-13. After regrouping, they defended the Blosville-Houesville area against German counterattacks, then advanced along the N-13 causeway towards Carentan. Among those identified are Private William Reed *(far left)*, Technician 5th Grade Robert Marois *(third from left)*, and Fox, Boddie, and Urbanczyk *(in the center foreground)*, all of Company H. *US Army via Ludwig*

Pouppeville

On D-day night, General Maxwell Taylor landed near Holdy and assembled a group of men. The first trooper he met in the darkness was Staff Sergeant Ed Haun (later KIA at Bastogne) of G/501st, who had lost his helmet on the jump. The general hugged the sergeant because he was so glad to see him. Taylor's group was totally confused about its location until dawn revealed the domed church steeple of St. Marie du Mont.

Taylor merged his HQ group with Lieutenant Colonel Julian Ewell's 3rd/501st men, mostly of G/501st. Captain Vernon Kraeger was there. He was mad as hell because two planes carrying men of his company had been shot down, and only 3 of the 36 men had survived. These three – Tetrault, Sergeant Word, and Art Morin – became the nucleus of the "Death Squad," which was later rebuilt and inflicted heavy casualties on the Germans.

One of the unique stories of Pouppeville actually took place on D-day night as the planes were flying over. Walter Turk of G/501st heard someone say, "One minute to the DZ," and doesn't remember what happened between then and 0600. He had jumped, but connector links apparently slammed him in the back of the helmet, dented it, and knocked him silly. Turk's buddies, David Mythaler and Fred Orlowsky, found him on the ground, disoriented and babbling incoherently. Fearing he would blunder into Germans, Turk's buddies tied a rope around him like a leash and led him around Normandy until dawn (they used the rope that each paratrooper carried to enable him to climb down in case he landed in a tall tree). Germans were all around and the men no doubt saved Turk from death or capture as they sought refuge in hedge ditches a number of times with a hand clamped over Turk's mouth.

Turk's first memory was at dawn as his buddies were asking, "Do you know where you are?" At this writing, he lives in Richland Center, Wisconsin.

General Taylor's group was top heavy with staff people and officers, but he decided to move his force toward the nearest divisional objective – Exit 1 from Utah Beach at Pouppeville. Leading them cross country south of St. Marie du Mont, he remarked, "Never in the history of warfare have so few been led by so many."

When the group hit the approach road to Exit 1, the men spotted a German platoon walking straight toward them, coming from Pouppeville.

The two enemy groups sighted each other and immediately took cover in roadside ditches east and west of the intersection. For several long minutes, neither side wanted to shoot. Then the angry Captain Kraeger jumped onto the road and walked toward the enemy, firing his carbine from the hip. Shooting erupted from both sides and Kraeger was hit in the arm but refused to leave (he was later KIA in Holland). Major Legere, the assistant division operations officer, was shot in the leg, and medic Edwin Hohl of 3rd/501st went onto the road to give him first aid. A German bullet ended Hohl's life as he was working on Legere.

Corporal Virgil Danforth, a G/501st man from Indianapolis, led the way into town, shooting a number of helmeted German heads as they bobbed up and

Lieutenant colonel Julian J. Ewell
Ewell graduated with the West Point class of 1939 and became CO of 3rd/501st. Pouppeville was his battalion's first engagement of WWII. *Author's Photo*

down in the ditch. (Interesting to note: John Boitano of B/506th was supposed to go to Pouppeville on D-day, but arrived a day late. It seemed like every dead German he saw there was shot in the head – probably victims of Danforth's marksmanship.) Danforth became one of the first twenty-five members of the 101st to earn the DSC. Private Meryl Tinklenberg, also of G/501st, knocked out a German machine-gun crew.

The group split in two directions to envelop the town; house-to-house fighting ensued. Curiously, prisoners taken in the town were from the 91st Division, with some Soviet Georgian volunteers and artillerymen present. Lieutenant Colonel Ewell coordinated the movement through the town and a bullet dinged his helmet as he looked around a corner. In the same manner, Lieutenant Nathan Marks of G/501st was killed by a sharpshooting German as he looked around a building.

A G/501st trooper named Bell came face-to-face unexpectedly with a German in a doorway. Bell had his bayonet fixed on his M-1 and executed a textbook thrust to the head, which caught the German under the chin, the blade coming out the back of his head. Bell reportedly swore off the bayonet after that incident.

Lieutenant Luther Knowlton
Knowlton, G/501st, met the first American tank to drive up cause way number 1 from Utah Beach on D-day afternoon. This photo was taken before Knowlton joined the 101st. At the time, he was a lieutenant in the 84th Infantry Division. *Grace Knowlton*

While this battle was going on, General Taylor sent Lieutenant Eugene Brierre around the town to make contact with the 4th Infantry Division, which was landing on the beach. Lieutenant Brierre met Lieutenant George Mabry of the 8th Infantry Regiment, which is now considered the first linkup of airborne and seaborne forces at Exit 1.

A better-known meeting took place late in the afternoon when a tank came up the causeway and arrived near the east edge of Pouppeville. Lieutenant Luther Knowlton and a trooper from G/501st opened fire on it, not certain if friend or foe manned it. Orange smoke and flag signals were exchanged and the first *official* contact was established with the Ivy Division at Exit 1.

Although previous D-day historians have made much of the meeting between the 4th Infantry Division and the 101st Airborne Division at Exit 1 of Utah Beach, this was neither the first meeting nor the most important. Probably the first meeting happened at Exit 3 in front of Audoville la Hubert, between Captain Ray Hershner of I/502nd, and Lieutenant Colonel Conrad Simmons, commander of the 1st Battalion, 8th Infantry Regiment. Exits 2 and 4 also established contact rather soon after H-hour and far more vehicles, men, and equipment came ashore at those exits than via Pouppeville. During the later battle for Cherbourg, on 24 June 1944, Lieutenant Colonel Simmons was killed in action.

14	# Bloody Holdy

Bloody indeed was the tiny hamlet (situated southwest of Sainte-Marie-du-Mont) from the time of the first landings near 0100 on D-day. The stick dispersion maps tell the story of a heavy concentration of 101st jumpers landing in and just south of Holdy. It was the intended DZ for 3rd/501st, HQ/101st, and the 506th minus 3rd Battalion, but many DZ A sticks were misdropped here (mainly 502nd troopers) instead of near their objectives (far north, near Saint-Martin-de-Varreville). The worst catastrophe resulted from the fact that intelligence had failed to pinpoint a German artillery battery, consisting of four 105mm cannons and their crews, situated in a field on the north edge of the hamlet. A stick from HQ/1st/506th landed in the tall trees on the edge of that field and were quickly slaughtered by the artillerymen. An unconfirmed story is that some 502nd troopers were also captured, carrying thermite grenades, intended for use in melting the breeches of the 122mm howitzers at their objective, which was near Saint-Martin-de-Varreville. The unfortunates who landed in this field were variously slashed with knives and bayonets, wrapped with their chute canopies and burned alive, or had the thermite grenades ignited between their legs after being bound with shroud lines. In any case, some who landed in the vicinity attested to hearing their agonized screams on D-day night. It was also near here that Donald Burgett of A/506th mentioned seeing a number of troopers lying shoulder to shoulder with their "manhood cut or shot completely away."

The guns and crews were captured in late morning by troopers of the 502nd, reinforced by Captain Lloyd Patch's troops of 1st/506th sent north from Culoville. These men later moved on to join the fight at Sainte-Marie-du-Mont.

One of Patch's men bore-sighted a captured 105mm and put a round through the domed church steeple of St. Marie du Mont, firing clear from Holdy that afternoon. The object was to root out snipers or artillery spotters, but they did chase First Sergeant "Buck" Rogers, HQ/1st/506th, and others from the steeple in a hurry.

Lieutenants Raymond Hunter and Bernard McKearney of E/502nd were left in charge of the artillery pieces when Patch's group moved on. Fearing the guns would be recaptured in a German counterattack, they began to destroy them one by one. A messenger came from Colonel Sink at Culoville to halt this because the 377th PFAB was devoid of weapons, but only one of the guns was saved. McKearney was also involved in burying the dead from the artillery field, but was unable to verify the stories of thermite torture.

Captain George Lage, surgeon for 2nd/502nd, established an aid station in Holdy and made trips between there and the division hospital at Hiesville all day. A Horsa glider, carrying members of Company HQ section, A Co., 325th GIR, 82nd Airborne Division, crashed east of Holdy, on the morning of 7 June, 1944. There were over 20 soldiers aboard, of whom 14 were killed in the crash. This disaster added to the bloody history of Holdy.

Treating Pows

A scene in Holdy on Dday morning. George Lage *(glasses, in center)* and his medics treat wounded Germans captured at the 105mm cannon positions. A later counterattack on the town from the opposite direction was repulsed in the afternoon. *Lage via Koskimaki*

Horsa Glider, June 1944

A view of the Horsa glider that hit tall trees growing from a hedge bordering a large field south of Holdy. The crash happened after daylight, on the morning of June 7, 1944. The towplane, unable to cut the glider loose, succeeded in making an emergency landing. The domed steeple of the Sainte-Marie-du-Mont church makes a good reference point. *US Army, via Hood*

Horsa Crash

The most famous scene of the Horsa crash, just south of Holdy, was published in *The Longest Day*. The bodies of eight of the 14 fatalities have been lined-up in front of the wreckage. Some had been thrown into the field across the road by the tremendous impact with trees. This detail was recalled by the locals, as well as the fact that the same field across the road was the site of an American field artillery battery a day or two later. From there, the battery fired on the town of Carentan. *US Army*

Hiesville and Château Colombières

Hiesville lies some distance inland from Utah Beach in the DZ C area, and was the predesignated location for both the divisional CP and hospital. Later, it also became the site of the divisional POW compound and the first temporary German cemetery behind Utah Beach.

Teams of surgeons and operating equipment came in by glider at 0400. The doctors were set up and working on casualties on the morning of D-day. Hiesville was also the rendezvous site where Pathfinders reported with their signaling equipment after they had performed their missions. Joe Haller and Lieutenant Albert "The Gremlin" Watson were DZ D pathfinders who made the six-hour trip north to drop off their Eureka equipment. *En route* they met, among others, Barney Momcilovic of HQ/1st/501st. Momcilovic recalls that as the group moved along hedgerows, the Germans kept flipping potato-masher grenades over the top at random intervals, hoping to catch paratroopers in the explosions. They seemed to have an unlimited supply. Watson was wounded by a concussion grenade *en route* to Hiesville.

Bill McMahon of I/501st landed somewhat north of Hiesville and made his way there by dawn. In the afternoon, McMahon set off, headed east toward the beach fighting. He encountered a young and frightened German soldier who was sheltering in a roadside ditch near Hiesville. McMahon talked gently and patiently to the German for about 15 minutes, trying to persuade him to surrender. Finally, the German walked out and handed his rifle to McMahon.

"He was shaking like a dog shittin' razor blades," McMahon later said. As he marched his prisoner back toward the 101st's POW collection point, some other sterling fighters assumed custody of the prize. McMahon felt powerless to stop them, and was later upset to learn that his successors apparently shot the prisoner out of hand.

The large Château Colombieres with castlelike turrets stood on the north edge of Hiesville and was used as the division hospital. It was the target of continual shelling, sniper fire, and bombing for the first four days. Supplemental hospital tents had to be set up outside to handle the overflow of patients. The hospital was bombed on the night of 9–10 June, when the *Luftwaffe* made one of its rare showings behind Utah Beach. Two large bombs landed near the hospital, with one detonating much later, apparently having been fitted with a time-delay fuse; there were a number of fatalities. Troops of the 501st assembled at Vierville were also attacked by air that night. An MP battalion billeted in a field between St. Marie du Mont and St. Mere Eglise took a number of fatalities from butterfly bombs that night.

Lieutenant Al Hassenzahl of C/506th was hit in the chest by a rifle slug and laid in the courtyard in front of the Colombieres hospital awaiting treatment. Mortar shells were hitting the roof while he lay waiting and orange slate pieces kept flying off and raining down on the wounded. Hassenzahl kept hoping fragments wouldn't hit him in the eyes and blind him. When a Catholic chaplain knelt above Hassenzahl and began to administer the last rites, the Lieutenant's eyes opened and he hissed through clenched teeth, "Get the hell away from me, Chaplain. I'm not going to die!"

So many shells hit Colombieres that the building had to be demolished and rebuilt after the war. Major Doug Davidson, the 502nd's regimental surgeon,

Airborne transport
Sergeant Hopp, 377th PFAB, at the reins of typical improvised airborne transport in Normandy. Troops who assembled at Hiesville loaded their equipment and souvenirs on wagons, bikes, motorcycles, tanks, and cavalry horses. As they later departed for the N-13 near la Croix Pan, they formed what *The Saturday Evening Post* called "the strangest military caravan of our times." ("Paratroopers of Purple Heart Lane," by Cecil Carnes and Bob Pick; 9 September 1944.) *Benecke*

Patheiger, Pangerl, and Leeds

After the fall of Carentan on 13 June, Lieutenant Joe Pangerl returned to Hiesville to take photos. This is a nice shot showing the front of the Château Colombieres with damage visible to the roof. (From left to right) Sergeant Fred Patheiger, Lieutenant Joe Pangerl, and Private Leeds, all of HQ/502nd. Lieutenant Pangerl says the troopers were in such superb physical and mental condition that they were "astounded when they were wounded and saw their own blood." *Pangerl*

revisited the place in the 1950s and found the chateau had been replaced by a modern-looking brick house, which stands on the same spot to this day. He found that only the original massive stone fireplace had been retained and is a part of the newer house.

Across the small dirt road facing the chateau are three stone buildings, arranged to form a courtyard. This became the POW compound for the 101st, and prisoners were recruited from here to work in a nearby field, digging graves for Germans killed in the fighting.

At the opposite (south) end of town is the Lecaudey family farm, which was the site of the 101st Division CP. General Taylor slept there the night of 6–7 June.

Colonel Robert Sink's D-day Ride

Although it is not at Hiesville, Culoville lies down the road from the Lecaudey farm. Culoville is not a village, but just a farm and courtyard formed by several buildings inside a walled area. Here, as predesignated in Field Order No. 1, Colonel Robert F. Sink established his regimental CP. The road in front of Culoville runs between Holdy and Vierville. Major Louis Kent, the 506th's regimental surgeon, had established his field hospital in the same complex of buildings. One of the patients there was a nine-year-old French boy, who had been shot by a German as he was helping paratroopers collect equipment bundles. The boy and his parents lived in Vierville.

Harold W. "Hank" Hannah, the S-3, wrote in his journal:

The barnyard became a most dramatic setting… certainly it had not been the scene of so many diverse happenings. A sniper shot a youngster and Major Kent performed a major operation. Much weeping and pathos on the part of the relatives of the little French boy being operated on. [The boy eventually died.]

Sink had no radio contact with his 3rd Battalion, which was supposed to be at Brévands. At 1000, he

Digging Graves
Sergeant Davis, a non-jumping member of the 377th PFAB, guards German POWs at Hiesville as they dig graves for their fallen comrades. *Benecke*

Hank Hannah, before and after

Major Harold W. "Hank" Hannah, of Texico, Illinois, in 1943 and a halfcentury later. Hannah was seriously wounded in Holland as division G-3, but continued to teach law until 1996. He passed away in his 90s, shortly after the turn of the millennium. *Author's Photo*

Ben "Chief" MCIntosh, B/502nd

McIntosh was a Pawnee Indian from Oklahoma who said, "We went on sort of a rampage." McIntosh was a professional light weight boxer who had fought in Madison Square Garden. *Dunwoodie*

commandeered a jeep from the 81st AAAB – which had come in by glider – and its driver, Technician Fifth Grade George W. Rhoden, A/81st. Sink also selected Amory Roper and Salvadore Ceniceros of the 506th (both later KIA) to accompany Major Hannah and him on a personal reconnaissance toward Brévands. The jeep went south for about a mile, hitting the D-913 in Vierville, then made a sharp right heading south. They eventually drove right through a sizable German unit whose men were resting in ditches on both sides of the D-913. The Americans fired their weapons and sped on, seeing more and more Germans. Making a swift U-turn at the first Angoville turnoff, they sped back up the gauntlet the way they had come. The Germans were reluctant to shoot as they were too busy ducking lead. Also, they might have shot their own men across the road. Hannah described the incident in his journal:

The colonel decided to borrow a jeep and go to the 3rd Battalion jump area and see if we could find out anything about them. A thousand yards past Vierville, we passed a German sentry guarding a picket line. Beyond him along the highway were several other Krauts, indicating that we were well past the mythical front line, which we had not commenced to think about as yet. I shot the sentry dead in his tracks with my .38 and Colonel Sink told the jeep driver to speed up. We drove for half a mile at 50 mph – I emptied my pistol, and the two boys with us mowed down several (with TSMGs). As we approached a corner, we saw several Jerries in the road; we fired, they took cover. We turned around and came back through the

"hostile boys" (as the colonel calls them) and shot up a few more before they could dive in their slit trenches along the road. A machine gun fired at us but missed. The Jerries use their machine gunss a lot, but they are not always accurate. After we passed into friendly territory again, we met a 501st platoon and told it to clean the hostiles out. Colonel Sink recorded the name of the jeep driver for a citation, and I had several offers for my .38!

On the morning of 7 June, combined tanks and paratroopers drove from Culoville through Vierville to Beaumont.

While at Beaumont, die-hard German defenders, firing from ditches along the road and the fields beyond, stalled the 1st/506th. Lieutenant Colonel Turner, the battalion commander, got up into the turret of one of the tanks and was directing its fire when a German shot him through the head, killing him.

In 1955, when Leo Conner was secretary of the 101st Airborne Association, he wrote a letter to Hank Hannah and mentioned Colonel Turner's death at Beaumont. Conner wrote:

I note that you arrived at Turner's CP on D plus 1 a short time after he was killed, and that you later took over his battalion. Turner was a personal friend of mine. I knew him in May 1942, when as a captain he commanded a tank battalion in the 8th Armored Division. I was at that time Executive of the 36th Armored Regiment and I did my damndest to talk him out of going Airborne. It was ironic that he should have been killed in a tank, as reported in *Rendezvous with Destiny*.

Vierville

16

Guarding a barricade
Steve Mihok and a buddy from HQ/2nd/506th man a fox-hole at a typical barricade (gap opening) in a hedgerow. *Mihok*

Although two gliders landed in the flooded fields east of Vierville, there was little activity in the town on D-day. An S-2 patrol from the 506th left Culoville on D-day, scouted in and beyond Vierville and reported that there were no German troops in the town. On 7 June at 0400, however, a task force of 1st/506th, supported by tanks, drove through Vierville from the north and encountered some resistance, but pushed on to continue the fight near Beaumont.

The 2nd/506th came down the D-329 a couple of hours later and encountered a veritable hornet's nest in Vierville. German paratroopers had circled around and taken up firing positions in the town. This held up the advance of 2nd/506th for some time. During the fighting, the battalion lost its brightest member, a Native American named Benjamin Stoney, who belonged to the S-2 section. Major Lewis Nixon had arranged for Stoney to be transferred into the intelligence section from E/506th back in the States when it was learned that he had an IQ of 147. Stoney charged across the D-14 to knock out a German machine-gun nest and reportedly fell dead across the two-man crew after first killing them.

Tanks returned to the village to drive out the *Fallschirmjäger* (German paratroopers) and many of their number lay in the ankle-deep water east of the hamlet, killed by canister rounds fired by the tanks. When Strayer's 2nd/506th moved on, the war was over for Vierville, and it became the assembly point for the 501st to regroup on 9 June. Jack Schaffer of F/501st manned a machine-gun outpost on the east edge of town from which he could see a glider in the distance. Schaffer took a number of photos, showing dead German paratroopers in the grassy area east

of the village. In searching the bodies, Schaffer noticed the bolts were missing from each German's rifle. At the time, he took this to mean that the Germans had thrown them away and were coming in to surrender when they were gunned down. More likely, the 506th had removed the bolts before leaving the area so the guns couldn't be used by other Germans if they were recaptured.

Schaffer also recalls a deep hog wallow in the backyard of the first house at the east edge of the village. A German had jumped into the wallow feet first to escape small arms fire and was stuck in mud up to his neck. Someone had walked up and shot him through the forehead. Some of Jack's buddies went to great effort to haul the German's body up out of the mud, to see if he was wearing a pistol or any valuables. They found none.

Another gory sight in the town remembered by many was a dead German who lay in the center of the D-913. A tank had crushed his head on the blacktop road. The man's head was flat as a pancake and about 18 inches in diameter. All of his facial features were distorted but recognizable.

A humorous incident happened at Vierville on 9 June. Ernest A. Robinson, HQ/3rd/501st Pathfinder, had discovered a German cap and uniform in a house. As his buddies sat in the grass, celebrating their survival with some Calvados, the fiery liquor of Nor-

501st Pathfinders, Vierville, D+4

Some of the 501st Pathfinders who survived included: *(standing, left to right)* O'Shaughnessy, Haux, Rofar, Robinson, Hunt, Larsen, Sarlas. *(Below)* Joe Bass, Ryan, Brazzle, Haller, Everly, and Lieutenant Faith. Captain Brown and Rich Beaver were in the building. Others who survived were still wandering. *Alice Larsen*

F/501st, Vierville, D+3

East edge of Vierville, 9 June 1944. Members of F/501st were recorded by Jack Schaffer, passing dead members of the *1st Battalion, Parachute Regiment 6*. This meadow was flooded with ankledeep water at the time. *Schaffer*

mandy, Robinson peeked around the corner of a building wearing the German cap and outfit. "Iss dot you, Fritz?" he said, then ducked back around the corner. In a minute, he reappeared saying, "Iss dot you, Fritz?" The third time he peeked around the corner, he ducked quickly back as Tommy gun bullets beat the wall near his head.

"Hey you guys, it's me, Robbie!" he said. A German cap and tunic were tossed around the corner of the building as a token of surrender.

Lieutenant Colonel Robert A. Ballard, CO of the 2nd/501st, was unique among the 101st's battalion commanders on D-day as he immediately recognized where he had landed. The large, wet fields southeast of Angoville were the DZ for his battalion, and most members were able to assemble quickly in the hedgerows between Angoville and les Droueries. The unit did not have an easy time, however, because the men were isolated and surrounded by German troops for the first two days. Also, they suffered from a lack of surgeons, having only a handful of medics to treat the many grievously wounded troopers from local fighting. Medics Kenneth Moore and Robert Wright established an aid station in the town church, rendering aid to friend and foe alike. Both were later decorated with the Silver Star for treating over 80 patients here in the first two days of the invasion.

Ballard was supposed to seize St. Come du Mont on D-day morning, but his battalion became heavily engaged some distance short of their goal, at the approach to les Droueries and at Gillis' Corner.

Indeed, there were casualties even *en route* to the assembly area. Staff Sergeant Leroy Pierce, F/501st, was shot through the head. T. V. Haddow received multiple shrapnel wounds, and the first two Fox Company patrols sent toward Saint-Come-du-Mont returned with casualties. Gutierrez was shot in the arm and came back with Sergeant Gainey.

Three men from 2nd Platoon fared no better. C. C. "Jumbo" Moore was the lone survivor when he, Huston, and Schinkoeth explored to the south. Huston crawled ahead on point, and held up his hand to indicate he had spotted the enemy. Moore saw one of Huston's fingers disappear like magic as a bullet severed it. More rounds passed through Huston's body, one splashing water from his canteen into Moore's face. Huston was dead and Schinkoeth was wounded. Schinkoeth crawled to the rear for aid, but never made it. A rifle grenade killed him *en route*. Moore spotted the German who fired at them in an apple orchard across the road, shot him, then pulled back.

Lieutenant Quincy M. Couger and Sergeant Leo Gillis of F/501st made one of the first successful forays a bit later in the morning (see the Gillis's Corner sidebar).

Gillis and Couger were dismayed that only a small percentage of the men assembled in the 2nd/501st area were taking an active part in the fighting on D-day. Gillis and First Sergeant Herschel Parks left the area at midday to search for Colonel Howard Johnson's force, which they located at La Barquette. After they left, Couger became infuriated with some of his men and waved his WWI .45 revolver in their faces. Shortly thereafter, he was killed by a German at point-blank range.

In the afternoon of D-day, F/501st made a circling movement and at day's end were coming back at the same crossroads they had fought for in the morning, but from a different angle. They were still far from Saint-Come-du-Mont, and Lieutenant Colonel Ballard received a radio message from Colonel Howard Johnson telling him to move his battalion to La Barquette. Ballard was too heavily engaged to comply and there were repercussions later, as Johnson felt Ballard had let him down.

Battered casualties wended their way back to the church in Angoville all afternoon, and there was fighting right in the town, with the aid station changing hands. The Germans who stormed in saw that their own wounded were being treated and left the medics undisturbed. In the evening, two Germans who were scared and had hidden in the steeple of the church all day, came down and surrendered to the medics.

There Was Death in the Air

Sergeant Leo Gillis, F/501st, said:

Let me tell you about this here … battle. On D-day, our guys saw some friends get shot up, guys bleeding…They're 4,000 miles from home and they start to wonder what the heck they're doing there. Then comes the realization that just like snapping your fingers, you could be off of this earth. It was obvious that you could be killed very easily, and everyone was cognizant of this.

There was death… in the air … you could not divert yourself from that death. It was like a faucet being turned on that drained your ability to function. It affected some guys more than others. You functioned with what was left. Of course, I could feel the feelings, too.

This feeling is impossible to imagine unless you're in the situation. Even then, you can't recapture the feeling yourself until you're in the situation again.

Everyone wanted to do the right thing, but some were not capable of doing it. They could not make themselves do it. Some guys would refuse to dig a foxhole, or throw their ammunition away. It's like in base-

Angoville church, 1990s
The church at Angoville has changed little since 1944. The 2nd/501st had a first aid station in this church on D-day and D+1. There is now a monument to the 501st across the road from the church, at the wall near the water pump. *Author's Photo*

Sergeant F. Leo Gillis, 3rd Platoon, F/501st, in a 1943 portrait. *Gillis*

Gillis's Corner

Sergeant Leo Gillis was born Francis Leo Gillis on 10 August 1923. He was born in Canada, but raised in the Fenkell-Dexter area of Detroit, Michigan. Like his alter ego, Leo Francis Runge in HQ/501st (born 8 August 23), Gillis acquired US citizenship. Both men were outstanding combat soldiers born two days apart under the zodiacal sign of Leo and both had "Leo" in their name. Gillis was not a garrison soldier and disliked military discipline, having a problem with those in authority. On his first day in combat, though, he suddenly became an important person in Ballard's assembly area. 1st Sergeant Parks, who had had little to say to Gillis in training and garrison life, sud denly found himself conferring with Gillis on the tactical situation. He found Gillis could draw diagrams showing the disposition of friendly and enemy troops, and he was at the forefront of the fighting.

Gillis, who was a crack shot with the M-1 Garand rifle ("I could shoot an apple off your head at 300 yards."), was moving forward along two parallel hedgerows that formed a line above les Droueries on D-day at dawn.

He saw Private James Luce of Philadelphia running back toward him, holding his wrist with the other hand.

"Lieutenant Couger wants to see you," Luce gasped, obviously hurt.

"Well, where is he?" Gillis asked.

Luce released his wounded wrist to point, and his hand fell on the ground, dangling only by tendons. Artificial-looking pink blood gushed from the wound on his wrist. Other men came to Luce's aid and sat him under a tree as Gillis moved forward to find Couger.

Gillis was anxious to get into action. He describes himself as a competitor ("I like to play, and I like to win"). Despite the shock of seeing Luce's wound, he was confident and he double timed forward. He could hear fast, ripping bursts of a German MG42 machine gun somewhere off to his left. Before Luce had arrived, Gillis had heard the gun and saw his buddy, Bob Gaitings, stand in the opening of a hedgerow at a wooden gate.

"Get the hell outta the way!" Gillis had shouted.

Gaitings had no sooner stepped aside than a long ripping burst of machine-gun bullets tore the wooden gate apart, wood flying everywhere.

Gillis reached the end of the dirt, two-wheeled lane and saw that it formed a "T" with a small paved road. Just across that road was a stone trough. On the left was a tall hedgerow that paralleled the lane. Couger was lying below the hedge, near the end of it, but was in a position from which he couldn't see around the hedge's corner. Across the path, Gillis saw web gear abandoned by Luce after he was hit. Gillis flopped prone where Luce had been. He looked to the right as Luce had, seeing large farm buildings 150 yards away at les Droueries. He deduced that Luce had been facing that way when hit by a bullet from behind. A German had stood around the corner of Lieutenant Couger's hedge and fired, but Couger couldn't see him. Gillis decided to face to the left instead, looking past Couger, down the road.

He could still hear the MG42, but due to the heavy foliage in the vicinity, thought the gun was about 200 yards to his left, near a visible road junction. A hay pile stood near the junction. As Gillis studied the hay pile, he couldn't believe it when three Germans jumped down from a hedgerow alongside the road, not 25 feet past where Couger lay. Couger couldn't see them, but Gillis had a perfect view of the trio. They didn't bother to look in Gillis' direction. One was holding the MG42 machine gun and all three started running toward the distant road junc tion by the hay pile. Two jumped onto the road and one was running away through the ditch. It was an easy shot for Gillis.

He later recalled, "I shot the man on the right side of the road, then the man on the left side of the road. Then I shot the man in the ditch."

The Germans never knew what hit them. Lieutenant Couger said, "Did you get 'em?" but he said it in a skeptical tone of voice, because he didn't really believe Gillis was shooting at anybody.

"Yeah, I got 'em," Gillis replied.

He later said, "It wasn't a very good feeling and I wasn't too excited about it. Maybe I was a little bit ashamed. I'll never forget that little curl of smoke coming up from the bolt of my rifle. I told myself, "Well, that's what I came over here for.""

Lieutenant Couger stood up and walked around the hedge and looked down the road.

"Boy, you did! You killed 'em!" "Yeah, I killed 'em." One of the Germans was still alive and Couger went over

and finished him off. They looked into the hedge where the Germans had jumped out, finding a pair of US binoculars with the name Huston on them, on a piece of tape.

James Luce died of shock on 8 June. Couger was killed later on Dday. We call the spot Gillis's Corner, because he avenged the deaths of Huston, Schinkoeth, and Luce there.

ball. You might have some good friends, but they're not players. You'd like for them to be players, but they're not and never will be. Combat separates people, too. Some guys don't appreciate me saying this, but it's the truth.

On 7 June, three 8-inch shells from the cruiser USS *Quincy II* off the coast landed in Company F's area, killing and wounding a number of men. Lieutenant Leo Malek of F's 2nd Platoon survived, but Gerard Bosscher, the regimental dentist, spent the afternoon picking stones, grass, and shrapnel out of Malek's legs.

Reenactment, Half a century later

From this vantage point, lying on the spot where Private James Luce was mortally wounded, but facing in the opposite direction, Gillis could see past Lieutenant Couger. In 1944, the earthen banks to the left of the road were heavily foliaged. In the early 1990s, the farmer trimmed them bare. Evidence of the Germans' hole is still visible atop the bank between the trees. When the three-man crew jumped down to change positions, they didn't know Gillis was behind them. He was able to shoot all three.

Blood on the Pews, 1990s

Half a century later, the ancient pews in the church at Angoville still show stains from the wounded who laid in them on D-day.

Schaffer's Masterpiece

This striking photo was Jack Schaffer's masterpiece of the Normandy campaign. Taken in the 2nd/501st assembly area in a hedgerow southeast of Angoville, the faces tell it all. Utter exhaustion and apprehension were heavy in the group. Closest to the camera is Harry Tice, Schaffer's buddy. Next is Charles Carlsen of Service Company. Note the variations in size of the diamond-shaped unit stencils on the helmets. Small rocks visible on the ground are from a 500 pound bomb crater nearby. *Schaffer*

<table>
<tr><td>

18

</td><td>

Migration

</td></tr>
</table>

"Où est le Boche?"
This may be the first photo snapped in Normandy by 501st photographer Al Krochka. Lieutenant Beamsley *(right)* and another 501st trooper question a Frenchman for details of their location and on German troops in the area. This was most likely in the area east of Basse Addeville. *Krochka*

Corporal Donald Robinson, F/502nd
Eddie Sapinski snapped this photo at an unknown location in Normandy. Note the dead cow in rear with legs sticking up in the air. Dead horses and cows were a common sight during the campaign and French farmers were kept busy trying to bury them. *Sapinski*

The tight V formations flown by each serial of planes had deteriorated after passing over the western coast of the Cotentin Peninsula. Initially, cloud banks had caused this dispersion. Soon, enemy flak batteries had opened up and, in the words of A/502nd trooper John J. Lee, the ack-ack parted the C-47's "similar to shooting a scatter gun into a flock of blackbirds."

Elements of the 502nd and the 377th PFAB were to land on DZ A, to concentrate on the two northern exits from Utah Beach and to eradicate the German artillery positions near Saint-Martin-de-Varreville. Most of these planeloads were dropped too far north, in the Saint-Marcouf-Ravenoville area, or too far south, near DZ C, in the vicinity of Sainte-Marie-du-Mont. Thus, throughout D-day and much of D+1, individuals and groups of varying size were making their way north or south, heading toward their assigned objectives. These cross-country migrations naturally resulted in dozens of battles when German machine-gun nests or dug-in units were encountered.

In Chapter 3, we saw how Lieutenant Colonel Robert Cole's group moved from a confused beginning at Sainte-Mère-Eglise back eastwards, eventually positioning itself near one of the beach exits. Also in that chapter, we saw how Lieutenant Colonel Strayer's 2nd/506th group left the Foucarville area, moving south toward their objective.

The planes carrying HQ/501st are a good example of how widely dispersed the planes from one serial could be. The plane carrying Lieutenant Werner Meier, the IPW (interrogation of prisoners of war) officer, and Sergeant Amburgey of S-2, dropped its human cargo near Carquebut, far west of the DZ. Another plane of that serial, carrying Colonel Johnson, dropped its jumpers near the Chateau le Bel Enault, near Addeville, the south edge of the airborne bridgehead.

The last man out the door of that plane was Sergeant Bill Canfield of S-2. Canfield landed somewhere in the canal de Carentan, above Brevands. Canfield nearly drowned before struggling free of his equipment. After having the hellish experience, he moved west, joining Lieutenant Beamsley's group, which was moving inland from the coast. Part of Beamsley's stick had landed near the Chateau le Bel Enault, also over Basse Addeville, and in the wastelands between there and the coast. They eventually joined forces with the 501st group at la Barquette.

Wrecked Glider, Vicinity of LZ E

Lieutenant James Haslam, who landed on DZ D with the 501st Pathfinders, took these photos two or three days after D-day, as he mistakenly wandered north toward Crisbec. The CG-4A Waco glider above came to rest after plowing through a hedgerow. Haslam's notation says that the jeep inside came forward, killing the pilot and copilot. "Never happened in training!" This glider was equipped with the protective "Griswold Nose." *Naslam*

Curious cows

Norman cows inspect the remains of another CG-4A, probably south of St. Marie du Mont. This glider was equipped with the protective "Griswold Nose." *Haslam*

Motley Crew, D-day

Al Krochka snapped this wonderful shot on D-day afternoon as his group paused in a hamlet somewhere east of Addeville. Two glider pilots in M-41 field jackets have joined the group, as well as a demolitionist from the 326th AEB. All others are from HQ/501st. Those standing include Jack Robins, Paul Biron, Dick Maurer, John Kildare, Earle Sheen. Kneeling next to the engineer are Warrant Officer Frank Wolf, Lieutenant Foster Beamsley, and Sergeant Bill Canfield. Biron, when interviewed, thought that the glider pilots were killed later that day. Canfield was acclaimed a hero in *Life* magazine later in 1944 for his participation in the famous "Incredible Patrol" in Holland. *Krochka*

19

Houesville

The group of houses designated as Houesville on the map lie just west of the N-13, north of Saint-Come-du-Mont. After moving west to la Croix Pan from Hiesville, the 502nd troopers moved south and established a line near Houesville. On 8 June, there were numerous German attacks on the area and a portion of the 502nd was surrounded there for a short time. Some 300 German troops were driven from the area by 9 June.

On 9 June, Lieutenant Colonel Robert Cole, the CO of 3rd/502nd, ordered a small bayonet charge at the south edge of Houesville, a preview of his more famous charge on 11 June. The charge at Houesville was led by Staff Sergeant Ward Faulkenberry of Company I, with members of Company H also participating. The attack disrupted German forces which were preparing an assault on Houesville, but Sergeant Norwood Cumming and another Company H man were lost in the attack.

Paul Dovholuk, the first sergeant of the 502nd's regimental headquarters company, was in the church steeple at nearby Blosville the same day, when an incident happened which resulted in Dovholuk receiving a battlefield commission. He wrote:

On the morning of 9 June, I proceeded near the edge of Blosville to look over portions of my company. An elderly Frenchman started talking to me in French and pointing to the back of the church. I couldn't understand him, but saw Wm. Bashlor and Robert McQueen of my company, coming our way. Coming down the road was a squad of men from I Company – I told them something was going on behind the church. Being a first Sergeant, I took command and asked the I Company squad to place themselves in position so as to crossfire their machine guns near the church.

Bashlor and I went up into the church steeple and observed the grounds behind the church. Bashlor said, "There's nothing there," and went back down the stairs. I kept observing the grounds as he was leaving. I spotted a German moving around and fired my submachine gun in his direction. As I started firing, more Germans were moving around. I kept on firing and soon the I Company squad began firing their rifles and machine guns. I fired a couple of magazines of submachine-gun ammo into the confused Germans. Next, I heard someone yell to stop firing. I did so and all was quiet.

I came down out of the steeple and lo and behold, the field adjoining the church was full of German soldiers. I immediately told the I Company machine gunners to move to the edge of the field and set up for a crossfire of the prisoners in the field. The riflemen stayed back from the prisoners in the field so they could shoot if necessary. I walked up to the German officer, who wouldn't put his hands on his head. He stated he was a German captain and took no orders from an enlisted man. He soon changed his mind because I pulled out my .45 automatic and stuck it up to his head and stated I'd "blow his damn head off." His hands went up fast. I also told him to relay to his men that if any of them tried to escape or throw a hand grenade, my gunners would start shooting. Nothing happened.

The best part is that the German captain started getting talkative. He told me he lived and worked in Detroit, Michigan, until 1938, when he went back to Germany and joined the army. This group of Germans had planned on hitting our regimental CP that night. We lined them up in a column of twos and sent for help to take them back to the beach. Quite a few were wounded – guess I got a few.

502nd Graves, D+4

This dramatic photo was taken by Red Larsen's camera at Houesville four days after D-day. The men pose over temporary graves of 502nd troopers killed in this area. Larsen stands at far left, Bill Gibbons is next, Joe Bass stands with hand on hip, and Dick Beaver is at far right. Larsen, Bass, and Beaver had landed on DZ D with the Pathfinders. Bass was killed in Korea in September 1950. *Alice Larsen*

"It's Okay – I Wiped it Off"

On 8 June 1944, Captain Cecil L. Simmons of H/502nd won a Bronze Star for leading his men in repulsing German attacks on Houesville. As the light began to fade that evening, the Germans called it a day, except for a two-man patrol that, unknown to the Americans, had sneaked into a clump of trees and bushes near the Company H positions. The trees were situated in a low spot just in front of the American line.

Simmons watched as one of his lieutenants walked down into the bushes to get some privacy for a latrine call. Shortly thereafter, he heard a great commotion and thrashing in the bushes. Simmons surmised that an enemy scout had jumped his officer in an attempt to kill or capture him.

Big Cec carried a British Fairbairn Commando knife strapped to the outside of his long left forearm. He grasped the weapon in his right hand. Then, removing his Case M-3 trench knife from his ankle, he was on the run, grasping the second weapon in his left hand.

Simmons jumped down into the bushes, straining his eyes to see in the dim light. He saw his lieutenant locked in a struggle with a German soldier. As he moved to assist, Simmons caught a movement out of the corner of his eye. Another German was rushing him from the flank. Simmons pivoted, thrusting his M-3 deep into the midsection of his enemy. Then, coming downward with a powerful right handed stab, he planted the British blade into the victim's face. Looking up, he could see that the lieutenant had finished his man also. As Simmons was about to remove his knives, he realized that he had thrust the Commando knife into the eye socket of the German, and now could not dislodge it, as it was buried to the hilt. Planting one foot against the corpse's skull, Simmons pulled and pulled, but could not get the knife out. Finally, he gave up, removing his M-3 from the corpse's gut and wiping off the blade before replacing it in his scabbard.

Captain Cecil L. Simmons, H/502nd.

As he walked away, Simmons glanced back at the dead man lying on his back, with the knife handle protruding from his face. He would later often wonder what the Graves Registration people thought when they came to bury this body.

The modern reader must bear in mind that these incidents happened long before the AIDS/HIV virus was known. This was one of Simmons's favorite stories, and the ending goes like this: The next day during a rest break, Simmons sat on the ground, broke out a K-Ration, and opened the small can of meat. Using his M-3 knife to serve as an eating utensil, he poked out little bites, eating them off the blade.

His aide, noticing this, was aghast.

"Captain, I can't believe you're eating with that knife!"

"Why do you say that?"

"Just think about where it was yesterday."

"Oh, that," said Simmons, pondering for a moment. "Oh, it's okay, I wiped it off." With a shrug and a grin, Simmons continued his meal.

Saint-Côme-du-Mont | 20

A number of activities took place near Saint-Côme-du-Mont on D-day, although it didn't become the focus of 101st operations until 8 June. Pathfinders of the 501st landed northeast, northwest, and southeast of the town.

Joe Beyrle of I/506th landed on the roof of the church, got free of his chute under fire, and got down to *terra firma*. He headed in the wrong direction for two hours and realized it when he hit the railroad line that runs from Carentan to Cherbourg. Reversing himself, Beyrle got back into St. Come, planted explosives on a power generator, then headed south. Shunning the flooded area below Dead Man's Corner, he headed west across the N-13 once again. Crossing one of the hedgerows in the area near dawn, he slid down into the laps of a platoon of German paratroopers. Beyrle was captured and the Germans marveled over all his equipment. "We had a mutual admiration society," Beyrle says, "that probably helped me to survive."

Beyrle was taken to a large underground room, dug into a farm field just west of the N-13 and south of Saint-Côme-du-Mont. The Germans had a CP there, and Beyrle was taken in and interrogated by an English-speaking intelligence officer. A blond woman sat nearby listening. She looked familiar to Beyrle, but he couldn't place her. Later, while marching south past Carentan, Beyrle remarked to a trooper walking beside him that he now knew where he had seen the blond before. She had been at a dance in England, several months before D-day, dancing with members of the 506th. *(See Chapter 29 for more about Joe Beyrle's POW experiences.)*

Fred Berke of C/326th AEB doesn't know Joe Beyrle, but he was taken to the same underground CP after being captured. Berke was told to lie in the grass outside the large hole, but was never taken inside for interrogation. At a 101st Airborne Division National Reunion in Washington, D.C., in 1990, Berke men-

Who Blew up the Steeple?

Sergeant Benecke, 377th PFAB, snapped this photo of the church steeple at Saint-Côme-du-Mont in mid-1944, before returning to England. Although church steeples across Europe were routinely blasted off by both sides to prevent the enemy from using them for observation, this church has a slightly different story. Gus Liapes and other members of Lieutenant Winan's "Ha-Ha" platoon (bazooka section, HQ/1st/506th) were up in the steeple on or shortly after D-day. They opened fire on a German armored car that passed below. Liapes believes this caused the Germans to eliminate the steeple. There are probably other versions of who blew the steeple off, and why.

tioned marching past Carentan as a POW, talking with an unknown trooper who was walking beside him. The trooper was telling him about a blond woman who sat in on his interrogation, and stated he had seen her in England before the invasion.

Berke also recalled seeing huge shells from the cruisers and battleships off the coast, tearing up the N-13 and the surrounding fields just east of the highway. He saw retreating cavalry and mule-drawn artillery troops, which looked like *Ost* volunteers, caught in the artillery. He saw mules, troops, and artillery pieces blown high into the air, twisting around in flight.

Ahzez "Jim" Karim of the 81mm Mortar Platoon, 2nd/501st, had landed right in the middle of the N-13 on D-day night, in the town of Saint-Côme itself. He barely escaped. Karim went on to lead a small group through enemy lines to Lieutenant Colonel Robert A. Ballard's assembly area, knocking out a German machine-gun nest *en route*. He was awarded the Silver Star.

On the night of the drop, Karim saw Corporal Elmer Glasser of his stick land in a tree in the middle of town, where he was soon killed. When the division moved south a few days later, Karim was in the town for a while. He recalls seeing another trooper, hanging in his harness from a light or power pole. "Each time the wind blew, the trooper's body would rattle against a building. This had caused German troops to fire into the man every time they walked past…He was full of holes."

Jim's platoon leader, Lieutenant Bill Russo, had also landed near the town close to a German CP. Totally alone and unable to move far, he spent the first day in hiding. He eventually located Private Daniel Martin, and they spotted a double concrete ramp, which they later learned was to be used to launch V-1 "Buzz Bombs." The bombs weren't there yet. Russo and companion rejoined the 501st on 8 June when they saw the 1st Battalion, 401st Glider Infantry Regi-

Captured Howitzer

This short-barreled 75mm German infantry howitzer was captured on the high ground between Saint-Côme-du-Mont and Carentan. This model was also popular with German paratroops. *Benecke*

ment (1st/401st GIR) attack vigorously through their area. Back in England, intelligence officers questioned Russo about the insignia worn by Germans at the buzz bomb site. On the night of 15–16 June, the first of these robot bombs fell on England. A few weeks later, 101st Airborne troopers located another V-1 launch ramp south of Cherbourg.

Many troopers of 3rd/506th had landed in the Saint-Côme area including Lieutenant Colonel Robert Wolverton, the battalion CO, who landed in an apple tree in a small orchard just east of the town; he was killed in his harness. His executive officer, Major George Grant, met a similar fate.

Captain Bob Harwick, H/506th, landed about 100 yards from the church, got out of his harness, and took shelter in a hedgerow. He lost his weapon and all equipment from the opening shock of his parachute and had only his cricket and trench knife. He was able to move only 300 yards before daylight, then took shelter in a "triangle of shrubbery at a road fork." Harwick later wrote:

I no sooner hid than Germans began passing. Germans, more Germans, and equipment! They even stopped and ate so close I could have stolen their black bread. I sweated it out from 5 A.M. to 7:15 that night, when a couple of Germans, looking for a place

Dead Man's Corner, 1990s
The large house on the corner, which was used as a German aid station, has changed very little. This is the intersection of the D-913 with the *Route Nationale* 13 (N-13). The corner got its name when an American tank was knocked out right in front of the house, where it sat for days, with the dead commander sticking up from the turret. The troops began referring to it as "the corner where the dead man's in the tank." This was shortened to "Dead Man's Corner," and it is still known by that name in France today. There are at least two versions of how the tank was knocked out. Don Burgett presented one in his book, *Currahee*, stating the tank was destroyed by German artillery on 7 June as it headed toward the D-913 to get more ammunition. Others claim the tank was knocked out by *Panzerfaust* fire from German paratroops sheltering in the ditch south of the intersection. *Author's Photo*

On left: **Unsung Hero**
Private Ahzez "Jim" Karim, HQ/2nd/501st, landed on the main drag in Saint-Côme-du-Mont. He won a Silver Star for knocking out a German machine-gun nest. *Karim*
On right: **Major Robert Harwick, H/506th**

to bed down pushed into the bushes, and there I was. He pointed a rifle at me and shouted "*Raus!*"

Harwick was searched and relieved of a short snorter dollar, 2,400 Francs, and a photo of his wife and daughter. "*Mein Frau and Töchterlein,*" he protested, but to no avail. As the Germans walked him south, they repeatedly searched him for cigarettes. He saw German paratroopers moving forward and was eventually pushed into a field with some other prisoners. He recognized a few and spoke to them and "got my first idea of what had happened; it did not sound good."

"I'll get the Sonofabitch out!"

The only gun of the 105mm battery captured at Holdy to be saved from immediate destruction. An assortment of 101st troopers hauled it south to the high ground above the causeway and began firing it toward Carentan. Some 377th PFAB artillery gunners were in on this as well as members of Lieutenant Winans's 1st/506th "Ha-Ha Squad" or "8-Ball Squad," which was an unofficial bazooka platoon where 1st Battalion mavericks were placed. Sergeant Ed Benecke, who took this photo, recalls that an empty casing eventually lodged in the breech and could not be dislodged. An engineer from the 326th AEB stated, "I'll get the sonofabitch out!" He tossed a live hand grenade down the muzzle, and sure enough, it blew the casing out. Shrapnel lodged in the bore, however. The next round fired exploded inside the barrel, blowing off half of the barrel and wounding eleven troopers. *Benecke*

Signs of Struggle

This remarkable shot was taken by Eddie Sapinski, F/502nd, after his lost group rejoined the company. This was approximately on 11 June, at which time 2nd/502nd was in reserve between Houesville and Saint-Côme-du-Mont. It looks like a struggle took place here, probably resulting in a trooper's capture. The rubberized invasion gas mask bag in the lower right corner suggests this happened Dday night, when the trooper landed, as most men threw their gas mask away immediately after landing. We can also see bazooka round containers, a cartridge belt, canteen, and Griswold Bag (which also would have been discarded upon landing). The helmet shows markings for 1st/506th. Most of the 506th PIR sticks landed in a concentrated area near Holdy, but strays came down far north or south of there. The trooper in the foreground is Corporal C. B. Williams, F/502nd, from Texas. In the 1960s, Williams served as campaign manager for Lyndon B. Johnson. *Sapinski*

Harwick still had an "escape kit pasted to the small of my back and a few toilet articles, which seemed awfully inadequate at the time."

He continued in his diary:

Just after midnight, they lined us up and started to march. As we got started, our artillery opened up along, on, and in the hedgerows by the road. The effect was terrible. Germans, horses, carts, trucks, all trying to leave at the same time. The crash of shells, yelling of men, roar of motors, diving for ditches, gave me a chance. I took off for the bushes and headed for the flooded area. I waded right up to the river, then back to a little bush dike, and hid. For a little over two days, I lay up to my hips in mud and water, sprinkling insect powder over me to keep the mosquitoes off. During this time, the battle ebbed and flowed by and near me, until I was so fed up I just didn't care. So at the end of the second day, I waded a ditch, ran past a German sniper, went into the river upstream, and eventually got to our lines. I picked up equipment abandoned along the road, outfitted myself, and rejoined the regiment. I found out then I was the only company CO left, and in command of 3rd Battalion. [Harwick's diary excerpts provided courtesy of Helen Briggs-Ramsey.]

As consolidated divisional elements fought their way south along the D-913 from the Beaumont-Angoville area, Don Burgett and a handful of A/506th men were the first to reach Dead Man's Corner at the intersection of the D-913 and the N-13. They had run through many fields and passed many hedgerows, thinking they were behind the main element, when actually they were in front.

Taking up positions just above the flooded area east of the causeway, they soon realized that a large German force had been retreating parallel to them, on the opposite side of the hedgerow. The troopers, inspired by the boldness of Sherwood Trotter, began piling up the retreating Germans as they crossed the N-13. Trotter was running back and forth, chucking hand grenades clear across the N-13. More troops from D/506th also piled in to the area, but things got too hot and the element pulled back, first to Dead Man's Corner, north of the intersection, then in darkness, they withdrew clear to Beaumont. This was after midnight, 7 June.

Before the 506th troopers withdrew in the night, a truck column driven by African-American soldiers pulled up on the road, headed south. Lieutenant McMillan of D/506th halted them and informed them that they were at the vanguard of the Allied invasion. A few more yards would put them behind German lines. The surprised truckers gratefully turned their convoy around.

Later in the evening, a German platoon moved in behind the American troops at Dead Man's Corner and formed their line, facing north at the intersection of the D-913 and the Saint-Côme-du-Mont turnoff. The bulk of 1st/506th was advancing toward them with tank support; firing erupted in the darkness.

Enemy rocket launchers fired at an American tank and hit it several times. The vehicle caught fire and two of the crew were wounded. The burning tank withdrew several hundred yards, causing a break in the column. Staff Sergeant Robert Mullins and Private Edward J. Murray, HQ/1st/506th, immediately brought light-machine-gun fire to bear on the enemy force, causing them to miss additional shots at the tank, and finally driving them away. They left behind two rocket launchers, an MG34, and several of their dead.

In the darkness and confusion, elements of the 1st/506th began to fire at each other across the gap. The fire on the tank had been extinguished and its crew began firing their machine gun south on the D-913. Mullins and Murray, realizing what was happening, volunteered to cross the gap to contact the forward part of the battalion. Heavy fire from both directions made crawling necessary most of the way, but Murray informed a tank crew ahead that they were firing at one of their own tanks, which had withdrawn. The forward tank lit an orange recognition flare and fire from the rearward tank ceased. The battalion rejoined forces, but the advance was delayed until D+2 (8 June).

After midnight, the Germans reestablished a line at the same intersection, again facing north, unaware of the A/506th and D/506th troops behind them at Dead Man's Corner. This force pulled back to Beaumont in the pre-dawn hours of the morning, walking right through the enemy line in the darkness. The Germans no doubt heard them, but must have thought it was their own troops advancing – there was no firing.

It was 0300 by the time Companies A and D got to sleep near Beaumont, a factor that would influence the coming "SNAFU Engagement" in the morning.

Both Staff Sergeant Mullins and Private Murray were later KIA. Mullins was awarded the Silver Star for his actions on 7 June.

Major H. W. "Hank" Hannah, the S-3 of the 506th, had started the tanks moving on this advance and on a number of occasions, was to personally untangle logjams in advances. He wrote in his diary:

There is just one secret to functioning well when the going is tough – that is, forgetting that you have any stake in life, and living only for the immediate situation.

The "SNAFU Engagement"

On 8 June, the division's objective was Saint-Côme-du-Mont, the last town on the N-13 before the Carentan Causeway. Most of the participants from Lieutenant Colonel Ewell's 3rd/501st and Colonel Sink's 1st/506th and 2nd/506th were so exhausted from the two previous days of fighting that they were

sleepwalking. Few troopers who landed on D-day can now recall anything of 7–9 June; they were so tired at the time that they were running on nerves.

The fresh 1st/401st GIR had come up to les Droueries from the beach and attacked briskly on Ewell's flank, but became engaged near Basse Addeville and remained locked in battle there for most of the day.

Elements of D/506th returned to Dead Man's Corner, then made a right turn and stopped in the fields just east of the N-13 and just north of the corner where they spent a mostly inactive day. Elements of A/506th were spread out, some moving east along the road between the D-913 and Saint-Côme-du-Mont, others moving south to Dead Man's Corner. *En route,* they passed the intersection of the D-913 and Saint-Côme turnoff. In a field on the southwest corner of that junction were dozens of dead Germans, many still lying in their sleeping rolls with blood trickling down from their ears; they had been killed by the morning's artillery preparation.

Charlie Hudson, First Sergeant of A/506th, recalls going into the large house at Dead Man's Corner and finding that the Germans had established an aid station inside. One of his men was shot dead upon entering the house. Shortly before this, the same trooper had commented to Hudson, "Sarge, I've never had so much fun in my life! You can shoot anybody you want around here and nobody cares."

Lieutenant Colonel Ewell found the N-13 near Dead Man's Corner. Looking north, he could see German troops and horse-drawn wagons pulling out of Saint-Côme-du-Mont, headed west. He decided to make a try for the Carentan Causeway, intending to block any German moves coming north. His unit fought all afternoon, blocking numerous German attacks. Later, he about-faced his troops to meet Germans attacking at the rear, coming south out of Saint-Côme-du-Mont. In a brilliant series of moves and counterattacks, Ewell crossed the N-13, took some high ground, and routed the Germans.

At 1400, the second bridge on the Carentan Causeway exploded. S. L. A. Marshall claims the Germans blew up this bridge over the Douve River. Frank Carpenter, C/501st, was at La Barquette with Lieutenant Farrell, the naval artillery liaison, however, and he claims to have witnessed Farrell calling in fire from a cruiser sitting off the coast, which destroyed Bridge No. 2. The destruction of this bridge was, after all, one of the division's D-day objectives.

The term "SNAFU Engagement" was coined by S. L. A. Marshall and in no way reflects negatively on Ewell's battalion. It refers to the lack of coordination by the attacking units on the morning of the attack. Exhaustion and a breakdown in radio communications were largely to blame.

Also on this afternoon, Captain Jere Gross, the CO of D/506th, was killed by an artillery round on the hill two fields east of Dead Man's Corner.

The fall of Saint-Côme-du-Mont set the stage for the advance along the causeway to Carentan. After crossing the N-13, A/506th encountered a horse-drawn supply wagon train still loaded with weapons and equipment that had been abandoned by the German *Parachute Infantry Regiment 6.* A sizable German cash payroll was also discovered.

The area was littered with dead Germans and dead horses. Charlie Hudson saw a live horse still hitched to a dead horse, dragging it as it walked along. "It was kind of a pitiful sight," he later remarked.

Exhausted troopers of 3rd/501st who survived the SNAFU Engagement on 8 June 1944, recuperate near Saint-Côme-du-Mont. *Krochka*

As Allied planners perceived it, the lock at La Barquette, over the Douve River, was of great strategic importance. Over a period of many months, the Germans had used the lock to flood the area behind the eastern Cotentin coast. In the case of a long siege behind Utah Beach, they could have continued to do so. As it turned out, however, the worst damage had already been done. Each time the tide came in from the Channel, the banks of the Douve would overflow because the Germans had closed the lock with huge wooden beams. (As of this writing, the beams were still in a barn beside the lock keeper's farmhouse.) Other written accounts have said that the Germans caused the flooding by opening the locks. Actually, they had closed them.

Colonel Howard Johnson, CO of the 501st, was to lead his regimental command group and his 1st Battalion in taking and holding this objective. They came over DZ D in the final serials of the 101st drop at about 0135.

Johnson's stick, landing across the Chateau e Bel Enault west of Basse Addeville, became fragmented, and the colonel barely escaped with his life. Making his way cross country, he assembled a force and moved on the lock at first light. A brief rush chased away the few Germans posted nearby and the lock was in American hands. It was evident that the Germans had placed a low priority in defending la Barquette. They knew well that they had already succeeded in flooding the lowlands as far north as Vierville; the floods even extended into the 82nd Airborne's area, west of the N-13. Now, the job of the 501st was to hold the objective until it came into the consolidated invasion bridgehead.

Throughout D-day, troops wandered into Colonel Johnson's perimeter. Many strays from the 506th PIR also arrived and were ordered to stay and reinforce the perimeter. The focus of defense shifted several times in the next few days. Initially, counterattacks were anticipated from the direction of Carentan or the N-13. These attacks never materialized, although efforts to reach Bridge No. 2 over the Douve at the N-13 were driven back. Destruction of that bridge was a D-day objective, but the bridge was not blown until D+2 (see Chapter 20).

A great debate rages as to whether Colonel Johnson made a personal visit to Addeville on D-Day afternoon or if he only spoke to Major R. J. Allen (in command there) via radio. Evidently, for some time the colonel left the lock area with a small group of men to search for more of his men. When his group returned to the area, they came under intense artillery fire from the high ground near Carentan.

This barrage came in where the road forks like the Y of a slingshot. Coming from Addeville, if one continues ahead, the road continues near the 3rd/506th's objective at le Port then swings up to le Grand Vey and beyond. Turning a sharp right at the junction takes one first to the lock service road or, if continuing straight, to the N-13 above Carentan. Much of the surrounding terrain east of the road junction was either impassable marsh or flooded pastures, devoid of cover. This Y-shaped intersection became known as "Hell's Corners" to the men who fought there. On D+1, a battalion of German paratroopers wandered into the fork of the Y while retreating from the vicinity of St. Marie du Mont. As a result, one of the largest pitched battles of the 101st Airborne in Normandy was waged at Hell's Corners.

The first American to die at Hell's Corners was Lawrence Ardrey, supply sergeant of the 501st. A sniper shot him on D-day morning and, without skilled surgeons to help, he died. (Major Francis Carrel, a 501st surgeon, arrived later on D-day and performed prodigious work at the lock on 6–7 June.) The only member of Service Company/501st to die in Normandy was Norman Dick.

En route to the lock area, Dick Gilmore and Clyde Bruders of the 501st's Service Company drew fire from a sniper in a distant tree. He was hard to spot because he had wrapped himself in the camouflaged nylon of an American parachute. Each trooper fired two shots into the sniper's tree and saw him drop out head first. They continued on to la Barquette and six days later were able to return and examine the sniper's body. He was wearing an American wristwatch and had American cigarettes and K-rations in his pockets.

There was much movement on D-day, and Lieutenant Bill Sefton's recon patrol started from Angoville in the early morning, fought through the afternoon in Addeville, and wound up at la Barquette in the evening. Major R. J. Allen's force in Addeville pulled out just before dusk to join Colonel Johnson's group at the lock. Father Francis L. Sampson, the Catholic chaplain of the 501st, stayed behind in Addeville to

Lock at La Barquette

The La Barquette lock over the Douve River, facing southwest toward the N-13 and Carentan. Half a century after D-day, the large wooden beams once used by the Germans to close the lock at la Barquette are still stored in the barn of the Parey family. Closing of the lock had caused the Douve River to overflow its banks at high tide from the Channel. This resulted in flooding the areas behind the Cotentin coast, an additional obstacle to invasion by air or sea. *Author's Photo*

mans had excellent observation of movement in the US perimeter, as Womer found out on D-day afternoon. At one point, he crawled out of a wheat field on his hands and knees, corning out onto a road. An 81mm German mortar shell landed right in front of him and the blast went up and just over him, only scorching the left sleeve of his M-42 parachutist jacket ("jump jacket"). Womer eased back into the wheat field. He later cut the burnt sleeve off his jacket.

On D+1, Womer climbed into the fork of a bare tree near his foxhole. He tried to spot a fat German soldier who had run across the road and was hiding among a group of cows. Suddenly, a flat trajectory artillery shell of 75mm or 88mm caliber streaked through the fork of the tree, missing Womer by inches. He came down in a hurry.

Lieutenant Farrell, the naval artillery liaison, had jumped into Normandy with the 501st troopers. He was able to radio the cruiser *USS Quincy II* in the Channel for support by her 8-inch guns. Farrell brought the devastating fire down on targets near Saint-Côme Du Mont and Carentan, and was able to reduce hostile artillery fire on the la Barquette area.

The Battle of Hell's Corners

On the morning of 7 June, elements of the *1st Battalion* of the German *Parachute Infantry Regiment 6* were moving south across country, retreating from their fight near St. Marie du Mont. The group still numbered nearly 500 and made its way cross country, guiding on the pointed steeple of the church in Carentan as its destination. Had the group reached Carentan, they could have reunited with their other two battalions for continued fighting. Standing in the road fork at Hell's Corners, one can look north and see the domed steeple in Sainte-Marie-du-Mont. With an "about face," one can see the steeple in Carentan.

The German *Fallschirmjäger* battalion passed by Lieutenant Colonel Ballard's force near Angoville, but, despite some fire laid on their flanks, they kept heading with determination toward Carentan.

Two members of the 501st had set off on a long-distance patrol that morning and happened to be east of Basse Addeville with a light machine gun when the German battalion approached across the open, grassy terrain. Lieutenant Fred Owens and Private First Class Leo F. Runge were in that position and opened fire on the German paratroopers, shooting until their machine gun jammed. They then began falling back in the face of the massive group, giving them harassing fire from an M-1 rifle. They ran out of ammunition so Runge and Owens stripped cartridges out of the machine gun belt, feeding them into the chamber of the M-1 individually, to keep lead flying at the Germans. Owens later got some bad press in certain historical accounts because he allegedly fired into the Germans during a truce, but Runge was very impressed with the bravery of this officer. (It is also worth noting that Owens received the Silver Star for this action, although he died shortly thereafter in the Bastogne fighting.)

It has been previously written that when the American lock-perimeter force opened fire, the Germans were totally surprised. It is true that they had no idea of how many US troops were dug in there, but they had been receiving American fire all along their route of travel. The delays caused by Runge and Owens enabled Colonel Johnson to move a number of machine guns, riflemen, and mortars into position facing the German approach – right at the fork of the roads at Hell's Corners.

Orders were passed for all on the line to withhold fire until a signal gun opened up. The German battalion

Souvenir Sleeve

Jack Womer was a demolitionist of the famous Filthy 13 from the 506th. Prior to joining the parachute troops in England, he had served with the 29th Division's Rangers. The left arm of Womer's jump jacket was scorched by the near miss of a German 80mm mortar round near Hell's Corners. He kept the sleeve as a souvenir when he discarded the beat-up jacket at the end of the campaign. In this 1992 photo, Womer displays the sleeve. Years of handling have diminished the powder burns, but the Dday elbow reinforcement is visible and the eagle patch is still in place. *Author's Photo*

protect the wounded. The entire aid station was captured by German paratroopers after Allen's group moved out, and Father Sam narrowly escaped death by firing squad. He was able to prevent the Germans from killing the wounded; his little aid station survived a heavy artillery shelling that night. They were liberated by friendly forces soon after.

Late on D-day, Sergeant Leo Gillis and First Sergeant Herschel Parks, of F/501st, wandered into the Hell's Corners perimeter. They found Captain Sammie N. Homan, their company CO, already there. Homan had led a patrol toward Bridge No.2 over the Carentan Causeway but was driven back by strong German forces. The Company F group dug in facing Basse Addeville (north flank). This would put them in a position from which they could not shoot at the German paratroopers the following day. Jack Womer, a 506th demolition-saboteur of the Filthy 13, was dug in on the same flank with a group of 506th strays he had helped organize.

En route to his objective at Brévands, Womer never made it beyond la Barquette. While moving in darkness the night of the drop, he had seen a column of American paratroopers freeze in the light of a flare, as taught in training. A German 20mm automatic cannon cut all of them down where they stood. The Ger-

came on, struggling through ankle-deep water and weeds, guiding on that distant Carentan church steeple.

When the group reached a point 350 yards from the road fork, the opening gun started firing and within a second, all guns on the line were blazing away. It was impossible to tell how many Germans were hit by the initial fire as the whole group disappeared into the water and weeds in a matter of seconds. Leo Gillis and Jack Womer's group were dug in facing directly toward Basse Addeville and could not participate in the firing, but turning around to their right rear, they could watch. A stray bullet struck a soldier near Gillis, killing the man.

Gillis later said:

The Germans looked like a big black cloud crossing that area—you could see them coming. When firing started, it was like shooting 'em in a barrel. They were trapped and they made a stupid move to begin with. They never should've been crossing an open area like that. They were in a foot of water anyhow.

Jack Womer said:

The Germans are coming from the beach – and they're running. I'm not over there, but I can turn around and watch – and it's a nice scene. Here they comin'—Christ, they're mowing 'em down like wheat. The 501st now, they're really putting' it to 'em! The wounded out there are wavin' to stay back… shooting their Goddamn arm off, shootin' every Goddamn thing.

The Germans pinned down in the swamp did return fire and succeeded in killing 10 and wounding 33 Americans during the battle. Bart Tantalow, of Lieutenant Sefton's S-2 section, was among those killed.

The German battalion was taking heavy losses and some 10 minutes after the shooting erupted, cries of "Kamerad!" could be heard coming from the swamp. Some Germans were throwing their rifles into the air, and some of those were reportedly shot by their own officers and NCOs for trying to surrender. Colonel Johnson was concerned that his troops might run out of ammo, despite the fact that they were winning.

Jack Womer said, "You can hear 'em: 'Cease fire!' Nobody wants to stop—they want to kill Krauts."

Two attempts were finally made to arrange the surrender of the surviving Germans. Readers of *Four Stars of Hell* (Declan McMullen Co., New York, 1947), *Rendezvous with Destiny,* and *Night Drop* will note a different cast of characters appears in the truce group in each account. We can be fairly certain that the last attempt, made by Private First Class Leo Runge, succeeded in bringing in the German battalion commander. The surviving German troops soon followed.

Because Runge – a Canadian national who had been born in Austria, but became a US citizen while serving in the US Army – could speak German, he wanted to meet with the German commander. Attaching an orange panel to his rifle, Runge walked toward the Germans, waving it. When he got to their positions, Runge saw the German major rise and walk toward him. Runge stopped near a wounded *Fallschirmjager* as the German commander walked toward him. The wounded man on the ground had been hit in the groin, but asked Runge for a smoke. Lighting a cigarette, Runge bent down and handed it to him.

It developed that the arrogant German major could speak English.

"You're trapped," Runge told him. "Our forces from the beach are coming up right behind you, and we have you outnumbered." Actually the German force was twice the size of the lock force and Runge had no idea of how distant the beach landing forces were.

At that point, firing erupted from both sides. The wounded German on the ground grabbed Runge by the leg and pulled him down, shielding Runge from the firing with his own body. The major laid down beside them. Leo pointed his M-1 at the major's throat and said, "You're my prisoner!" He took the Luger pistol from the major's holster and when the shooting tapered off again, marched the German back into the American lines. The major was highly upset when he saw the small number of Americans manning the US line. He wanted to go back, get his battalion, and just walk over the lock force, but it was too late. The major was shoved into a horse stall at the Parey farm, and before long some 350 men of his battalion walked in in small groups to surrender. Some 150 more had been killed or wounded in the swamp.

According to German historian Paul Carrell, only 25 of the German paratroopers from the battalion escaped that day, making their way around to their CP on 9–10 June.

The 350 prisoners were lined up on the road that leads to Peneme and German artillery spotters in the distance saw them. Thinking that it was an American group, they began throwing mortar and artillery rounds on the road.

Hero of Hell's Corners

Private First Class Leo Runge was born in Austria, but was a Canadian citizen who joined the US Army and later became an American citizen. A member of the 501st's regimental Demolitions Platoon, Leo could speak German and captured the German major commanding the *1st Battalion, Parachute Regiment 6*. After the war, Runge lived in Laureldale, Pennsylvania, where he operated a plumbing business. He received the Silver Star for his actions of 7 June 1944. Runge died in 1990. *Runge*

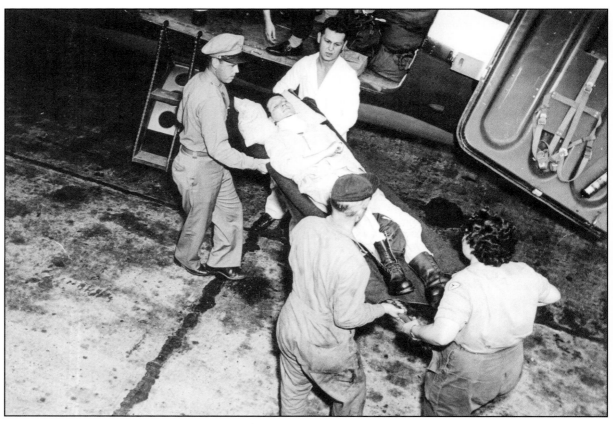

Shot in the Neck

Rich Reinhold, of the 501st's S-2, arrives back in the States with a brace on his neck. While out in the swampy area northeast of Hell's Corners looking for German wounded on 7 June 1944, Reinhold was shot by a wounded German paratrooper lying in the shallow water and weeds. "It was the dumbest thing he ever did," Reinhold said later. Several of Reinhold's buddies riddled the German with bullets a second after he fired. The German slug had entered just below Reinhold's chin, coming out the back of his neck, narrowly missing his spine. In the years after WWII, Reinhold made a full recovery, and his wound was not apparent to anyone who saw him. *Reinhold*

Jim Purifoy had been among those guarding the Germans and he dove into the roadside ditch to take cover from the enemy fire. Several German parachutists piled in atop Jim and nobody cared anything except to escape the fire. A number of Germans were killed by their own guns here and Captain McReynolds, the 501st adjutant, was killed while attempting to keep order under the shelling.

Before the shells came in, the prisoners had been stripped of their equipment, including fancy parachutist gloves, smocks, and jump knives. A pile of photos on the ground grew to several feet in height.

Gillis said, "These guys were queer for pictures – every one of them had enough photos in his pockets to fill an album." Womer said, "Then their own artillery came in on 'em – tore their ass up … we loved it!"

The two wooden bridges that crossed the Douve River at intervals of several hundred yards were situated in the hinterlands near the small town of Brévands. Only a few primitive roads circumvent the area. In June 1944, much of the surrounding area was also flooded by the backup from nearby la Barquette. At any time, the area is also laced with deep, flooded ditches and tall marsh reeds. It is nearly impossible to cross by foot unless one follows the two-wheeled cart paths or dirt roads that wind through the region. Any effort to send German reinforcements north from the N-13 – between Carentan and Isigny – would logically be done via Catz, coming up through the Brévands area across the two bridges. What exactly the Germans had in the way of reserve armor, troops, and supplies was not certain, but the plan to seize the bridges had a simple objective.

Troopers of 3rd/506th were to capture both bridges (the southwest bridge was a footbridge, the northeast bridge was a vehicle bridge) and, if possible, were to gain a toehold on the opposite (southeast) bank.

Under perfect conditions, the rest of the division would be aware of the situation there, and the troops holding the bridges would be guided by higher headquarters, as well as by circumstances. If the Germans began crossing the bridges in force, sending reinforcements toward Utah Beach's defenses, the troopers were to demolish the spans. If they could be held in the event that German troops were unable to force a crossing, they could be used to shuttle US troops and vehicles across, as soon as the invasion front reached that area.

On D-day, however, the scenario was far from perfect. With staggering DZ casualties (see Chapter 3), 3rd/506th sustained the highest rate of KIAs and POWs of any US airborne battalion in the Normandy operation. Of the 723 personnel who jumped, fewer than 150 made it to the objective in the first two days.

As mentioned in Chapter 20, Lieutenant Colonel Robert Wolverton, the battalion commander, and his executive officer, Major George Grant, were killed upon landing. All the company commanders in the 3rd Battalion were either killed or captured. It fell to one of the battalion staff officers, Captain Charles Shettle, to lead the survivors in holding the bridges. Shettle landed far north of the objective, near Angoville, but knew where he was. He made a beeline straight for the objective, cutting down secondary roads on a 45-degree angle, picking up troops along the way. Enroute, he saw an officer and trooper of the 506th charge and destroy the crew of a German antiaircraft gun; both men were killed in the process.

Shettle's small group reached the objective before dawn. As day broke through, he realized his line would be the 20-foot-high earthen berm, which retained the Douve during high tide. Arriving troopers cut foxholes into the side of this sandy dike and quickly learned that looking over the top was hazardous. Such silhouetting would draw fire from the German side of the river. Also, to stray too far behind the dike was dangerous, as much of the ground on the German side of the Douve was considerably higher. This fact afforded the Germans with a view of

A Mighty Warrior
Staff Sergeant Fred Bahlau entered Normandy as Company H's supply sergeant. In addition to Bahlau's organizational and leader-ship skills, he proved to be a mighty warrior. He was one of the few men of the regiment to earn two Silver Stars and also received a field commission. Here, he strikes a pose for the camera, facing away from the Douve River. Although the Germans across the Douve were the main concern, there was also fighting from the opposite direction, most notably the action in which Lieutenant Charles Santarsiero earned his DSC. *Bahlau*

movement behind the earthen berm. Private First Class James Martin of Company G found this out when he and others sheltered in a large depression about 150 yards northwest of the line. German mortars were laid on the position, which was visible from a hill across the Douve. Explosions bracketed the crater, killing and wounding a number of men. Jim Martin and the survivors moved up to the line at a dead run.

H/506th Troopers

This photo was made with a German camera captured by Staff Sergeant Fred Bahlau. *(Left to right)* Lieutenant Hegeness, Sergeant Bahlau, Sergeant Phil Parker, and Private First Class Gordon Yates, all of H/506th. Parker and Yates are armed with Lugers. Note the extra pocket on the lieutenant's shoulder. Bahiau had rubbed foot powder on his jacket in England, to avoid having it gas impregnated (the foot powder gave the jacket the appearance of having been gas treated)

Lieutenant Turner Chambliss

In postwar correspondence to George Koskimaki, James Martin related a tragic story that happened just after daylight at Brévands. Martin's platoon leader was a very tall (6 feet 4 inch) lieutenant named Turner M. Chambliss. Chambliss was an Army brat and also a January 1943 graduate of the US Military Academy at West Point, a fact he mentioned often. Martin considered Chambliss to be "the most idealistic person I ever knew… very GI, strict, but fair." It seemed evident that the other officers were envious of Chambliss, since they pumped the men for any lapses they might have used against him; there were none.

The tragic gag began back in England, when Martin had conceived the idea of asking "Are we Army or West Point?" since Chambliss was so "West Point" about everything. Martin had stenciled the words "West Point" on the chest of every man's jump jacket in the platoon.

The troops, who had expected an uproar, were disappointed at the next formation. Chambliss gave no reaction and didn't even let on that he had noticed. Thus did the entire 2nd Platoon of Company G jump into France with "West Point" emblazoned on their chests. The end of this story is best told in Martin's own words, as told in Koskimaki's book *D-day with the Screaming Eagles*:

[Lieutenant Chambliss] got to the bridge before most of us. During the fighting in the exposed area near the bridge, he suddenly stood up and was shot twice through the mouth. I'm ashamed to tell you what happened next, but I must. As he lay dying, he asked if there was anyone there from the 2nd Platoon, and when told there were none, he told the H Company sergeant who was cradling his head that he would like to know why we put "West Point" on our jackets. He wondered if we were mocking his background. I cried tears of shock and frustration and shame as his body was carried past our position. I keep wondering how he could have failed to perceive the great pride and affection we felt for him.

Meanwhile, Captain Shettle, at the southwest footbridge, could look approximately 500 yards to his left and see a German 88mm-dual-purpose gun on the hill adjacent to the town of Brévands. He called the available Company H men together and asked for volunteers to cross the bridge to estimate German strength on the opposite shore. First to volunteer was Private First Class Donald Zahn who ran right across the top of the bridge armed with a Tommy gun. Alone, Zahn worked to the left about 70 to 80 yards after crossing. He encountered no Germans, but visual checks of a wooded area indicated that German troops and gun emplacements were present. He proceeded along the river cautiously, until he could see the rear of the wooded area, finding it well fortified.

Zahn made his way back toward the bridge after a solo half-hour recon and met Sergeant George Montilio who was just coming across. They discussed the situation and were joined by approximately ten additional troopers led by Lieutenants Rudolph Bolte and Kenneth Christianson. Also in the group were Sergeant Harry Clawson (later KIA in Holland and a Silver Star recipient) and Private First Class Hank DiCarlo.

While the group was formulating a plan for attacking the German positions, the enemy, aware of their presence, struck first. A P-38 pistol was fired through a nearby hedge, and the 9mm bullet struck DiCarlo in the back, exiting his right chest. Zahn sprayed the bush with his Thompson, killing the German, whose pistol was recovered.

More German troops charged the hedge, yelling as they came. The Americans began tossing grenades across the hedge. Mingled with the explosions, they could hear screams. Without further friendly casualties, the American group recrossed the Douve, working hand by hand along the lower bridge supports to avoid enemy fire. Training at the old obstacle course at Camp Toccoa paid off here. The wounded DiCarlo was also brought back to the friendly bank.

The reader of *Night Drop* by S. L. A. Marshall will find a different account of this action, including many facts the participants could not verify. Marshall cites two troopers who crossed the Douve first, hauling a light machine gun. He writes that both were killed. He was probably mistakenly referring to Zahn and Montilio, although neither was killed here. Zahn is positive that no one brought a machine gun across that day. Also, German casualties are given as 13 killed and three machine gun nests destroyed. Zahn says, "If we killed three or four, we were lucky." When interviewed, Christianson also felt the figures were high and stated an accurate body count was impossible under the circumstances.

During the return trip across the bridge, the group could see that demolitionists in scalplocks and war paint were already wiring the bridge for demolition.

Most of the available troops were from G/506th and H/506th because I/506th had been decimated by plane crashes and misdrops (see Chapter 3). Most of the Company G men were at the northeast bridge, which they held with fewer than seventy troopers for the first three days.

On D-day afternoon, Lieutenant Charles "Sandy" Santarsiero of Company I brought in a group of 26 men. Santarsiero had landed way up near Sainte-Marie-du-Mont. His arrival was perhaps the luckiest thing to happen to Shettle's group.

Shettle's consolidated force was on the extreme southern flank of the Cotentin invasion. In addition to manpower shortages, it was plagued by an absence of radio equipment, making it impossible to communicate with the regiment, the division, or the fleet offshore. (Shettle made a personal call on Colonel Johnson at la Barquette and used his radio to report the status of 3rd/506th to the cruiser *USS Quincy II*. The information was not forwarded to 101st or 506th HQ, nor to the command Center in the UK.)

When a personal reconnaissance by Colonel Sink – as well as radio calls – failed to raise any information from Shettle's group, it was concluded that 3rd/506th had been destroyed. It was further concluded that the bridges were in German hands and that they must be destroyed by an air strike. Three P-51 fighters, loaded with bombs would depart England on D+1 to accomplish that mission.

Before noon on 7 June (D+1), the three P-51s flew in low, bombing the two bridges and strafing the foxholes northwest of the Douve with machine-gun fire. Some friendly casualties were sustained. There would have been many more had it not been for Staff Sergeant Ed Shames of Company I, and the chaplain, T. S. McGee, who set off orange smoke grenades on the road bridge and waved a recognition scarf at the planes. The P-51s broke off the attack without strafing US positions north of the Douve River. Donald Zahn found one paratrooper sitting upright in his foxhole, dead. A large piece of timber from one of the exploding bridges had impaled him.

A spectacular tragedy occurred at the north (highway) bridge, as one of the planes flew in so low that a wing tip struck the parapet of the bridge. Lieutenant Santarsiero saw the aircraft burst into flames and come apart, scattering debris halfway to Utah Beach.

Lieutenant Richard Meason (pronounced *May-son*; nicknamed "Flash Gordon") the acting CO of Company H, led a patrol in search of communications equipment on the northwest (friendly) side of the Douve. The first German they spotted was about 100 yards away and running. Meason fired a reflex shot with his .45 pistol that miraculously hit the German, dropping him in his tracks.

This patrol eventually returned with 12 to 15 prisoners some of whom, Captain Shettle recalls, were Hungarian volunteers. Zahn recalls there was some talk of doing away with the prisoners, in accordance with the preflight verbal directives concerning "no prisoners for the first three days." However, arrangements were made to accommodate them and, in addition, a battalion aid station was established in the nearby Fortin farm.

The troopers near the north bridge had been pounded by direct fire from the 88mm gun on the hillside near Brévands, which worked up and down the embankment, trying to blow the Americans out of their foxholes. The German gunners succeeded in killing numerous cows behind the embankment. American dive bombers (not the same planes that bombed the bridges) eventually took out the 88mm gun.

A One-Man Army at Brévands

Lieutenant Charles Santarsiero of Scranton, Pennsylvania, represented part of Company I at the north bridge. On D+2 (8 June), he earned the DSC for the following action.

Santarsiero was using binoculars to scan the area behind his Douve position, watching for the anticipated approach of friendly troops from the eastern Cotentin coast. Instead, he saw several German companies marching toward the bridge in retreat. They were unaware that US forces held the area. Santarsiero alerted his troops, who remained concealed until the Germans approached to a distance of 75 yards. When he ordered the group to commence firing, they achieved total surprise. Most of the Germans in the forward companies were taken out, and the rear company scattered into a large field surrounded by hedgerows.

Santarsiero decided to throw the enemy off balance before they could regroup to attack. Leaving Lieutenant Linton Barling (KIA-Holland) in charge of the bridge, Santarsiero ran forward to the first hedgerow. In it, he found a perfect position that someone had previously dug. It was a slit trench, with a V-cut into the hedge. Fifty yards ahead, Santarsiero could see two German officers shouting to a group of men. Included in this group were six American paratroop prisoners, carrying stretchers. Santarsiero opened fire on the Germans, dropping many of them. The POW stretcher bearers scattered in three directions, still dragging the now-empty stretchers behind them; Santarsiero never saw them again.

A German MG42 crew opened fire on Santarsiero's position, showering him with dirt and rocks. Then for some unknown reason, the MG42 stopped firing.

In squad strength, the panic-stricken Germans began to run from left to right in front of Santarsiero's position. He fired at the last in line, working his way up to the first. Then another squad would run past, and Santarsiero reversed the procedure, traversing right to left. Santarsiero took a heavy toll, firing until he ran out of targets. (Santarsiero had been a weapons

One-Man Army

On 8 June 1944, Lieutenant Charles "Sandy" Santarsiero led elements of 3rd/506th in engaging several companies of retreating German troops. The citation for his award originally recommended the Medal of Honor, but was reduced to a DSC due to an old feud within the 506th officer corps. In 25 days of actual WWII combat, Santarsiero was seriously wounded in action twice, and personally inflicted nearly 100 enemy casualties with small arms fire.

instructor at the Fort Benning Infantry School. He told the author he used an M-1 rifle in this battle and used up a bandoleer of ammunition. Firing rapidly at less than 100 yards, most of his bullets found their targets.)

Three Germans with a white flag appeared. Santarsiero walked out to meet them and began to render first aid. Soon the field was "alive with Germans and wounded, wanting to surrender." Santarsiero pointed them back toward Captain Shettle's position, then heard the word *Kamerad,* coming from his right. It was the MG42 crew that had fired on him earlier. The gun, loaded with a full belt, was pointed at him. Luck was with Santarsiero as the crew could have easily cut him down. Instead, they had remained concealed, watching the surrender, before giving up themselves. These prisoners were added to those being held near the southwest bridge and Santarsiero gave the MG42 to the bridge force to increase their firepower.

In talking things over with Captain Shettle, Santarsiero learned that the 3rd Battalion was still out of radio contact with regiment and division. He and Lieutenant Barling set off across country, heading northwest, in an attempt to shoot their way through

to headquarters. They took separate routes, and Santarsiero reached Utah Beach. He flagged down a jeep driven by an officer of the 81st AAAB and got a ride to Hiesville, where he briefed a worried General Anthony McAuliffe with news about 3rd/506th. (McAullife is of later "Nuts" fame at Bastogne. At this time, he was the divisional artillery commander.) After listening to Santarsiero's story, Mac took him by the arm and said, "Charlie, you have brought great news!" He showed the lieutenant the last entry he had made on the situation map, which read:

No word from 3rd Battalion, 506th. Unable to contact by radio. Sent numerous patrols out, but unable to get through due to enemy forces. We can assume that the 3rd Battalion has been annihilated.

Santarsiero Leads the 327th GIR to Brévands

Lieutenant Santarsiero talked with Lieutenant Colonel Joseph H. Harper as he led Harper's regiment down the winding dirt roads to Brévands. (Harper replaced Colonel George S. Wear as CO of the 327th GIR. Wear was relieved early in the campaign for unsatisfactory performance.) Deep, water-filled ditches also crisscrossed the area. A short distance from the Brévands bridgehead, Santarsiero spotted several German marines setting up an MG42 machine gun to ambush their column from the flank. He pointed out the Germans to Harper and said, "Give me your best BAR man. One good burst should get them all...."

A young glider infantryman armed with a Browning Automatic Rifle was brought forward and followed Santarsiero into the reeds beside the road. They flopped into some brush and Santarsiero pointed out the targets.

As the lieutenant prepared to command the gunner to open fire, he glanced over at the gliderman and noticed that the lad had a death grip on the weapon, his knuckles turning white with the strain.

In a patient voice, Santarsiero asked, "Son, have you killed anyone yet?"

"Well, ...no, Sir."

"Would you rather that I did it?"

"Okay," said the soldier as they traded

"When I fire, open up, then we'll rush them."

The tense youth nodded.

Santarsiero opened fire and his aim was good. The enemy crewmen were all struck by bullets. A lieutenant, hit in the arm, stood up, clutching his wound and wanting to surrender. Santarsiero and the kid were running up full speed toward him. One of the German gunners, although wounded, was still trying to aim the machine gun. Santarsiero came sailing in on top of him and the other wounded gunner. He grabbed the throat of one German, pushing his head into the water-filled ditch, drowning him. At the same time, Santarsiero produced a razor-sharp knife and slashed the throat of the other German. The Marine lieutenant still stood nearby, watching as he clutched his wounded shoulder. The young BAR man was also standing nearby, vomiting. The Marine lieutenant was taken prisoner and the 327th GIR completed its trek to Brévands, where it relieved 3rd/506th in their bridgehead positions and assumed control of the prisoners.

When Lieutenant Santarsiero reported in to Captain Shettle, the front of his jumpsuit looked like a butcher's apron.

"My God, Sandy, where are you hit?" Shettle asked.

"That's not my blood," Santarsiero replied.

Nineteen officers and 117 enlisted men, the survivors of Captain Shettle's battalion, marched to Hiesville to regroup. During three days of fighting at the bridges, they had lost 7 killed and 21 wounded. In *Rendezvous with Destiny,* Rapport and Northwood credit the battalion with 60 to 70 German "casualties" as well as 258 prisoners. (Presumably 60 to 70 killed, as the wounded were counted with the prisoners. Of the 258 POWs, Santarsiero claims 179 were captured in his fight on 8 June.)

At Hiesville, an additional 4 officers and 100 troopers who had been lost rejoined 3rd/506th. On 9 June, Captain Harwick of Company H, the only surviving company CO (who had escaped from captivity near Saint-Côme-du-Mont), returned and assumed command of 3rd Battalion.

The 327th GIR Continues the Fight at Brévands

Soon after relieving the 506th, elements of 1st/327th GIR began scouting the area for a means of crossing the Douve River. Engineers brought up rubber boats. Also, Lieutenant Carlton Werner, Private First Class Gordon Hatchel, Private First Class George Groh, and Private William Webb located and salvaged a ferry from the far shore. (Werner was KIA at Normandy; Hatchel was KIA at Bastogne; Groh was WIA at Bastogne; and Webb was POW at Bastogne.) They brought the ferry across to the northwest bank and a patrol of A/327th's 2nd Platoon crossed to the enemy shore. They were soon ambushed, losing one man killed and five wounded.

When the shot-up group returned to the Douve, they found the ferry wouldn't work, so they swam across. Two of the men began to drown, but were saved by Private Arthur Mayer, who was shot in the arm and the leg during the rescue. Mayer became one of the first 25 men in the 101st to win the DSC.

After dark on the night of 9–10 June, C/327th crossed the Douve on rubber boats, followed by the rest of 1st Battalion. By morning, the entire regiment was across. The 1st/401st GIR (which fought as the third battalion of the 327th GIR, since the 327th only had two organic infantry battalions) came across at low tide in the morning, wading in the then-shallow water.

German artillery had inflicted numerous casualties, but most of the Brévands defenders faded back. In the coming days, the 327th helped liberate Carentan, coming in along the Bassin-a-Flot canal from the northeast. Other elements would make contact with the 175th Infantry, 29th Division at Auville-sur-le-Vey, which was the first known contact of troops who landed at Utah and Omaha beaches at 1400, 10 June 1944.

The 327th would fight on through Catz, St. Pellerin, and Montmartin en Graignes, where they collided with elements of the German *17th SS Panzer-Grenadier Division* on 12–13 June.

The Continuing Ordeal of Hank DiCarlo

Meanwhile, Hank DiCarlo of H/506th, was lying in the Theophile Fortin farm, where a provisional aid station had been established to treat members of his battalion. DiCarlo had been shot on D-day on the first Douve crossing, but had somehow been left behind when elements of the 101st Airborne left the area. DiCarlo lay alone for what seemed like days, until a regular infantry outfit moved into the area and loaded him into an ambulance. Hank had received

no real medical treatment since being wounded and his chest cavity was filled with blood. Breathing was difficult for him, and he was relieved at the prospect of evacuation.

However, due to the confusing road network in the area, the ambulance took a wrong turn and eventually wound up at the front line. Before he knew what was happening, DiCarlo was ordered out of the ambulance, handed a rifle, and told to join an attack which was about to jump off. He took the weapon and began charging across the field. Halfway across, he passed out, dropping unconscious to the ground. Finally, the battered eagle was moved to Utah Beach and sent to a hospital in England. The rugged DiCarlo would fight again at the epic battles in Holland and Bastogne, and was seriously wounded again.

A Note from the Author Regarding 3rd/506th at Brévands

As official historian of the ETO, S. L. A. Marshall did superb work in documenting many of the major battles of the WWII 101st Airborne Division. Most notable are the accounts of Summers at XYZ; Lieutenant

The Politics of Rank
How History Was Distorted for Propriety

Yet another example of distorted history follows in the saga of Zahn and Montilio. As previously described, Private First Class Donald Zahn, 3rd/506th, was the first member of the 101st Airborne to cross the Douve at Brévands and was alone on the enemy shore for at least half an hour. Sergeant George Montilio was the second man across. It is no reflection on Montilio's courage, but the battalion adjutant felt it was more appropriate to award the DSC to a sergeant than to a private. Thus, before leaving France, Montilio received the medal instead of Zahn. Montilio declared he wouldn't wear his medal until and unless Zahn received one also. Zahn recalls, "Montilio and I had a very good understanding about the D.S.C. He probably felt more disturbed about the initial outcome than I did. He was the second man across the bridge, and I have no qualms in sharing the medal with him." Montilio never lived long enough to wear his medal. A trig gerhappy replacement killed him in a case of mistaken identity the night of 19 April 1945. Montilio was one of the last WWII battle fatalities of the 101st Airborne. A park in his hometown of Quincy, Massachusetts, is named in his honor.

In mid-1945, Donald Zahn, now a lieutenant in Company C, finally received his DSC for being the first man across the Douve footbridge on D-day. He credits his former CO, Major Bob Harwick, with pushing the write-up through. To add insult to injury, as General Maxwell Taylor awarded the medal, the pin broke.

Colonel Robert Cole's causeway battle and bayonet charge; and the battle at Best, Holland. In the case of these battles, Marshall's technique was to assemble a quorum of survivors and let each man tell what he saw or did, in the presence of the others, who would add, clarify, or interject. By this method, a picture of the whole battle would emerge as if by assembling pieces of a puzzle. Time and circumstances didn't always permit use of this technique, and it was notably not used when he assembled his accounts of 2nd/501st and 3rd/506th in Normandy. In the case of these units, Marshall relied on official after-action statistics and the testimony of battalion staff officers who may have embellished or distorted the truth to make better-sounding reports.

This author was acquainted with S. L. A. Marshall, via telephone conversations in the early 1970s, while Marshall still resided in Birmingham, Michigan. As Marshall stated in *Night Drop,* he had set his 1944 notes aside for 15 years before resurrecting them to write the book. In the case of his notes on 1st/502nd, and 3rd/502nd, his notes were and will remain forever unsurpassed in accuracy, as they were derived from the group testimony sessions described above. He did admit, however, that there might be inaccuracies in his reporting of the la Barquette battle, the Angoville-les Droueries fight, and the Brévands actions as he had not used the group-talk method with the involved survivors of those actions.

In the case of the Brévands fighting, he relegated it to an odds-and-ends chapter entitled "Other Screaming Eagles" complete with the inaccuracies culled from reports and the testimony of commanders.

Rapport and Northwood as well as George Koski-maki came closer to the truth in their accounts, but certain nonexistent elements that crept into early accounts have been repeated in each new account. John Keegan in his *Six Armies in Normandy* (Middlesex, England: Penguin, 1982) describes Private First Class Donald Zahn firing a light machine gun while across the Douve. Surely Zahn himself would remember had he fired such a weapon while over there. Also, Zahn remembers patrolling with Lieutenant Richard Meason later in the day, but didn't see him across the Douve. Thus, Meason's name has been omitted in the account of the crossing although he is credited with crossing in two other works. (Neither Kenneth Christianson nor Hank DiCarlo remember Meason crossing.)

In talking with survivors, their testimony frequently contradicted the official and previously published versions. Different individual perceptions, also influenced by the passage of time have to be considered. Some men, like Zahn, felt that estimated German losses were far higher than actual. The actual figures will probably never be known. It is also regrettable that so little has been mentioned about Lieutenant Santarsiero's action at the north bridge, probably the most significant action in this sector, in terms of enemy losses.

These factors have been mentioned here not to discredit the brave deeds of 3rd/506th, but to show how easily the truth can get distorted, the myths growing with each retelling. It is even more interesting to imagine cadets at West Point or Sandhurst critiquing such actions as the Douve incursion, armed with such misinformation. The main fault had arisen from not talking to the actual participants. Their testimony contradicts the official account with amazing frequency. (This afterword has also been included to justify why the author has dared to dispute the venerable accounts that have preceded this one, a fact which will surely raise some eyebrows.)

On the opposite side of the coin, almost nothing has been mentioned of the 8 June fight at the north bridge, an action of far greater consequence (in terms of casualties) than the bridge crossing. Lieutenant Charles Santarsiero has never received credit in the written accounts for his leadership by example in that engagement.

The small Norman village of Catz lies east of Carentan and southeast of the wooden bridges of Brévands. Catz is no smaller than most of the brutally contested villages to the northwest, but was spared from most of the fighting by a quirk of geography. The town is situated at the base of the peninsula and is somewhat outside the consolidated airborne bridgehead area.

After the 501st had consolidated and moved south from Vierville, it crossed the Douve River near Brévands and followed the single, winding access road to Catz. The approach from this direction is difficult, with tall marsh grass and floods impeding travel unless one stays on the road. The only other approach to Catz is east along the N-13 from Carentan, then north on an auxiliary road. Catz was a passing point for advancing troops of the 327th GIR and the 501st, which were forming up to encircle Carentan from the east. On 12 June, the 327th advanced along the Bassin-a-Flot, and the 501st attacked Hill 30 from St. Hilaire Petit Ville and linked up with the 506th, which was coming from the west to complete the encirclement.

Sergeant Ed Benecke, again armed with his camera, passed through Catz with the advancing units. This demonstrates how fragmented units were even as late as 10–11 June. Benecke of A/377th PFAB, was at Catz, while other 377th men like Sergeant Art Parker were far west at the causeway north of Carentan, joining other scattered elements (including the 326th AEB) in Lieutenant Colonel Robert Cole's bayonet charge.

In the first week of the invasion, Catz had played only an incidental role. German troops contesting the Brévands bridgehead had shuttled through it and stray paratroopers had passed through or near it. In their hasty withdrawal, the Germans had abandoned some weapons and equipment in Catz, including a *Nebelwerfer* found by Sergeant Benecke.

A more poignant discovery was the grave of a lone trooper who had wandered into the village on D-day and was killed there. His helmet stencil indicates membership in the 506th, although the battalion tic is not visible. The marker did not give the trooper's name, but the French people had buried him neatly and mounted his eagle patch on the cross. Like all the Americans killed on the peninsula, he was later reinterred in the US cemetery behind Omaha Beach or returned to the United States in 1947.

A stick dispersion map indicates that one planeload from HQ/1st/506th dropped its men south and east of Brévands. Some of these men wandered into Colonel Johnson's lock position and fought the Battle of Hell's Corners. It is possible, even likely, that the dead trooper in Catz was one of the last of this stick to exit the plane. Or, we might surmise that he belonged to one of the 3rd/506th companies and simply got lost in the confusing terrain. Supply Sergeant Fred Bahlau's H/506th stick landed just north of Carentan and the survivors drifted into the Brévands bridgehead after wandering the rugged hinterlands in darkness. Bahlau received a field commission after Normandy.

This is the grave described in the text, carefully prepared by French civilians at Catz for the misdropped 506th man who was killed there. *Benecke*

"Screaming Meemie"

Sergeant Ed Benecke at Catz with 150mm *Nebelwerfer* 41 abandoned by retreating Germans. This five-barreled rocket launcher fired 75 pound high explosive projectiles at targets up to 7,330 yards (4.2 miles) away. The weapon was electrically fired and when reloaded could sequentially fire five rounds every 90 seconds. The "Screaming Meemie" shells made a lot of noise enroute to their targets and upon detonation, but their eerie howling sound while in flight did more psychological damage in flight than the physical damage caused by their warheads upon detonation. *Benecke*

24 Cole's Charge at the Carentan Causeway

On the afternoon of 10 June 1944, members of Lieutenant Colonel Cole's 3rd/502nd began moving south along the Carentan Causeway (N-13), passing over the four rivers on the approach. Initially, their ultimate goal was to pass through Carentan and occupy a rise known as Hill 30 at the southeast edge of the city. This would set the stage for linking up with elements of the 29th Infantry Division, attacking east from Isigny. (It developed that Hill 30 was far too ambitious of an objective and it wasn't taken until 12 June by 3rd/501st troopers.)

Lieutenant Ralph Gehauf of the 502nd flew reconnaissance missions over the area in a Piper Cub. The ground troops crossed the Jordan River then the Douve, using an improvised crude bridge of ropes and planks over the Douve. The planks soon disappeared and the troops were hauling themselves through the waters of the Douve by hanging onto a rope only. While crossing, the troops were under intermittent mortar and artillery fire. Lieutenant John P. Painschab of the 502nd was shot dead during this approach and Lieutenant Raymond "Whispering" Smith, who could be heard from a long distance, suffered a mysterious wound to his posterior.

Company I of the 502nd led the way, strung out along the elevated causeway. The lower ground on both sides was mostly flooded, but the Germans had established sniper positions and machine gun nests on islands of dry ground in the midst of the swamp. These banged away at the advancing troops, taking a toll, along with the mortar and artillery shells. By nightfall, the Americans were exhausted. Many fell sound asleep and slid down into the water, not even waking up. The hard sides of the embankment were too hard to dig into, and officers moved up and down the line, waking the troops up to separate the living from the dead and keep them moving up. Private First Class Theodore Benkowski of G/502nd was among the many men hit by German fire on the approach. He later counted himself among the fortunate because he wasn't killed. A German sniper shot one of his eyes out.

Some time after midnight, a German Stuka dive bomber came screaming north on the causeway from Carentan, firing its machine guns. A number of men were hit, and the bullets made sparks on the blacktop road as the plane came on. Halfway up the causeway, another German plane flew from east to west, perpendicular to the other plane's flight. This plane dropped some bombs that killed and wounded a number of men from Company I. The planes crossed paths so quickly that most of the survivors were only aware of the one that came up from Carentan. During this approach, fighting was done on the flanks in knocking out German positions that were firing on the causeway.

The 3rd Battalion came on, crossing le Groult (Bridge No. 3) then arriving at Bridge No. 4 at the Madeleine River. Here, the Germans blocked the way by placing a large iron "Belgian Gate" across the small bridge. Troops were forced to squeeze past it, one at a time, as bullets from zeroed-in machine guns clanged off the iron of the gate, making sparks in the darkness. Companies G and H and part of HQ/3rd followed Company I through the gap and troops began to shelter in ditches north of a cabbage patch. Art Parker and a number of strays from assorted units, including the 101st Recon Platoon and the 326th AEB, also arrived. All through the night, men squeezed past the Belgian gate at the rate of one per minute.

Beyond the last bridge was a large, open field. A farmhouse on the far side was a German CP. The hedgerow on the south edge of the field had been prepared with German troops and numerous dugouts in the field were manned by enemy troops. Near morning, Company H came through the gap at an accelerated rate, numbering 84 men and officers. HQ/3rd Battalion had 121, and there were 60 left in Company G. Item Company had been reduced within 24 hours from 80 men and 5 officers to 21 men and 2 officers. Lieutenant Colonel Cole ordered Company I to the rear, although Lieutenant Bob Burns stayed on until wounded.

Medal of Honor
Lieutenant Colonel Robert George Cole (West Point, 1939) of San Antonio, Texas, commanded 3rd/502nd. He ordered and led the first bayonet charge of the Normandy invasion on 11 June 1944. Cole was awarded the Medal of Honor for this, but before it was awarded, he died of a sniper shot in Holland in September 1944. *US Army*

Some troops made lemonade from the packets in their K rations and had a snack. Others even got a few minutes of sleep before daybreak. Lieutenant Gordon Deramus of HQ/3rd's 81mm mortar platoon spent the rest of the night just east of Bridge No. 4 with Sergeant G. F. Verley. At daybreak, it was evident that a large battle was about to take place. Verley cracked one of the GI jokes of the day, "*Heil* Hitler, in case we lose."

At first light, Lieutenant Colonel Cole was pacing back and forth south of the Madeleine bridge, giving commands in full view of the Germans. The only thing that saved him, besides God's providence, was the fact that the dug-in defenders had strict orders to hold their fire, lest they give their positions away. Private Bernard Sterno of Company H remembers that his CO, Captain Cecil Simmons, was whispering to his troops as he gave instructions to deploy them.

"Dammit Simmons," said Cole, "you don't need to talk so low! Those damned Heinies know you're here!"

Private Albert Dieter of Company H advanced to the first hedgerow beyond the bridge and a fusillade of German bullets was fired at him. With one arm shredded by fire, he calmly walked back for first aid. Two men with Dieter had been killed and the German fire continued, wounding and killing a number of others. Lieutenant Colonel Cole conferred with Captain St. Julien Rose-mond of the 377th PFAB. Some artillery was in position back near Saint-Côme-du-Mont and smoke shells were requested. Cole passed the word down the line, "Fix bayonets and prepare to charge the farmhouse upon the blast of a whistle." Many of the men never received the order.

The Charge

By all accounts, Cole's charge got off to a sporadic start. In the first place, many men hadn't clearly received the order, most didn't hear the whistle, and the enemy fire was murderous. Sergeant Elden Dobbyn, of Company H was among the first to rise.

"C'mon! C'mon!" Dobbyn yelled, waving his arm.

Sterno joined him and more and more men began to get up and run toward the Germans. Another group off to the right was moving along spurred on by Lieutenant Colonel Cole. Much of his group hit the ground when the first heavy fire came at them, but the colonel worked on each man, urging them on. He kept firing his .45 wildly in the general direction of the Germans, yelling, "Goddamn, I don't know what I'm shooting at, but I gotta keep on!" Despite all the danger, some of the men who heard him couldn't help laughing.

The attackers snowballed, leaping a waterfilled ditch into which Cole fell, led by Major John P. Stopka, the 3rd/502nd executive officer.

Sterno and Dobbyn came upon a German crouched in a hole and fired on him at the same time. A cord led from the German's body to a P-38 pistol.

"I got that one!" Dobbyn yelled as he ran on. Sterno wasn't sure if he or Dobbyn or both of them had shot the German, but he paused to get the P-38 pistol. As Sterno lifted the gun, something bumped his hand. An armor-piercing .30-06 round had passed clear through his trigger finger. Sterno was wearing a glove and saw blood coming out both sides of his index finger.

A medic gave Sterno first aid but the medic himself went down shortly thereafter. Sterno treated another wounded man, then firing the P-38 with his left hand, ran on to the farmhouse, now in American hands. Other troopers had carried the fight into an apple orchard behind the house. Lieutenant Colonel Cole saw Sterno's bloody hand and ordered him to

German bunker

The fields along the N-13 contained many German dugouts like this one, which was only partially completed. Members of the 502nd inspect the bunker as a former tenant lies in front. *Dovholuk*

move back toward the bridge for more medical treatment. *En route,* he was hit on three separate occasions. This became known as "The Odyssey of Private Sterno" as related in *Night Drop* and *Rendezvous with Destiny.* (These accounts slighted Sterno as being "runty" and "not the brightest." Neither description fits him. Sterno didn't lose his finger as reported, and the German weapon was a P-38, not a machine pistol as reported.) With men dropping dead and wounded on all sides, Sterno survived to tell his story.

Back at a ditch near the road, Sterno encountered three wounded men. He sat near them, then heard three "whumps" of mortars being fired from the German lines. Sterno dove for cover, but still received multiple shrapnel wounds on the back, crotch, and legs. The other wounded men were killed by the blast.

One of them, a member of Company H, had a large handlebar mustache. Sterno recalled how Eisenhower had paused to ask the man at the airfield on 5 June, "What did you do before joining the army?

"I was a waiter in a restaurant in Pennsylvania, Sir."

"With that mustache, I thought you might have been a pirate," Eisenhower replied.

Now Sterno looked at the trooper sitting upright with the top of his head missing from the nose up.

Engineers had cleared the iron gate from the entrance to the bridge and Sterno could see Lieutenant Bob

Above: "Mad Major"

Major John Stopka, known as the "Mad Major" of D-day, led a mixed force isolated in a large chateau near Ravenoville Plage from 6 to 8 June. At the forefront of Cole's Charge, he was later awarded both the DSC and the Silver Star. Here, he displays a trophy of the Normandy fighting, a German MP40 machine pistol, often referred to by American soldiers as a "Schmeisser." Stopka was killed 14 January 1945, north of Bastogne. In a tragic mix-up, he and other US troops were killed by a misdirected P-47 air strike. *National Archives*

"The Odyssey of Private Sterno"

Private Bernard Sterno belonged to the 1st Platoon of H/502nd. Company H probably contributed more men to the bayonet charge than any other. Sterno was hit by bullets and shrapnel on four separate occasions on 10 June 1944, during the bayonet charge and while moving back for medical attention. He lived to tell about it, too. Sterno's experience has been described in *Night Drop* and *Rendez-vous with Destiny* as "The Odyssey of Private Sterno."

Pick of HQ/502nd driving a weapons carrier under heavy fire over the bridge. Pick made numerous trips, bringing up ammunition and taking out the wounded. Sterno eventually walked back during an afternoon truce.

Before the bayonet began, Captain Cecil Simmons was knocked unconscious by a close explosion. While unconscious, he had an out-of-body experience, floating up over the battlefield and looking down on his own body and watching the battle. He saw one of his men ram the bayonet on the end of his rifle into a German, then lift him clear off the ground while impaled.

Simmons drifted back to consciousness about 15 minutes later as one of his men was shaking him. Simmons and the man trotted across the field where heavy firing was still going on. Simmons reached the far hedgerow and came upon a German lying on his belly firing across the field. Simmons shot the German and the dying man made a face which Simmons

later thought humorous, his tongue protruding out of his mouth as he died.

It was written that only two men who made the charge are known to have used bayonets – T/5 James O. Brune, the mail clerk of H/502nd, and Lieutenant Edward A. Provost. Brune was later killed, and Lieutenant Provost was evacuated with a serious face wound. Certainly, each individual who made the charge lived his own personal epic, and many didn't survive to tell about it.

Company H's first sergeant, Kenneth Sprecher, had been the first to enter the farmhouse after shooting the lock off the door. He was awarded the DSC for his part in the charge. Cole and his command group moved in and occupied the house.

As the day wore on, much small arms, mortar, and artillery fire was exchanged. Lieutenant Homer Combs arrived from 1st/502nd, which had begun crossing Bridge No. 4. Most of them deployed to the south on both sides of the highway in and near the cabbage patch. Combs pushed west toward the railroad line with a small group of men where they fought a small war of their own for most of the afternoon. Combs was later KIA.

A truce was called in the afternoon to evacuate the wounded, and Major Douglas Davidson, regimental surgeon of the 502nd, went down the N-13 waving a white flag. He carried a message to the German commander in Carentan, suggesting that he surrender his force. The German declined, but with less flair than General Anthony McAuliffe displayed six months later when the ultimatum was reversed at Bastogne.

During this truce, Lieutenant Wally Swanson, now CO of A/502nd, was captured while snooping around German lines. Several German soldiers jumped out of a hedgerow, overpowered the big man, and bound him with ropes. He wasn't aware of the ceasefire and had more or less blundered into captivity. When Major

Davidson returned from Carentan, the fighting resumed with a new ferocity. The Germans untied Lieutenant Swanson and gave him a shove back toward his lines (many German soldiers believed in following the rules of warfare). He went on to fight the rest of the war with the 502nd.

The German troops laid down a terrific base of fire in the afternoon and advanced to one hedgerow from the US bridgehead. Sergeant Harrison Summers of B/502nd, who had earned the DSC on D-day, was among those who helped hold back the Germans. Just when the situation looked hopeless for the paratroopers, an American artillery barrage from nearby Saint-Côme-du-Mont fell on the front line, killing some friendly troops but crushing the last powerful German attempt to drive the 502nd back across the Madeleine River.

During this day-long battle, the ditch along the east side of the causeway was a sight to behold. It was a solid line of bodies of dead and wounded troopers. The surviving Americans passed ammunition forward from hand to hand for hours, like an old bucket brigade.

By late afternoon, the German force had been broken and with orders to "defend Carentan to the last man," the Germans pulled back. They would later counterattack in conjunction with the elements of the arriving *17th SS-Panzer-Grenadier Division*, but they would leave only a token force to defend Carentan itself. The might of the German *Parachute Infantry Regiment 6* had been spent trying to stop the 502nd on the northern approaches to Carentan.

At this writing, a visitor to the N-13 above Carentan will discover that the town has expanded right up to the southern edge of Bridge No. 4. The historic farm field where Cole's charge took place now has a warehouse built on it. The Ingouf farm, which was the objective on 11 June, still stands and is occupied by descendants of the family who lived there in 1944.

A Peugeot car dealership now stands on the site of the old cabbage patch. In front is a small marker dedicated to the 101st Airborne. The marker states that at this cabbage patch American parachutists "swept" the Germans away from Carentan.

The Aftermath of Cole's Charge

Late on 10 June, 2nd/502nd moved up along the causeway from their reserve positions to relieve the 3rd Battalion. Hans Sannes of Company D was among them. Half a century later, he recalled seeing the water in one of the rivers still red with blood.

"Some things just stick in your mind," he said, "and that bloody water always stuck in my mind."

As the survivors of Cole's battalion – once about 700 strong – formed up in an orchard for a head count at 2000 hours, they now numbered 132. A last salvo of artillery shells burst among the apple trees, killing three more and wounding eight. The battalion marched north to go into reserve with 122 men. The survivors were given a recuperation period near Boutteville where ETO historian S. L. A. Marshall formed small groups and recorded testimony of their experiences. As each man spoke, the others added or corrected, until it was clear what had actually happened. Some 15 years later, Marshall resurrected his notes from his attic and wrote *Night Drop*.

It is true that no great quantity of medals for valor were awarded in the 101st Airborne Division in WWII. Many of the men would have met the standards for the DSC as it was awarded in some other units, but exceptional feats were so commonplace in the 101st that many individuals who deserved at least the Silver Star received nothing.

It is also rumored that General Max Taylor wanted only one Medal of Honor per campaign to be award-

Medic Jack Rudd

Born 29 December 1921, Technician 4th Grade Jack Rudd was "itching to go" to combat as a paratrooper. The medic from Gloversville, New York, was so determined to get overseas that he didn't even turn himself in for treatment when he was seriously injured on one of his qualifying jumps at Fort Benning in 1943. Rudd had landed while oscillating and suffered severe pain in his lower back when sitting or if he looked downward while standing. It wasn't until several years after the war that a doctor informed him he had broken his tailbone. Rudd suffered in silence throughout his combat time, afraid only that the injury would prevent him from serving.

On D-day, Rudd had landed near Foucarville and was with his wounded company CO, Captain Cleveland Fitzgerald.

On 10 June, immediately after Cole's charge, Rudd came up to the cabbage patch area with 1st/502nd. During the hottest part of this action, Rudd ran into the open with only a Red Cross arm brassard to protect him and dragged or carried several wounded men back for treatment. He later found half a dozen nicks on his clothing and equipment where slugs had barely missed his flesh.

One badly wounded trooper evacuated by Rudd was nicknamed "Candy" in the company. Jack felt that the man would survive despite serious eye damage. Much as in the case of Lieutenant Bernard Bucior (see Chapter 8), Candy vanished before reaching England – perhaps through the same circumstances?

Medic Jack Rudd B/502nd, receives the DSC from General Omar Bradley, CG of US First Army, near Cherbourg, July 1944.

Survivor's of Cole's Charge
Some of the key figures who survived the charge posed a few days later at Marmion. *(Left to right)* Lieutenant Colonel Cole; 1st Sergeant Hubert Odom, G/502nd; Sergeant O'Reilly (later captured at Bastogne); and 26 year-old Major John P. Stopka, later KIA at Bastogne. S. L. A. Marshall conducted his post-battle interviews here. *National Archives*

Hill 30, Today
Just south of Carentan near la Billonnerie is a sizable rise 30 meters above sea level. This Hill 30 was defended by Ost volunteers and is not to be confused with the Hill 30 near Chef du Pont where the 82nd Airborne fought. On 12 June, the 3rd/501st stormed up this hill as its ranks were decimated by direct fire from 20mm automatic cannon. Private James W. Bowie, of HQ/3rd/501st, of Bowie, Colorado, claimed to be a direct descendant of the Jim Bowie of Western legend. He was shot to death by an Ost volunteer near the crest of the hill. Few, if any, prisoners were taken. This photo, taken half a century later, shows how Hill 30 looked to the troops who charged up. Two DSCs were earned in the fighting here. *Author's Photo*

ed within his division. Thus, Staff Sergeant Harrison Summers, Lieutenant Richard Winters, Lieutenant Charles Santarsiero, and others who perhaps deserved the Medal of Honor did not receive one. Lieutenant Colonel Robert Cole became the first member of the 101st to receive that distinction and was to be the only member of the 101st to be awarded the medal for action in Normandy. Cole would have received his medal around December 1944, but a sniper's bullet ended his life in Holland, 18 September 1944.

On 13 June 1944, Captain Cecil Simmons of H/502nd wrote his first letter from Normandy, saying:

Dearest Folks,

I've got the first rest since I landed in France and as I may get it in the next battle, I've got to hurry up and write while I can.

I think I've seen Hell face to face and have come through it O.K. for the present. I'll guarantee you that on last Sunday morning with my body prone in the mud of France, a dead man in front of me and some of my wounded behind me, I made some vows to God that if He would get me and mine out alive, I certainly would keep… He did… and I intend to keep them, too.

Dad, … you have always admired a German Luger pistol and it might interest you to know that I fought a German parachute captain for his. When we were finished, he didn't need his anymore, so I have it now. Hope I can hang onto it. I think I've nearly caught up to my quota and got one for every one in the family. It seems for the present that our armies are victorious and for another hour of freedom I can look on a blue sky and green fields.

On 18 June, Simmons wrote:

You may be sure that the men I brought into combat are a good deal different than the men I am taking out with me. On one occasion, my first sergeant and I had our bodies in a ditch and our heads buried in the mud for five hours, with machine-gun bullets ripping our shirts and piercing our first aid packets on our belts. When we got out and the battle had been won, one of the first things I said was, "Chaplain, I swear I'll go to church with you every Sunday, from now on."

Two men of Simmons' battalion wrote an epic poem about the battle of the Carentan Causeway and now it had a name: Purple Heart Lane.

Purple Heart Lane
by R. D. Cready & R. H. Bryant

We drink to the men so bronzed and tan, Who marched down the road to Carentan. We were the ones who so long had to train To fight this battle of Purple Heart Lane. Yes, this is that road stretched 'cross the plain, This piece of Macadam called Purple Heart Lane.

Why was it called this, you may want to know? Well, "Jerry" was there to give us his show. He had mortars, machine guns, and 88s, too, With plenty of armor to back up this crew. Then there were snipers that we could not see. They kept firing at us, my buddies and me.

We had laughed at crawling, keeping close to the ground, But we did it and liked it right up to the town. Then came the charge that led to their guns. We beat back those "Jerries," those invincible huns. Invincible, they say, and they weren't far wrong,

But we made them sing another sort of song.

The long battle over, we trudged up the hill. There we paused to look back at our comrades so still. We think of the boys who died not in vain, Our pals, yes, the heroes of Purple Heart Lane.

(To the memory of the men of the 502nd who died at Carentan)

Carentan

25

Off Limits

Typically, soon after Carentan was taken, the city was placed off limits to the troops who fought to take it. *Devasto*

A sizable city located at the bottom of the Cotentin Peninsula, Carentan had to be captured for the troops from Omaha and Utah beaches to link up. Troppers of the 101st Airborne broke the main German resistance on 10–11 June in the causeway battles north of the town. Only a token rear-guard greeted the troops who entered the town on 12 June.

Entering the town was expected to be more difficult and involved an envelopment from three sides, with the 327th GIR coming in from the northeast along the Basin-a-Flot canal. The 501st was to come across the Vire Taut Canal from Saint-Hilaire-Petit-Ville on the east, storming Hill 30 and linking up with the 506th

south of the town. The 1st Battalion of the 506th had already reached la Billonnerie south of Carentan in the pre-dawn of 12 June.

The Carentan region is rich with history. Roman troops had used the peninsula as a staging area in their ancient raids on England. Napoleon's troops had built the canals that nearly surround the city, as he once hoped to make it an island, virtually surrounded by waterways.

Many troops of the 101st never got inside the town itself, merely bypassing it and taking up defensive positions to repel the counterattacks that were soon to come.

81st AAAb, Carentan, D+6

On the N-13 on the south edge of Carentan, not far from the railroad station, a British six pounder anti-tank gun of the 81st AAAB heads west past the point where the N-13 turns north toward Cherbourg. Crews of the 81st took up defensive positions south and west of town and were instrumental in holding back attempts by tanks of the *17th SS Panzer-Grenadier Division* to retake Carentan. Although practically identical in every way to the US 57mm ATgun, early versions of the British six-pounder had a shorter barrel, enabling them to be loaded into a Waco glider. For this reason, the 81st AAAB obtained a number of them in time for the Normandy operation.

Some troopers went into town to get haircuts at the local barbershop. The big event in Carentan took place on 20 June when an awards ceremony was held in the town square in front of the WWI monument. German artillery fire interrupted the ceremony twice, killing a small French girl. In another incident, a time bomb left behind by the Germans exploded, demolishing a city block.

Recalling the award ceremony, Fred Bahlau wrote:

Artillery fire broke up the presentation twice. Pictures and a movie were taken of the ceremony. A small girl was killed just after the presentation. She was one of the little girls presenting the flowers.

During the ceremony, they didn't have a bouquet of flowers for me, so another girl ran into one of the buildings on the square and ran back out to present one to me. Of course, this was a big deal to the French and it was all photographed.

Carentan, D+6

A Marder ("Marten") selfpro pelled 75mm anti-tank gun was abandoned in front of the Carentan church by retreating Germans. Perhaps they had run out of fuel, ammunition, or both. Before leaving, they had removed the track to render the vehicle immobile, It is believed that this is the same mobile artillery piece that fired straight up the causeway during the 3rd/502nd's approach several days earlier. It may also be the same gun that scored a direct hit on D/506th's CP (approximately on 8 June), killing Captain Jere Gross and others. The hill where they died, near Dead Man's Corner, is plainly visible with binoculars from Carentan. *Pangerl*

Silver Star Ceremony

Representatives of companies throughout the 101st Airborne Division stand at attention before the WWI Victory Monument in the main square of Carentan. This Silver Star ceremony was interrupted a few minutes earlier by German artillery fire. Note damage to buildings. (Standing left to right) Private Walter Sanderson (D/502nd; KIA), Private David Gifford (D/502nd; KIA), Staff Sergeant Bruno Schroeder (HQ/506th), Staff Sergeant Harry Clawson (H/506th; KIA), and Staff Sergeant Fred Bahlau (H/506th).

Battleship Barrage

A view of the railroad station at the south edge of Carentan. The tracks were hit by 14-inch shells from the battleship *USS Texas*. *US Army*

Captured German Paratroopers

Two *Fallschirmjager* of the *6th Parachute Regiment* captured on a recon patrol near Carentan by members of F/502nd. Joe Senger (left) and Laurence J. Welsh pose with the prisoners. Senger was killed in the liberation of Holland. *Pistone*

Who Sold Us Out?

On the foxhole line south of Carentan, Lieutenant F. E. Sheridan watched with concern as his troops guzzled liberated bottles of Calvados, cider, champagne, and wine. Suddenly, the exasperated troop leader shouted, "The next man who pops the cork on a bottle will be shot." Shortly before this episode, two of Sheridan's men, Lowell Whitesel and Eugene "Red" Flanagan, had walked to and from Carentan, returning with armloads of alcoholic beverages. Flanagan was a crusty, colorful character, a bit older than most of his buddies. A confirmed tobacco chewer, Flanagan was known for spitting from one side of his mouth, and talking out of the other side.

Like many others who had landed on DZ D on Dday, Flanagan wondered why the antiaircraft fire had been so heavy and why the waiting Germans had seemed so ready to repulse the airborne landings. In retrospect, we know that the DZ D serials were the last 101st sticks to jump. Word of alert and alarm had long since arrived from Germans in the DZ A and DZ C areas to the north.

As Flanagan and Whitesel walked out of Carentan, they observed the famed war correspondent Ernie Pyle standing along the edge of the road holding a microphone. A nearby newsreel cameraman recorded the process as Pyle interviewed passing soldiers.

Spotting the battle weary troopers, Pyle called out to Flanagan, "Hey, paratrooper! Do you have anything to say to the folks back in the States?"

Red walked right up to the camera, spit a stream of brown juice, and said, "Yeah! Who the fuck sold us out?"

End of interview. Flanagan never liked correspondents anyway.

Eugene "Red" Flanagan, Bazookaman

During the later part of June, the 501st and 506th were in position to defend Carentan from counterattacks launched from the south or west. During this time, companies were dug in in static positions, but sent out many patrols to keep informed of enemy strength and activities.

One such patrol went out in daylight from D/506th. Art DeMarzio was along and Johnny Dielsi was walking point. They approached some farm buildings that at first looked quiet and unoccupied.

As the Americans checked the farm buildings, a platoon of Germans suddenly charged out of the nearby wooded area firing their weapons. The troopers immediately returned fire but were outnumbered about 8 to 1. Dielsi was struck by a number of bullets and dropped to the ground. As DiMarzio said, "He was flippin' around on the ground and we thought he was dead, and we left him there." The American patrol fell back to report on their contact with the enemy.

John Dielsi was, in fact, alive. The Germans bayoneted him and left him for dead. In a scenario more reminiscent of WWI trench warfare or a South Pacific battleground, the battered eagle began crawling in a long, agonized journey, and was eventually found by another company. He was given first aid and survived the war. Back in the States, Dielsi suffered nervous problems, especially during thunderstorms.

"Kidnap CP"

Officers of the 501st move into the former CP of the 506th in Carentan – note the "Kidnap CP" sign at left. ("Kidnap" was the radio call sign for 506th units.) Standing is Lieutenant Werner "Mike" Meier, the 501's IPW officer. One of the officers has acquired a German paratrooper helmet, which is draped from his folding stock carbine on the wall. *Haslam*

98

Future Congressman

Lieutenant Jim Haslam took this photo outside Carentan using a German camera he found on a dead man in the ditch along the D-913 above Dead Man's Corner. On the French-made Renault R-35 light tank of *Panzer* Battalion 100 are Lieutenant Hugo S. Sims, E/501st, and Lieutenant Arthur Cady, HQ/501st, as well as a canine friend. Sims later became the youngest member of the House of Representatives. He appears to be wearing a dagger of the German Air Raid Protection League *(Reichsluftschutzbund, or RLB)*. *Haslam*

Dead German Paratrooper

Eddie Sapinski recorded this dead German paratrooper near the Madeline River – his pistol and binoculars have been pilfered.

On to Paris

In the main square in Carentan, members of the 327th indicate where they'd like to go.

The best-known counterattack on Carentan happened on 13 June 1944, when armored elements of the *17th SS-Panzer-Grenadier Division* pushed up from Saintény and east from Auvers. But on 12 June, right after the fall of Hill 30, the 501st swept around the south edge of Carentan and began moving down the old Roman highway toward la Billonnerie and beyond toward Eau Partie.

The 2nd/501st group led off, with Company F crossing fields east of the road and Headquarters Company moving right along the road. They collided head-on with a battalion of the *SS-Panzer-Grenadier Regiment 38* at midday, and a fierce clash ensued.

Company F, with Captain Sammie N. Homan back at the helm, had been reduced to three officers and about seventy men. They saw *SS* scouts and deployed to firing positions left and right of a hedge gap on the left (east side) of the highway. The 3rd Platoon of Company F was strung out along a hedge on the left flank, with 2nd Platoon in the middle and 1st Platoon on the right.

Soon, dozens of *SS* panzer-grenadiers appeared marching in single file towards Company F's positions. A file of *SS* troopers came on toward the left flank with their hands raised, as if to surrender, but they still had weapons in their hands.

Another bunch was walking straight toward a gap in the hedge that separated the 3rd from the 2nd Platoon.

Set up in the gap with a light machine gun was Stanley "Pappy" Green who had already accounted for more than his share of enemy kills in the campaign. Green, in his early thirties, was one of the oldest members of Company F.

Crouched above Green holding his M-1 rifle was Leo Gillis (see Gillis's Corner in Chapter 17). Beside them was Walter Malten of Chicago who had been born in Essen, Germany, and spoke German fluently.

Gillis told Malten to yell at the Germans in their own language and tell them to drop their weapons and surrender. The *SS* troops never missed a step, despite the clear warning from Malten's booming voice.

"What's the idea telling them there's only eight of us here?" Gillis asked, chuckling. Malten frowned.

The Germans kept coming and Pappy Green looked up, saying, "Anytime you're ready, Gillis, an-y time."

Gillis was impressed by Green's demeanor – he seemed totally without fear. Gillis drew a bead on the lead man in the approaching file and said, "Don't shoot yet – when I fire, then you start shooting."

Gillis squeezed off his first shot, from a range of less than 30 yards, putting the round squarely through the lead German's chest. The first three men in the file dropped and Green's machine gun opened up, slashing through many *SS* men before the determined survivors finally sought cover. Green's bullets sought them out, shearing through the sparse grass that concealed them and hitting more of them. The others who were foolish enough to get up and charge were quickly mowed down.

Shooting had erupted all along the line and as John Penta walked out to accept the apparent surrender of the *SS* troops on the left flank, they brought their weapons down suddenly and shot him dead.

The firing went on for perhaps 15 minutes, with those who participated moving up and down and firing from different positions to keep from getting hit in the head. Sergeant Joe Bass caught a bullet in the head and was knocked unconscious, but not killed. His buddies, Schaffer and Tice, dragged him back to the battalion aid station.

Eventually, the *SS* men began waving white flags and Captain Homan ordered his men to cease fire, thinking the Germans were ready to surrender. This was another ruse, however, and when Lieutenant Raymond Oehler of 2nd Platoon rose up to observe the surrender party, a German fired at him with an MP40 machine pistol and a 9mm slug hit Oehler in the

Three SS Troopers, One Shot

This shot of Gillis was made on Mt. Currahee in early 1943. He holds his favorite weapon, the incomparable M-1 Garand .30 caliber semi-automatic rifle. This weapon would shoot through 18 inches of pine boards at 300 yards, or three SS troopers at 30 yards. Gillis

throat, severing his spine and killing him instantly.

The battle resumed, hot and heavy, with C. C. Moore and Chuck O'Neill manning a machine gun not far from Green's. They returned fire, shooting at any movement in the grass and received heavy counterfire that hit the tripod of their machine gun.

Members of HQ/2d Battalion, 501st arrived to help hold the line, but the *SS* panzergrenadiers kept creeping up and built up a devastating base of fire that was clipping the leaves and branches off the top of the hedgerow. Captain Homan asked his forward observer from the 907th GFAB to call for support, but the man was too frightened to speak in the radio. Homan picked it up and ordered the barrage himself.

Allen Hurd of HQ/2d Battalion was with Gillis when a German slug wounded Hurd in the shoulder. A bullet hit the root of a tree near Gillis's arm, spraying his forearm and face with fragments and splinters. Around that time, *SS* troopers were trying to turn the left flank. Gillis ran over to Captain Homan and said, "There's just too damn many of 'em! We've got to pull back to the next hedgerow."

At that time, a general withdrawal began and Company F moved toward the path in the center of their position and ran back two hedgerows from there. Artillery began to fall on the field and aided in covering their withdrawal.

Before pulling back, Sergeant Clem Jahnigen of 3rd Platoon parted the hedge bushes to take a peek through. He was utterly shocked when he came face to face with an *SS* man who stood on the other side doing the same thing. A potato masher sailed over but the toss was long and the concussion of its explosion merely jolted Jahnigen forward into the hedge. Jahnigen ripped a grenade from the D-ring of his suspenders, depressed the spoon, ripped out the pin, and popped the grenade barely over the hedge. He heard the blast and a scream, then ran to join the others in the retreat.

In the retreat, Private First Class Jimmy Lamar of 2nd Platoon was almost back to the safety of the next hedge when a slug caught him in the rear end. He went into a long flat dive, sliding face first through a hog wallow before reaching cover.

German mortar rounds followed the American retreat and Private Al Lisk of 3rd Platoon was hit in the butt also. Staff Sergeant Leon F. "Country" Evans of 2nd Platoon had a large portion of his skull blown off by a large mortar fragment. Mortally wounded, he offered up his wristwatch to "Jumbo" Moore before dying.

The company dug in on a new defensive line. More mortarrounds came in, one killing Private First Class Leroy Prahm. Prahm had won a lot of money gambling before the invasion and had been mailing it home a little at a time because he wanted to go to college when the war ended.

The American artillery eventually forced the *SS* to pull way back. This was the closest they would ever get to Carentan on this flank. Company F/501st went forward to survey the damage and found about 30 dead *SS* troopers in front of Pappy Green's former position. Leo Gillis found a badly wounded *SS* man lying in the grass, mumbling in German. He raised his M-1 rifle butt to finish off the dying German, but Blanchard Carney grabbed his arm and pushed him aside. The German died on his own shortly thereafter.

Battle of Bloody Gulch

Elements of the 506th collided head on with the *17th SS* on the afternoon of 12 June, and dug in near Douville. During the night of 12–13 June, Sergeant Louis

Pass the Ammunition
This item promoting War Bond sales was syndicated in camp newspapers across the country in 1943. Gillis and his buddy, Merritts, discussed the odds of such an occurrence, wondering if they'd ever get to make such a shot. Gillis duplicated the feat on 12 June 1944, near la Billonerie, France.

Truax of D/506th heard *SS* troopers shouting insults and challenges at the 101st troopers. He even saw some *SS* standing on the roof of a farm building in the darkness. They were smoking in full view of the American line, hoping to draw fire so their comrades could pinpoint US positions.

The events of the following day were a shock to both sides. Part of Colonel Sink's regiment jumped off early on 13 June in a westward attack, and found themselves passing tanks and infantry of the *17th SS,* headed east in an attack of their own.

Communications Sergeant Louis Burton, a member of the Headquarters Section, F/506th, awoke to a shout of *"Krauts!"* followed by an explosion and shooting. His company had received air drops of candy and cigarettes, but were low on ammunition. They found themselves directly in the path of the German armored onslaught. When attempts to reach battalion headquarters by radio failed, Burton was sent back to personally report on the situation to Lieutenant Colonel Robert Strayer. Company F was forced to retreat, which exposed the flanks of the companies on either side of them – a fact that was strongly resented. Certain company-grade officers lodged bitter complaints, resulting in the relief of Captain Thomas Mulvey as CO of F/506th. This was a blow to Mulvey's men, who had served under him since Camp Toccoa. Most of the other companies who fought on 13 June didn't even see any German tanks. In mitigation, it might be stated that the other

Premonition of Death

Lieutenant Eugene "Iggy" Knott (at left, holding the mortar shell) was a tough, wiry man who had once led the 81mm mortar platoon of 1st/506th. He had a premonition of death shortly before being killed at Bloody Gulch on 13 June 1944. *Don Straith*

companies might have fared no better than Company F did, had the tanks hit their sector of the line.

Company F suffered many casualties that day, but one of their rifle grenadiers, Ostrander, made a one-in-a-million shot, arcing a grenade that dropped right in the turret of a German tank and dragging the commander down inside before exploding. Despite brave fighting, F/506th was pushed back almost to Carentan before being relieved by elements of the 2nd Armored Division.

West of Carentan is a terrain feature that resembles a dried riverbed or gully, with grass and bushes growing in it. This became the scene of much bloody fighting on 13 June. Members of the 506th variously refer to it as "Bloody Gulch or "Bloody Gully." This gully runs perpendicular to the railroad embankment west of Carentan.

Lieutenant Charles Santarsiero, who had distinguished himself a week earlier at Brévands, led I/506th's attack westward past the gulch on 13 June. His companion for a while was a forward observer from a 155mm howitzer outfit who was to provide supporting fire. This man later went up onto higher ground and called the big shells in right in front of the US positions. Lieutenant Linton Barling helped Santarsiero circle a German machine gun position but disappeared after his canteen was shot off. A trooper from another company told Santarsiero, "I want to fight with you." Santarsiero never got to know the kid's name. When the *SS* began swarming in, the young soldier kid was captured and spent the rest of the war as a POW.

Santarsiero also encountered Lieutenant Eugene "Iggy" Knott at C/506th's positions. Knott looked pale and apprehensive.

"What's the matter, Knott?" Santarsiero asked.

"Oh – I'm scared," Knott said. Bullets were flying all around.

"Well Jeez, aren't we all?" Santarsiero replied.

"Not that...If I get it, I hope it's quick."

Shortly thereafter, Lieutenant Knott was hit right through the neck and killed.

Santarsiero recalled:

While I'm going up to the gully, someone threw a grenade and knocked me down. I got up and stepped around a tree. The guy is behind the tree and I gave it to him in the stomach. I look up – as far as you could see – Germans coming. I opened up with the M-1, emptied a clip at all I could see. Then an MG42 burst went between my legs, but one round came up into my thigh.

Santarsiero hit the ground and fired at another *SS* man, hitting him in the back. The man spun around and was hit by fire from a German machine gun – the one which had already wounded Santarsiero. The wounded *SS* man was "screaming bloody murder."

Germans were coming up on both sides of the bank and Santarsiero had his hands full. Santarsiero spotted and shot the machine gunner who had shot him. Santarsiero wounded another *SS* trooper who was almost right beside his hole. To add to the bedlam, the 155mm shells came in. "What a mess that was," said Santarsiero. The nearby wounded German tried to crawl into Santarsiero's hole to surrender to him. He wanted to escape the artillery fire. Santarsiero beat the German away with his rifle.

After the artillery barrage, Santarsiero was fortunate to be evacuated for treatment of his wounds, but before that, he says, "We stood there and got the situation under control."

Staff Sergeant Jerry Beam of I/506th saw more chaotic fighting at the gulch. He was with Corporal Bryan when an *SS* trooper jumped up, threw his helmet, rifle, and backpack down, yelled "*Heil,* Hitler!" and ran away. Beam saw Bryan fire seven shots with his rifle at the fleeing German, missing every shot.

"I defy him to try that again... I'm going back to a Tommy gun!" Bryan said.

As Sergeant Beam changed positions, he saw one German firing an MP40 from the hedge and sprayed the German with his Tommy gun. He ran back, jumping over three dead troopers (American) whose machine gun had been hit by a mortar round – Beam saw that their gun was twisted as he jumped over them.

In the confusion of the fighting in this area, Len Goodgall of I/506th accidentally shot First Sergeant Gordon Bolles of H/506th with his Tommy gun, but most of the rounds were deflected by Bolles's equipment. Bolles returned to H/506th in England after Sergeant Fred Bahlau had already been promoted to first sergeant to replace him. So for a brief, awkward time, Company H had two first sergeants. Bahlau was moved over to HQ/3rd/506th, which solved the duplication.

At a 506th reunion some forty years after the war, someone pointed out Bahlau as the former first sergeant of H/506th to Len Goodgall.

Goodgall humbly approached Bahlau and asked, "Were you the first sergeant of Company H?"

"Yes," answered Bahlau.

"I'm awfully sorry, I've felt bad about it all these years, but – I'm the man who shot you at Bloody Gully."

"Oh no, that wasn't me," Bahlau told him.

"The man you shot is standing right over there." Bahlau pointed out Gordon Bolles, and Goodgall was able to speak to him about the unfortunate incident. Bolles, who has since passed away, was reportedly most gracious about it.

God Takes a Hand

While moving up to rejoin his company on 13 June, Sergeant Lou Burton crossed numerous hedgerows. One in particular will always remain in his memory. As Burton was about to hurdle himself over the top, "someone" grabbed his combat harness from behind and jerked him violently backwards. Stunned, Lou landed on his back, just as a burst of German machine-gun bullets shredded the leaves at the top of the hedge – right where he would have been. The mysterious part of the story is that when Burton looked around to thank the man who had saved him, there was no one there. Even more curious was the fact that he had been pulled back so strongly that there were red burns on his shoulders from the web suspenders scraping against them.

In the afternoon, vehicles of the 2nd Armored Division arrived and took the pressure off the 506th. They were from Combat Command A (CCA), 2nd Armored and included the 66th Armored Regiment, 14th Armored Field Artillery (AFA) Battalion, 195th Anti-aircraft Artillery/Automatic Weapons (AAA/AW) Battalion, and 3rd/41st Armored Infantry Regiment. Sergeant Jerry Beam of Company I felt that the 2nd Armored "had more tanks and vehicles than we had men." Also, German forces attacking north on the highway from Sainteny had been stopped cold, largely thanks to the 57mm guns of the 81st AAAB whose gunners would not retreat in the face of tanks.

In the afternoon, the Germans pulled back but continued tossing in occasional mortar and artillery rounds.

Sergeant Burton was talking to a group of his buddies when he saw Yochum, another Company F man, standing about 75 yards away. Yochum was waving and calling him to come over and talk. Burton left the group he had been standing with and walked over to see what Yochum wanted.

When Burton asked what he wanted, the puzzled Yochum answered, "I didn't have anything to say to you."

"Well then why the hell did you call me over here?"

"I didn't call you over here."

At that moment, a mortar shell exploded amidst the four troopers from whom Burton had just walked away. All were seriously injured by shrapnel and concussion.

Reinforcements had been requested by 2nd/506th, and Captain Legs Johnson's F/502nd was sent to help. The 2nd/502nd launched a counterthrust without waiting for the promised support by the 2nd Armored. Captain Johnson led F/502nd in a rampage through numerous fields, until they suddenly found themselves outnumbered and almost surrounded by SS troops. He recalled:

When we jumped off, F Company was jumping, hollering, shooting, and we got too far in advance. We did some crazy things in F Company, even put up some white flags to surrender, but the bastards would shoot them out of our hands. It was pretty hot action.

At that time, the rumbling of tanks was heard and at a distance of 200 yards, five tanks of the 2nd Armored could be seen moving up. The lead tank, however, veered off to the south before reaching the besieged Company F. In approved fashion, Captain Johnson ran toward them with Lieutenant Don Alexander, periodically hitting the ground, then dashing on. The two officers had trouble attracting the attention of the tank crews and finally resorted to firing their weapons at them. "What the hell are you guys shooting at us for?" the commander of the lead tank asked. The tanks then followed Johnson to relieve F/502nd and the tanks remained for the rest of the day.

Johnson and some of his men clambered aboard the lead tank, which turned left after chasing the Germans away. They headed toward the Carentan-Baupte road on a sunken lane along a hedgerow. When less than 75 yards from the road, the American tank encountered a small German armored vehicle coming from the direction of Cantepie. The paratroopers jumped off and took cover as both tanks stopped to duel. The turret of the American M-4 Sherman tank traversed a bit faster than the German's, enabling the US gunner to fire first. The 75mm round

Carentan-Baupte Road, D+22
Two weeks after the turret was blown off this tank by an M-4 Sherman of the 2nd Armored Division, two 502nd lieutenants stopped to pose for a photo in the chassis. They are Lieutenants Larry Hughes and Joe Pangerl. *Pangerl*

Counterattacks on Carentan, D+7

This photo was taken along the D-971, just south of the D-223 intersection, facing north, toward Carentan. Road debris, including the destroyed Sturmgeschütz 75mm assault gun at right, is from the failed attempt of the *17. SS-Panzer Battalion* The American antitank crew, armed with a 57mm gun is from the 81st AAAB, whose Battery A was credited with knocking out three German tanks on 13 June 1944. This highway was also the boundary between the 501st and 506th.

A Half-Century Later

Site of the 13 June 1944 counterattack by panzergrenadiers of the *17th SS-Panzer-Grenadier Division* and an assault gun. The Germans were stopped here by troopers of the 81st AAAB. The D-971 was designated 171 in 1944. *Author's Photo*

tore the turret clean off the German tank and sent its commander flying out. As the paratroopers rushed forward, Captain Johnson saw the enemy commander lying with his intestines exposed. "He was still alive and his guts were wriggling – it was the first time I had ever seen anything like that."

The troopers tossed a couple of grenades into the opening atop the German tank chassis, and finished this encounter. The *17th SS-Panzer-Grenadiers* were on the run and eventually pulled back beyond Auvers. The 502nd established a new line, and with the 506th went into holding positions a mile outside of Carentan. While at au Vers, the 502nd was able to get some rest and recuperation and to mingle with the friendly French population. Children at the town orphanage became acquainted with the paratroopers.

Lieutenant Donald C. Alexander, a Rebel from Tennessee, was a bit older than most of the troopers and had a total disdain for the enemy. As he result, he didn't bother to crouch when running from place to place under enemy fire. He was fatally shot on 19 June and posthumously received a Silver Star for attracting the attention of the 2nd Armored tanks on 13 June 1944.

At la Billonnerie

At this area south of Hill 30, the 501st dug in for an extended holding period. Lieutenant William J. Russo

commanded the 81mm mortar platoon in HQ/2nd/501st. Lieutenant Russo's men were under frequent artillery fire and on one occasion, some ancient coins were unearthed by the shelling along the old Roman road. Russo's men brought some of the curious, black, oval-shaped coins to him and asked, "What are they lieutenant?" Russo looked at a bull's head design on the coins and realized that they were ancient gold coins of Roman origin. Not wanting his troops to abandon soldiering in favor of treasure hunting, Russo told them, "These are of no value men, get back to your positions."

One is often reminded of the great loss of property, homes, and lives that the French people endured during the battles for their liberation. In Normandy, these losses were especially hard to endure because the Norman people had suffered relatively little from the German occupation. Their simple life of dairy farming had gone on, and even in 1940 when France capitulated, the early war battles had not touched their region.

Major Harold W. Hannah, S-3 of the 506th, wrote in his journal:

The French are neither friendly nor unfriendly. They are quite noncommittal, as though they didn't know they had been liberated! There is a preponderance of young and old and not many intermediate. They are shy and shocked—so many things have happened so suddenly before their eyes… their homes shelled and bombed, their livestock killed, their homes used by soldiers, their yards and fields stinking with dead Germans and dead Americans. To me it is a sort of abstract and matter of fact reality – to them it must seem a terrible nightmare.

Lieutenant Russo will never forget a dramatic scene he witnessed while walking along a fenced field near la Billonnerie. In the field, a pregnant cow had been mortally stricken by artillery fire. A French farmer was pulling a stillborn calf from the dying cow. He looked at Russo, shook a bloody fist, and said in English, "Why did you come here?"

Beyond Hill 30 with the 501st

To say that Russo was well liked would be an exaggeration, but his men respected and feared him, and one who meets him feels pity for the Germans who faced him.

As Russo put it years after the war, "A lot of sorry bastards who wore mouse gray regretted the day I joined the Army." Russo was a no-nonsense, all-business type of leader, very competent in all aspects of 81mm mortar operations. He insisted on the same level of competence from his men.

Bill Russo had joined the CMTC (Citizen's Military Training Corps, founded originally by Calvin Coolidge). He had joined at 15 years of age, before the outbreak of WWII, receiving early training from WWI veterans of the 14th Machine Gun Battalion, who instilled a strong sense of professionalism. After being commissioned in September 1942, he served with the infantry before volunteering for airborne duty and joining the 501st. Russo had great respect for the 81mm mortar as a weapon. He knew he could walk HE (high-explosive) rounds methodically through a village or city and destroy it more thoroughly than could an aerial bombing raid.

He later said, "If they had listened to me, it could have been done right… It could have been done so right." The commander and staff of the 501st had declared before D-day that each of the three battalion mortar platoons would get 120 rounds of 81mm ammo in equipment bundles. Russo was incensed: "Do you know how fast I can use that up? My guns can fire a round every second and half, and we can do it all day long." Russo wanted to establish an ammo dump so his gunners wouldn't run outthe first day. If each trooper in the battalion had jumped carrying one round, he could have had his dump. "But they wouldn't listen to me."

By the time the 2nd Battalion faced the *17th SS* in holding positions south of Carentan, Russo was getting 81mm ammo by the truckload. He built up his ammo supply at last. He had his four mortars laid on what he suspected was the CP of the *17th SS,* about 800 to 900 yards beyond the front line. He later said:

You can figure the enemy as you figure yourselves. How far behind the line will they have these men fed, if they're eating hot meals? How far are you going to get away from that position? Not too damn far, right? With the mortars, you can move a yard at a time… short, down, left, right. I could do 360 degrees in less than a minute. I had pieces of string from the bipod out to aiming stakes. I was pretty good with geometry. If I miss you, it will be the first time only, then I'll be right on you.

One afternoon, via binoculars, Russo saw a motorcycle dispatch rider turn at a distant intersection, then approach the suspected HQ of the *17th SS.* The next day, the cyclist was careless enough to approach in the same way. Four of 2nd/501st's mortars sent 81mm shells on the way. They blew the motorcyclist sky high, just as he was pulling up to

Child of Auvers
Mike Milenczenko, F/502nd, is charmed by a pretty girl at the schoolhouse in Auvers. This pretty *girl* was actually a boy named Roger, who still resides in Auvers in 2003 His parents dressed him as a girl because they always wanted to have a girl instead of a boy. The 502nd paratroopers never discovered this was actually a little boy. *Pistone*

the German headquarters. Those who witnessed that incident still talk about it.

Of this period when ammo was abundant, Russo said:

Maybe at noon, I'd say, "Give 'em twenty-six rounds!" Sit down for a while. "Give 'em another fifteen." All night long. Nooooo rest buddy. You don't feed anybody…You don't move any thing…Nooooo way…To walk on any road in the area would be *ab-so-lute* suicide. There'll always be one gun popping away. I could make you wish you were never born. I mean that. I've seen woods and areas I've worked on. One time I caught those bastards inside a convent. The nuns weren't there. What a ball they had! HE light walking around the stone wall, 16-pound white phosphorus shells in the courtyard. You talk about a ball! That's what a mortar can do to you!

To deceive the enemy on his source of fire and thus avoid counterbattery fire, Russo used more tricks. The Germans would time the interval between launch report and explosion to estimate range. But Russo said:

I used "Charge Six." That's the most powerful charge there is. It'll launch a round three miles! And maybe I'm shooting at a target 300 yards away. Cheeeeoooh!

IPW Team, D+14

Sergeant Fred Patheiger (driver) and Lieutenant Joseph Pangerl, German-speaking interrogators of the 502nd's IPW Team, paused at the west edge of Auvers. At this spot, the N-803 takes a sharp right turn from the Carentan-Baupte road. Two MPs ride "shotgun" on the back. A very tall crucifix stands here, the base of which is visible above the hood of the jeep near the left edge of the house. *Pangerl*

Master of the Mortar

Lieutenant William J. Russo, 2nd/501st's 81mm mortar platoon leader, in a 1943 photo. Wherever he served, he took a heavy toll on the German Army. "Their cute tricks cost them a lot of men … that's a fact," he said. *Mole*

It's gone for a week. You don't know where it is! Even if you hear them coming in on you. They're all up there . . . then down they come. You could get eighteen of them on you at once—a second and a half apart. The world blows up.

When word came that we were pulling out, I had ammo all over the place. They said, "You'll be required to carry your ammunition back with you." I said, "Yeah? That's what you think!" I bet those Krauts still think another war started. It was just search and traverse… with that Charge Six, I never had to worry about friendly troops. We were south of Carentan about 1,000 yards. Near la Billonnerie.

Before returning to England, Russo's men were stationed near Cherbourg. One rainy night, he made a surprise inspection tour of a farmhouse where they were sheltering and discovered some contraband hidden there. To this day, his men believe Russo himself planted it there as an excuse to get his platoon out in pouring rain for a half hour of close-order drill.

Lieutenant Russo jumped into Holland with D/501st and later went to C/501st as a rifle platoon leader for the duration of the war.

SS Panzer Troops

Elite, black-jacketed SS panzer troops of the *2nd SS-Panzer Division "Das Reich"* and the *17th SS-Panzer-Grenadier Division "Gotz von Berlichingen"* drove north from stations in France far south of the invasion front. These reserves were released by Hitler to help repulse the Allied landings, although other elite SS units were held in the Calais area until Hitler's forces in Normandy were doomed.

This photo, captured later by Bill Canfield, 501st's S-2 section, shows SS panzer troops of the *17th SS* conferring with Army and Waffen-SS generals in front of the bank in Parthenay. They were presumably on the move to Normandy at the time. Both *Das Reich* and *Gotz* suffered casualties in men and vehicles *en route* to Normandy, thanks to strafing attacks by American fighters. These *"Jabos"* (short for *Jagd-Bombers* or hunter-bombers) were feared by the Germans. The planes delayed the arrival of these mighty

German units at the invasion front and greatly reduced their striking power. The *2nd SS* held positions from southwest of Caen to la Haye du Puits, arriving in Normandy near the beginning of July. Gotz went up against the 101st at Carentan. Baron von der Heydte, commander of the *Luftwffe's Parachute Regiment 6*, was placed with his survivors under command of the *17th SS* on 11 June. They were to counterattack at Carentan and drive the invasion back into the sea. Major General Werner Ostendorff, commander of the *17th SS*, was overly confident that he could "get that little job cleaned up all right." Delaying the counterattack for an additional day, he told von der Heydte that his paratroops would manage until then. "And surely those Yanks can't be tougher than the Russians," he said.

"Not tougher," von der Heydte replied, "but considerably better equipped, with a veritable steamroller of tanks and guns." The clash of 13 June would tell the tale. *Canfield*

When the 101st Airborne landed in France, they came in immediate contact with Germans of the *709th Infantry Division* who were manning defenses at and behind Utah Beach. Included in Lieutenant General Karl von Schlieben's order of battle was *Cavalry Squadron 795,* a battalion of horse-mounted former Soviet volunteers. Although their home base was in Turqueville, these *Ost* volunteers surfaced in the fighting at Pouppeville, near St. Come du Mont, at Hill 30, and as far west as la Fiere. Many miscellaneous nationalities served in the *Ost Battalion 649,* also part of the *709th Division.* Many of those had Asiatic features, which at first caused the troopers to speculate that they were Japanese advisors on loan to the Germans to teach them about camouflage techniques. As mentioned elsewhere, some men of 3rd/

506th had landed in the bivouac area of an *Ost* unit on D-day night, resulting in a no-holds-barred slaughter by both sides.

Reports of the fighting efficiency of the *Ost* volunteers varies, but members of D/502nd were tied up for hours on D-day, shooting it out with them near Turqueville. Hans Sannes recalls that the first dead German he saw was actually an *Ost* volunteer who looked about 6 feet 6 inches tall stretched out on the ground.

The Georgians at Turqueville had taken some prisoners, as was discovered when they surrendered the village on 7 June. A Russian-speaking GI from the 4th Infantry Division persuaded them to give up the town, at which time 23 American parachutists were liberated.

Opposite: **SS-Panzer-Grenadier**

The pitiless visage of a grenadier of *SS Panzer-Grenadier Regiment 38*; this photo was found south of Carentan. *Urbank*

Below: **German Grenadier**

The first enemy soldiers encountered by the 101st in Normandy belonged to the *709th Infantry Division*, like this grenadier killed near Houesville by Lieutenant Charles Matson, H/502nd. The German had a premonition of doom, writing in his diary before D-day, "We are going to be like birds going after the enemy and it will mean everyone will be in blood." He knew this would be his last battle. Note the chicken-wired helmet for attaching camouflage. *Matson*

SS Recon Trooper

SS Mann Eduard Kaermarck, *SS Reconnaissance Battalion 17*, killed on 12 June 1944, south of Carentan. Kaermarck was among the first members of the *17th SS Panzer-Grenadier Division* to die in battle with the *101st Airborne*. After passing Hill 30 on 12 June, John Urbank, G/501st, saw Kaermarck leap out of a hedgerow south of Carentan and spray an American tank point-blank with an MP-40 machine pistol. This suicidal attack was answered by fire from the tank's machine gun, which quickly ended Kaermarck's life. Urbank witnessed this from across a field about 200 yards away. He crossed to search the SS man's body after the tank drove away. Urbank kept this photo and some insignia from the dead man and turned his *Soldbuch* over to the battalion S-2 section. The interpreter read an insert in Kaermarck's paybook which indicated he was a *"Volksdeutsche"* (ethnic German) recruited from an east ern European nation, and that his conduct was to be scrutinized and his loyalty evaluated. This may explain his overzealous and fatal combat debut. *Urbank*

Fritz Bein

Fritz Bein of the *3rd Battalion, Parachute Infantry Regiment 6*, as he looked in 1944 (left) and Herr Bein on a visit to Sainte-Mère-Eglise for the forty-fifth anniversary of the invasion's front battles, 5 June 1989 (right). *Author's Photo*

The outlook for the *Ost* volunteers was hopeless – all who were not killed in battle were forcibly repatriated to the Soviet Union after V-E Day. There were suicides and mass rioting in the prison camps and all who returned to Russia were either sentenced to years of forced labor or, in the case of officers and noncoms, summarily executed.

Two Russian-speaking interpreters had been attached to the 101st Airborne before Normandy, specifically for the purpose of interrogating these *Ost* volunteers. Lieutenants Ermoliev and Judels were their names according to Joe Pangerl of the 502nd's IPW Team No. 1. Ermoliev was a large, impressive-looking man who had been involved in moviemaking in Hollywood before the war. Judels was quite the opposite in appearance.

One afternoon in the CP, the duo were examining some captured weapons at the table of a French farmhouse. The pistol that Judels held fired accidentally, striking Ermoliev with a fatal wound to the head.

It is well known that General von Schlieben, who commanded the *709th Infantry Division,* retreated north to Cherbourg where he finally capitulated, although he refused to pass the surrender order on to his troops.

The German *91st Air Landing Division* had moved into the Cotentin area shortly before D-day, causing the reassignment of DZs within the 82nd and 101st Divisions. Many *91st* troops also engaged 101st troopers. The *91st's* commanding general, General Wilhelm Falley, was ambushed and killed in his car by 82nd Airborne troopers of the 508th PIR at Picauville on D-day morning as Falley was speeding back to his CP from war games in Rennes.

The *243rd Infantry Division* had been located on the west side of the peninsula to protect it from possible landings. A few days after D-day, its *Grenadier Regiment 922* was rushed east to help push back

the Utah Beach landings. The 101st met them also, as verified by captured German documents. Other German units included *Machine Gun Battalion 17* stationed near Brévands. (It was a member of this unit who put his boots on the wrong feet in the excitement of D-day night, as described by Cornelius Ryan in *The Longest Day* (Simon & Schuster, New York, 1959), although he wasn't shot by a downed British flyer, as shown in the movie.) The 3rd/506th probably met these troops as well as German naval infantry units who had been stationed near le Grand Vey.

To cover the causeway, the German Army's *Artillery Regiment 191* had provided the twelve 105s and *Army Coastal Artillery Regiment 1261* manned the XYZ complex at Saint-Martin-de-Varreville.

In his combat journal, Major Harold W. Hannah of the 506th wrote, "Our first enemy was the German *6th Parachute Regiment* – most of the soldiers were young and they gave up easily – hey were not tough fighters."

Art "Jumbo" DiMarzio disagreed with this in 1989 when he said, "The only soldier that could stand up next to the American paratrooper was the German paratrooper." There might be some Airborne boastfulness involved here, but consider the performance of Sergeant Alexander Uhlig's platoon of the *Parachute Infantry Regiment 6* a month later. Uhlig earned the Knight's Cross of the Iron Cross when his forty men wiped out an entire battalion of the 90th Infantry Division near Périers (Seves Island), taking over 300 prisoners, including the battalion CO. French historian Henri Levaufre of Périers is currently preparing a book on this little-known battle.

The Far Flung

Nearly a thousand paratroopers of the 101st Airborne landed so far from their intended DZs that they could be considered beyond the consolidated bridgehead. The troop carrier pilots had scattered them from just south of Cherbourg to just north of Saint-Lô and as far east as Pointe du Hoc. The initial effect of this from the standpoint of grand strategy was positive, as it led the Germans to believe that the invading force was much larger than it actually was. For the unfortunate misdropped individuals, however, it became a nightmarish struggle to escape and survive. The epic of these lost men, without food and constantly stalked and outnumbered, is part of the essence of a paratrooper's war.

One little-known group from I/506th jumped from a crippled plane over the Pointe du Hoc. The lieutenant of the stick (Lieutenant Floyd Johnston) landed topside on the cliffs and was wounded in the arm. Len Goodgall and Ray Crouch, two other jumpers, landed in the shallow waters near the base of the the cliffs. The group had never been briefed about the Pointe du Hoc or the significance of the cliffs and their gun emplacements. Goodgall and Crouch roamed up and down the beach all night, puzzled as to where they were and hearing bombs explode topside as planes flew over. Their plane, which was losing altitude as the men jumped, dropped the rest of the stick farther out in the Channel, where they drowned.

At dawn, Goodgall and Crouch saw landing craft coming toward them and thought, "Great, they're sending a rescue party to get us." It was, in fact, the 2nd Ranger Battalion coming to assault the positions atop the cliff. They landed and began firing their ropes and grappling hooks up to the top.

"If you wanta get outta here, Mac, come with us!" they said.

Goodgall and Crouch climbed the cliff with them and fought with the rangers for several days. Both were cited by a ranger officer for their excellent combat performance.

A B/506th stick was misdropped in the wasteland between Isigny and Carentan. This lost group was supposed to be at Pouppeville on D-day and obviously never reached its objective. Included in the group was a tough sergeant named Edgar Dodd who had been a member of the original Parachute Test Platoon back in 1940.

This group eventually joined forces with a ranger platoon led by a lieutenant. There was some friction between Sergeant Dodd and the ranger officer.

"Come to attention and salute me," the lieutenant said.

"Go to hell," Dodd told him, "You think I'm going to salute you in the field? You're crazy!"

Another stick led by Lieutenant Robert Saum of I/501st came down just north of Saint-Lô and worked north for a week, moving mostly at night. Despite some close calls, they reached Carentan without making contact with the German forces.

Sergeant Dennis McHugh of that group recalls their only casualty was a man who wanted to stay behind and surrender. He eventually stabbed himself in the leg with a trench knife and was captured by the Germans. In the battles of the subsequent weeks, the same man was recaptured and, once liberated, came back to the 501st.

One plane of H/501st crash landed two fields east of Dead Man's Corner (see Chapter 20). The plane had strayed to the south and was trying to correct its flight path, but lost altitude as its men dropped out in the flooded area near Baupte. A group of the men, including their lieutenant, assembled and hid in the boondocks throughout D-day. On the morning of 7 June, the lieutenant called his men together and told them to shave ("It's an old army tradition to shave, even in the field").

At this point, Sergeant Norman N. Nelson stood up on a tree stump and addressed the group:

Men, it appears to me that we're suffering from a lack of leadership here. We have more important things to worry about and we've got to do something soon. If you follow me and let me lead you, I'll get us out of here. If you want to shave, go over there with the lieutenant. Lieutenant, you're welcome to come along, but I'm in charge.

With that, Nelson, who had been in the Regular Army since 1937, strode off and the men followed him. The lieutenant and Sergeant Joe Cardenas trailed along behind them. This group hid out at Raffoville, then made contact with Maquis (French Resistance) leader Jean Kapitem, a salty man in his thirties with a scarred face. Kapitem had been waging war against the Germans since France was conquered in 1940. He led the group to his village at Sainteny, on the Carentan-Periers road. The group hid in the outskirts as the Maquis supplied them with water, meat, and bread. Also in the area were misdropped men from 1st/501st.

Harry Plisevich and Leonard Morris of H/501st were also in Sergeant Nelson's group. While hiding at Sainteny, everyone in the group was reported MIA. They saw endless columns of German vehicles and some tanks speeding up the highway. It was the 17th SS Panzer-Grenadier Division coming up to the line in darkness. The enemy were too numerous and well equipped; attacking them would have been suicidal. Nelson's group eventually worked north by night, making contact with the 2nd Armored Division after the fall of Carentan.

Other sticks from 3rd/501st had landed near Baupte, and Captain Hotchkiss, the CO of I/501st, was ambushed in a courtyard in the town and killed along with Private First Class Joe Gonzales, a member of his company.

After a brisk firefight outside the village of Baupte, more 3rd/501st troopers were killed and captured, including Corporal Johnny Clapper (KIA) and Private First Class George King (POW). Captain Albert W. Mitchell, S-2, and Sergeant Clarence E. Spangler did a splendid job, reportedly shooting many Germans between them before they were wounded and captured. Captain Mitchell had grown a magnificent handlebar mustache before the invasion, which extended from ear to ear. Colonel Johnson, who had "banned" mustaches in the 501st because they made the men look "old," had ordered him to shave it off. Mitchell, who waxed the mustache proudly each day, had refused.

Somewhere in Normandy, Jack Breier, H/501st, photographed these members of his group, including Fritz Niland, Corporal Charles Starnes, Staff Sergeant Clarence Tyrell (later KIA), Technician 4th Grade John Posluszny, and an unidentified man. *Breier*

Medic Leo Westerholm, H/501st, was among the prisoners near Baupte, when Mitchell and Spangler were brought in. He wrote in his diary:

First Sergeant Spangler and Captain Mitchell came in all beat to pieces. The Jerry was mad as the dickens at them and we found out later why. The Jerries told us they had "murdered" an officer and two men. The captain and sergeant told us they didn't expect to see the end. They were taken to Cherbourg, interrogated, and shot. Their bodies full of lead were found later in a mud hole. That's war, I know, but I know both were married and the sergeant had two children.

Many troopers of the 377th PFAB had landed in the Valognes-Montebourg area and some were soon killed or captured. Felix "Doc" Adams, the 377th's surgeon, landed on the roof of a German CP east of Valognes and was knocked unconscious from the impact. He awoke to find himself a POW. Doc Adams did a lot of good work, giving aid to other prisoners and was soon liberated in the fighting near Cherbourg.

Elton Carr of HQ/377th landed up near Quineville and was captured on D-day afternoon. He says First Sergeant Ralph E. Odom landed in the ankle-deep shallows of the Channel. As he stood unfastening his chute harness, Germans walked out to take him prisoner. After being captured, Carr was in an unknown village and saw an open-backed German truck drive through loaded with dead German soldiers. The 101st troopers in that area had taken a heavy toll, despite sustaining many casualties and despite the fact that many of these fierce fighters were artillerymen. When the 101st returned to England in July 1944, only 218 of the 450 troopers of the 377th PFAB who jumped on D-day were available to go back.

Two sticks of B/501st troopers, along with a company sized-element of 3rd/507th (82nd Airborne Division), became legendary when misdropped at Graignes, France. The occupied the town, established an aid station in the church, set up roadblocks, and outposted the swampy ground facing Carentan. This heroic group fought in isolation for almost a week after D-day, until the town was taken by overwhelming German forces. Captain Loyal Bogart of B/501st had been wounded in the plane, but jumped anyway. He was eventually captured by the Germans who executed him along with two local priests. Frank Juliano, B/501st, was trapped in the town, but successfully hid from the Germans by concealing himself in the stone oven of the town baker. The oven is still there.

Yet another group under the Division Operations Officer (G-3), Lieutenant Colonel Raymond Millener, landed far west of Carentan. These division headquarters troops joined with men from HQ/501st and inflicted serious damage on the Germans in the Saint-Jores-Pretot area. The list of far-flung actions is extensive.

Adventures of Sergeant Arthur Parker

Sergeant Arthur Parker was one of the group of 377th PFAB troopers badly misdropped between Montebourg and Valognes *(see Chapter 3)*.

My name is Arthur Parker and I was a sergeant in the 377th Parachute Field Artillery. I parachuted into Normandy on 6 June 1944 as a survey and instrument man. I was to map the targets we were to fire on and help the infantry when needed.

The history books show that the 377th PFAB got little credit for what we did as infantrymen. I, for one, was in the fight for the causeway above Carentan as were many men from other outfits, as their helmet markings indicated at that time. Many soldiers in the bayonet charge were not in the 502nd. We strays who couldn't find our own regiments or battalions just fought with any outfit we came across that had food and ammunition to give.

I know we can't change history, but somewhere, someone can insert facts that will make history a little more accurate. The following concerns my small role in the Normandy invasion…I hope that all those lost and forgotten paratroopers that fought with other outfits at least get a mention.

I started down the flight path, knowing eleven men jumped behind me. After wandering, I heard men talking, gave them the cricket, and located four men from the 377th PFAB, but none from my plane. We huddled around a map and one man said he had crossed a blacktop road off to the right. I suggested we go there, where we picked up six more men of the 101st, but not the 377th. One of them suffered from a head wound and asked that if we have to leave him, to kill him first. I told him that he goes where we go, and nobody gets left unless he is dead. I took charge of this group because I was the oldest man there; I was the ripe old age of twenty-six.

Heading toward the sound of firing on the road, we challenged a group from the 82nd Airborne with a cricket. We received a voice reply, as they had no cricket. It was a captain from the 82nd and three men. I think his name was Russell. We had another huddle and looked at his map, which was different from mine. We still didn't know where we were. It was starting to get light and I knew we had to get off the road soon or the Germans would be on us. The captain said that there was a big barn down the road where he came from and he wanted to go back there and hide out until daylight or until we found out what kind of troops were in the area. I told him we were going out in the fields and have a little cover and room to move around if we had to. I told him I was against going to the barn as this was one of the first places the Germans would look when they found all the empty parachutes in the fields. He said he could order us to go, but he was taking his men and we could go wherever we wanted, seeing as we were 101st.

The 101st men said they didn't like the barn idea and would rather be out in the open. We moved to the left of the road about two small fields over. Everyone was dead tired, but I insisted that one man would have to be on guard and another to lay on top of the hedgerow to watch the road. There was traffic on the road, and it was all German. Myself and another man crawled over to the next field and got a .50-caliber machine gun, complete with ammo, from an equipment bundle under an orange parachute. We were hoping the bundle was food and water as we were starting to hurt.

We brought the machine gun back and cut the orange chute in pieces and gave each man a piece to use as a friendly recognition signal. We changed bandages on the boy with the head wound and it didn't look good. We had no water left to wash his wound, and he wanted more morphine, but I couldn't ask the other men for theirs. One of the men volunteered to give half a shot of his morphine to ease his pain. My lookout on the hedgerow motioned for me to come up to him and pointed over the road where six German soldiers were marching Captain Russell and his men down the road. I knew that the barn was not a good place to hide.

We saw three P-47 fighters open up on someone on the road and when they came back, I got the men out in the open and we started to wave our orange rags. The planes saw us as they flew over and tipped their wings, but they circled back and came back at us with every gun blazing. They churned up the field with those machine guns in the wings. Lucky for us they were bad shots as none of us were hit, but they did scare the shit out of us.

We began to move east, which was a big mistake; the planes must have radioed ahead to one of the cruisers off the coast. We heard big, heavy shells whistle toward us. When they hit, they would leave a crater about 50 feet across. Four shells came in the first volley, but they were a little short. We ran to the nearest hedgerow to get behind it. As I crawled through the hedge, I fell in a foxhole with a German soldier in it. We were too close to use guns. I got my knife out of my boot and gave him a jab in the liver, and he went down without a sound. The next four shells came in right where we had been a few minutes ago, but on the other side of the hedgerow. There must have been a spotter plane that could see us and was calling fire down on us. We laid in the hedgerow for a while and no more shells came in.

We regrouped near the foxhole with the dead German and searched him for food. He did have a canteen of water, which we all shared, and a few pieces of hardtack with caraway seeds, which tasted very good to us. According to the dead soldier's pay book, he was only fourteen years old. He had cut shelves into the side of his foxhole and lined them with books. His rifle wasn't loaded.

Even though it was daylight, we figured we were spotted now; we collected our machine gun and moved on. We figured German patrols would be out looking for us, but headed southeast. We still didn't know where we were or where we were going. We crossed a field that had green oats growing in it. We tried eating these green oats; they were milky and bitter and had a hard green spike on them. They were very hard on the mouth, but everybody did eat a few handfuls.

We went through a hedgerow and found six paratroopers from the 101st Airborne who were as lost as we were. They said the way we were going, we would run into a lot of Germans, as they lost ten men in a fight they had that morning. They also led us to a small wooded area where we found four paratroopers tied to trees, with their penises cut off and left to bleed to death. Those Germans were mean bastards! We didn't know what division the dead men were from as the Krauts had cut off their shoulder patches and arm flags for souvenirs. [Most units of the 101st didn't wear the armflag in Normandy, so the dead men were probably with the 82nd Airborne.]

We headed south, hoping to find friendly troops. We now numbered sixteen, and had a regular machine-gun crew for our .50 caliber. Before that, we were thinking about ditching the heavy bastard as we did not have enough men to carry the gun and ammo and two men to carry our wounded man, who was now going blind on us but could still walk with help. His head wound was now infected, and yellow pus was running down the side of his head. We asked him again if he wanted to be left by the side of the road where the Germans would find him and give him first aid. He said again that he would shoot himself if we left him. He said he knew he was slowing us down, but would try to keep up. By now we were all giving him our morphine, hoping we wouldn't need it for ourselves if we got hit. Water was still our big problem, next to food.

We pushed hard all day and made five miles, which doesn't sound like much, but with the country we were going through, dodging German patrols and having a blind man with us, I thought we did great.

We found this little farmhouse and watched it for an hour with our machine gun set up to cover it. We saw no wires coming from the house, so we knew that they had no phone to report us if they decided to. Four of us approached the house and knocked on the door. A real old man opened the door and stood there with his mouth open. For never in his life did he see four American soldiers with dirt streaked faces and dirty clothes, our beautiful jump boots worn and ragged, and four rifles stuck in his face. We showed him the American flag sleeve patch and he yelled for mama to come see the sight of the saddest looking bunch of American soldiers anywhere. They jumped around like kids, hugging us, and laughing and crying.

We asked if there were any *Boche* around; he pointed a full circle around his house. We then made motions like we were drinking, we wanted water. He thought we wanted wine or brandy and he brought out a bucket of Calvados. We indicated washing, and he understood and brought us a bucket of water. After we drank our fill, we took the water to the other men outside and everyone got their water. We brought the wounded man into the house and the French mama clucked over him like a mother hen. She washed and dressed his head wound, which made us sick to look at. There was a little spring house out back with a cement tub used to cool milk. We used the old hand pump to fill the tub and we all washed, soaked our feet, and put on clean socks.

We got our maps out and with help of the old man, located our position by St. Mere Eglise, which was on our maps, and indicated we were near Valognes, which was not on our maps. He pointed the direction to St. Mere Eglise and indicated he saw five troopers from the 82nd yesterday, but they didn't stop, He drew two AA [the 82nd Airborne patch has an AA in the center, meaning "All-American"] on a piece of paper, and 5, and gave us two big round loaves of bread and a jar of apple jelly. We made him take a handful of invasion money and indicated he should hide it if the Germans came. We asked the wounded man if he wanted to stay with the Frenchman, and he said no.

We said good-bye to the old French couple, and headed south. We seemed to be between two paved roads, as we could hear traffic from both directions. After a few hours, we came to the railroad tracks, which we thought was miles from our position. We had to decide if we should cross the tracks or stay on the side we were on. Another sergeant and I crept up and saw there was a light coat of rust on the tracks, so no trains had used them for several days. We took turns covering each other as we crossed the tracks. We also pulled down the wires that ran along the tracks.

About a half hour later, we ran into trouble; mortar fire started to come in on headed toward the embankment, but the fire followed us. The Germans had us under observation. We made the embankment and worked along the ditch by the tracks. The mortar fire let up for a minute, and we thought the Germans lost us. Working down the ditch, we found that we were getting squeezed by a river on our right and the railroad on the left. There was no chance of crossing the river in daylight, so we were forced to get on the other side of the tracks again. This time, the machine gun opened up on us, as each man tried to cross, but about ten of us made it across.

Mortars came down again and we were split into two groups. Our machine gun was with the small group on the other side of the tracks. Machine gun fire was now raking the embankment, and I knew it would not be long before a patrol would follow up their fire and try to flank us. One of the men, Sergeant William Crowley, said that he would try to get our machine gun over to our side and to watch where the Ger-

mans were going to attack us from as he raced across the tracks. We spotted the machine gun that was firing at us and I shouted to Crowley to move back up the tracks a ways. I said when we fired at the enemy gun to try to get back across to us with our gun. After a few minutes, we opened fire on the enemy and drew their fire. Crowley and his group crossed the tracks, bringing the machine gun and the blind man.

We crawled south a few hundred yards down the ditch. One of the men spotted seven German soldiers heading across a field toward us. The German machine gun was still firing short bursts, but they were way behind us. The patrol was heading toward us. We split up, some going left and some going right, and quickly set up our machine gun on the edge of the ditch. We got it ready to fire.

I took a few men with me, and we crawled down the ditch. We had to stop on the right flank of the patrol or they would be in the same ditch with us. The German machine gun went silent, as they were getting close to our own men. The patrol wasn't sure where we were, as they kept firing their machine pistols in a sweeping fire in our direction. I told my men to put all their fire on the right flankers when our machine gun opened. Our machine gun started firing and we laid our fire on the flankers. The Germans hit the ground fast; I was surprised how seven men could hide in a few inches of grass. Two of them made a dash toward us, while the others gave them covering fire. Our machine gun just cut them down. The right flanker made a dash for our ditch, but he had a long run and before he even got close, the machine gun cut the legs out from under him. We now had to worry about the left flanker, as he was close to our ditch when he went down. We lobbed a few grenades in the direction where we thought he was. We still had three or four Germans lying out in front of us. Our machine gun raked the ground in front but we saw no movement and heard no outcry.

After what seemed like hours of waiting, two of the Germans jumped up and made a break back to their own lines. At least ten rifles and the machine gun stopped them dead in their tracks. We only had one or two Germans to worry about now. A Sergeant Swan said he would crawl out and see if he could find out if any Germans were alive out there. He crawled out and was gone about 15 minutes. We heard a loud whisper "Don't shoot!" Sergeant Swan crawled back into the ditch. He said that all the Germans were dead, and he had a German pistol to prove it. A few of the men wanted to go out in the field and look for pistols and I reminded them that there was a German machine gun out there and one German that we didn't account for. We were all excited as we had met the enemy for the first time and beat him.

The missing German must have gotten back to his own lines or they knew their patrol was dead, as they opened up on us again. We fired a few bursts from our machine gun just to make them keep their heads down. We heard the cough of the mortars again as rounds began to walk across the fields toward us. Some of the rounds fell among their own dead. We made haste to get out of there and work our way south in the railroad ditch. We spotted a bridge that crossed the river (we found out later it was the Merderet River); we knew the Germans wouldn't let us get across that bridge. Heading east along the bank of the river, we began to receive direct fire from a tank or self-propelled gun. Two of our men were killed by the first round. We headed for the shelter of the riverbanks. As we crawled along the banks, the fire continued, but went over us. We came to another bridge. The river made a half circle and we were back to the railroad again.

Hearing all the firing, the Germans guarding the bridge were waiting for us to show up. As we dashed for the railroad ditch, the Germans opened fire with machine pistols and rifles. They did hit two of our men. We didn't know if they were killed or wounded and captured. We made the ditch, set up the machine gun, and fired at the bridge. The Germans didn't know we had a heavy machine gun; their firing stopped real quick.

We followed the tracks south until we met a paved road running at a sharp angle away from us. We got in a triangle-shaped field and found signs of a large firefight. Spent cartridges and bloody bandages were lying around, plus a lot of steel pots with 377th markings on them. These men were probably wounded and captured, no graves or bodies were around. We heard heavy firing off to our left and started in that direction, but picked up fire from the self-propelled gun again. So we reversed directions again.

We knew we would have to cross the paved road before dark. Sergeant Crowley and another man scouted around for a good place to cross. In a while, they returned and said we could cross at the railroad tracks, as it was unguarded. We set up four men with the machine gun, covering the road and tracks. We all made it across without drawing any fire. The men were all tired and wet and wanted to stop and rest. I told them the self-propelled gun would get us if we stopped, as they knew this area and we didn't. Sergeant Swan and another man went to scout off to our left to see who was fighting there and what town we were near. We never saw them again.

We were now down to ten men, and one was blind. We took the machine gun apart, throwing the pieces in the ditch as we walked along. We were running out of ammo for it and it was getting heavier with every step we took.

Using the railroad ditches as good cover, we moved the rest of the day and most of the night, with only a few short naps. We didn't understand why the Germans didn't come out in force against us, as they knew we were in the area. We later found out that the 82nd Airborne was off to our left, and they had the Germans tied up. Still heading southeast, we were having trouble staying on our course as the ground was getting swampy. We had to keep bearing to our left, where we could hear the sounds of heavy fighting.

We ran into a German patrol that was guarding the railroad and had a short firefight with them, and three of our men were killed there. We were real short of rifle ammo, no shortage of hand grenades. We had to get in the swamp to get away from the Germans, which made it slow traveling, but at least we had water to drink. Not very good, but it was wet.

We worked east along the edge of the swamp; that was the only direction open to us without going back the way we came. We heard light firing ahead and hit the ground. Two men went forward to see what the situation was. They returned in about half an hour and said they thought there was an American outpost ahead, but they were not sure. We all went forward on our bellies and watched for a while. We saw nothing but freshly dug foxholes. We clicked the old cricket a few times, no reply.

We saw a helmet and the barrel of a rifle come up from a foxhole. It wasn't a German coal bucket helmet. We hollered that we were Americans, and someone asked for the password. The only password we knew was a week old, but we shouted "Flash" and got a reply of "Thunder." The voice told us to stay

down and crawl toward him. We got to about 50 feet and could talk without shouting. He asked which outfit we were from and I gave him our code name of Kite, which meant nothing to him. I asked him his outfit and he answered, "The Deuce." I asked, "You mean the 5-0-Deuce?" and said we were 377th. He said we should stay where we were for the time being as there were Germans close by.

He must have had to phone someone and said in a few minutes they would open up with their machine guns to cover us and to move to the right side of the hole. When the guns opened up, we crawled into the front lines of the 502nd. These were the first Americans we saw in five days. A lieutenant took us back to a dugout they were using for a CP and questioned us, while we ate K-rations and smoked our first cigarette in a long time. A medic came and took our blind man away. The lieutenant told us he heard the 377th PFA was wiped out and had only one gun in action of the twelve we parachuted in with. I asked where Headquarters Battery was and as far as he knew, there was none, although some of our officers were with one of the regiments, south of St. Come du Mont. He pointed it out on our maps. We drew some ammo and I swapped my carbine for an M-1 rifle, and the four of us took off to try to find our battalion or some of our officers, so they could report us alive.

Here ends the ordeal of Art Parker and his group in getting back to American lines. Their experiences were somewhat typical of those who made it. Many misdropped troopers moved and hid alone for hours, days, or weeks until killed or captured. Ken Putterbaugh of B/501st wandered alone until 20 June before being captured. He had been dropped far southeast of Carentan.

As Parker mentions, food and water were a prime concern to the far flung and halizone pills were dropped into stagnant water taken from puddles, which killed some of the bacteria, but did nothing to improve the taste. John Kolesar, a 377th PFAB buddy of Parker's, relates that he even ate a raw chicken in his struggle to survive the long trip back to friendly lines.

It is interesting to note that 377th PFAB men were not eligible for the Combat Infantryman Badge (CIB) because they were artillerymen. Art Parker became an exception to the rule because of a special exploit in Holland in September 1944 wherein he knocked out two German tanks with a bazooka. He was awarded both a Silver Star and a CIB, which appears on his discharge. Around 1988, Parker received a letter from Washington, DC, stating that he was no longer eligible to wear his CIB!

As we can see, members of the 377th PFAB did plenty of infantry-style fighting and they feel that this was one of the great injustices of the military system in WWII. Members of the 326th AEB also did plenty of fighting in the infantry mode; they were also ineligible for the CIB because of their "engineer" designation. The qualifications for a CIB in the US Army remain the same in 2003.

To amplify the German atrocities (certain grisly details were removed in editing) reported by Parker, it can be said that another 377th PFAB man who landed in the same vicinity (Lamar Weeks, Battery B) entered a barn and discovered another war crime. Hanging from the rafter of the barn were two paratroopers and a French boy about 10 years old. The Germans had apparently discovered the US soldiers hiding in the barn and executed the boy who lived there as punishment for aiding the Americans.

Of the handful of troopers who survived the trip back in Parker's group, one was later killed at Bastogne and two others have passed away since WWII. Art Parker is indeed a survivor. When Art reached the N-13, he headed south along the Carentan Causeway from Dead Man's Corner in search of his battalion. He remembers seeing a billboard advertising Singer Sewing Machines on the east side of the elevated causeway road and farther south, on the same side, a large yard full of cattle skeletons from a slaughter-house-type operation. He made his way across the four bridges, along the hard-sided, elevated cause-way embankment and had more close calls.

501st Strays at St. Georges du Bohon

Several planeloads of troopers from 1st/501st were misdropped south of Carentan, north of Sainteny, in the vicinity of St. Georges du Bohon.

Major Phil Gage of Atlanta, Georgia, was among the first casualties in the area on D-day night. He heard what he thought was a cricket signal and replied with his own. He received a blast of gunfire in response, which nearly severed his hand at the wrist. He was captured and the Germans finished amputating his hand while he was a prisoner. After playing hide and seek for half the night and into the day, the German *Fallschirmjäger,* superior in number, began to close in. Bill Spivey, a Texan from A/501st, lost an eye when a grenade exploded in his face.

A mixed group of troopers from HQ/1st Battalion and A/501st found themselves in a ditch, with their backs to a hedgerow, firing across a field at German para-troopers. Sergeant Alex Haag was firing his carbine across the field when suddenly a hard object thumped him on the back. It was a German *Eiergranate* (egg-shaped grenade, as opposed to a stick grenade) with blue smoke sputtering from it. A *Fallschirmjager* had gotten behind the Americans and was moving along the rear of their hedge, tossing grenades over at intervals. Haag rolled away, but the grenade exploded and knocked him unconscious. When Haag awoke some 15 minutes later, he was surprised to discover the fight still going on. He retrieved his carbine and resumed firing.

Haag understood the German language but wished he didn't when he heard a German officer shout the command to close in and finish off the Americans. The paratroopers were outflanked and outnumbered, so Captain William Paty, who was wounded, stood up to signal surrender of the group. All prisoners in the area were taken to the local church, which was about 300 yards from the location at which most of them were captured. The Germans had observers in the church tower who had helped seal the fate of the Americans in the area.

Joe Taylor, a native American trooper from A/501st, was among the men captured and saw a number of wounded troopers lying in the aisles of the church. Major Phillip Gage was among the wounded and had not received any medical attention.

Taylor wrote, "The surviving troopers were ordered to bury our nine men killed in action. I knew only two of the nine and they were from A Company." He recalled that his group also buried Germans killed in the engagement in the grounds near the church. There were more dead Germans than Americans, and it seemed to Taylor that each German had been shot between the eyes or in the center of the fore-head. For Joe, Alex Haag, George Brown, Allen Lyde, and others this was the start of a long ordeal as POWs. Major Gage, who was also wounded in the stomach, looked "like there was no way he could possibly survive," but he survived to become rank-ing officer at *Stalag* 221 at Rennes and was fortu-

nate to be liberated there on 4 August 1944.

An interesting footnote to the action at Saint-Georges is that the church was later completely destroyed by shelling and bombing and the remains – just a stone floor, a stone doorway, and altar – still stand as a monument. A new church of a different design has been built across from the mayor's office in town. The new church steeple is more pointed than the original Roman-style steeple. That steeple contributed to the death of 1st Sergeant Wilburn Ammons of A/501st. On the night of the jump, Sergeant Ammons' parachute caused him to oscillate into the side of the steeple, breaking his neck. He was among those buried in the church grounds by the POWs.

Before the division returned to England in July, word reached Lieutenant Sumpter Blackmon of A/501st that the bodies of some men in his company had been located by the ruins of the church at Saint-Georges, and he took a detail of men there to retrieve the bodies. They were interred in one of the US ceme-teries at Sainte-Mère-Eglise, later to be reinterred at Saint-Laurent, above Omaha Beach.

Many years after the war, Lieutenant Thomas John-son, a former surgeon of the 501st who had been captured near Saint-Georges, returned to the small village and visited the local priest. He left with the priest a drawing showing the flight of US planes over the village on D-day and a few artifacts, including one of his dog tags. These items are now displayed in the Airborne Museum in Sainte-Mère-Eglise. The priest donated them to the museum around 1990.

Captain Robert Phillips' Group

Several sticks from 1st/501st landed far south of Carentan and assembled under the leadership of Captain Robert Phillips, CO of C/501st. Traveling mostly after dark, the group scored an impressive number of victories against enemy groups in their week-long trip back to friendly lines.

Some far-flung groups were constantly hounded and pursued by enemy troops. Others managed to avoid contact completely in their trip back. Phillips' group was perhaps the most brilliant of all, as they inflic-ted enemy casualties continuously while suffering only one of their own. Phillips later wrote:

I can truthfully say I never considered surrendering. This did happen to others. Perhaps the circumstances were such that we never had to consider such a proposition, but we did engage the enemy on nume-rous occasions at close quarters. We were stealthy, cautious, and bold at the proper times.

Phillips' group eventually joined up with other troop-ers led by Lieutenant Edwin Hutchison of B/501st and Lieutenant Chuck Bowser of C/501st. They even-tually comprised a group of 18 men and 3 officers.

Lieutenant Bowser later wrote:

When I jumped, my chute opened just before my feet touched the ground. The plane seemed to be losing altitude when I jumped. I often wondered what hap-pened to the other men in my stick. I knew them all, and knew them well, but don't recall seeing any of them on the ground.

Of the trip back, Phillips wrote:

At night, a patrol of four or five would move to the nearest road where traffic was noticeable. The patrol would then ambush vehicles by means of Hawkins mines. Horses, ammunition carts, and men would go sky high. We had over twenty boxes of machine-gun ammunition and three or four machine guns. We were so loaded with ammunition and guns that walking was a real chore.

The group had continuous skirmishes with Germans and eventually left one machine gun and half of their ammunition in a barn, then fled across some fields. Phillips wrote:

I looked back and swarms of Germans were scouring the fields. In some fashion I can't recall, I later learned the Germans found our ammunition and burned the barn and farmhouse to the ground.

The group came under fire from two German motorcyclists who spotted them and opened fire with machine pistols. Captain Phillips killed one of them with a carbine after flanking him. A column of German vehicles then came up the road and the American group ambushed them. Phillips wrote:

We caught them in a crossfire from both sides of the road and they emptied fast. The Germans who weren't killed in the trucks were running down the road madly. One of our men jumped on the lead truck and, using the machine gun mounted over the cab, opened fire on the Krauts. The excitement was enervating and exhausting.

The group moved some distance and sheltered in a field surrounded by densely foliaged hedgerows. Phillips wrote:

One hour or so before dark, some Germans had moved into position around our thicket. They raked the area pretty continuously with machine gun fire, fired some mortar rounds, and made it seem like a big operation. The bullets were much too high to do us any harm, and we had the protection of the earthen base of the hedgerows. We just sat tight and silent. No fire was returned. The enemy fire ceased.

Writing about Lieutenant Edwin B. Hutchison, Phillips remarked:

Lieutenant Hutchison was one of the most courageous and gutty men I have ever seen. He liked to roam by himself at night, and I cautioned him several times. It developed he was the only man we were to lose.

By D+5, the group had reached the vicinity of Baupte, west of Carentan. A small, elderly Frenchman suddenly appeared through a hedgerow opening bearing bread, milk, and a leg of pork. He said that he knew the group was in the area and apologized for the meager rations, but explained he was trying to help refugees who had fled from the heavier fighting to the north.

The group had spent many cold nights without blankets, always posting sentinels, while the rest of the group slept. At a place where railroad tracks cross the Douve River, the group had its final battle before rejoining friendly forces. Phillips deployed his men and machine guns behind the railroad embankment as a group of 75 to 100 Germans approached. He wrote:

They were retreating from Carentan. They appeared somewhat carefree, helmets off and sauntering along talking. We deployed along the tracks on both sides of a small utility-type house. Frankly, our aim was to destroy them all. Starting with my hand signal, one machine gun opened fire, and each individual weapon fired simultaneously. If it weren't so deadly a business, it would have seemed funny to see that mob scatter like a bunch of wild men. I assumed our engagement lasted about 30 minutes. The Germans organized and started their attack. They advanced on our position; Lieutenant Hutchison kept exposing himself. I was in and behind a small house. I cautioned him several times to observe from behind cover. The last time I saw him he had stepped out the door of the house with a grenade in his hand. Just as he threw it, several Germans were as close as 20 to 25 yards. I saw him reel around. I was about

5 yards from him. He was hit in the stomach with what I later thought to be some sort of pistol grenade, because he was ripped wide open.

Captain Phillips then ordered a retreat, which soon left the Germans behind. Before pulling out, he paused to look at Hutchison, "He was done for!"

As the group made its final approach to Carentan on D+6, Phillips saw:

German and American machine guns and ammunition and other abandoned equipment dumped all over the place … craters the size of homes, apparently from the naval gunfire offshore. As we entered the town, I saw a group of children who had been caught in the artillery. This was the most shocking scene of the entire week. I tried to guide our column away from it.

The Combat Diary of Private First Class Carl Beck

Private First Class Carl Beck was a machine gunner in 3rd Platoon, H/501st. His specialty was the M-1919A4 light machine gun. The jumpmaster of Beck's plane was Lieutenant Felix Stanley of Waco, Texas. Their plane was hit by flak and losing altitude when the pilot turned the green light on over a flooded area near Baupte, France, west of Carentan. (So severe were the floods in this area that one farmer used a rowboat to paddle around his farm fields. It is believed that Beck's plane crashed after the paratroops bailed out.) Beck's day-by-day account gives us a harrowing look at the ordeals of yet two more of the far flung in their efforts to survive and rejoin their outfit.

6 June 1944. I went to sleep over the Channel and woke up over the French coast. All kinds of stuff coming up at us … beautiful 20mm tracers, red, green, blue, yellow … they make a sickening thud each time they hit the plane, and she rocks like a corpse. We went out the door at 0113 on the nose…This is the first time I've been shot at on a jump. Those damn tracers reach out like fingers, then slip away as fast as they come. It's sure windy, and I can see the hedgerows, orchards, and houses slipping away below me like a map. Hit the ground in a ditch, with my rear end off the ground a couple inches and my feet almost straight up in the air. Took me about 30 minutes' struggle to get out of the chute. Paul Petty was on the other side of the hedgerow… I told him to meet me at the end. Right after that, I heard a prolonged burst of machine gun fire. Petty didn't show up. Chalk one for Kraut.

I headed for a spot where I saw the equipment bundle light land … realized I'm unarmed, except for fragmentation grenades. After I fell in the ditches about a dozen times, I met Robert M. Johnson and we teamed up. We have only one rifle with ninety-six rounds, a long WWI-type bayonet, and four fragmentation grenades to protect us.

Still a lot of stuff being thrown around in every direction, all small arms. We wandered around until about dawn and decided to hide and wait [for] developments. Slept off and on during the night…About 0400, we heard the naval barrage beginning and the whole sky is lighted just like you see in the movies. We don't have a compass, but we know the direction of the gun flashes is east to west.

About dawn, ate a K-ration and Kraut has spotted us moving in the hedgerows. Slugs are zipping all around with a horrible regularity. We crawled down the hedgerow about 50 feet on our bellies, then crawled over, there we could stage and run. Found the equipment bundle, but somebody had already been there. Picked up a Demo kit, don't know why.

We went back to a corner of two hedgerows, crawled under some brush and went to sleep. The night was the same as last night, gun flashes and a distant roaring. God, we must be half way to Paris. Haven't seen a living soul but we know the Krauts are all around us.

7 June 1944. Got out of our "home," as we call it, and went snooping around. Found where Raul Seva dropped his paybook. There's a lot of GI equipment lying around, like a struggle, maybe. Found lots of Hawkins mines lying around, but every time we tried to mine the road, a vehicle came along. Finally gave it up as a lost cause. We found a better hiding place for a while, but I got to messing around with a booby trap igniter and it goes off like a pistol and is promptly answered by a burst of machine gun fire. Boy! Those Krauts are sure on the ball. Those machine gunss are firing at about 800 yards, but they sound like they're right on top of you. I never heard anything like it in my life.

We moved back to our old "home." Johnson gave me the rifle and ammo and I'm in the lead on all our excursions. We both read our New Testaments and prayed we'd get out okay. I hope the Big Boss isn't ready to scratch our names yet. I never knew how consoling the Bible could be, especially the 23rd Psalm. During our snooping, we found a signpost that said we were 3 kilometers from Baupte and 13 kilometers from Carentan. Boy! We're really lost. I have a hunch I know the directions, but I'm not sure.

8 June 1944. This morning, Kraut woke us up with a long burst of machine gun fire about 0600. A big police dog came sniffing around but for some reason he didn't see us. I could have reached out and touched him. I had to hold my mouth shut so my heart wouldn't jump out. Oh, Lord! Was I scared. We decided it's about time we got out of here, so we take off north, we hope. We're going to try to swing around Baupte and make the coast. The idea was pretty vague, but we've got to do something. We're out of food and water, except for a D-ration apiece. I'm so thirsty and hungry, I can feel myself getting weaker all the time.

We moved north about a mile and a half, then ran into a puddle of water that had green slime covering it. We scraped off the scum and filled our canteens, but couldn't wait the half hour for the halizone to take effect so we drank it anyway and ate our D-Bars. We rested awhile then swung west, dodged two Krauts and some trucks at a main road. We crossed the road after some delay, threw the Demo kit and bayonet away as we're getting weaker. We have to stop more often and we're praying at every stop … following a trail that a large group of men made over the countryside, but no sign of them. We ran into some Kraut positions on a hill which an 81mm mortar crew knocked them out of. Saw my first dead trooper today. He was Sergeant Albert Schill of Headquarters Company, 3rd Battalion shot through the left eye. There was no weapon on him, so we still have only one rifle…

Ran into two women pushing bicycles down the road… Johnson jumped out of the brush before I could stop him. The women were almost scared to death. All they could say was *"Boche,"* and point. They took off… A Frenchman came down on the road behind us and caught us. I covered him before he could squawk, but he seemed unruffled, and came toward us, making the V sign and saying, *"Vive la France."* He shook hands with us, fed us, and introduced us to his wife. He showed us where to leave the sunken road, and we hadn't walked a hundred yards 'til some Krauts went walking by on the road. They were laughing and playing the harmonica. I

1st Lieutenant Edwin b. Hutchison

Hutchison was killed outside Carentan just before Captain Robert Phillips' group rejoined the 101st. Hutchison was a member of B/501st and Phillips called him "one of the most courageous and gutty men I have seen." *Hamilton*

could have flipped a grenade and gotten them all.

It began to rain shortly after and we got soaked to the skin. We could hear a Kraut mortar plunking in the distance, so we knew we were headed in the right direction. By now I'm so tired I don't give a damn if we get caught or not. About 1600, we saw several Frenchmen and women digging an air raid shelter. They were sure scared. After a lot of bickering, the oldest one signaled for us to follow him. We walked through several hedgerows then he motioned for us to wait. He left us and it began pouring rain. He was gone about a half hour and came back; we were about to leave if he hadn't showed up. He took us to an old barn with part of the roof missing, and took us up into the loft. He gave us some hard boiled eggs, bread, pork, and wine. He left us and we pulled the ladder up into the loft after us. We crawled out of our jump suits and ate. We felt much better and went to sleep then, but I sure had some horrible nightmares.

9 June 1944. We woke up about 1100 today and finished the rest of the wine and food, which didn't help much. We got our equipment in shape, ready to scram at any time. I've lost so much weight that I can slip my ring off my finger without any trouble. The Frenchman came back about 1700 with a little chow and a paper written in English with French equivalents; we figure it was dropped to them by our planes.

10 June 1944. We're getting a little restless just laying around here… About noon, a Kraut staff car rolled into the courtyard, fired a shot, then jabbered something in Kraut or French, fired another shot, then pulled out like a maniac. We just lay in the barn with-

out hardly breathing, until they left. The Frenchman came back with more food and two pint bottles of Calvados and coffee. I got about half stewed because Johnson couldn't stand the stuff so I had it all to myself.

11 June 1944. Today (morning) a few shells started coming over; they're plenty big, too. I'm sleeping like a rock and Johnson keeps waking me, telling me to quit snoring. The Frenchman didn't come back today. Johnson is in favor of going out and digging in, but I figure they're using these buildings as an aiming point for the artillery.

About dark, the tempo of the shells has increased 'til the shrapnel is bouncing off the walls like rain. Right after dark, the Kraut started fading back along this small road beside the house. They're under fire from 155s and 16-inch naval batteries. The Krauts sound like a mob of endless proportions going by. It's too dark to see them, but it sounds as if they're all fouled up.

The shells are screaming down now, but I'm so tired I don't give a tinker's damn whether they hit here or not.

12 June 1944. This morning the shelling ceased entirely and about 1000 the Frenchman came back and signaled for us to follow him. We followed, but halfheartedly. We walked about a half a mile and stopped to drink a gallon of milk apiece and pass our cigarettes around to the civilians. Most of the women didn't smoke, but I guess they took one just to be polite. They sure had a helluva time.

1130. We rounded a bend and saw at the crossroads one of the most beautiful sights I have ever beheld. There, taking a break, was a column of American infantrymen. They turned out to be 2nd Platoon, F Company, 508th Parachute Infantry Regiment, 82nd Airborne Division. We walked to the head of the column, spoke to the Battalion CO, Lieutenant Colonel Shanley. We found they didn't have any rations because they left their musette bags behind when they forded the Douve River. They had tangled with four tanks the night before; they got two and ran off the others.

1205. We are all set to attack the town of Baupte with F Company on the left, jumping off 5 minutes after D Company on the right. E Company is in reserve. We jumped off according to schedule in one of the most beautifully conceived attacks you could ever read about.

1245. Knocked off a 20mm gun and crew, otherwise no resistance.

1305. Entered town and almost shot a priest who came out of a house we were searching.

1330. Met resistance from behind a railroad embankment almost 200 yards to flank. Approximately one company enemy infantry, with two 20mm guns in support.

1335. Krauts, about 40 of them, come over the embankment, making like they're going to surrender. But before they get too close, we see pistols and grenades in their hands, and yell for them to drop them, but they keep coming. The whole battalion opens fire at once, and Krauts pile up like jack straws. Don't know how many I got, but it wasn't less than a dozen.

1340. Found an A-4 machine gun that the crew didn't know how to use, so I set it up. Those enemy can't get away without swimming because there's a dammed-up lake behind them. We've got 'em where the hair's short now.

1345. Keeping up continuous fire … men are getting picked off all around, just me left on the gun.

1355. 20mm gun makes a break for it, pushing gun along R.R. track. Opened up long burst, saw tracers and armor piercing rounds hit men and gun breech. Got eight of the bastards on that burst and occasionally can see a helmet disappear behind the embankment. Must have got at least twenty Krauts in that position.

1400. Shooting's all over now and we take score. On our right flank, D and E companies with P-51 support get twenty tankettes (French), and 10 *Panzer IV*s all in a pack. We destroy a dump of gasoline, which burns all night. E Company in reserve, was committed to help D, which was having a hard time on our right.

1405. A tankette drove into view firing a 37 and a 31 [*sic*], coming hell bent down the street. It is hit with a 57mm AT, but keeps on charging down the street. Another guy and I are in a doorway when he comes by, so I heave a Gammon grenade, which goes over the tank and hits the side of the house across the street and blows it in.

The other fellow's Gammon hits the turret and stops the tank. One Kraut crawls out the turret and I shoot at him, but I can't get a bead cause a slug knocked off my rear sight. He runs into a Gammon, and a guy cuts loose from behind a hedge with an M-1. When we go to search the bastard, he's dead, I swear he is, but when we turn to walk off, the son of a bitch raised up and moaned. I had my back turned and he scared me so bad, I turned and pumped 10 rounds in him before he could hit the ground. Now I know the S.O.B. is dead.

1430. Still flushing Krauts but not many. Saw one when a Gammon hit behind him and blew open his bowels and his shoe was about 10 feet away, with his foot in it.

Spent quiet night under Kraut overcoats and blankets, gasoline dump still burning. Not such a hot MLR. Going to change machine gun in the morning.

13 June 1944. Moved the MLR today and have a Kraut 20mm gun on my left covering the road. I have nine boxes of machine gun ammo in a good Kraut position. Went looking over the town today and it's beat up pretty bad…Everybody is well fed on Kraut rations and French Calvados and champagne. Set up a new defense in an area to the west; we're not expected to stay here long. The French men and women are looting the Kraut food and clothing dumps. Picked up a Schmeisser [*sic*] machine pistol with ammo today. Tried it on outpost and she works okay. A Frenchman brought me about three-fourths quart of Calvados and some roast duck and I filled my gut.

14 June 1944. Pulled out today and rode until almost dark. We passed through the 505th area, don't know where we're going or why. Ran into Kraut about 2400 and had a little skirmish. Moved the machine gun about three times 'til we found a position to suit us. Patrols started going out tonight to Cretteville, recons only.

15 June 1944. Same positions, not much new. A couple of the boys came back from the hospital, sporting their Purple Hearts. One got it in the back and the other got it in the leg. Not bad, but bad enough. That makes our squad five men, counting Johnson and me. Today, the lieutenant wanted me to be squad leader and Johnson assistant, but the colonel gave him orders to get us back to our unit. They still don't want us to go, and we don't want to go, but after all, a colonel is a colonel.

Patrols reported several dead Krauts in an armored car that were stringing wire. We must have got them last night. Today two tanks moved out in front of the

A Rare Luxury

Paratroopers somewhere in Normandy sleep in the tiers of a farmer's barn. This shelter from the elements was considered a rare luxury, even though the roof was blown off before they arrived. *Krochka*

positions and cleaned out Krauts in front of us. They clattered around for about an hour, then came back.

16 June 1944. Platoon on a combat patrol to Cretteville today. The way those 88s are singing over makes me discouraged. Orders to go to Hill 67 and try to knock out any resistance there. If there's no resistance we are to swing south and skirt the edge of a swamp.

1300. Jumped off with mortars and machine guns; the 88s are heckling us, but still no casualties.

1330. Came across some Frenchmen and they gave us some cider and it sure hit the spot on such a hot day.

1445. Kraut giving us hell from the Cretteville hill, no resistance from Hill 67, so we swing south again.

1615. While crossing open hill on our return north, Kraut spots us and gives us heavy 88 fire. Johnson was carrying the machine gun and I swear he jumped an 8-foot hedge without touching it with 35 pounds of machine gun cradled in his arm. It's not funny, but I still had to laugh. I could have knocked off his eyes with a stick.

1700. Pulled into area with no casualties; why, I don't know. I guess God is still with us. Still intermittent shelling going on. They don't have our positions, so they are only heckling us and putting the fear of God in us. Found out tonight that the shells going over are knocking out the bridge at St. Saveur le Vicomte. Those poor engineers are working their balls off. I feel for them, but I can't reach them. Had to throw away my Schmeisser [*sic*] after that patrol; it's just too damn heavy, especially after toting a machine gun all the time.

17 June 1944. Got our walking papers today, bright and early. The colonel wrote us up a slip, saying we'd been with them all this time. I swiped a Schmeisser [*sic*] from his motorcycle before I left. Got to division about 1200, hungry and dry. Those boys eat like kings there, so we weren't hurting long. The POW cage is here; division HQ was still at Hiesville, right alongside a battalion of 240s. [240mm howitzers, the largest towed artillery piece in the US Army invento-

ry in WWII.] One of them has "Widow Maker" stenciled on the barrel. It's good, but not as good as "Jivin' Joan" [Beck's personal M-1919A4 light machine gun].

18 June 1944. Got a Kraut *Volkswagen* down to 501st, and it was raining. We were forced to take a flask of cognac on the way and it was quite dry by the time we got there (both the flask and the weather).

Found Klondike rear but not forward. After messing around 'til afternoon, they finally got us down to Blue [code for 3rd Battalion; 1st was Red, 2nd White], and then it took an hour to find the company. The boys were just about to move up and relieve Kidnap on the line, so we had a hand-shaking fest. [Kidnap was the radio call sign for the 506th. Each regiment had a call sign beginning with K; that is, 501st – Klondike, 502nd – Kickoff, 327th GIR – Keepsake, 101st Division was Kangaroo.] Johnson and I coming back make the total officer and E.M. company strength (H/501st) thirty-nine. Most of the boys are missing in action. Aubin, Donst, Bray, and Captain McKaig have been evacuated for wounds, also several others. Spitz, Gray, Pegg, Petty, Petzolt, and plenty others are KIA.

We returned to the 1st Squad, 3rd Platoon, and "Jivin' Joan." Duffy and almost everybody else were missing from 24 hours to 9 days. The family is not half complete, but I guess we're lucky to be here. Pumphrey, Duffy, and I are on the gun together. The boys have had a pretty rough time around Carentan. Not much to do here except pull guard, two on and four off.

19 June 1944. Not much cooking today, intermittent shelling, mostly air bursts. They seem to be getting zeroed in, but that's about all. No casualties.

20 June 1944. There's not much cooking these days, so I'll close this diary until we tangle with Kraut. We moved on the 28th with a regiment [*sic* - probably a battalion] of 155s backing us up. The company is covering about 400 yards of front with thirty-nine men. It's not too rough though. The 79th Division relieved us there and we moved to Cherbourg and left the continent about July 12.

Carentan, 12-14 June 1944.

View of the town center of Carentan, the hospital units continue moving towards the level crossing and the road to Périers where the front line is. Pictured here is a German ambulance captured by US paratroops. *US Army via Heimdal*

Below on left: More shots picturing troops and medics moving down the Rue Holgate towards the level crossing and the Périers road. The destruction is worse on the left, east side of the street. *US Army via Heimdal*

Below on right: A little further on, rounding the street corner, we come to the street leading to Saint-Mère-Eglise and Cherbourg. The GIs have captured a German *Kübelwagen* previously used by the German paratroopers – the «WL» is a *Luftwaffe* registration.*US Army via Heimdal*

Largely thanks to the misdrops that put many of the Screaming Eagles miles into enemy territory and well outside the consolidated assembly areas, some 665 members of the 101st Airborne Division were listed as MIA at the end of the Normandy campaign.

There was no disgrace in being captured under these circumstances and many troopers wandered for weeks with almost no ammo, food, or water and were eventually caught.

Some captured Eagles were liberated by friendly troops in minutes, hours, or days after being captured (their stories alone would fill a book). Others who were sent to Rennes, France, with serious injuries were liberated as early as 4 August 1944.

For Joe Taylor of A/501st and many other POWs, the Normandy invasion was soon followed by an eight-month ordeal in German captivity. Taylor, who is still bone thin, has stomach problems to this day as a result of his time in the POW camps. "I just knew I would starve to death," he recalls. During moves from camp to camp, meals and Red Cross parcels were scarce. Taylor resorted to eating grass, tree bark, and charcoal from fires just to stay alive.

After being incarcerated at St. Lô, the original groups of POWs from Normandy were marched through the city of Paris where German civilians from the embassy put on quite a show, jeering, spitting, and hitting the prisoners as they walked the gauntlet. These were dark days for the prisoners and many in the crowd were actually French civilians who didn't like Americans at the moment. German loudspeakers broadcast to the onlookers that these American "Terror Bandits" were actually convicts of the worst sort, who had been released from prisons in America to wage "dirty" warfare against the heroic German forces.

George Rosie and his buddy Jim Bradley had belonged to HQ/3rd/506th and were unfortunate to be in one of the groups that was paraded through hostile civilians in Paris. George later recalled:

As we marched through one section, this one gal was running down the column, spitting in men's faces. As she came up to Jim "Mr. America" Bradley to spit in his face, he spit in her face! Jim was right in front of me. I thought, "Boy, are we gonna get hell now," but the guard just pushed her back into the crowd, and we moved on.

Reg Alexander at Prétot

One of the most grueling ordeals borne by any 101st POW was that of Reginald Alexander of H/501st. On a 1st Platoon plane jumpmastered by Lieutenant Robert Curran (later killed at Hill 30), the plane was badly hit by flak and crashed after the troopers bailed out. Like other planes of the serial, this one had drifted south after emerging from the cloud banks and being dispersed in flak. Alexander was struck above the eye by shrapnel before leaving the plane. When he jumped, his chute streamered and he hit the ground on his feet at almost full force, shattering both his legs.

Alexander's buddies, Don Metcalf and Bob Beachy, soon found him but were forced to leave him. They alerted French civilians in a nearby church at Prétot, and a priest and nun arrived to carry Alexander to shelter.

Alexander's mission had been to meet Brigadier General Don F. Pratt, the assistant division commander, at Hiesville. Alexander was carrying important invasion maps to give to the general. The French hid these maps and Alexander's uniform. (Pratt had been killed on the glider landing and Hiesville was many miles from where Alexander landed.)

Several days passed and the French decided to dress Alexander in civilian clothes and attempt to move him eastward toward American lines. He sat in the seat of a farm cart pulled by one horse, as two young Frenchmen led the cart down a road. German troops intercepted them, and Alexander revealed his identity. After much excitement, he was taken into German custody and the French youths were led away. It is unknown what became of them.

Alexander found himself in a chateau, where he lay on the floor in great pain. A German SS man, berserk from shell shock, was brought in and lay on the floor in the same room. When the SS man learned that Alexander was an American, he viciously assaulted Alexander, kicking him repeatedly in the head. Alexander began to yell, and an English-speaking

"Hungry Hill"

US Airborne prisoners look up at Allied planes flying over Saint-Lô in the "Starvation Hill" or "Hungry Hill" area. Here, their diet consisted mainly of "Whispering Grass" soup made from turnip greens. When the POWs arrived in the area, the city was intact; when they left, the city was in rubble from air raids. Second from left is Captain John T. McKnight, erstwhile CO of I/506th. He survived and was liberated in 1945. *via Winters and ECPA-France*

Above on left: **Liberated by the Russians**

This POW mug shot for ID purposes was taken of Joe Beyrle, I/506th, while he was at Stalag XII-A, Limburg, Germany, as a POW, following the Normandy drop. Joe Beyrle landed on the roof of the church in St. Come du Mont on Dday night and was taken POW during D-day. A German took his dog tags and uniform and tried to infiltrate through the lines. The German was killed, prob ably by another German, who mistook him for an American. The body was buried in a US cemetery and Beyrle's parents received a telegram that he was KIA. Beyrle's camp (he was transferred from XII-A) was liberated by Soviet troops, and he fought for months with a Russian tank crew, equipped with a Lend Lease M-4 Sherman tank. Thus, Beyrle has more combat time with the Red Army than he has with the US Army. He visited his own grave after being liberated and is still welcomed as an old comrade on his return visits to the Russian Federation. *Beyrle*

Above on right: **Reg Alexander**

This 1943 photo shows Reg Alexander, H/501st, wearing his regimental pocket patch proudly on his jump jacket. The insignia was usually worn on the left chest. *Alexander*

German doctor intervened and ordered the SS man restrained with ropes.

Alexander eventually began the long trip back toward Germany via ambulances. During this time, his column was strafed at least once by British Spitfires. Also, French civilians, angered by Allied bombing raids, would sometimes pound on the outside of Alexander's ambulance when it stopped in various towns.

Alexander was kept in a cave near Saint-Lô for a time, then continued on, eventually being placed on a cot in a basement in a town with canals. Some 104 days after D-day, an American armored division liberated the town and Alexander was sent to a traction ward in England before being shipped home.

Liberation of Stalag 221, 4 August 1944

The Germans had established a special POW camp in the city of Rennes, the gateway to the Brittany Peninsula. The camp was a departure from the normal German POW camps for a number of reasons. First, it was not located inside Germany. Also, the camp was reserved for wounded prisoners only. Unlike most *Stalags,* enlisted men and officers alike were housed here. (Officers were usually segregated in officer camps, or *Oflags.*) Some British and Canadian prisoners were kept here as well, and the ranking officer was Major Phillip Gage of 1st/501st who had lost a hand when captured near Saint-Georges du Bohon on D-day. The *Stalag* was situated in or near the famous Jean Mace School, and the lucky prisoners liberated there were able to rejoin their units or return home almost a year earlier than the prisoners who were taken to Germany.

Liberation

Two wounded 101st Airborne paratroopers, who had been held prisoner in *Frontstalag 221*, stand in front of the Hotel de Ville in Rennes, France on the day of their liberation (4 August, 1944). Ludwig Wirtheimer and Charles Egger of G/506th posed with French friends US Army photo. *US Army*

Propaganda

A publicity photo staged by the Germans for the international press photographers at St. Lo shows American POWs eating more than they normally ever got. POWs writing to their families were always required to state that they were being well fed. Not so. *Winters/ECPA*

30	# The Journey Back

Back to England, 10 July 1944
Members of the 501st PIR are ready to board an LST for the voyage back to England where they will train and prepare for their next mission. Many companies sailed back with less than 70 remaining men. *Krochka*

After pulling out of the Carentan perimeter in late June, the 101st Airborne moved west then north up the Cotentin Peninsula, stopping briefly at Saint-Saveur-le-Vicomte, Pont le Abbé, and Tollevast, below Cherbourg. An ammunition crisis had plagued VII Corps, due to the Channel storm, but this had little effect on the 101st, which did little shooting during its last two weeks in Normandy. Most of its time was spent in resting, getting cleaned up, and eating, as shown on the following pages. The 82nd Airborne would also return to England in July, but was engaged in fighting on the peninsula for more days than the 101st.

Cherbourg

The large wall sign that greeted those entering Cherbourg from the south is still there. The city had already been captured by regular infantry outfits before the 101st arrived. (Left to right) Bill Kowger, Lee Estep, and Stanley J. Rogers, all of A/377th PFAB. *Benecke*

124

Calvados

The delighted troopers in Normandy discovered a form of homemade apple brandy popular in the Cotentin, known as Calvados. Having a fragrance and taste similar to cognac, Calvados was preferably sipped like a potent liqueur. Potent it was, and batches aged less than 10 years could reportedly take the skin off one's throat if consumed too quickly. Even small amounts had a distinctly mindaltering power, and the taste made it much preferable to Benzine, hair tonic, or Buzz Bomb Juice, which the diehard alcoholics had consumed in a pinch.

Pee Wee Martin of G/506th likes to relate how his bunch moved into a farm area and after a brief but intense period of scrounging, located the farmer's stash of alcoholic beverages that had been secreted in a hole inside his barn and covered over with other materials.

"The Germans have been here four years and didn't find my liquor!" said the distraught Frenchman as he helplessly watched the troopers guzzle his stash. "You Americans have been here less than a week and are using up everything!"

An officer reportedly mollified the farmer by writing him a promissory note that the debt would be repaid by the US government.

While in the St. Saveur area, Captain Cecil Simmons of H/502nd caused another minor uproar with a French farmer. Simmons had located a large kettle used by the farmer to brew Calvados. Simmons was ttying to get the foul odor of the gas impregnation chemical out of his jump suit. He filled the kettle with water, tossed his jumpsuit in, and began stirring it over a fire. The Frenchman ran out yelling, very excited.

Another Calvados story happened in Sainte-Marie-du-Mont. Lieutenant Gordon Deramus of HQ/3 502nd was standing in the street when a medic rode up on horseback, holding a long Calvados bottle.

"Want a drink, lieutenant?" the medic said.

"Sure," said Deramus, about to have his first taste of Calvados.

"I'm not sure, lieutenant, but as long as this stuff holds out, we're gonna whip hell out of 'em!"

« Wow! What's that?»

Joe Pistone takes a long pull on a Calvados bottle while fending off John "Hollywood" Hromchak. Ed Jacobson *(kneeling)* ravages a 10-in-1 ration. *Pistone*

Opposite: Washing Up

501st troops at a washing trough in Normandy. Al Krochka wrote in his album, "Finally came the day when we could wash clothes heavy with mud, sweat, and blood." *Krochka*

Below: Taking in the View

The fort atop the hill at Cherbourg afforded a panoramic view of the French coast. Officers of the 501st take in the view. *Krochka*

Nothing a Good Battle won't cure

General George S. Patton at an awards ceremony where 25 101st Airborne troopers received the DSC. His nemesis, Viscount Montgomery of the British Army, was also present. *Krochka*

Saint-Sauveur-le-Vicomte

Sergeant Ed Benecke stands in front of a building in Saint-Saveur-le-Vicomte. The Germans painted the name of each town in bold white or black letters on a prominent house at each approach to town so their troops would immediately know their location – the French had a nasty habit of turning or removing road signs to confuse the *Boche*. *Benecke*

White Bread

Cherbourg, July 1944. A mess sergeant holds aloft the first loaf of white bread seen in the 502nd in months. *(Clockwise from lower left)* Captain George Buker, S-2; Evans Thornton, S-1; Lieutenant Bob Pick, S-2; Captain Henry Plitt; and Captain Frank Lillyman, Pathfinders. *Buker*

England Again

More troops, having just debarked their LST, march into waiting buses. The location is Southampton, England, taken on approximately 14 July 1944. *Musura*

War Trophy

While aboard an LST bound for England, a group from the 502nd PIR displays a trophy captured in France. *Dovholuk*

Rest in Peace

The dead from American Cemeteries No. 1 and No. 2 at Sainte-Mère-Eglise were reinterred at Saint-Laurent behind Omaha Beach several years after WWII. At that time, families had the option of having the deceased returned to the States for burial in a local cemetery. James Luce rests under a typical cross at St. Laurent (right), while Freddie Lenz has been returned to Dundee, Michigan. The 19-year-old who ran away from home to join the Army lies under a typical rectangular government marker (above). *Author's Photo*

Glidermen of C/401st

A glider with a load of glider infantrymen of C/401st in England. This group flew to Holland on 18 September. *At far left,* standing, is Captain Joe Brewster, S-2 of 1st/401st. *Left to right (standing) are:* Technical Sergeant Grayson Davis, Sergeant George Naegle, unknown, Private First Class Ben Molinaro, and Private First Class Charlie Ratkic. Kneeling *(left to right) are:* Private First Class Frank Lombardino (KIA), Private First Class Ray Vigus, Private First Class Leonard Waddlington, and Private First Class George Miller (MIA). The tall officer standing at far right is Captain Preston Towns, the company CO, who died of wounds near Bastogne in December 1944. The C-47 towing this glider was crippled by flak some 12 to 15 miles short of the LZ, so Captain Towns broke the plexiglass windshield out of the glider and cut off the tow rope with his trench knife. *US Army*

Members of the 101st who had survived the Normandy invasion without serious wounds were returned to England in July 1944. The official casualty list indicates 868 men were KIA, hundreds more were missing in German POW camps, and the number of wounded was in the thousands. The picture was grim, but gradually, many of the wounded trickled back from hospitals, and even a few MIAs miraculously rejoined the unit.

Sergeant Ed Hughes of F/501st had been wounded near Angoville and evacuated to England before the bulk of the division returned. When he met a bus containing the survivors of his 2nd Platoon, only 12 men got off.

"Where are the rest?," he asked Chuck O'Neill.

"This is it. There are no more."

Johnny Gibson of HQ/3rd/506th had been captured just above Carentan on D-day in a group with George Rosie and others. Gibson was a medic and unwounded, and the Germans used him to treat their own casualties as they retreated south. The Germans were so lacking in medical supplies that they were boiling and re-using gauze pads. Mercurochrome and crepe paper was the only dressing available to cover wounds. Gibson eventually was transferred to *Stalag* 221 at Rennes. This was a bit of good fortune, as Rennes was liberated on 4 August 1944, releasing Gibson and others, most of whom were badly wounded and ZI'd (sent to the Zone of Interior, or the continental United States). Gibson was ready for more action and returned to his battalion, in which he would serve until badly wounded in the Bulge.

The 101st had had its baptism of fire in Normandy, and most importantly from a psychological standpoint, had taken the measure of the German soldier and his capabilities.

Lieutenant William J. Russo of 2nd/501st later remarked:

I think they (the Germans) had gotten so used to their terror – you know, scare the shit out of everybody in Poland, the Low Countries, Russia. They got onto terrorizing this and terrorizing that ... well, when you meet people who don't terrorize, you're up shit creek. It all goes the other way, really.

They used to drop us those *[propaganda]* pamphlets in Holland and Bastogne: "If you don't give up right now, you know, that this is gonna happen and that is gonna happen..." Best toilet paper we ever had! *[Laughs]* Ahhh, that was comical.

A Holy War

Certainly, casualties were always considered, and the troopers worried more for their families than themselves. Transfers out were available, but to most troopers, the only honorable way out was through death or the "million-dollar wound," which would send them home. As a handful of survivors made it through each future battle, they came to view themselves as "fugitives from the law of averages." Yet, they continued to face whatever was in store for them. Carl Beck, H/501st, said, "This war was viewed as a crusade against evil. Therefore, do your part in the crusade."

Lee Parrish, G/501st, had survived the nightmare of Normandy including a knife fight with a German paratrooper that he had encountered while getting water from a stream. "I wasn't much of a soldier until I accepted the fact that I was just a dead man, walking around, waiting to find out where I was going to lie down for good," he said after the war. "Once I accepted that fact, I became a fairly decent combat soldier."

The fear of being maimed and surviving may have been greater than the fear of death. Don Burgett of A/506th gave an insight into the philosophy that helped him to function. Asked how he overcame his fear of being shot in the head when raising up from cover to return fire in a shoot-out, Don remarked, "Well, look at it this way, if you did get hit in the head, you wouldn't have anything to worry about."

"I Promise you another mission"

On 31 August 1944, another mission took 101st troopers as far as the airfields before the mission was canceled. General Maxwell D. Taylor (above) assembled the division, apologized, and promised the troops another mission. Someone booed. Lieutenant G. W. Sefton, HQ/2nd/501st, later commented, "I never could understand how anyone as obviously brilliant as Maxwell Taylor could overlook the enlisted man's point of view so far as to assume that every private, noncom, and junior officer there was just as anxious to return to combat as he, a West Point general, was." *Musura*

"No thanks, General"

What General Taylor saw. Note the ambivalent facial expressions of the troops.

Opposite: Another Canceled Jump

Corporal Harold Bice and Private First Class Lyman Allen Hurd, both of the 2nd/501st's S-2 Section, preparing to board their plane in England on 17 August 1944. The troops were assembled and sealed off at airfields, and issued ammunition, rations, and French currency, but the jump was canceled. The 101st was to land in position to help close the Falaise Pocket, but General Patton's armored forces arrived so quickly that the mission was rendered unnecessary. Although the men have been issued the new quick-release T-7 parachute harnesses and combat boots, they still wear the gas impregnated M-42 jump suits. *Beyer*

32

Market-Garden Plan and Marshalling Areas

During the summer of 1944, the First Allied Airborne Army was born, under command of General Lewis H. Brereton (US Army Air Forces). This Army included the British 1st and 6th Airborne Divisions, the US 82nd and 101st Airborne Divisions, and would later include also the 17th Airborne Division. The latter US divisions constituted the US XVIII Airborne Corps, under General Matthew Ridgway.

Order of Battle, 101st Airborne Division, 1944

Although listed as a full division on paper, the 101st Airborne was down to about 12,000 men after many of those wounded in the Normandy invasion had recovered and returned to their units and replacements had been incorporated. The division consisted of the Division Headquarters Company (HQ/101st), Signal Company, Recon Platoon, and Military Police (MP) Platoon; the 501st, 502nd, and 506th PIRs; the 327th GIR; the 1st/401st GIR; the 326th AEB; the 377th PFAB; the 321st and 907th GFABs; the 81st AAAB; the 326th Airborne Medical Company; and the 426th Airborne Quarter-master Company.

The *Market-Garden* Plan

Field Marshal Montgomery wielded considerable political clout in the coalition of Western allies and insisted finally that his grandiose scheme to end the war before Christmas be implemented. The plan, called *Market-Garden* (*Market* was the airborne assault and *Garden* the ground offensive) would use the First Allied Airborne Army to jump at intervals along a highway extending forward from the current front line, deep into the Nether-lands. A number of bridges were to be seized and held by the airborne troops as Monty's Guards Armored Division raced northward to Arnhem. In mitigation, Monty wanted to drop his British 1st Airborne troops in the northernmost spot, at Arnhem, but the end result would be "a 50-mile salient leading nowhere," as one critic called it. Indeed, the entire plan was perhaps doomed

to fail in reaching its ultimate goal, and this could have been predicted based on Monty's record thus far since D-day. His ground forces had never moved rapidly forward in anything like the lightning thrusts needed to make MARKET-GARDEN a success.

In theory, if Monty's armor had reached the bridge at Arnhem in time, it would have pivoted eastward and driven straight toward Berlin to overthrow the Hitler regime at its nerve center. This maneuver also would have bypassed the Roer Valley and the Siegfried Line defenses of Hitler's *Westwall,* but to discuss what was hoped for is now idle speculation.

The American airborne survivors of this operation are, of course, cynical about the sacrifices of their buddies and the heavy losses sustained with questionable gain, but each engagement was a toe-to-toe confrontation with the enemy. Each encounter was thus fought accordingly. Any local victory, no matter how small, was viewed as bringing the war in Europe one bit closer to an end. Some of the American troopers who survived this operation complain that the ultimate failure of the mission was due to factors having nothing to do with them. As they truthfully point out, all their assigned missions were accomplished in short order, yet few will actively fault the dedication or courage of their British and Common-wealth comrades in the battle. The sacrifices and skill of these warriors was evident at every look.

The British Army had its strengths (especially the artillery, which was accurate and timely) and its weaknesses (mainly tactical and procedural), and these factors would become very evident to the members of the 101st Airborne in the coming fight in the Netherlands.

Thus, with little time for plans or preparation, the 101st was to drop between Son (sometimes spelled "Zon") and St. Oedenrode, and also in the Veghel area, to open a corridor for the armor of the British XXX Corps.

Captain Cecil Simmons

Simmons, with his stick from HQ/502nd on 17 September. The 4U marking on the nose of the C-47 identifies it as a part of the 89th TCS, 438th TCG. Also visible in the photo is Sergeant Fred Patheiger. Flak damage (possibly from the recent Southern France invasion) is evident on the side, below the cockpit. *Pangerl*

Issue of New Equipment

By the time the 101st troops actually entered the Nether-lands in Operation *Market-Garden*, their over-all look had changed notably from their look in Normandy. New-version jumpsuits issued in late 1944 were actually the standard M-43 combat suit, green in color instead of tan, with rectangular pockets and a sateen finish. Actually, the Army was undergoing an elimination of all nonstandard uniforms and footwear. Jumpsuits were no longer to be worn and were actually recalled in some units. Many troopers hid a set in the bottom of their barracks bags, to be used later. Jump boots were also nonstandard and were to be replaced with the recently introduced two-buckle combat boots.

The only thing making the paratrooper look different from a regular infantryman at that point was the addition of cargo pockets to the upper legs of the M-43 combat trousers, thus converting them to jump trousers of a sort. The parachute riggers were put to work making these conversions of canvas material, and tie-down straps were also sewn on to help secure the load. Many troopers considered the straps a nuisance and cut them off.

A new cap patch for the overseas cap was also introduced, incorporating the parachute and glider – red for artillery and blue for infantry – all in one patch. Paratroopers immediately balked loudly at wearing a patch with a glider superimposed over their parachute and in some units (notably the 502nd), refused to wear the new patch until close to V-E Day. There was a distinct feeling that all this standardization was unnecessary and a suspicion that it was brought on more by jealousy than any other factor. The jump boots, M-42 suits, and cap patch had been definite status symbols, unique to the parachute troops, and now the Army was taking them away.

Of all these take-aways, only the jump boots were eventually restored. There was, after all, a safety factor involved in the wearing of jump boots. They had been designed to offer special support to the ankles, which had to twist hard during the execution of a parachute landing fall, and the buckles that protruded from the combat boots could potentially snag on a suspension line in event of poor body position upon leaving the plane. All manner of malfunctions could be imagined.

Unlike the issue of the smaller, gauze arm flags, which had been only spotily issued for the Normandy jump, all troops of the 101st entering Holland were issued with an armband printed on oilcloth. This larger brassard was issued with two steel safety pins, and although it was made with numerous holes punched in it to facilitate securing to the upper arm with string, it was usually folded and pinned on the sleeve.

New helmet nets, reputed to be of British manufacture, were also issued having a mesh between ¼ and ½ inches. These were noticeably different from the wide-mesh (1 inch) nets worn in Normandy. It became fashionable to wear the new net with a paratrooper's cloth first-aid kit tied to the front, although HQ/501st would soon publish a memo banning the practice. Photographic evidence indicates that it continued to flourish in the 502nd, even into the Bulge era.

Probably the most important change in equipment for the average jumper was the adoption by the US Army of the quick-release parachute harness. This consisted of a round metal disc that could be rotated and slapped to instantly release the front harness straps of the main parachute.

Initially, this arrangement (later designated as the T-7 harness) was sewn by riggers onto the existing T-

Creased Skull

Sergeant Ed Pieczatowski, G/327th, in England, summer of 1944, displays the helmet shot off his head by an SS trooper near Montmartin-en-Graignes in Normandy. The slug creased Ed's skull and knocked him down, but he was not seriously wounded. This happened to Ed a second time at Bastogne, with the same result. Such close calls became commonplace among the Screaming Eagles. *Pieczatowski*

5 harnesses to replace the clip fasteners used in Normandy and on earlier jumps.

Ironically, the quick-release mechanism was invented and patented by the American Switlik Parachute Company, but was used first by British paratroops in Normandy. After numerous complaints were lodged about the tightening-up of the T-5 harness and the slowness in removing it in combat, the US Army finally embraced the quick-release design.

Photographic evidence indicates this arrangement was worn to the airfields for the jumps that were canceled in the summer of 1944, prior to Holland. Worn in combination with them were the M42 jumpsuit and the combat boots.

Another American jumping device that made its combat debut in *Market-Garden* was the leg bag for heavy equipment, which was jumped attached to one leg and released before landing to dangle below the descending jumper on a 15- to 20-foot rope. This enabled the heavy equipment (which could be a radio, machine gun, or bazooka) to land before the jumper did, diminishing the danger of broken legs.

On the Normandy drop, American paratroopers used a British-made bag for this purpose, which was lowered by rope after one's chute opened. But during the summer, Master Sergeant Joe Lanci of the 501st's Parachute Maintenance section invented a more sophisticated gadget that the Americans would later mass-produce and call their own. This bag incorporated a ripcord that enabled a jumper to drop the bag by pulling the handle.

Colonel Howard Johnson, the 501st CO, recognized the significance of this enduring contribution to the airborne, and recommended Lanci for the Legion of Merit medal, which he did receive.

Although the M-1919A6 light machine gun was introduced at this time with carrying handle, bipod, and shoulder stock added, many gunners preferred the wider, faster traverse afforded by the tripod-mounted 1919A4.

Combat Jumpsuits – old and new

In 1944, Giles Thurman (left) modeled the M-42 tan jumpsuit (this example is reinforced). His buddy wears the new green M-43 combat suit, modified by riggers with cargo pockets and tie-downs on the legs. *H. Moulliet*

Malfunction Junction

Injured on a practice jump in England are John Cipolla, C/501st; Lieutenant Ed Defelice, B/501st; and Lieutenant Joe Wasco, G/501st. As a lieutenant colonel commanding 2nd Battalion, 327th Infantry in the Vietnam War, Wasco distinguished himself in battle. *J. Cipolla*

Tex McMorries, Super Machine Gunner

Melton "Tex" McMorries, the G/501st machine gunner, was twice recommended for the DSC but never received the medal. *Doris McMorries*

"The Greatest All-Around Machine Gunner the War Has Produced"

Private Melton "Tex" McMorries joined G/501st as a replacement before Market-Garden and was soon to establish himself as one of the deadliest gunners in the 101st Airborne.

Like all good gunners, Tex would adjust the traverse and elevation mechanism on his weapon when setting up at an anticipated killing ground. When the attackers came-in, he usually found them to approach on an oblique angle, rather than directly toward him. He would use the swivel tripod to advantage and start firing in front of each enemy target, swinging the gun in toward the man, instead of merely lead ing him. Thus, the bullet dispersion would usually find its target. "This could make the difference between a hit or a miss," he said.

Tex also felt that instinct and common sense had a lot to do with a machine gunner's success in battle, and he said, "A smart sharpshooter would score more kills than a dumb expert."

By the time the 101st was pulled out of Holland, Tex McMorries had scored such an impressive string of kills that Lieutenant Colonel Julian Ewell selected him to be the main instructor for new machine-gunners joining the 501st.

In introducing McMorries to a class of replacement gunners, Lieutenant Jack Cranford said:

You are all well trained in machinegunnery; many of you are experienced. We can help you only a little more, but this little can save your life or turn the tide of battle. You need courage and skill. We can only help you with the latter. Mac is the greatest all-around machine gunner the war has produced. He has many times turned almost certain defeat into victory. With the use of his skill and courage, he has killed more enemy than many of you will ever see, so try to learn a little more.

Tex McMorries was tall, lanky, and part Apache. Some of the events described in the Holland and Bastogne battles will help demonstrate how he gained his reputation.

The Flight Across and the Jump Drop Zones Son, Eerde, and Heeswijk

33

Due to the short notice before *Market-Garden* was launched, the troops participating received much shorter briefings than they had before Normandy. The survivors of D-day, however, now knew what to expect of combat. Experience had taught them to leave much unnecessary equipment behind, so many troopers were dropping with a lighter load than they had borne in Normandy.

Charlie Eckman, the intrepid warrior of HQ/2nd/501st's Light Machine Gun Platoon recalled, "My buddies and I gathered together, nicked our fingers with knives, and mingled our blood. We swore we would fight to the death for each other."

After crossing the Channel, planes bearing 101st Airborne paratroopers would turn left and head north along the European continent, crossing the front lines near the Belgian-Dutch border, then dropping their sticks along the road that would become known as "Hell's Highway."

This was the first major American airborne operation that would be carried out in daylight, rather than under the cover of darkness. It would make a big difference to the accuracy of the drop and the ease of assembly afterwards.

The 82nd Airborne, flying a different (northern) route, would land just below the British near Grave and Nijmegen. Drop zones A and A-1 for the 101st were below the 82nd's area, near Veghel and Eerde, Holland. These troops would land shortly after 1300, followed by the 506th troops dropping on DZ C, just above Son, Holland. The 502nd would come in last just above the 506th at the northern edge of the same

Second D-day
General Brereton waves to his troopers as they prepare for their second D-day. *Musura*

field, south of Sint-Oedenrode. The 326th Airborne Medical Company with 52 personnel and a surgical team, would land on landing zone (LZ) W in the center of the same field, along with elements of the 327th GIR and miscellaneous headquarters units. Airborne engineers and gliderborne artillery would also land on LZ W. Of the 377th PFAB, only Battery B jumped, landing on DZ C two days later.

On 17 September, troop-carrier planes departing England from Aldermaston, Chilbolton, Membury, Welford, and Chilton-Foliat, would deliver 6,641 troopers in 424 C-47s.

HQ/502nd

Members of HQ/502nd at their marshaling area in England. Several members of the S-2 section are visible in the foreground. *Musura*

Airborne General
On 17 September, General Maxwell D. Taylor (second from left), CO of the 101st Airborne Division, adjusts his reserve chute as Lieutenant Colonel Pat Cassidy (second from right), CO of 1st/502nd looks on. Note the cuffs of Taylor's M-43 jacket, evidently a prototype or experimental model. *US Army*

When Lieutenant Bill Sefton's plane, bearing a stick of D/501st, got airborne, he saw the men nod at each other. As if by signal, they all reached down and unfastened the two buckles on each of their combat boots, The flaps fell off and dropped to the floor. This revealed them all to be wearing jump boots, contrary to pre-flight orders. To comply, they had cut the flaps off their combat boots, buckled them around their ankles, then disposed of the objectionable flaps as soon as they got airborne.

General Taylor had personally requested that Major Hank Hannah, formerly S-3 of 506th, be moved up to division G-3. He was on a plane to Holland in that capacity when the C-47 was hit by flak. He wrote in his journal:

When we passed over the British Second Army and into hostile territory, the flak commenced raining on us from Eindhoven. My plane was hit in the left engine and left tail section, and some of it came through the floor at the front of the plane where no one was seated. The fire became so intense that the motor cut out, and we had to jump prematurely. However, the pilot held on so tenaciously that we were able to jump within the edge of the DZ. The crew chief jumped out after we had gone (I saw him in Son later), but the plane went down in flames. I haven't learned about the pilot, copilot and navigator, but I'm afraid they didn't make it – perhaps because they stuck it out for us.

VIP Transport
Pasaaic Warrior is the nose art of this B-17 Flying Fortress, which was the personal plane of General Lewis Brereton, First Allied Airborne Army. General Brereton flew in this fortress along with the C-47s laden with paratroopers. He witnessed the drop from his personal plane on 17 September 1944. A few days later, he was on the ground and moving up Hell's Highway to confer with his commanders on the ground. *Simmons*

Mishaps at DZ A

Due to the shot-down pathfinder plane that was to mark DZ A-1 between the canal and the Aa river west of Veghel, Lieutenant Ian Hamilton's battalion was misdropped some distance farther west. The Drop at DZ A-1 was conducted at 400 feet. Despite the wrong location, 1st/501st landed in a compact area, assembled quickly, and moved on to Veghel with few casualties. Father Francis Sampson, Catholic chaplain of the 501st, landed in the moat of Heeswijk Castle. Captain William Burd of HQ/501st was left behind with a rear guard to cover 1st/501's withdrawal. Burd was killed, and most of the rear guard was wiped out.

Troopers of 2nd and 3rd/501st had the ideal jump onto sandy, plowed fields near Eerde. Ground fire was minimal, and the troopers jumped at between 1,000 and 1,200 feet altitude. Inevitably, as in any mass combat jump, a few individuals experienced problems.

Lieutenant Bill Sefton of HQ/2nd/501st's S-2 section had decided to make the jump with a fully assembled M-1 Garand rifle cradled in his arms. Approaching the DZ, Sefton was "not altogether sure I could keep my breakfast down." At the green light, Sefton exited his plane at a long thrust, holding the M-1. As his suspension lines were deploying, one wrapped around the muzzle of his rifle, just behind the front sight. After the chute opened, Sefton looked up to see his rifle dangling from just below the skirt of his canopy. Upon landing, Sefton ducked his head and heard the rifle hit the ground nearby.

Most of the injuries sustained on DZ A were caused by jumpers being struck by their own weapons, worn disassembled in a Griswold Bag, tucked at an angle across their chest, or beneath the reserve parachute. In many cases, the weapon bag would straighten into a vertical position from the opening shock. The trooper, too distracted by his surroundings to notice, would hit the ground, at which time his knees drove the bag rapidly upward into his face.

Joe Lamber of F/501st was making his first combat jump that day. Joe's main parachute seriously malfunctioned, failing to open. Joe pulled the ripcord on his chest-mounted reserve, but as it deployed, the second canopy wrapped around his streaming main. Joe was falling to a certain death when an equipment bundle below him, filled with weapons, oscillated into his path. Joe struck this shock-absorbing device so hard he was knocked unconscious, but he floated safely to the ground, draped across the bundle. A surgeon who had watched the incident unfold, revived Joe on the ground and explained to him how he had arrived intact.

Hayden Faulk, also F/501st, jumped with one of Sergeant Lanci's new leg bags containing a light machine gun. After the opening shock, Faulk was twisted around in his harness so badly that he couldn't reach the ripcord to release the bundle from his leg. To make matters worse, Faulk was drifting toward the only house for hundreds of yards around. Faulk crashed right through the roof of the house with the gun attached to his leg, breaking the instep of his foot. He eventually limped into Veghel and collapsed in the town.

Harold Paulson recalled a mishap that occurred on DZ A-1. Franics Beavers, one of Paulson's C/501st buddies, landed in a tall tree, from which he dangled upside down, unable to free himself. Due to the height of the tree, his buddies were unable to get him down. Beavers was left behind and was captured by the Germans.

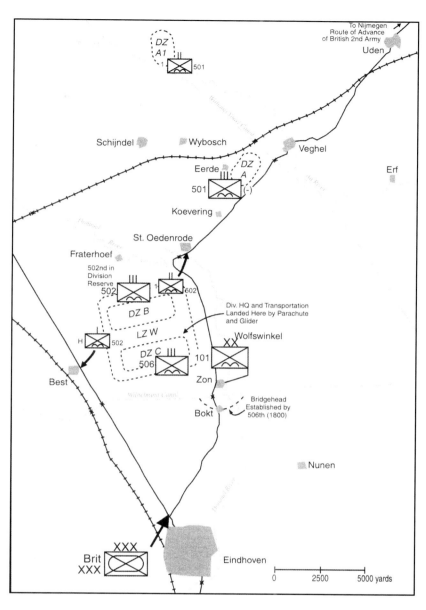

Division Landings & Positions. Operation *Market-Garden* 17 Sep. 44.

DZ C – Son, Holland

The wide-open expanse above Son provided ample space for DZs B and C, plus glider LZ W. Soon after the 506th got on the ground, glider serials began to land, with medical, HQ, and artillery elements.

Don Burgett of A/506th landed on DZ C and provided a narrative describing some details of the flight and the jump:

We took off and circled as the planes gathered in formation. We were at a higher altitude than on the Normandy jump. I recall looking out the left side of the plane and seeing the white cliffs of Dover; they looked about an inch high. We were really up in altitude.

Going across Europe, we really received no antiaircraft fire. It was a beautiful sunny fall day.

We got the red light signaling that we were approaching the DZ. Everybody stood up and hooked up. We took up a jump attitude near the DZ, and we began to receive flak. Not as much machine-gun fire as in Normandy, but a lot of 88s. I saw a couple of planes go down.

The tall young blond trooper in front of me was of Polish descent and had recently transferred to the paratroops from the ski troops. He looked out to the port and said, "Is that flak?" I said, "Yeah. Look out there. You can see it exploding." About that time, a hole appeared in our port wing, maybe 2½-feet wide and about 4–6 feet long. It's strange. You see the surface of the wing. It's there, and all of a sudden it disappears; you don't even see the metal leaving. So there was this big hole there, and this ski trooper said, "Let's get out of this damned thing!" We got the signal to go, and we went.

I learned later from Sergeant Vetland that the trooper behind me didn't jump. He froze in the door and Vetland hit him real hard and knocked him to one side and the trooper went back to England on the plane. The man tried – he had battle fatigue and should have been treated accordingly, but of course he wasn't.

After the opening shock, we had plenty of time. This was the first time we jumped with the quick release. All the planes kept tight formation and maintained proper altitude despite heavy flak. The troop-carrier crews were right on the ball on this one. A plane near me was hit and losing altitude. I got down on the field and met Phillips and a few of the others.

On the Normandy drop, some guys had been killed on the ground before they could get out of their chute, so on this drop the guys had the quick release. A lot of 'em wanted to get out of it in a hurry, so they had the safety clip undone, and some even had the release disc twisted. A tap on it after that and three of the straps would drop away. They also had their belly band off; that way when they hit the ground, all they had to do was unclip the reserve chute, hit this thing, and it would fall off.

Well, one of the guys… his chute opened and he came out of the chute; the chute drifted off by itself. The guy came down without a chute at all, hit the thatched roof of a haystack, ricocheted, and hit the ground. You could see his arms and legs windmilling,

Ritzler and Maguire

Ready to load up on 17 September are Chuck Ritzler and Walt Maguire, both of D/501st. Note the extension added to Maguire's Griswold Bag, enabling him to jump with his M-1 rifle fully assembled. *Ritzler*

Marshaling at Membury

Gus Liapes snapped this photo of two of his buddies before takeoff. John Grispan *(left)* lost a limb in Holland but survived WWII; he has since passed away. Charles Dickey *(right)* from Saint-Louis, Missouri, was, according to Liapes, "the bravest man I have ever known. His twin brother was killed on the Dieppe raid. He was always at my side or after a Kraut." Dickey was KIA in Holland. Both Dickey and Liapes had been wounded twice in Normandy. *Liapes*

Trooper taxi
A plane of the 89th TCS, 438th TCG, ready for takeoff. *Krochka*

and they kept getting smaller. All his bones were breaking.

I was with Doc Saint, our medic from New York. I asked him, "Are you going to him?" He looked and said, "Ain't no sense in going to that one."

About 35 feet above our head, two gliders were trying to get into the same field. One was above the other. The lower one's right wing hit the left trailing edge of the one up above. He spun, made a quarter turn, and hit the road. The jeep broke loose and came forward. The other glider spun out the other way, and he went down.

We stopped to try and get the survivors out. I was on my knees trying to break some plexiglass when someone said "We got a mission. We gotta be there," so we left as others were working on the wreckage. [Burgett's mission was to seize the bridge at Son over the Wilhelmina Canal.]

Winner Take All

The troopers of A/506th set off south through the woods at the east end of the Zonsche Forest, toward the canal. Company B of the same regiment was also landing on this DZ. Sergeant Herb Clark and his buddies had pooled money ($5 each) in England until they had a pot of over $200, winner take all. The trooper with the first kill after landing would win the pot, but he had to have witnesses or proof of the kill.

Clark's group was on the ground, getting out of their harnesses, when a lone German in the trees at the edge of the forest began firing at them with a rifle. Lieutenant Herb Viertel, Clark's platoon leader, was armed with a carbine, which fired erratically due to a worn sear. The weapon sometimes fired two or three shots in a burst with a single pull of the trigger. Viertel fired at the German and hit him through the chest with a two-round burst. He went over and removed the *Soldbuch* (paybook) from the dead man's pocket; the two bullets had gone through the book right through the ID photo of the man's face. The dead German was a member of *Flieger Regiment 53*.

Doomed Trooper

Swamped with equipment and parachutes on 17 September is Joe Mero, a former layout man for a Long Island newspaper. Mero, a clerk in HQ/2nd/501st, was married and would lose his life after heroic fighting in the Veghel area. *Baynes*

"This Yellow S.O.B. Won't Get the Honor of Jumping into Battle with You Brave Men!"

Lieutenant Ian Hamilton of B/501st was a Normandy veteran who recalled that he pencilled-in a last minute replacement on the jump manifest for his plane. This soldier was a boxer and apparently a tough guy. As the C-47 was taxiing along the runway for takeoff, the replacement intentionally fired the carbine in his leg scabbard. The bullet went clear through one of his feet and out the open door of the plane.

The aircraft was picking up speed for takeoff, but Hamilton grabbed the trooper by his harness and dragged him close to the open door of the plane.

Hamilton faced his stick and bellowed, "This yellow S.O.B. won't get the honor of jumping into battle with you brave men!"

With that, Hamilton flung the trooper out of the moving plane and he thumped and bounced along the runway, to be retrieved by medics on the ground.

Following the campaign, a Board of Inquiry was convened at Mourmelon to investigate the incident. After testimony was heard, Hamilton was ruled justified in his action that day.

17 September 1944, a "stick" of paratroopers en route to Holland. *Krochka*

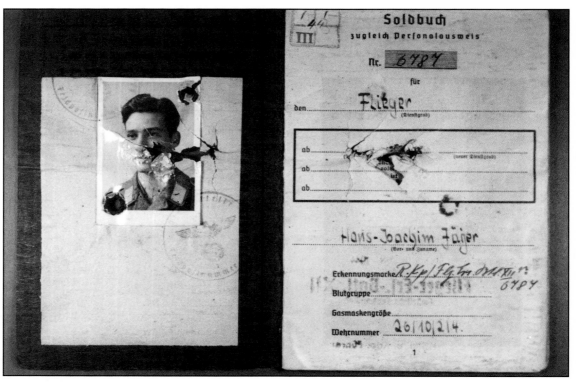

First blood
The owner of this pay book, a German soldier of Flieger Regiment 53, had the dubious honor of being the first enemy soldier killed by B/506th in Holland. Note bullet holes through inside of front cover. *Clark*

Son to Eindhoven

34

When the 506th moved south from the DZ above Son, their objective was to capture the Son Bridge over the Wilhelmina Canal before the Germans could destroy it. The 2nd/506th went down Hell's Highway, passing through part of Son *en route*. John Lindsay, a bazookaman, knocked out an emplaced 88mm gun near the St. Aloysius Boys school. The 1st/506th was paralleling second to the west, cutting south through the Zonsche Forest. As they neared the canal, mighty explosions thundered through the treetops, showering the troopers with deadly steel fragments. Don Burgett at first thought the men ahead had stepped on boobytraps, but several 88mm guns were positioned just north of the canal, west of the Son Bridge. Firing into the trees where 1st/506th was approaching, they inflicted heavy casualties.

Captain Melvin Davis, CO of A/506th, was hit by shell fragments. A medic knelt above him to give him aid. Two more shells banged in, wounding the medic once and causing additional injuries to Davis. Turning to the medic, Davis said, "You better hurry, boy; they're gaining on you!"

Burgett recalled, "The shells kept hitting and slamming us, and they kept saying, "Keep going! Move forward; we've got to take the bridge!"

Lieutenant Bill Kennedy had jumped in with B/506th. He recalled seeing General Max Taylor near the canal. Taylor remarked to one of the 506th officers, "Now is the time for your men to be heroes." He was referring to a mad rush to capture the bridge intact.

Burgett and many others were up and running and Paul Carter and Earl Borchers had set up a light machine gun before being hit by shell fragments. Paul Carter was killed instantly. Borchers walked back past Burgett. Borchers was dazed and in shock

and his buddies later learned that the blast had embedded the contents of his leg pocket into his upper leg. Among the items surgically removed were a two-cell flashlight, potted meat in K-ration cans, chewing gum, and other odds and ends. His legs were shattered, yet he would rejoin the 506th months later in Germany. According to Burgett, "In any other war in history, the man would've been sent home."

Burgett saw his buddy, Phillips, but Phillips ran to the right while Burgett went to the left, near the North Brabant Sanitarium, a tuberculosis hospital. Shell blasts were raining down large shards of glass from the windows of the hospital. Burgett found another buddy dead there; his face had been sliced vertically in half as if cut by a band saw.

Burgett paused to take the dead man's ammo, then joined in a charging group who were yelling, "Let's go!"

Burgett recalled:

We broke out of the woods and went running toward the guns. The only chance you've got is to take the people who are trying to kill you. If you stay there long enough, they're going to kill all of you. We ran toward three 88s in sandbagged encirclements on our side of the canal. One gun disappeared completely when the crew spiked it to prevent its capture. The blast also killed them. The sandbags, gun, and crew all disappeared. I ran toward one gun, which fired at us, flat trajectory. I felt the shell go past and heard it explode in the woods behind me. I went over the sandbags, and the crew immediately quit. [They] couldn't reload and had no arms except pistols. One guy fell on his back saying, *"Nein, nein, nein,"* and he was crying like a baby. I came down with my bayonet to impale him, and he just put his arms up behind

DZ A, 17 September, 1944.
A 501st trooper in the foreground is gathering his equipment after landing. Scores of additional troopers can be seen dropping in the background. Al Krochka snapped this photo between Eerde and Veghel. *Krochka*

Fire on IZ W

Sergeant Ed Benecke stands beside the CG-4A Glider that carried No. 1 gun of A/377th to Holland on 17 September. Ed's nine-man crew was also aboard. The Germans had set fire to the grass of the peat bog on the LZ and succeeded in setting several gliders aflame. Parts of the 377th were forced to land by glider instead of parachute on this mission due to the loss of crews and guns on the Normandy misdrop. Only B/377th would parachute into Holland – two days later. *Benecke*

his head. I don't know how I stopped in time, but I did. This crew and the other one surrendered.

The troopers were almost to the bridge, when the Germans blew it. Burgett recalled:

I haven't been in too many explosions that were that big. It was a wooden bridge, and the whole bridge disappeared. Phillips was with me, and we hit the ground. I remember rolling over on my back. I looked up and saw what looked like a piece of a toothpick; I could see it twisting very slowly. I said, "Hey Phillips, look at that,"

He said, "Yeah, that really went up high." It started coming back down, getting bigger and bigger. I started getting scared because it's coming right down and you don't know which way to run. But this thing was huge, and it didn't hit more than 40 or 50 feet from us. You could feel the shock waves from it when it impaled right into the ground. It was about 2½-ft square, about 3,040 feet long.

Lieutenant Colonel LaPrade swam across the canal, and with the help of some engineers using planks, a crude footbridge was formed to move the 506th south toward their next objective: Eindhoven.

Eindhoven

The 1st and 3rd/506th went halfway to Eindhoven along Hell's Highway, then stopped along both sides of the road for the night. Some additional Germans were killed in the vicinity of Bokt, and young Dutchmen quickly retrieved Mauser rifles to aid in the fighting. These Dutch resistance fighters tied a white armband around their upper arm, to signify that they were friendly to the Allied cause.

Don Burgett later said of the first night spent near Bokt, "We didn't dig holes that night, just lay down in the weeds and fell asleep. In the morning we got up like a buncha dogs, with dew dripping off our helmets."

The attack toward Eindhoven jumped off, with one platoon of A/506th staying behind to guard the tem-

Blasted by a Bazooka

Somewhere in Holland, a member of HQ/326th AEB surveys a former German machine-gun nest. The gun and its crew were blasted into the ditch by a bazooka round. *Krochka*

Conference at DC C
On 18 September 1944, General Maxwell Taylor (standing near center, facing toward left side of photo), confers with a British Army officer and members of the 101st divisional staff. To the right of the British officer is Major Hank Schweiter, assistant G-2, and to the right of Hank is Colonel Carl Kohls. *Taken by Flight Officer Bob Hamilton (glider pilot), via C. Shoemaker.*

porary crossing at Son. The 3rd/506th led the way into Eindhoven.

The British armor, which was supposed to be at the Son Bridge by 1800 on 17 September, was still below Eindhoven, and the paratroopers would have to fight their way south to meet up with them.

Captain John Kiley, CO of I/506th, was fatally shot by a sniper on the approach to Eindhoven. Members of H/506th and I/506th attacked, with Company H advancing through a cabbage patch to the edge of town. Lieutenant Rudolph Bolte was killed in that area, along with Jon Hanson. Charlie Kier was shot through the chest while going through a gate.

Hank DiCarlo considered James Tarquini to be one of the best combat men in H/506th. He saw Tarquini crash through a plate-glass window, circle through a building, and come up from behind to knock out a machine-gun position. Sergeant Frank Padisak was also instrumental in the fighting.

Coming into Eindhoven from the north, Staff Sergeant Jerry Beam and Lieutenant Charles Santarsiero engaged an 88mm gun position, but were halted. The 2nd/506th entered town from the east. Rifle grenadiers from F/506th, including Robert Sherwood and Homer Smith, joined Staff Sergeant John H. Taylor and others in knocking out two 88s from the flank.

It was surmised that much of the German garrison had left Eindhoven to join the big fight at Best.

Clearing out high-rise buildings was a new experience to these paratroopers who were experienced mainly in hedgerow fighting. The giant Phillips Electric building was searched floor by floor by members of H/506th. A/506th men were assigned several high-rise buildings and rode by elevator car to the top of each. The troopers operating the elevator would say, "Floor please," and take them up. Exiting at the top, they worked their way down, checking each office, but finding no Germans.

Members of H/506th entered a park within Eindhoven and encountered an outhouse. Luther Myers entered for some privacy, but the Germans had booby-trapped the toilet. When Myers pulled the handle to flush the toilet, the outhouse exploded, miraculously leaving him seated on the throne, unharmed. DiCarlo recalled seeing him holding the handle with his pants around his ankles, surrounded by smoke.

In the afternoon, British scout vehicles entered Eindhoven and proceeded north toward Son. Two of them

Wounded in the Jaw
Private Oscar Mendoza had been wounded in the jaw while floating to the Eerde DZ in his parachute; he refused to be evacuated, and as evidenced by this photo, set out to gather equipment bundles from the DZ with a Dutch pedal cart. *Krochka*

C-47 Crash on DZ C
The wreckage of the same plane that Don Burgett watched crashland: the plane did not burn, but the crew did not survive (they are buried nearby). *Krochka*

HQ/506th men resting in sugar beet patch along Hell's Highway, en route to Veghel from Eindhoven. *Reeder*

would contact Lieutenant Wierzbowski's H/502nd platoon near Best. The British armor would reach Son and erect a Bailey Bridge over the Wilhelmina Canal by 0600 on 19 September. By then, the operation was already seriously behind schedule.

Massive celebrations with the civilian populace ensued. Sandwiches, beer, and fruit were lavished upon the liberators. Some would spend the night in town while others pulled security on the east and west outskirts, and some 506th men joined British tanks in a push toward Nunen, Holland, well to the east. An air raid hit Eindhoven that night with the *Luftwaffe* making the first of increasingly strong bombings.

Don Burgett recalled that some young Dutch girls brought food and blankets out to the US foxhole line that night. They walked along until they saw a troop-er who looked attractive to them, then got into the foxhole and spent the night.

Back to Son

On 20 September, the Germans made a concerted counterattack on Son, coming along the south side of the canal from the east. The 1st/506th was rushed north to assist elements of the 326th and HQ/101st personnel in repulsing the attacks. The Germans were using Panther tanks, and Colonel Ned Moore succeeded in hitting one with a bazooka. The German unit had recently arrived from a quiet sector and was reluctant to pursue its attack with a total effort. They did manage to kill a number of 506ers who were dug in along the dike.

The 1st/327th GIR, as well as elements of the 81st AAAB joined the fight, and division headquarters was moved north to the Henkenshage Castle at Sint-Oedenrode.

The strain of battle shows on the faces of these three exhausted HQ/506th officers resting in Eindhoven. They have been identified as *(left to right)*: Lieutenants Schrable Williams, Bruno Schroeder, and Robert Haley. This location has been identified as the side of the Vlokhoven church. *Reeder*

Fresh Milk

Fresh milk, a treat rarely seen by the WWII paratrooper, is enjoyed by an unknown 506th soldier in Eindhoven. *Dutch Airborne Friends*

A/506th Machine Gunners

Two A/506th machine gunners were photographed by a Dutch civilian in Eindhoven, who gave a copy of the photo to Frank Anness, D/506th, on a visit after the war. The trooper at lower left has been identified as Harold Boye, a young replacement who won the Silver Star before being killed near Opheusden in October 1944. *via Anness*

Panther Hunters

An *Ausführung* Mark V Panther, from the *Panzer Brigade 107. Dovholuk*

Collaborators

In Eindhoven, Dutch girls who had slept with German soldiers had their hair shorn off in public as a form of retribution. They were then banished from their hometown. The men labeled as collaborators faced a worse fate – prompt trials, usually followed by summary execution. *Musura*

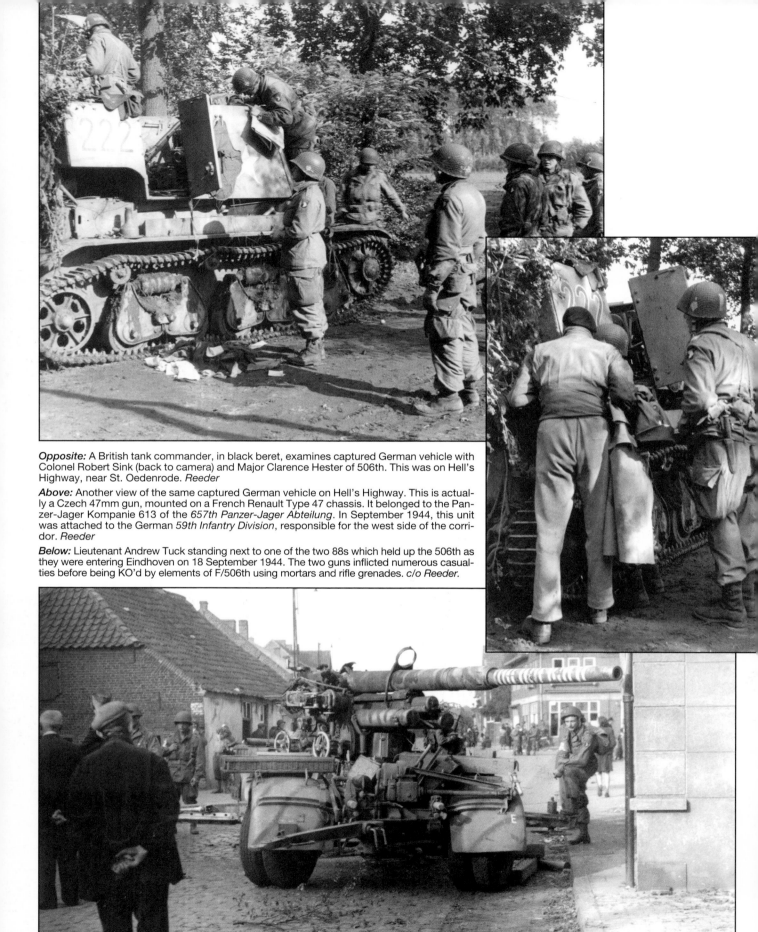

Opposite: A British tank commander, in black beret, examines captured German vehicle with Colonel Robert Sink (back to camera) and Major Clarence Hester of 506th. This was on Hell's Highway, near St. Oedenrode. *Reeder*

Above: Another view of the same captured German vehicle on Hell's Highway. This is actually a Czech 47mm gun, mounted on a French Renault Type 47 chassis. It belonged to the Panzer-Jager Kompanie 613 of the *657th Panzer-Jager Abteilung*. In September 1944, this unit was attached to the German *59th Infantry Division*, responsible for the west side of the corridor. *Reeder*

Below: Lieutenant Andrew Tuck standing next to one of the two 88s which held up the 506th as they were entering Eindhoven on 18 September 1944. The two guns inflicted numerous casualties before being KO'd by elements of F/506th using mortars and rifle grenades. *c/o Reeder.*

The village of Best, Holland, lies almost four miles west of Hell's Highway, and like Son, is situated near the Wilhelmina Canal. Upon landing on 17 September, it was learned that the two bridges near the main Son Bridge had been destroyed by the Germans shortly before the jump. When the main Son Bridge was destroyed in the face of approaching paratroopers, it seemed like a good idea to General Taylor to send a force west to try and capture the alternate bridge over the canal south of Best. This was initially deemed a mission suited to a company, so H/502nd was detached from 3rd/502nd to capture and hold the bridge — if it was still intact.

Charlie Company at St. Oedenrode

The 1st/502nd, commanded by Lieutenant Colonel Pat Cassidy, was sent north to capture Sint-Oedenrode. Captain Fred Hancock's Company C led off, and after a brief, but brisk, skirmish, the defenders were killed or driven off.

The next two days in that sector were relatively quiet, and some of Hancock's men published a mimeographed one-page daily newsletter for the local troops, entitled *The Charlie Chronicle.* On 17–18 September, things were so slow for C/502nd that its first edition said:

This headquarters is contemplating laying airstrips to get back out. There doesn't seem to be enough action here for tough Airborne men. So far on this cakewalk old Charlie has done pretty good… Some time this PM Maxwell was seen talking to Pat at a prominent road junction – maybe we will get another bite of those Germans. I know you are disappointed with the slight action we have seen so far, but Germany hasn't capitulated yet.

In the second edition, the situation was already rapidly changing:

Jerry tossed a few kitchen sinks over here in the early morning hours but had the wrong range. Patrols were sent out from the 3rd Platoon to try and locate their guns but had very little success. However, I believe from the sound of their muzzle blasts, the guns were sitting in behind our lines and the patrols were out to their front. Unconfirmed report that Jerry is approaching our positions from four different directions and so many that we couldn't count them with an adding machine. The Dutch are just trying to be helpful when they give you these reports, but try to get some confirmation of them before sending them in – I can't sleep nights with such reports. Those five hundred Krauts just up the road have increased to eight hundred. Should we send the British up there or write home and tell them to sell the outhouse?

Despite the dire forecast, the situation in Sint-Oedenrode would never approach the magnitude of the fighting near Best. Aggressive patrols went out continuously, however, like spokes of a wheel, mostly to

Foxhole correspondents
Two members of the 502nd in a foxhole near Best. One is reading an old letter from home as the other writes a letter home. Note they are both on guard for the enemy at the same time: one holds his carbine and the other a .45 pistol. The next day, these troopers moved to a different location. The hole shown was dug beside a large haypile. Shortly after they moved away, a shot-down C-47 crashed right where this photo was taken. *Swartz*

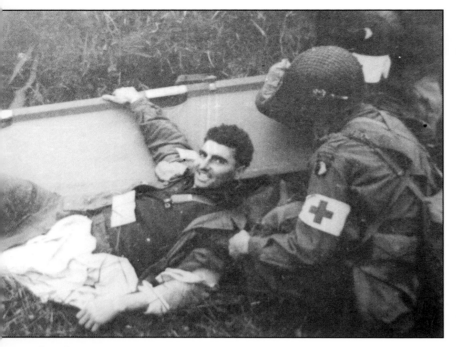

Smit Saves His Buddies

Lieutenant Morton Smit, a platoon leader with C/502nd, was wounded in the intense fighting near Sint-Odenrode on 19 September 1944. An exchange of hand grenades and small arms fire took place at very short range. Smit, crouched behind a hedge and suddenly saw a German concussion grenade sail in. He batted down the German grenade with his carbine, and it exploded, setting off an American fragmentation grenade on his belt. The grenade blast broke Smit's arm in several places and shattered his left hip, which has required a number of surgeries to correct since the war. This photo was taken as Smit was about to be evacuated to a field hospital. He is smiling because he is happy to be alive and because he was feeling the effects of morphine. Captain Fred Hancock, Smit's CO, snapped this photo. *Smit*

the west of the town. The C/502nd, sometimes supported by a tank from the Irish Guards, pushed repeatedly northwest along the road to Schijndel. The B/502nd went roughly toward Olland, to the west, while A/502nd probed toward the southwest in the direction of Donderdonk.

Despite the smaller number of casualties near Sint-Oedenrode, the local casualties were adding up and the small actions were close up and furious.

Jay Nichols of B/502nd recalled losing his captain, "Buck" Rogers, wounded and evacuated, as well as Private Redmond Wells, KIA. Captain Fred Hancock, C/502nd CO, caught a machine pistol round through the chest. Spitting blood, he walked a quarter-mile back to the aid station. Although evacuated from Holland, Fred would return to the 502nd in a few months.

A Gathering Storm at Best

On 17 September, Captain Bob Jones had led H/502nd to the western edge of the Zonsche Forest. One platoon, under Lieutenant Harper, was sent west to try to enter the town of Best. The platoon became pinned down. During a lull in the shooting, a German truck convoy drove down the road between the two sides, seemingly unaware of the situation. Someone shot the motorcyclist who was leading the convoy, and the trucks stopped, disgorging dozens of German infantrymen, who joined the battle.

Another H/502nd platoon, under Lieutenant Duffy, had probed south through the forest, but was also halted and driven back. The company was alone on the western edge of the airborne bridgehead, and the enemy concentrated all the fury of their artillery on that section of the woods. Throughout the night,

shells bursting in the tree tops rained steel and wood fragments down into foxholes, and American casualties multiplied.

On the first evening, a platoon led by Lieutenant Ed Wierzbowski had set off to the south, determined to seize and hold the bridge over the Wilhelmina Canal south of Best. With that platoon was part of Lieutenant James E. Watson's 3rd Platoon of C/326th AEB. This group broke out of the woods some 500 yards east of the bridge and following the slippery embankment parallel to the canal, worked slowly west toward the bridge. The group paused only 30 yards short of the bridge, which was still intact, but guarded by two German sentries.

At this time (according to S. L. A. Marshall), the American group numbered 18 men from H/502nd and 26 from the 326th. One of the scouts, Joe Eugene Mann, went forward to the bridge, at a crawl, with Lieutenant Wierzbowski. The duo was nearly spotted by one of the sentries and had to lie still for over a half hour, during which the larger group behind them was wondering what to do. Finally, a mixed group of engineers and H/502nd men stood up and ran for the rear.

Mann and Wierzbowski used this confusion to jump up and re-join the group at the base of the embankment. Having decided to stay, the stage was now set for a last-stand battle by Wierzbowski's group. Any thought he might have held of capturing the bridge was soon eroded by the ever growing numbers of German troops entering the area. But the fighting spirit of this group was not diminished. Vincent Laino of the engineers was a machine gunner. He had his gun and 500 rounds of ammunition. There was also a bazooka with five rounds and a 60mm mortar with six rounds.

It rained hard during the night, and Wierzbowski's group had been located by the Germans. It was just a matter of time before they would close in to finish the group off.

At 1100 on the morning of 18 September, the Germans demolished the bridge over the canal south of Best. There was no way for Wierzbowski's group to communicate this fact to their company or battalion headquarters.

The Death of Lieutenant Colonel Cole

Back at H/502nd, Captain Jones had pulled his troops more deeply in to the woods to try to avoid some of the heavy mortar and artillery shelling which was decimating his men. Lieutenant Colonel Cole's position was also under heavy fire, and he had called for air support. P-47 fighter-bombers were to bomb and strafe the nearby woods where Germans were firing on his battalion. A shell killed Technician Fifth Grade Robert Doran, Cole's radio operator, and the first P-47s to arrive strafed Cole's positions by mistake. Just as Cole was about to run into the open to readjust the aircraft recognition panels in front of his positions, Sergeant Graham Armstrong arrived with an S-2 patrol. Armstrong told Cole that Colonel Michaelis wanted to know whether the bridge over the canal had been captured.

"Screw the bridge!" said Cole, who was preoccupied with the immediate problem of friendly planes attacking his men. Cole ran out into the field and was shot through the head. He died instantly. Bob Cole was thereby robbed of the honor of being presented with his Medal of Honor. It would be announced a few months later for the bayonet charge he had led back in Normandy.

Joe Mann Sacrifices Himself for His Buddies

After the bridge over the Wilhelmina Canal was blown, Mann and Hoyle had moved the bazooka to a mound west of the platoon position and fired at a German ammo dump. The second round blew it up. Six Germans attacked their position from the north. Mann and Hoyle were able to shoot them all, but the attackers succeeded in wounding Mann in both shoulders. Hoyle then used the bazooka to destroy an 88mm-gun position 150 yards away.

Men wounded in this fight were being placed in a separate hole from the men still fighting. Joe Mann was wounded two more times, and his arms were both placed in slings, but he refused to join the wounded, begging to remain with the men still fighting.

During that night, two British armored cars appeared across the canal and a platoon from D/502nd joined Wierzbowski's group, but both units pulled out before the Germans counterattacked the next morning.

On the misty morning of 18 September, Wierzbowski saw a German officer leading a file of men toward his position. He yelled to Betrus, who tossed a grenade, but German grenades were already sailing in. A chaotic flurry of activity began, with paratroopers tossing out live grenades and firing furiously at available targets.

Lawrence Koller was shot through the head, and Laino was taking a heavy toll of the attackers with his machine gun. A German ran up from the right, firing a sweeping burst with a machine pistol at a downward angle toward Laino's head. A 9mm slug imbedded itself in Laino's jaw, but he lifted the machine gun, swinging it around and firing a long burst. He saw several tracers pass through the German before the enemy fell. A German grenade flew in, and Laino grabbed it, throwing it back just before it exploded. The blast took out one eye and blinded Laino in the other. He called for a medic, but Orvac, the only available aidman, was busy working on Koller.

Yet another grenade thumped on the ground behind Joe Mann. Sitting with both arms in slings, he was unable to toss it out. He yelled, "Grenade! I'm taking this one!" He laid back on the explosive just as it detonated. The concussion lifted him, and shrapnel hit several others in the hole. But Mann's sacrifice had saved their lives. He reportedly said, "My back is gone," then died without a moan. Mann's action earned a posthumously awarded Medal of Honor.

Soon after the explosion that took Mann's life, the group capitulated. They were out of grenades and low on ammo. The survivors were marched north to a field hospital near Best. Later that day, they grabbed weapons when the Germans weren't paying attention, captured the hospital, and returned to American lines to fight again. (Note: This account differs in detail from that given by S. L. A. Marshall, but it is based on the testimony of Vincent Laino, who described the experience to Bob Granche in a hospital ward soon after the events took place. Granche related the story to the author.)

Bob Granche's Roadblock

Like other men in 3rd Platoon, C/326th AEB, Bob Granche (pronounced "Granchee") was tall. He didn't relish combat, but like his fellow machine gunner Vince Laino, he took pride in outperforming his opponents. Granche liked the M-1919A6 light machine gun with bipod and shoulder stock and carried it in Holland, along with a carbine.

On the night of September 18–19, shortly before midnight, Granche was selected to lead a three-man patrol north to where a path formed a "T" with the Son-Best road. He was to establish a road block near there. Starting out along the path with two other troopers, Granche reached his objective around midnight. The American trio walked right up to three Germans who were standing there in the dark. The Germans didn't realize the approaching troops were Americans until Granche sprayed some bullets at them from his carbine. He succeeded in dropping two of them.

Working quickly, Granche led his buddies east along the tree-lined road for about 100 yards, then selected a tall oak tree on the north shoulder to blast with C-2 explosive. The blast brought the tree down, blocking the road. He then dragged the two dead Germans to a sitting position, and propped them up with their backs to the tree, facing toward Best. He also put their helmets on them.

Granche placed his machine gun in the northern ditch about 20 feet west of the felled tree. Granche and friends were brought under fire within ten minutes by German infantry. At a range of less than 50 feet, hundreds of bullets flew furiously across the road. Granche and friends had several grenades apiece. They threw all of them across the road and fired their weapons. Bob burned through 500 rounds of light machine gun ammo. There was a lull in the fighting for a couple minutes.

A group of 14 additional German troops, including a man dressed in civilian clothes, exited a house 100 yards west of the roadblock and joined the men in the southern ditch. Firing resumed. A German grenade sailed across the road, thumping Granche in the chest. He reached down, feeling in the dark for the deadly object. Seconds elapsed, and Granche had not found it. He dove for cover behind a large oak tree, just as the grenade detonated. The tree

Tree of Life

In September 1994, former 326th AEB machine gunner Bob Granche, returned to this spot in Holland for the first time since WWII, 50 years after this oak tree shielded him from the blast of a German grenade. Before returning to Holland, he had not attended reunions or talked about this incident because his citation says he killed a Dutch civilian who was mixed in with the Germans that night. Talking to Dutchman M. Sanders in 1994, Granche learned that the man in civilian clothes was a German soldier who had gotten fedup with the war and had begged the clothes from Sanders so he could desert to Germany. *Granche*

Airborne Artillerymen

New arrivals – possibly members of the 377th PFAB – greet Dutch kids in Sint-Oedenrode circa 19 September 1944. Note that the trooper at left is equipped with a M-1928A1 Tommy gun and has acquired an A-2 leather flight jacket, which is tied around his neck by the sleeves. *Nichols*

saved Granche's life, but one of his feet was mangled by the blast. The other troopers fled east and north, leaving the position.

Despite his painful wound, Granche crawled back into position behind his machine gun. Several Germans arose from the ditch across the road and began walking toward his position. Evidently, they assumed the grenade had killed him.

Granche swept them all down with a burst of fire.

Things got quiet, and Granche realized that all the enemy soldiers across the road had been killed. He crawled back to the T-intersection, then made his way south for a distance of three hundred yards to inform his commander that the roadblock was no longer manned. A patrol was sent back to the spot, guided by Granche. An officer liked Bob's touch of propping the dead Germans against the fallen tree. A few more were added, and Granche later received the Silver Star for this action.

As mentioned in the previous chapter, even the German garrison in Eindhoven had been diverted to the area near Best, to participate in the growing conflict there.

The 2nd/502nd left their reserve position near Wolfswinkel on 18 September and moved west to join the battle at Best also.

**"I Told You Guys
Not to Go in That Barn!"**

Corporal Joe Pistone was with his platoon leader, Lieutenant Robert Banker, during the move to Best. Pistone's 8–10-man group began to fall behind the company advance when his group and their horse-drawn supply wagon came under fire.

They moved on into the hamlet of Molenkampen. There, in a bunker behind a farmhouse, they found 30 Dutch civilians hiding from the firing.

As dusk began to settle in, Pistone looked for a place to spend the night. He moved several hundred yards east, to a house on the edge of the DZ. Parachutes were strewn all over the field, as were a number of gliders. The nearby farmhouse had a barn attached, and in it were a number of wounded with attending medics and the 502nd's chaplains, Reverend Raymond Hall (Protestant), and Father Andrejewski. Pistone found a parachute canopy and decided to bed down for the night in a ditch near the farmhouse. His men complained that they were cold and wanted to go into the barn for warmth.

"That's the first place the Germans are going to look," Pistone warned them. "For Chrissake, stay out here!" The men drifted away in the darkness and later did go into the barn.

Pistone was comfortably wrapped in his parachute canopy when he was awakened by some "loud stage whispers," around 0100. He heard equipment clanking and then one shot was fired near the barn. About 35 American troops were in the barn. A voice shouted in English, "Either you surrender, or we'll burn the building down!"

Many of the troops in the barn had removed their boots, and they filed out and marched away into captivity in their stocking feet. This group would remain captive for the duration of the war. Pistone was in the ditch, "really scared," as the group walked away in the darkness. He was afraid to shoot because he couldn't distinguish friend from enemy in the darkness. Other German troops crossed the ditch to search some of the gliders, their boots thumping the embankment of the ditch, right beside Pistone's head.

After everything quieted down, Pistone spent a scary night alone in the ditch. At dawn, he approached the barn and encountered Lou Zotti of HQ/2nd/502nd. Zotti had spent the night on the opposite side of the building.

"What happened?" said Zotti.

"My whole squad is missing," said Pistone.

As they stood talking, Father Andrejewski came out of the barn. He had hidden deep in the hayloft and had evaded capture.

Sergeant Earl Cox, F/502nd's operations sergeant, made an entry in his journal that day, listing some of the men who were missing as a result of the above described incident: Silfies, Bolkus, Crosby, Dellande, Franklin, Gallagher, Milineczenko, Smith, Turner, Weston, Fellers, Moore, and Wilson.

Pistone rejoined F/502nd near Best. He could hear the fierce fighting from a distance, and he located Lieutenant Banker. Banker was infuriated and wanted to know where Pistone and his squad had been. Pistone was finally able to calm Banker down and relate the story.

Some members of Pistone's squad were liberated before V-E Day and came to visit the 101st before returning to the States. Joe's first words upon seeing them again were, "I told you guys not to go in that barn!"

German troops kept pouring in as the fight for Best continued. They were members of the *Fifteenth Army* who had been diverted from their trip to the German border to join the battle, as well as units transported from afar to aid in the fighting.

British tanks reinforced 2nd and 3rd/502nd on 19 September. In a drive along the western edge of the Zonsche Forest, a climax of sorts ended the first phase of fighting there. Over 1,100 prisoners were rounded up and marched east, away from the fighting. Even so, the Germans continued to hold the town of Best itself for many weeks to come.

Private Sterno's Second Odyssey

Private Bernard Sterno, H/502nd, was a fortunate survivor of Cole's immortal bayonet charge at the northern edge of Carentan. Sterno was wounded on four separate occasions on that single afternoon of 10 June 1944 and was still hospitalized for his multiple wounds in England when he heard news of the MARKET-GARDEN operation on the radio. Sterno left the hospital and headed for his old base camp to see

A/506th troopers aboard a British XXX Corps Cromwell tank of the 15th/19th Hussars, headed toward Oerle, west of Eindhoven on the morning of 19 September 1944. *Reeder*

A British XXX Corps Cromwell tank pauses in Sint-Oedenrode along Hell's Highway. *Musura*

**Pows,
18 September 1944**
Members of C/502nd outside Sint-Oedenrode with German prisoners.
Smit

about catching a plane to Holland to join his buddies. Thus began Sterno's second, lesser-known odyssey, as told in his own words:

A trooper named Bluett from A Company got out of the hospital the same day as me, 17 September, a Sunday. We said, "Darn it, we missed the invasion." We made our way back to Chilton Foliat to our base camp, near Hungerford. I wanted to catch a plane ride over to Holland so I could jump in and rejoin my outfit. I heard the voice of my sergeant, J. B. Cooper, and didn't want him to see me (I knew if he found out about my plan he would put me on restriction or something).

We heard that Sergeant Kremer and someone else were going to London to try to catch a boat ride to the continent. We learned that resupply planes were taking off daily from Ramsbury. There was a quonset hut full of weapons, ammunition and grenades, so we equipped ourselves and slept that night away

from Cooper and the old barracks. We went to the airfield at Ramsbury and approached a C-47 crew that was preparing to load equipment for a resupply mission.

We walked over like we belonged there.

"Which one of these damned planes are we supposed to be on?" I asked.

"What do you mean?"

"We're supposed to get combat jumpmaster experience on these darned things."

Some young flight engineer or something, said, "I could sure use some help on my plane."

"Doesn't matter which one of 'em I'm on, as long as I'm on one of 'em."

"I'll get you some parachutes and flak jackets."

A little while later, a jeep pulled up with two white canopied pilot-type parachutes and two flak vests.

German Light Tank
A German light tank knocked out by fire from an RAF Typhoon fighter near St. Oeden-rode. The troopers aboard it are from 1st Platoon, C/326th AEB. Originally a French Army vehicle, at the time of its destruction, this Hotchkiss H39 light tank belonged to the Hermann Goring *Ersatz* and *Ausbildungs Abteilung* (a training and replacement battalion). *Crilley*

An officer of the 506th PIR, on his
Cushman 53 Airborne Scooter. This
was on Hell's Highway between
Uden and Veghel about a week after
the jump. *c/o Reeder*

Where'd you get that Jeep?

Troopers lucky enough to swipe a jeep usually beat the numbers off the front fender and some times christened the vehicle with a new name. This jeep was acquired by the 506th's regimental S-2 section, and one of them is applying the new name. *Palys*

We sat there about an hour or two before takeoff. The crew chief was looking at us and said, "I don't know about you guys. I'm kind of leery that you have plans of some kind."

He didn't say anymore. We got on the plane and he said, "We're going to take a lot of flak when we drop this off, when we make our turn to come back; before we get there we'll get a lot of flak."

Beautiful sunshiny day, I was lyin' on the floor, looking out the door of the plane.

Halftrack Ambulances

Halftracks pressed into medical evacuation service in the vicinity of Sint-Oedenrode. *Crilley*

We got to the drop zone and threw the bundles out. Bluett, the guy who was with me got sick; he was throwing up in his helmet. I told him "You'd better not jump," and he didn't.

We were looking down and I said "Where do you think we're at?"

The crew chief pointed down at Hell's Highway, which was lined with vehicles and said, "I don't know, but that's the British supply line there." I stood in the door and some impulse hit me, and I just dove out.

Instead of the three-thousand count, I did a five-thousand count, and pulled the ripcord.

Coming down, I could see people coming from all around – some in the distance looked like Germans, some looked like civilians.

I landed, dropped the ripcord handle, and two 12-year-olds walked up with their hands out. We shook hands. I handed one of 'em my carbine while I unfastened my harness, then took it back. They picked the chute up and took it away. So all these other people from the village were there. Girls were hugging me, and an older man drove up on a bicycle, all excited.

He got me on the back of that bicycle and started riding me toward his village. He got tired, stopped to wipe the sweat off. He made me take off my helmet, and I held it low with my carbine. I had nice long flowing blond hair then. We went past a hedge, and he waved, and I waved… were those Germans? Can't be.

We got in the village. This priest came out and hugged me. This lady, about 35 years old, walked right down the street toward me.

"Are you American or English?" she asked.

"I'm American."

"We must get you out of here—Germans everywhere," she said in perfect English.

She asked if I would visit this old man who was dying, who hadn't seen an American in five years. I said, "Certainly." I went in the building. She translated, and I shook hands with him. They poured me a drink, and I drank it. A Dutch Underground man wearing an orange armband and rifle arrived. They got me a girl's bicycle. The Underground man rode ahead of me. At each curve, he would stop like a scout, then motion me on.

We got to the main road, and a couple heads bobbed up behind a machine gun that was pointed right at us.

Armored Casualty

Another German armored casualty along Hell's Highway was this *Sturmgeschütz III* assault gun equipped with a short-barreled 75mm main gun. Vehicles of this type were not frequently seen by 1944. This is an early C model vehicle, belonging to the *Hermann Göring Ersatz* and *Ausbildungs Abteilung. Benecke*

"Yank," they said, "there's Jerries over there." I asked them about the 101st.

"Oh, your blokes are down that way," they said. I pedaled up along all these English trucks which were stalled on the highway.

Coincidentally, some regimental medics of the 502nd came up, and one guy recognized me. They gave me a ride down to the regimental area, and I slept that night on a stretcher.

In the morning, I asked where was third battalion as I walked along past all these machine-gun and rifle positions. I found the H Company CP in this farm building by a large pile of hay. They were heating up coffee and stuff for breakfast. When I walked in, they all looked shocked and surprised. I walked up to First Sergeant Harry Bush and said, "I want to get on the morning report."

"Good, what's your rank now?"

"I'm a buck private. I'm AWOL. I just took one of the Air Corps' parachutes."

"Don't worry about that, they're laying all over the country here."

First Sergeant Bush promoted me to buck sergeant on the spot; they needed squad leaders because of all the casualties. The guys I knew were all around talking to me. One guy said, "We killed a lot of Germans." About half our guys were wounded or dead. Weren't too many left.

They gave me some K-rations and grenades, and I swapped my carbine to somebody for a grease gun [M-3 submachine gun].

The next morning was September 21 and we moved out. I was walking with Jack Dunwoodie about 3:00 or 4:00 in the afternoon, when someone told me to take the point and go pick up some wounded Germans. I started walking down this road, and where

Part of a British convoy destroyed on Hell's Highway during a tea break. *Benecke*

153

Mike Marquez painting 506th DEMO markings on a European-made Ford truck, captured from the Germans. *Reeder*

The Supa Dupa Paratrooper
Mike Musura took many of the photos in this book as one of the 101st's division photographers.

it curved, I never saw so many Germans in my life. I raised the grease gun overhead with both hands to signal those behind me the enemy was in sight. The large group walking toward me hadn't spotted me when I dove in the ditch for cover. But at the same time, a group across the field opened fire on me. I was wondering why my people didn't come to help me. Maybe they were thinking I got riddled or killed. Every time I raised up, a bullet would hit near me. So there was a brick building across the road from me, and I saw two of them walking beside that building. I know now why that guy swapped me the grease gun. I fired three shots, knocked that one German down, and the other one screamed; he went crawling through the bushes. I pulled the bolt and shot at him several times. Whether it killed him or not I don't know—I never heard any more from him anyway. So the ones in front, they didn't see me yet. They kept getting closer and closer. I didn't know what I'm gonna do. One raised up, saw me, ducked back down, I said "Oh, hell." I heard a noise. Chic, like that. I knew what it was—the cord being pulled on a potato-masher grenade. I looked up and there it was coming. I put my head between my knees, crumpled down, and it went off. That was almost as bad as when that shell hit near me in Normandy. It blew my helmet off . . . my eyes, I couldn't see nothing, thought I was blind. I heard a voice, *"Kommen, kommen, kommen."* I rubbed my eyes; I could see a blur. Finally, after getting tears out of my eyes to where I could see, there was a German squatting there, with a rifle pointed at me. So I got up and walked toward him. He just put his rifle on his shoulder and told me to follow him. I know why he wasn't worried about me because that whole ditch, all the way down, was loaded with Germans.

He stopped, pulled an apple off the tree, and I stopped, pulled me one off, and we got to the German first-aid station there. The German officer there could speak English fluently. They treated me real nice there. I asked for some water, he said "The water is no good, could you drink some milk?" I said, "Sure"

I found out after the war that when I didn't come back some of the guys said, "He's in trouble; let's go get him!" But some lieutenant said, "NO, we gotta keep going."

Although Sterno escaped German captivity twice, he was destined to spend most of the duration of WWII as a POW in German captivity. He had a remarkable series of adventures that would require a separate book to tell. He jumped out of a boxcar on a moving train for his first escape, evading the Germans for six days before being recaptured.

This remarkably courageous trooper was eventually liberated by the Red Army. He was discharged after V-E Day. Two and a half years later, he reenlisted and served an entire career in the military.

Two Tanks in One Day

Lieutenant Kenneth Shaw (later KIA at Bastogne) of the 377th PFAB got word one afternoon that German tanks were approaching on a sunken lane east of Hell's Highway. He went into the woods overlooking the lane from the south with Sergeant Art Parker acting as bazookaman, and two machine gunners. A line of Panther tanks appeared, with infantry riding atop them. The machine gunners dusted off the infantry as Parker fired his first rocket down against the lead tank. The rocket bounced off. The second round stopped the tank, halting the tank column. Art fired into the second tank, also disabling it. The rest of the German armor was forced to halt the attack and back all the way to their line of departure. Two tanks in one day—not bad for a survey and instrument man from the field artillery. Art was awarded the Silver Star for this action, but always regretted that the lieutenant and machine gunners didn't get any credit.

Military Intelligence

Harry Silver, S-2, 502nd, examines a knocked out German self-propelled gun on Hell's Highway. This vehicle is selfpropelled Czech 47mm antitank gun, mounted on a captured French Renault R-35 tank chassis. *Pangerl*

Hordes of Pows

By 20 September, the 502nd had captured over 2,000 prisoners from the German Fifteenth Army in the Best-St. Oedenrode area. Hordes of POWs were marched to waiting trucks. The prisoners were driven south, transferred to trains, then boarded ships that took them to the United States. A trooper named Olsen from G/502nd accompanied a large group of POWs all the way back to the States—naturally, without authorization. *S.C. photo c/o N. Wierzbowski*

Troopers of 3rd/501st enter Eerde. *Krochka*

The small village of Eerde lies southwest of Veghel, and the loamy plowed fields in between became DZ A for 2nd and 3rd/501st.

The 2nd/501st would remain mostly in and around Veghel during the first two weeks of the campaign while 3rd/501st moved immediately to occupy Eerde and outpost the highway to Sint-Oedenrode. The 1st/501st would act as a mobile force, circulating in many villages north and west of Veghel.

A large windmill marked the north end of town, and a church with a sizable marble statue of Christ in front stands in the center of town. German forces moving toward Hell's Highway from the west soon recognized the strategic importance of Eerde and as a result, the tiny village became an important focal point of the fighting.

In the early fighting, 3rd/501st was in and out of Eerde, and 1st/501st took up positions near the railroad track north of town, where tall sand dunes dotted the landscape. The dunes were visible both from the church steeple in town and from the large windmill. On 24 September, a German attack supported by tanks attempted to enter Eerde from the dunes and A/501st went into the dunes to clear them in face-to-face fighting. This encounter has been well documented in both the regimental and divisional histories.

The Windmill at Eerde

A fine shot of the windmill on the edge of Eerde near the sand dunes, showing a trooper of the 501st below it. Jacob Wingard was killed while observing from an upper window of the windmill. *Krochka*

Elite Intelligence Unit

An S-2 patrol from HQ/501st is about to depart on a reconnaissance mission from Eerde, Holland, late September 1944. The trooper at far left with the BAR is Robert Nicolai, one of Colonel Howard Johnson's bodyguards. Second from left with Tommy gun is Sergeant Eugene Amburgey. The oil-cloth American-flag invasion arm brassard is visible on both of these men. In the center of the photo is Dick "Smokey" Ladman, and behind Ladman, holding a radio, is David Smith. The staff sergeant is John F. Tiller. Colonel Johnson considered his regimental intelligence platoon an elite corps; they would soon win international fame for conducting the Incredible Patrol in October 1944 on the Island. *Canfield*

"Old Glory" and the Sand Dunes

One of the enduring folk legends of the town concerns the use of the steeple of the church to observe artillery fire into the dunes.

After a forward observer from the 907th GFAB refused to mount the steeple due to the hazzards of German artillery fire, Paul Bebout of HQ/1st/501st, climbed up there with a radio and binoculars. Enemy artillery soon blew the steeple down,a nd Bebout was dug out of the rubble, dazed and slightly wounded. He later received a Bronze Star Medal, but was ordered not to resume that activity.

Frank Carpenter, C/501st, described what happened next:

The Germans started the day off by firing down on us from the high ground, with the notion of taking Eerde. I remember looking back on the village shortly after the fight started and saw someone climbing the church spire and attaching the American flag to a pole on top of it. The Germans, taking issue with this show of impudence, pulled up a tank and blew down the top of the church, flag, pole, and all. Shortly thereafter, there again was the flag waving from the topmost point—and again it was blown down. All through the morning this act was repeated, with neither the German tank crew or the trooper [Lieutenant Howard] giving up. A platoon of British tankers were sent up to help us take the dunes, but the German tanker knocked them all out before they got off a shot. Shortly, we got word to take the dunes, and we did. I still remember looking back at the village, from the dunes this time, and seeing "Old Glory" waving from the top-most point of what was left of the church spire. It was a sight I will never forget as long as I live. Oh yes, we got the German tank that night with a WP barrage from division artillery.

(Harry Howard was a career soldier who died in the 1970s. His heroic defiance of the Germans provided great inspiration both to his comrades and the Dutch onlookers. He has become one of the legendary figures of the WWII 101st.)

The Night Attack on Schijndel

The success of Lieutenant Colonel Harry Kinnard's sweep in the Heeswijk-Dinter area had convinced Colonel Johnson of the need to disrupt German staging areas west of Veghel before organized attacks could be mounted. Dutch resistance fighters had brought word that the Germans were massing troops in Schijndel, west of Eerde, and Johnson ordered 1st and 3rd/501st to attack that village on the night of 21–22 September, with short notice and no prior reconnaissance. Lieutenant Colone Ewell of 3rd/501st was so agitated by the order that he wanted to "turn-in my soldier suit." Attempts to reach the regimental commander by radio were unsuccessful, and the attack jumped off as ordered, with 1st/501st coming into town from the east and drawing the first enemy fire. A German flak wagon delivered devastating fire and after bedeviling 1st/501st, the vehicle moved around to fire at 3rd/501st.

Ewell's battalion crossed the railroad tracks and came at Schijndel from the southeast, skirting the towns of Hoeven and Berg en route.

Melton "Tex" McMorries of G/501st described the Schijndel attack as follows:

I don't know the name, but this village [Hoeven] was occupied by civilians, and we could plainly hear the weird sounds of many voices. These voices picked up, and all the villagers joined from one length to the end, which I suppose was prayers. Of course this

Duel with A tank

Harry Howard, 1st/501st, defied a German tank repeatedly to drape the American flag from the Eerde church steeple and to observe artillery fire. *Homan*

Below: **Site of the duel**

A view of the church steeple from which Lieutenant Harry Howard draped the Stars and Stripes. German artillery damage is apparent. *US Army*

Lieutenant colonel Harry Kinnard

In front of the Eerde church is Lieutenant Colonel Harry Kinnard (West Point, 1939), one of the greatest field commanders to serve the 101st in WWII. Beside him is his executive officer, Sammie N. Homan. Homan had commanded F/501st in Normandy and would return to 2nd/501st as its commander for Bastogne and the duration of the war. *Homan*

automatically pointed out that somewhere ahead of us lay the enemy.

First Battalion to our right was the lead attack battalion, because although enemy machine-gun fire opened up on the entire area at the same time, the first American guns started up somewhat to our right. One of the books [*Four Stars of Hell* by Lawrence Critchell, McMullen Publishing, 1947, left a bad impression on the conduct of the troopers on the approach to Schijndel. [The book said the troopers were cowering in the ditches, kicked-up by a few officers, and so on.] No doubt everyone was hunting cover, as the fire was murderous. But believe me, most of the men conducted themselves in the true tradition of the trooper.

I knew the heavy machine-gun fire we were receiving came from a slightly raised position or a small hill. It came in a solid sheet from directly ahead and also down a line to our slight left. As we moved forward, the heaviest fire seemed to be edging slightly to our left, which would indicate we were moving at an angle in relation to the fire. The intensity of the fire changed little, which indicated if they moved any machine gun, they did it fast. I thought I saw a set of tandem tracers, tracers very close together, but not close enough to be coming from the same gun. Naturally, it was impossible to tell about rifle fire at this time. I moved forward at a run for a short distance, then I saw the railroad tracks and subconsciously knew this was it. The guns had stopped using tracers once they established their zeroing in.

2nd/501st At the railroad crossing

This famous railroad crossing outside Eerde was occupied by numerous 501st troops of assorted companies, as well as by German troops during the see-saw fighting in September. When this photo was taken, 2nd/501st's Light Machine Gun Platoon was holding it. *Krochka*

One of the ammo bearers left 500 rounds of machine gun ammo in the open field, swept by machine-gun fire. I turned my machine gun on him and told him he had 10 seconds to retrieve the ammo. Donald Kane, a squad leader, jumped up, and ran for it, saying, "I'll get it." Suppose he figured the ammo bearer could not muster the nerve, and he would die. Somehow, Kane made it.

Then I heard the Germans, and although they used every device to hide muzzle flashes, I saw a very light spot and moved for it at a dead run.

The double bunker with two machine guns was not entered by cowing troopers nor by officers, but by me and close behind me came Carl Tennis.

I suppose someone was decorated for this kicking up the troops, etc. Perhaps they deserved it, but not at the expense of trying to create the impression that the truly great troopers of the 501st froze up.

Then we moved almost dead right into Schijndel, which by this time was alive with the noise of battle. I think this was a couple hours before daylight. By daylight, only some sniper fire was going on. I set up on a corner by a building, and sometime later, a noise tapped on the window near me. As I looked, I heard some low muttering and a hand stuck through the window containing some bread. I assumed it was a civilian, too uncertain to make his face visible. I was hungry, but didn't trust the bread to eat it.

A little after daylight, we attacked out of Schijndel, and for a short time as we crossed an open space, it looked like we might be in trouble, but our fire turned the tide, and we broke into their artillery. I am sure you have heard how helpless artillery [units are], once their infantry is stripped, and this turned into a regular turkey shoot. We were using POWs to carry ammo for us as we broke into their artillery. I had one with two bullet holes in the calf of his leg. Finally, Captain Stanley suggested I let him go as a regular POW, as he was going to bleed to death.

Carl Beck of H/501st wrote in his diary of the night attack, saying:

Sept. 22: Field orders came down… the battalion is to attack Schijndel. Jumped off about 2300 and everything was quiet until we reached the 155 phase line, then all hell broke loose. We had to dig Krauts out of holes and houses with WP grenades. Kraut wouldn't come out of several places, so we blew him out with bazookas. Krauts had a 20mm gun about 1,000 yards away. We went after him with a bazooka and machine gun, but he got away.

During the house-to-house fighting, Bob Baldwin of G/501st saw Lieutenant Colonel Julian Ewell shoot two Germans in a Dutch living room, using his .45 pistol.

Most resistance in Schijndel ceased before dawn, but a German motorcyclist drove into the village, unaware that the place was now in American hands. He entered an open-air urinal, and a grenade was tossed inside as he was using it. According to Al Luneau of C/501st, the mortally wounded German wrote a haunting dying declaration on the porcelain wall using his own blood: "*Schwartzes Hand*" (Black Hand).

In retrospect, the attack on Schijndel was a short-lived but successful foray. The original plan had called for the 3rd/501st to hold the place until elements of the 502nd, driving up the highway from Sint-Oedenrode, could link up. Unexpected pressure on the 502nd, however, plus sudden strong attacks against 2nd/501st from east of Veghel, prompted Colonel Johnson to withdraw his two battalions from Schijndel to consolidate the corridor area once again near Eerde and Veghel.

The attack on Schijndel had netted 250 German POWs, plus 170 wounded and an unknown number killed.

"Fire a Few Rounds at Their Feet!"

Pete Tessoff had joined I/501st as a replacement after Normandy. He received a facial wound during the fighting around Eerde. As Pete walked through the village, guarding two German POWs, the trio passed Colonel Johnson, who was standing on the verge of the road.

Seeing the blood from Pete's wound, the colonel's concern for one of his boys surfaced.

"Did they hurt you son?" the colonel asked. "Fire a few rounds at their feet!"

Later, angered by lack of concern of the British tankers to keep on schedule, Colonel Johnson had words with a tank commander of the British Guards Armored Division on Hell's Highway. The colonel interrupted the tank commander's tea break, saying, "If you don't get moving, I'll have one of my boy's come out with a screwdriver and a pair of pliers and have him take your tank apart!"

Attack on Eerde

Although the village of Eerde changed hands several times in the early fighting, the most concerted German effort failed against G/501st on 24 September.

Tex McMorries was recommended for the DSC for his actions in repulsing the attack on 24 September. Using his M-1919A4 machine gun, he was credited with 38 kills that day. Tex was responsible also for knocking out two MG42s and a 20mm cannon and crew.

Tex wrote about certain details of the event:

Our position served as a roadblock and the point of an inverted-V defense line. Our lines ran along the road for a ways, then left the road and swung back towards the windmill. My position was farthest north or northwest on the road. On 23–24 September, they estimate the Germans dropped over 600 mortar rounds near our gun. We had heard a tank, and having no mines, we dug out in front before the attack, simulating burying mines. They had a tank with this attack; it came in very close, gun down, firing at us, supporting their infantry. The tank stopped almost as if it had spotted mines. This attack came four times, the first three determined, the last disheartened.

We ran very low on ammunition in my position, which I believe was receiving the brunt. Captain Kraeger or someone sent word, and they were stripping rifle ammo and reloading it in belts for me.

The Germans made a bad mistake – they should have attacked farther north or farther south, then they wouldn't have exposed their troops to our perfect field of fire. Perhaps in the beginning they picked this because of their use of tanks, but when they failed to go all out in gambling the loss of their tanks, they ended up with a very bad place to attack. Also, they perhaps had too much confidence in their artillery preparation for the attack. It failed to eliminate many gun positions. It appeared every few yards was hit by a shell, but only direct hits or real close shells were effective.

You see, nobody had a better view than I did. In fact, later, a few other people made their way up to my position to get a better report and view of the scene and the spoils of the battle. The killing grounds lay on the road, in and near the ditches, from 50 to 200 yards north or northwest of our position. We coun-

ted over 100 weapons laying on the ground in front of us, from 20mm to pistols, from 25 yards out to almost 200 yards.

Tex's objective narrative omits much of the drama of this battle, but bear in mind that the enemy began the attack with numeric superiority and tank support, being halted only by infantry small arms fire and tactical superiority. The outcome was definitely in question, but this was to become a common scenario in the 101st Airborne's late-war battles.

Twice during MARKET-GARDEN, McMorries was recommended for the DSC, but his platoon sergeant and squad leader, Haun and Case, respectively, stated they wanted to rewrite the citation before submitting them. When Bastogne came up unexpectedly, Haun was killed and Case was blinded, and the write-ups were never sent through channels.

The outcome of other attacks on Eerde were no less uncertain until the battles had been won, and the coming narratives concerning Carl Beck and friends on a different flank are a good example.

Prior to MARKET-GARDEN, two officers of the 501st who had served with Service Company in Normandy, were transferred into 3rd/501st as rifle platoon leaders. They were Lieutenant Francis Sheridan and Lieutenant Charles K. Davidson. Both officers proved to be outstanding in combat, but Lieutenant Davidson didn't last long.

Carl Beck's combat diary again sheds light on further German attempts to take Eerde from the west flank:

Visiting his Flock
Father Francis Sampson, the 501st's Catholic chaplain, visiting members of his flock on a motorcycle in September 1944.

Peter Frank and a German Paratrooper
Sergeant Peter Frank served on IPW Team Number 9 with the 501st. A German Jew from Berlin, Frank spoke Basque French, as well as German. Note the tough-looking *Fallschirmjäger* POW leaning against the wall at left, wearing a boat-shaped overseas cap (*Schiff*). The pocket for his gravity-blade jump knife is visible on his right leg. *Musura*

Airborne Artillerymen

A 75mm pack howitzer crew from A/377th PFAB man their gun in Holland. *Left to right:* Charles Eckert, Frank Waas, and Orland "Pappy" Fry. *via Benecke*

Sept. 25: Made contact with the Herman Göring Division [*sic*] … they were on a combat patrol … sure went around and round 'til after dark. Duffy got a slug in the pack, and I got my beanie turned around on my head by a bunch of machine-gun fire. Darn close. Finally got knocked back into the ditch when a sniper's bullet hit a tree right beside my head. Knocked me coo-coo for awhile and a few splinters in my face, but nothing serious. Two wounded Krauts in our ditch … finally pulled back with one prisoner and left all wounded. No casualties, but Lieutenant Davidson got slugs through his pack and patch pockets and canteen. He sure is in solid with the platoon now. I didn't think anyone could move, but he sure did. We are sure proud of him.

Sept. 26: Moved up to take over part of the line between I Company and 2nd Battalion. Ran right smack into an element of German paratroopers. Met them halfway and sure got a mess of them. A corporal in the 1st Platoon is dead and another private, besides. Lieutenant Davidson, Aubin, Duffy, and I were out abreast of the 3rd Platoon and Lieutenant Davidson was killed by a light machine gun in the chest. Aubin got his .45 … took us about two hours to drive them off and there are dead Krauts laying all around–sure was hot for awhile. Must have got about 35 Krauts. Johnson was killed by a machine pistol, but Schleibaum got that Kraut. Pulled back about a hundred yards and set up final protective line … dead Kraut laying here and we had to cover him with sugar beets. Got Kraut parachute wings and a wallet with Kraut FPL in it. Turned it in to S-2. Quiet night after we got dug in.

Sept. 27: Krauts hit us with one company and a light machine gun platoon in support. Fired about 2,000 rounds, and then it started to rain. Stayed in a squatting position for about 3½ hours. Bones was shot between the eyes and Wilks tried to fix his eyes. About half the 1st Platoon was wiped out by the first 12-round barrage. Ground looks plowed over and the bark is torn off all the trees. Got a new platoon leader today but didn't see him during the whole battle … a few Krauts out this morning and Laf Otis reported no activity after taking out a patrol. Carried Bones out and Turner got his pistol. Poor guy. One of the spark plugs of this platoon.

The Lost Division

Company H had sustained so many losses in repulsing the Germans that Company D was sent over from 2nd/501st to reinforce their line. Sergeant Jurecko wrote in his diary:

Sept. 28: A beautiful day today, but last night, it rained very hard and with the rain came death to eight of our men. We pulled in here (my platoon) last night to help out H Company who were taking a terrific beating. Along this road lined with high trees, enemy shells hit the trees and threw shrapnel right into the men's foxholes and killed or wounded quite a few. It's a helluva bloody mess along this road – bodies lying everywhere, both of the enemy and our boys. Its been eleven days since we jumped here. How I would like to take off my boots and wash my feet or even shave my face. The men are very tired and worn out. They need rest bad.

Other Jurecko diary entries from Holland:

I got a hold of a *Stars & Stripes* and they have us in print as the "Lost Division." Well it seems that we are lost. Very little food, sleep, or rest; the men have been fighting hard and being wounded or killed. Yet they keep fighting and will not stop until the British infantry reach us.

Also:

Yes, I saw men of steel with tears in their eyes. The day Sergeant Choate, my first sergeant was shot through the head, and I told Sergeant Koss of it, his best friend … there, amidst the hell and furious noise along the front lines of battle I saw tears come to the eyes of the bearded young sergeant and watched him break to pieces at the loss of his comrade.

After the Battle

After the 101st left the Eerde area, Canadian engineers reportedly plowed the sand dunes flat to convert the wide open area to a temporary airstrip.

Today, the windmill at the north edge of town still stands, although the top portion, including the wind blades is missing. A small but attractive monument to the 501st, with a stone mosaic of the Geronimo insignia, stands right in front of the windmill.

The city of Veghel was at the top of the 101st's initial bridgehead. Two bridges were seized there – over the Willems-Vaart Canal at the south edge of town and the Aa River, in town. Members of the 501st's S-2 section ran into Veghel from the DZ near Eerde, and Chief Sayers and friends were the first to arrive. They shot up a German cyclist and captured a few members of the local German garrison. Chief then entered a house to celebrate. He discovered a bottle of orange liquid, exclaimed, "Apricot brandy!" and gulped the contents. It turned out to be orange dye, which left Sayers' lips, tongue, and teeth a strange color for the next two weeks.

Dutch residents started filling the streets and celebrating their liberation in what Lieutenant Bill Sefton calls "a comic opera war." Priests handed out beer and pretzels, girls danced with the soldiers in the streets, and Dutch resistance men flocked in with information on German troop movements.

There was brief excitement as a group of Germans tried to escape from town in a bus. The vehicle was riddled with bullets and crashed. One of the passengers was a 14-year-old Hitler Youth in full uniform. Sefton recalled, "He was so snottily defiant that I think the majority of our group shared my great desire to turn him over my knee and paddle his ass with the butt of a weapon."

Sefton also saw a German tank struck by a perfectly aimed bazooka round as it approached Veghel from the south. The round hit the tank's turret, then went up in the air because the gunners had forgotten to pull the pin in the nose of the rocket. The Nazi tank drove into the square, then fled from town with no casualties to either side. Being the farthest north of 101st units, the job of the 501st at Veghel was to defend the town against German counterattacks, holding open this section of the corridor.

Hand-to-Hand

Unknown to the Americans who had occupied Veghel so easily on 17 September, a battalion-sized German force was encroaching on the town from the direction of S'Hertogenbosch, along the canal. This powerful thrust would fall squarely on the perimeter of E/501st in the wee hours of the morning. A small German probe came into the A/501st sector to the north near the Aa River.

Frank H. Whiting, an A/501st replacement, was spending his first night in combat. Frank had spent most of 17 September doing a lot of marching, without encountering the enemy. At 0200 of 18 September, he was about to have a hairy baptism of fire. Placed in an outpost in a swampy area near the railroad embankment, the exhausted trooper soon dozed off. He awakened when several German pointmen crawled into his hole. They grunted in German and informed him with prods of their weapons that he was their prisoner. Leaving one man behind to guard Whiting, the German scouts continued on qui-

Resistance Fighters meet Glider Medics

Combat medics from the 327th pose with Dutch resistance fighters near the corner facing the Veghel church. *Dutch photo via Hopke*

etly to the east. Whiting was still awakening and comprehending his predicament, when he heard the voice of Sergeant Bruce Fess from Chicago call out to see if he was OK. The German guarding Whiting panicked and fired a rifle shot toward Fess. Whiting grabbed the Mauser rifle, trying to wrest it away. Both men rose from the hole, grappling for possession of the weapon. Fumbling and pawing, they dropped the weapon and rolled into the swamp. Whiting's comrades behind the embankment could hear the commotion, but in the darkness, could only guess at what was going on.

With frenzied thrashing in the muddy water, neither opponent could attain a good grip on the other. They bit flesh and gouged at each other's eyes. Whiting choked the German almost unconscious, but received a bite in return, his finger being chewed almost to the bone.

Thinking that Whiting had been killed, Fess and Morris Bull Bear tossed grenades over the embankment. During his struggle, Whiting could feel and hear the explosions on either side of him. Then, he remembered the rifle. Exhausted, he broke free of the German and crawled, groping for it in the blackness. He located the rifle and swung it like a ball bat, striking the German in the head repeatedly. Exhausted but victorious, hands greasy with mud, Whiting staggered to his feet, worked the rifle bolt and aimed at the German, who had raised up to all fours from the ground. He fired a round into the German's back, putting him flat on the ground.

Lieutenant Mosier ran up and asked, "Are you OK?"

Whiting could only point at the prone figure and let the rifle drop.

Mosier quickly withdrew his M-3 knife and dropped on the German, stabbing him several times.

Frank Whiting would go on to fight through MARKET-GARDEN, and the Battle of Bastogne, but this was his first and last hand-to-hand fight. Members of E/501st were about to experience point-blank fighting near the canal.

Night Attack

The German group that marched along the canal the night of 17–18 September was a mixed battalion minus one company, with some paratroops attached. Their route of travel brought them directly to the outpost line of E/501's 2nd Platoon. Behind this at the railroad embankment was the front line. Behind the frontline was a large building housing a phosphate factory.

When E/501st scouts reported hearing voices and footsteps to their front, Staff Sergeant Frank McClure went to investigate. He later recalled:

I went down the road about 100 yards with "Guadalcanal Clark," past Garcia and Moore, who were dug in beside the road. I heard voices and Garcia said, "Halt! Who goes there?" That was the start of the fight. Garcia jumped into the canal because a grenade went off right on the edge of his foxhole. When I saw him later, it had blacked his eye and the whole side of his face. He swam to safety on the other side. The Germans had them little stinkin' grenades on the end of their rifles, similar to ours, but they looked like a little CO_2 bottle sittin' there. Those things would come in, and they'd really jolt you. Clark and I dived over the roadway, started running, and ran into a fence. The fence knocked us down, which probably saved our lives. Well, the momentum of these people was terrific. They just kept coming, they came on, they spread out…The attack eventually flowed north. It couldn't go south because of the canal and

The Well-Dressed Paratrooper

Sergeant Adam Slusher of C/326th AEB demonstrates what the well-dressed paratrooper was wearing in late 1944. On his head is the knit wool cap, commonly worn under the helmet. He wears an O.D. wool shirt under his sleeveless knit-wool sweater. The 101st Division shoulder patch is visible on his left shoulder. He wears the Air Corps-type suspenders with leather end loops to secure his M-43 combat trousers along with a captured German belt. The trousers have been modified into jump pants by adding a canvass cargo pocket to each leg, as well as tie-down straps. An M-3 trench knife at the ankle and jump boots (contrary to prevailing rules) complete his accouterments. A Thompson submachine gun is his weapon of choice. *Slusher*

couldn't go forward because of Lightfoot's machine gun. Clark and I went through the pasture, came back through Joyner's squad, then back through the factory, and back around in behind Lightfoot. By that time, everybody was involved in the fight. There was some hand-to-hand stuff that went on because they had actually rolled right up on Joyner's people.

Harry Mole, the E/501st wire corporal, was with Lieutenant Joseph MacGregor when the shooting began. MacGregor ordered Harry to stay in position with Russell Waller, to maintain a 2nd Platoon CP, then vanished into the dark to join the fight. Soon thereafter, Waller became worried about his friend, Walter Olender, known as "Geezel."

"I've got to find him, he's never been in combat without me," Waller said.

"But MacGregor said to stay here 'til he comes back…."

Waller ran off toward the right to look for Geezel. He was caught in the fight and never returned. In the light of morning, he was found dead, lying next to his buddy Geezel.

Company E eventually withdrew behind the railroad embankment and Harry Mole found himself alone on the enemy side at dawn. He realized he was maintaining a platoon CP without a platoon. He later recalled "hightailing it back to the tracks, and I think

Above: After the withdrawal of the mixed battalion that attacked E/501st from S'Hertogensbosch, some German survivors were rounded up as prisoners on 18 September 1944. A barrage of 60mm mortar fire had dazed and demoralized many of them. *Krochka*

Opposite: A paratrooper of E/501st inspects some German POWs. *Krochka*

body dead without any marks on them. Of course everybody was real jittery after that. It was a scary thing; I remember that spooked everybody real bad for a long time. We kept moving out and thinking we were going to get into another big fight, but the 1st Platoon started rounding up prisoners, and whatever happened, there was no more fight left in them guys.

Lieutenant MacGregor had been shot through his helmet and sustained a horrible head wound. He was barely alive when recaptured, and the Germans left him for dead. As medics carried Mac from the battlefield, his men examined the bloody, bullet-holed

Captured Machine Guns

Some of the machine guns captured from the German battalion that struck at E/501st the first night in Holland are displayed by their captors. *US Army*

Rounding up Pows

A 501st trooper rounding up Germans in Veghel.
Krochka

helmet, and doubted that even Mac could survive such a wound.

A large, dynamic leader of men, MacGregor was a Scottish citizen who had lived in the Bronx before the war. He had been an outstanding soccer player and had won the title "Mr. New York City" for his weightlifting accomplishments. Miraculously, he would be back for more fighting.

E/501st' s action was the first of many desperate battles to hold Veghel against German attacks.

Sergeant Leo Gillis of F/501st had been put in charge of an outpost on the east edge of town. On the second day, he saw a tremendous German artillery barrage work across Veghel, and "it looked like they were going to blow the town right off the map."

Gillis rounded-up his troops, and they headed west to link up with friendly forces. He recalled:

We had seen hundreds of Dutch civilians, all wearing orange, heading into Veghel. We tried to talk to them, but they smiled and kept walking; they were going to have a big celebration. When them people were all in that town, the Germans started to shell it, and it was just fantastic. That town caught fire, and there was smoke and shells, and it just seemed like they were going to blow the town right up – completely. It really got bad. We stopped a couple of times because I didn't want to get in too close to that artillery. I remember down in these sewers and pipes, women and children were down there, and they were crying. That artillery had a habit of making people cry – especially women.

Cummings Wins a Silver Star

By 21 September, the 327th GIR had been moved north from the Zonsche Forest to join the fight at Veghel. On that day, Technical Sergeant Ernest Cummings of C/327th earned the first of two Silver Stars he would collect in WWII.

Losing one man of his squad killed in an ambush, Cummings sent the others to the left while he circled to the right. Advancing to within 15 yards of an enemy machine-gun nest, he destroyed it with grenades and Tommy-gun fire. He then led his squad in an attack, killing 20 Germans and capturing 30 more. At dawn on 22 September, Cummings and his squad repulsed a German counterattack. Cummings crawled out

under fire to rescue a wounded comrade.

Elements of the 506th moved up from Son to assist in the Veghel fighting, with 3rd/506th doing much infantry fighting. Other elements moved beyond to Uden to the north, and some were surrounded there briefly, under command of Colonel Charles Chase. The 1st/506th was sent south to Koevering on 24 September to reopen the highway when the British convoy there was wiped out.

Hitching to Nijmegen

During this period, a number of men from the 501st's regimental S-2 Section hitched a ride north with the British convoy to Nijmegen (in the 82nd Airborne's sector), which was still occupied by the Germans. The group established themselves in a hotel, and were discovered. They then shot their way out. In the escape, King R. Palmer was killed.

Heavy German attacks crashed against Veghel on 22–24 September with 3rd/506th and elements of the 326th AEB and the 327th GIR holding the south and west approaches. During one attack, Private First Class Anthony Yodis of H/506th crossed the canal and went forward eagerly to meet the advancing Germans. He was killed in that action.

The 501st met most of the attacks from Erp to the southeast and generally held the east sector. Jack Rider, a 2nd/501st cook, knocked out a German tank with a bazooka. Clerk Joe Mero engaged the enemy near a grain elevator and killed many. His binoculars were shot away during the fight. A day or two later, he was fatally wounded.

The Veghel fighting proved that infantrymen with small arms and bazookas could sometimes prevail against tanks, as a matter of necessity. This lesson would prove invaluable in later fighting at Bastogne.

Kinnard's Cannae

On 20 September, Lieutenant Colonel Harry Kinnard (CO of 1st/501st) maneuvered the entire battalion on an aggressive sweep toward Dinter and Heeswijk, to disrupt and rout enemy troops massing there to counterattack Veghel. Using Headquarters and Companies A and B to advance north of and parallel to the Williams-Vaart Canal, Kinnard also positioned elements of Company C in a backstop position to inter-

Troopers of C/326th AEB

Members of C/326th AEB paused for a photo between Veghel and Uden, Holland. *Top row, left to right:* Onsbey, Gaston, Minar, Adam Slusher, and Hanko. *Below, left to right:* Lawson, Cawley, Albert Kouba, and McCarthy. *Slusher*

"Holy Christ! He's Gonna Take Over This Joint!"

On patrol outside Veghel one afternoon, several men from F/501st, including Leo Gillis, encountered a hard-core German non-com who wished to negotiate a truce to pick up wounded. This German sergeant didn't think he should have to surrender his pistol. Jim Nadeau was also in the group that captured him. The German was taken into HQ/2nd/501st. Bill Russo recalled:

I was at battalion HQ; they had taken the man's gun. They had not blindfolded him. This guy was infuriated, because if you're not blindfolded, you can't go back. You should have heard him – believe me. I thought, "Holy Christ! He's gonna take over this joint!" He had the Iron Cross, buddy, and you could see that he had earned it. He looked soldier, he acted soldier, everything he did was soldier! I thought: My God! Thank God they don't have too many of them floating around!

He said, "My men will think I deserted them! Do you realize what you're doing?" You know, like, "You dumb sonsabitches." He was somethin'. I think anybody who met him—they met a soldier!

"I Don't Think We Should Do That, Soldier"

One afternoon in Veghel, General Taylor saw Eugene "Red" Flanagan marching a German prisoner purposefully toward the Willems-Vaart Canal. Sensing something was amiss, Taylor noticed that the German's hands were bound behind his back.

"Where are you going with that prisoner, trooper?"

Flanagan pointed to the brown American jump boots on the POW's feet. "Gonna drown this bastard in the canal, general."

"I don't think we should do that, soldier," said Taylor, as he gently removed the POW from Flanagan's custody.

dict the German retreat. A total encirclement, reminiscent of the Carthaginians' destruction of a Roman army at Cannae in 216 B.C., was accomplished, with 418 prisoners taken; another 40 Germans were killed. The herd of German POWs was paraded through Veghel later that day, down streets lined with jeering Dutch civilians.

A paratrooper from 2nd/501st guards two *Luftwaffe* prisoners carrying a stretcher along the Willems-Vaart canal in Veghel, Holland, September 1944. *B. Beyer*

More Defensive Action

In one defensive action by 2nd/501st, Charlie Eckman and Gleason Roberts set up their gun in support of a squad led by Asher Hetrick, E/501st. Eckman recalled:

We set up our gun near a shoe factory on the edge of Veghel and got into some hellish fighting there. Asher Hetrick of E/501st was to my right; he had seven guys with him. He said, "Don't worry about the fourteen Krauts that's coming up the lane; we'll get them with the first volley." I never even gave those Germans a thought, because I knew they'd get them. Gleason and I opened up. He used the machine gun, and I used the Thompson sub. My God, they were just comin' in waves. They even shot ack-ack at us, and they knocked out our machine gun. That's where

Tactical Conference in Veghel
Colonel Bud Harper, CO of the 327th, with Major General Maxwell Taylor. *Krochka*

I got some more shrapnel in my leg, but it wasn't bad, just bleeding and stuff. Those cannon shells explode, and that damn stuff cuts all through the trees. When they take it out of you, it grinds. Going in is no problem. Two of Hetrick's guys got killed, … but by Jesus, we just kept firing and for some reason, they didn't overrun us and kill us. We didn't have anything left to fight with. Hetrick's men had killed all the Germans on the lane, and it looked to me like on the field that Gleason and I had killed twenty-some before they stopped coming. Hell, they had tanks and ack-ack, and they could have overrun us.

Taking Ten
Albert A. Krochka, then one of the 101st's divisional photographers, "takes ten" on a Dutch street. He has replaced his torn jump suit with the M-43 model and is armed with an M-3 "Grease Gun" submachine gun. *Krochka*

The German Paratrooper's creed

Exerpts from the German Paratrooper's Creed follow:

You are the chosen ones of the German Armed Forces. You will seek combat and train yourself to endure any manner of test. To you the battle shall be the fulfillment.

Cultivate true comradeship, for by the aid of your comrades you will conquer or die. Beware of talking. Be not corruptible. Men act while women chatter. Chatter may bring you to the grave. Be calm and prudent, strong and resolute. Valour and the enthusiasm of an offensive spirit will cause you to prevail in the attack.

The most precious thing in the presence of the foe is ammunition. He who shoots uselessly, merely to comfort himself is a man of straw. He is a weakling who merits not the title of paratrooper.

Never surrender. To you death or victory must be a point of honor.

You can triumph only if your weapons are good. See to it that you submit yourself to this law – first my weapons and then myself.

You must grasp the full purport of every enterprise, so that if your leader be killed you can yourself fulfill it.

Against an open foe, fight with chivalry, but to a guerrilla, extend no quarter.

Keep your eyes wide open. Tune yourself to the topmost pitch. Be as nimble as a greyhound, as tough as leather, as hard as Krupp steel, and so you shall be the German Warrior incarnate.

> From *Saga of the All-American*, W. Forrest Dawson.,
> comp. and ed. Atlanta: Albert Love Enterprises, 1946.

Eckman's account is somewhat typical of the many desperate battles to hold Veghel. The soft sandy soil in the area enabled men to dig deep holes with ease, and many tunneled in sideways as well. Artillery experienced from the inside of such a hole was doubly terrifying, as the whole earth seemed to shift and move.

Lieutenant Werner Meier, the 501st's IPW officer, kept a list of the name, rank, and branch of every prisoner taken in the Veghel-Eerde area for the first two days. The first day's bag of 25 Germans included a paymaster, one lieutenant, three *SS* troopers, one Hitler Youth, and two Dutch civilians. On the second day, the list had more than doubled to 55 POWs. After that, the list was so long that Meier didn't bother to list all the POWs individually.

Reopening the Highway

When the Germans wiped out a long convoy of British vehicles south of Veghel, near Koevering on 24 September, an estimated 300 British soldiers were killed by 40mm antiaircraft guns and swarming infantry. Afterward, 1st/506th came down from Uden to reopen the highway. Spending the night in fields west of the highway were A and C/506th. It rained during the night, and a small group of German paratroopers got lost and wandered into an American position. Someone fired on them with a Tommy gun, and the survivors bolted over a hedgerow, dropping right into the laps of a C/506th group under Lieutenant Albert Hassenzahl.

One of Hassenzahl's men, Robert Wiatt, was standing in a ditch below the hedge when he heard the shots and realized that men were hurtling over the hedge into the ditch with him. In the extreme darkness, he kept quiet because he couldn't tell if the intruders were friend or foe. One of the new arrivals lay on the bottom of the ditch with his arms wrapped around Wiatt's feet. Suddenly a voice spoke in German, and a wild melee erupted in the ditch. Lieutenant Hassenzahl found himself fighting with a pot-bellied German. He punched the man in the midsection, heard him deflate like a balloon, then grabbed his trench knife and plunged it into the German, although the wound wasn't fatal.

Wiatt kept trying to kick his legs loose from the arms of the prone German. Wiatt grabbed his M-1 rifle, to which he had previously affixed a bayonet, and plunged it downward into the German. The next day he discovered that the blade had taken the man through the throat. Several Germans survived the confused brawl to be taken prisoner. Wiatt and others looped parachute suspension line around the neck of each prisoner, linking them together in one line.

A few troopers began marching them to an area along the highway. This movement in darkness was difficult and while climbing over a fence, one of the Germans tripped and fell, dragging the others down, too. Thinking that the American paratroopers had killed one of their number in cold blood, the others began letting out with terrified screams. Somehow, the prisoners were handed over to a headquarters unit for safekeeping.

The next day, both A and C/506th encountered some Sherman tanks that had been captured from the British and were now being used by the Germans. Leonard Benson of A/506th noticed a black cross painted on a Sherman that was driving alongside his platoon. He mounted the tank, banged on the turret and captured the entire German crew.

Sergeant Bill Knight of C/506th saw another Sherman drive out of the woods with crying Dutch civilians on the outside. The tank fired at the Americans,

C-47 Crash

Sergeant Benecke paused on the trip to the Island to photograph this crashlanded C-47 of the 79th TCS, 439th TCG. It is probable that this plane was delivering gliders bearing the 325th GIR (82nd Airborne) to the Overasselt LZ when the flight was aborted short of the LZ. Note the glider in rear. The Cherokee Strip nose art title is visible on the plane. *Benecke*

Opposite: Generals Taylor *(left)* and McAuliffe *(right)* visit Colonel Howard R. Johnson *(center)* at his S-2 office in Valburg, Holland. Johnson lost hearing in one ear due to a close exploding shell, and this may have contributed to his death a week later on the Island, as he seemingly ignored warnings shouted by a nearby trooper. *Mihok*

then backed out of sight into the woods again. The Germans had evidently coerced these women and children to perform the role of shields against retaliatory gunfire.

Knight saw another enemy Sherman flipped over by an exploding Gammon grenade. He and Corporal George Rollyson caught a large group of German infantry by surprise in a long ditch. The pair of Americans shot dozens of Germans there in less than a minute, but were never recognized for the feat.

After a total of 44 hours, the highway near Koevering was open once again.

Elements of the division began moving north, beyond Uden and Grave in the 82nd Airborne's sector and then on to Nijmegen. Crossing onto the island between the Waal and Neder Rhine Rivers, the 506th and their supporting artillery – the 321st GFAB – led the way. After staging near the Zetten-Andelst railroad station, they moved west on the Island to occupy an insignificant Dutch town already held by the British Army. The town was called Opheusden.

The 501st, led by 1st Battalion, would cross the Nijmegen Bridge, then head east to Coffin Corner east of Driel, to take up positions along the Neder Rhine.

A whole new phase of the 101st's history was beginning – the saga of the muddy, bloody piece of land that became known as The Island.

Captain Joe Pangerl in Holland in September 1944, with M1A1 carbine.

A 20-foot-high dirt embankment with a road running along the top extends from the south shore of the Neder Rhine just below Arnhem, westward past Driel, Heteren Rankwijk, and Opheusden. Although this dike, which runs parallel to the south shore of the Neder Rhine, is there to withhold any drastic flooding of the river, it is, at places, several hundred yards from the water's edge. The dike and road run fairly straight while the river zig-zags such that at some spots the river is fairly close to the dike and at other spots is a considerable distance away.

Traveling west along the dike road from just below Arnhem, the situation is much the same geographically, as one passes under the railroad bridge that crosses the dike at right angles, after crossing the Neder Rhine, between Arnhem and Driel, then continuing past Heteren and beyond.

The spot where the then-destroyed railroad bridge passes over the dike road became known to 101st paratroopers as "Coffin Corner." The area north of (on the water side of) the dike was held by German troops, with their backs to the Neder (Lower) Rhine. The area east of the railroad bridge was also held by German troops, and continued to be during October and November. Thus, US troops in the area were faced with Germans to their front and all along their right flank—the railroad embankment being part of the German front line.

When 1st/501st moved up in an orchard near Coffin Corner in the darkness of 4 October 1944, the corner was relinquished by Commonwealth troops, who had held the area very tentatively against local German efforts.

The Germans in the area belonged to *Panzer-Grenadier Regiment 60* of the *116th Panzer Division*.

James Calvin, an enlisted replacement in C/501st for the Holland invasion, described the early fighting at Coffin Corner:

We marched about six hours in the dead of night to relieve the British just below Arnhem, between the two rivers in what we called the Island [due to the fact that the land mass is completely surrounded by the Neder Rhine and Waal Rivers]. In October, we had a defense line set up about 40 yards behind and parallel to a dike. As I remember it, we called it the Coffin Corner. They stopped our advance a few hundred yards from the position we were supposed to occupy. They called the officers forward to reconnoiter the position. We had fallen out to the side, and I had my back against an apple tree. I remember at the time seeing Captain Robert Phillips, who equaled and even surpassed the essence of all great leaders, coming up through the orchard, walking as though he was not afraid to be killed. He shouted out orders to the platoon leaders, telling them what he wanted them to do. In looking back, I am certain that the Germans thought he was directing the actions of the battalion and not of the company. It was for this reason that I believe now, and have through the years, that they pulled back – thinking a battalion was on the attack.

We relieved the British within 30–40 minutes, and we occupied this position for the next three or four days.

The next morning, just about daybreak, a sniper in a farmhouse to our right rear zeroed in on one of our people, Staff Sergeant William R. Roark. I will never forget this. Roark was a fine individual. I heard the shot, and I heard that awful sound that told me it hit some kind of target; we called for Roark, and he didn't answer. I took my rifle off my shoulder; he was three or four foxholes from me. I crawled down the line to his position, and he had slumped down into his foxhole. When he did, his helmet slid over the front of his face. I reached down and pulled the helmet back, and I saw immediately that Roark didn't know what hit him. He was dead. I returned to my position.

Within 30–40 minutes, Captain Phillips called for this man, Sergeant Milton F. Nelson, from Minnesota. I'll say at the outset that Nelson was no doubt the greatest, the bravest combat soldier I ever knew. He reported to the CP on a dead run. Within 5–10 minutes, he returned and announced he needed to take two people on a recon patrol. I didn't say anything, but I knew I would be selected. I don't think there was a GI anywhere who went on more patrols than I did, and I have to admit, I ran scared every step of the way.

Aerial view of Coffin Corner
Coffin Corner is visible where the railroad bridge crosses the road on the south edge of the river. The curve near the upper right of the photo is where the Germans detonated an aerial bomb to blow open the dike and flood the area as far west as Opheusden. *Coby de Hartog*

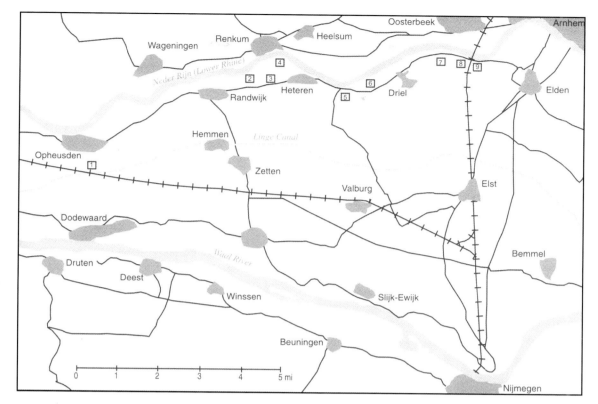

« The Island »

  Key to map references:

1. Opheusden railroad station and bridge across Linge Canal
2. Point of return of 138 British Airborne and 4 American pilots, 22/23 Oct 1944
3. Windmill at Heteren. Destroyed but never rebuilt
4. Point of return of "Incredible Patrol," with 32 German prisoners on 1 Nov 1944. Their overnight point was only half a mile east of a German 18(?)cm battery which always shelled the Island and killed, among other things, staff members of the jam factory at Dodewaard.
5. Start point for "Incredible Patrol" on 30 Oct 1944; also monument for 101st Airborne, unveiled 25 Sep 1982
6. Korevaar Brickyard (southside), Doorwerth Brickyard (northside); also memorial on the dike honoring 42 men of 7th Battalion Royal Hampshire Regiment, KIA 22 Sep–24 Oct 1944
7. Point of return of British Airborne, 25 Sep 1944, 2163 men.
8. "Coffin Corner," site where a StuGIII was destroyed; railroad bridge blown on 17 Sep 1944
9. Dike blown up by Germans in late-Nov 1944, flooding the Island. The Germans intended to drive the Allies out by blowing this up, but got themselves in trouble west of Opheusden, where the water level rose higher than they had anticipated.

Nelson selected Casada, and by then I already had my combat equipment on, because I knew he was going to holler for me.

Captain Phillips wanted Nelson to return to the orchard, which was visible, and draw their fire, so that he could ascertain the probable enemy strength in this farmhouse.

Our mission was simply to parallel to the right to a hedgerow, then proceed to the front of the orchard, then return back up the exact route we took the night before. When we came to the front of the orchard, I was in the center, Sergeant Nelson was on my left, and Casada was on my right…They opened up on us with machine guns, and I don't honestly know how we got out of that orchard alive. We returned to our lines in the same way that we came in. Casada dropped off at his platoon, and I continued on with Sergeant Nelson. We were no more than 30–40 yards from our CP when I heard the shot. Nelson was running to the right and a few steps in front of me. I heard this awful sound, and I knew that the bullet had found its target. Nelson was shot through his left arm, through his chest, and out his right side. He fell like a ton of bricks. They sent people out from the CP to help me bring him in. When we brought Nelson in, he was cussing like a sailor. This was the bravest man I ever knew. But before he died – and I'm sure his lungs were filled up with blood – he did not cry out loud, but I saw tears from his eyes. Bless his heart; he was the greatest individual I ever knew.

Two or three weeks later, Captain Bob received a letter from his mother after she had learned of his death. In the first paragraph, she designated that she wanted this letter to go to whomever was with her son when he was killed. They gave me the letter and I carried it. When I was wounded at Bastogne, it was severely enough that they cut my clothes off and I lost her letter, her address, and all my notes. But I would dearly love to meet with this lady and tell her what a great, great individual, and what a courageous son she really had. I don't remember her first name, I remember only Nelson.

When Nelson was killed, they made Crews the squad leader and made me assistant squad leader. This was no more than a corporal's stripes. I had been in the Army over four years and had already reached the grade of staff sergeant before I transferred into the paratroopers. But with all of the promotions I had up until that time, this promotion meant the most to me, simply because I gained it in combat.

With the frequent shifting of companies and regiments along the dike, 1st/501st was eventually replaced at Coffin Comer by D/506th. Frank Anness recalled moving into the area, along with an airborne artillery battalion.

A pesky German with an MP40 machine pistol was dug in on the railroad embankment on the right flank. Each evening at exactly 1800, he would raise up in his hole and spray a full magazine of 9mm into the American positions, then duck back out of sight.

A *Sturmgeschütz III* KO'd by Frank Carpenter of C/501st.

Anness consulted with an artilleryman about this situation and together, they bore-sighted a 105mm howitzer on the precise spot where the German popped up each evening. When the German made his next appearance, he disappeared in a burst of flame and debris as the howitzer crew took him out.

The only serious attack against American positions at the corner was made by a 75mm *Sturmgeschütz* assault gun and some grenadiers one evening while C/501st held the area. Frank Carpenter of that unit bore-sighted an abandoned British six-pounder anti-tank gun at the assault gun when it rumbled through the underpass below the railroad bridge and turned south, exposing itself broadside to American fire. Frank chambered a round in the cannon and didn't know how to fire it. He began striking every lever in sight until the weapon discharged. The round streaked directly into the armored vehicle, knocking it out. Expert riflemen of the 501st picked off the grenadiers. Frank Carpenter was later decorated with the Silver Star for this action.

After reaching the area known as The Island, 3rd/506th moved from the Zetten-Andelst area westward to the town of Opheusden. The 2nd/506th occupied the dike facing the Neder Rhine river on a line extending eastward toward Randwijk. The line west of Opheusden ran south, crossing the east-west railroad line at right angles. Company H held this line on either side of the track, with G/506th extending from their right flank into the town and around to the east along the dike.

The 1st Platoon of H/506th was along the road that crosses the track, which then goes north into Opheusden from the southwest. Moving into the area was easy, and the British troops who pulled out at that time remarked that it had been a quiet sector. It was 4 October 1944, and the Germans would begin a furious drive to capture Opheusden the next morning.

Attack on 5 October

Hank DiCarlo, Joe Harris, and other H/506th men were near a blockhouse made of railroad ties, west of the road and just south of the track. At dawn on 5 October, they were aware of Germans moving to their front. Small arms fire came along the track from the west any time someone moved next to the blockhouse.

Major Oliver Horton, CO of 3rd/506th, came up that morning to look the situation over. He peeked around the corner of the blockhouse, and Harris yelled not to walk out by the track, as the area was under fire. Horton ignored the warning, walked out near the railroad track, and was hit by enemy fire. A medic gave him aid, but he died within an hour. Major Robert Harwick was 3rd/506th CO once again.

Over on the right flank, north of the railroad track, the 2nd and 3rd Platoons of Company H were experiencing devastating mortar and artillery fire (the British said it was the worst barrage since El Alamein), followed by wave upon wave of attacking infantry. Sergeant Charles Richard's squad was overrun by weight of numbers, and the survivors circled around to rejoin the company. Lieutenant Alex Andros and his men piled up scores of German bodies in front of their positions.

Some German troops made their way into town for house-to-house fighting. Ed Slizewski of G/506th was in a building in town when his buddy John Androsky staggered in the door and said, "Polack Eddie, I've got a gut full of lead." He then dropped dead to the floor.

Joe Harris saw a badly wounded runner of G/506th in the battalion aid station. The wounded man told Harris to go to the house used as G/506's CP to look for a musette bag behind the boiler in the cellar. Someone had blown the safe in the brick factory across from Wageningen and had placed the paper guilders in this bag, hiding the loot in the cellar of the CP. Upon checking the location out, it was discovered that someone had tossed a white phosphorus (WP) grenade into the cellar, and the bag of money had burned up.

The 1st/506th was moved forward to support 3rd/506th in holding Opheusden. Lieutenant Bill Pyne was CO of C/506th. He went up onto the main dike to have a look toward the river and was struck by an exploding shell, sustaining a serious chest wound. While waiting for the medics to evacuate him, Pyne smoked a cigarette. His men saw smoke come out of the hole in his chest each time he inhaled. He was evacuated and did survive. Lieutenant Hassenzahl took command.

Silver Star
General Matt Ridgway, XVIII Airborne Corps CG, looks on as General Lewis Brereton awards the Silver Star to Sergeant Ralph Bennett. Bennett served as a squad leader with H/506th at Opheusden. *US Army*

Ambush Site

A group of 101st troops in front of the Opheusden railroad station, where First Sergeant Fred Bahlau, Ben Hiner, and Lieutenant Weisenberger ambushed a company of Germans. *Krochka*

The town of Opheusden was pounded continually with mortar and artillery fire, and there was more skirmishing with the German infantry. Company C was reduced to new commander Lieutenant Al Hassenzahl and 26 men in a day.

Sergeant Bill Knight of that company lost three weapons that day. Two rifles were struck by bullets, and a third was disabled by shrapnel. Another shell fragment lodged in the metal at the top of his bayonet scabbard. Miraculously, Bill was not wounded by any of the flying metal.

Ray C. Allen's 1st/401st was brought up from the Veghel area to assist in relief of the 506th. Colonel Allen's force was frequently used as a fire brigade within the division and seldom received due recognition for their heavy fighting.

Withdrawal

Allen met with his longtime friend, Colonel Robert Sink, who wanted him to take up positions right where the 506th was currently holding. Allen refused, stating that Opheusden itself held no strategic importance. Sink was concerned with the heavy losses his regiment had sustained in holding the town and didn't want to give up the real estate. Sink threatened to courtmartial Allen, but cooler heads prevailed and backed Allen up. After all, the division's mission at the time was to defend the corridor and the highway between Arnhem and Nijmegen. Opheusden was far west of there and indeed held no strategic value in itself.

A plan was agreed on to form the 1st/401st in a new line 1,200 yards east of the current line. The 1st and 3rd Battalions of the 506th would then fall back through the 401st.

When the battalions withdrew that night, Don Burgett of A/506th was left behind with several men and some machine guns, to act as rear guard. As the last of the battalion troops moved past, Burgett got a real

"lonely feeling." Lieutenant Tony Borelli was in charge of the rearguard group, and at dawn, Burgett and friends kept asking, "Can we go now, lieutenant?"

Lieutenant Borelli was a cool character, well liked by his men. He kept saying, "A little while longer."

At daylight, the group packed up their weapons and hiked to the rear. *En route,* they passed near a large enemy force who must have thought they were prisoners or their own troops. No shots were exchanged. Shortly thereafter, a massive German attack by a battalion driving toward Nijmegen came from the west. The 1st/506th, fighting from an apple orchard, helped repulse the group. A large number of Germans also entered a gap between companies of the 1st/401st, and scores were ambushed with little loss to the Americans.

Also that morning, Lieutenant Hassensahl's 26-man company maneuvered against the rest of the German battalion, who were reported in a nearby woods. Sergeant Mariano Sanchez, "who had eyes like an eagle," called fire onto Germans in an open field, from the battalion's 81mm mortars. He then directed the mortars to walk fire through the woods. Sanchez received the Silver Star for this action, but was killed at Bastogne. The Germans in the woods realized they were trapped and saw elements of the 327th GIR coming up from the other direction.

As Hassenzahl's company approached the woods, Lieutenant Hatfield, leading half the group, lost contact; Corporal Harold Forshee, the lead scout, was shot dead; but dozens of Germans began coming out of the woods with no helmets and hands on their heads. Hatfield fired his .45 at them and they ran back into the woods. Eventually, they came back out to surrender. Sergeant Bill Knight had admonished the lieutenant not to shoot at them, and a surrender of nearly 250 Germans was accomplished.

Knight confiscated a whistle that one prisoner kept blowing, and another German was found in possession of a British commando knife, engraved with the name "Captain Harold Van Antwerp." Van Antwerp had parachuted into Normandy as CO of G/506th. He had been found dead on DZ D. This prisoner who was found with his knife was taken aside and shot. Hassenzahl felt, "This may or may not have been the right thing to do, as the knife could have changed hands four times or more since Normandy." Of course, even if the German had looted it from van Antwerp personally, legally speaking, it was far from a capital offense. Another 40 to 50 dead Germans lay in the field near the woods, victims of the mortar barrage called in by Sergeant Sanchez.

Three Troopers Ambush a Company

That night, First Sergeant Fred Bahlau, Staff Sergeant Ben Hiner, and Lieutenant John Weisenberger of HQ/3rd/ 506th walked through German lines, returning to the Opheusden railroad station to recover some battalion baggage. All three were armed with Thompson submachine guns, and they planned to spend the night at the station. Bahlau spotted a company-sized group of Germans approaching in the dark, but the group veered left and cut across the track, heading for Opheusden. Hiner went up into a window of the house on the left. Weisenberger entered a barn to the right. At a given signal, they opened fire on the flank of the enemy company, which was passing them broadside, at a range of 100 yards. A German machine gun returned fire, knocking shingles off the roof of the station, but the bulk of the enemy unit kept moving ahead as if bent on a mission. After some grenades had been hurled at the enemy force, the last 40 men in the group dropped back and came in, surrendering to the three Americans. An unknown number had been killed. The prisoners were marched to the rear.

Fred Bahlau's Second Silver Star

The next day, Major Robert Harwick was riding in a jeep with the driver and Lieutenant Heggeness when the jeep was ambushed by a German machine gun. The driver was killed, and the jeep crashed into the Linge Canal. The officers escaped and Harwick supplied Sergeant Bahlau with another jeep and driver, directing them to return to the ambush site and recover his map case, which had been left in the shot-up vehicle.

In a daring daylight move, Bahlau and driver sped down the road, located the shot-up jeep, retrieved the map case and the body of Harwick's driver, and returned successfully. They had to shoot their way out of that spot. Bahlau was awarded his second Silver Star Medal for this incident.

Probing into Opheusden

In the following days and weeks, the western edge of the perimeter of the Island was largely taken over by the 1st/401st and the 327th GIR. Although Opheusden was back in German hands, numerous American patrols probed into the town almost daily.

Sergeant John R. Gacek was seriously wounded and left behind on one of the patrols. The next day, a patrol returning to that location found Gacek still alive. He was evacuated, but died. The CO of C/401st dispatched a patrol across the Neder Rhine in rafts to reconnoiter and look for a prisoner. The patrol was uneventful and returned empty handed. Another effort to cross in a raft by Lieutenant Fred J. Rau and Chinese-American Staff Sergeant Gilbert M. Chinn was ambushed while in the water; both of the glider troopers were killed.

Battlefield Commission

Fred Bahlau served with HQ/3rd/506th in Holland and earned a second Silver Star at Opheusden. The ribbon with cluster is visible in this photo. Not long thereafter, Fred received a battlefield commission and was transferred into C/506th as a lieutenant for the duration of the war. *Bahlau*

Tex McMorries and the Battle for the Dike

When 2nd and 3rd/501st relieved British troops on the Neder Rhine dike between Heteren and Driel, the Brits were glad to go. The sector had been quiet because the Brits had enjoyed an unspoken truce with the Germans – a reciprocal no-shooting policy.

The Germans held two brick kilns down near the water and had their backs to the Rhine, but several hundred yards of pasture separated the shoreline where the kilns were located from the road on the main dike. The landward shoulder of this main dike became the front line for troopers of the 501st. They dug their foxholes just below the shoulder of the road and could hear Germans digging and talking 30 feet away, on the opposite slope of the dike. Only the road atop the dike separated the opposing sides, and the Americans stirred up a fight as soon as they arrived. As a result, the quiet period ended.

A concerted effort began to drive the Germans from the opposite slope of the dike. The Americans found that their artillery could not be effectively employed against reverse slope defenses less than 50 feet away. Someone tied a bunch of boot laces together, attached a fragmentation grenade to one end of the long string, pulled the pin, then tossed it over, while

On the Dike

Parachute infantrymen from 3rd battalion 506th in position on the dike facing the Neder Rhine between Opheusden and Randwijk in October 19-44. *US Army*

holding on to the other end of the string. This prevented the grenade from rolling to the bottom of the reverse slope before exploding. Next, it was realized that a length of parachute suspension line would more conveniently serve the same purpose. Finally, someone realized that WP grenades would be ideal for burning the Germans out of their holes. At dusk on the evening of 5 October, a jeepload of WP grenades and salvaged parachutes arrived, and the 501st resolved that there would be no Germans on the dike by morning.

In G/501st, Tex McMorries and Bob Baldwin (as usual) had drawn a diagram of the troop situation in the area and had concluded that because of the inflexible nature of the front line on the dike, the safest place to be would be in the midst of the enemy front line. When the troops began tossing their WP grenades across, two G/501st men crossed the dike. Tex, firing his light machine gun from the hip, was joined by Private Rowland. Tex shot one German in his hole, then jumped into it and began firing the machine gun to the right along the enemy slope and then to the left. Then he would duck as the enemy troops on either side returned fire. As he and Baldwin had expected, this caused chaos in the German line. Tex spotted a sizable group of German reinforcements rushing up on the right flank and sent Rowland back across to the friendly side to alert the men on the American line.

Tex had been blown off his feet by German concussion grenades while originally crossing over the dike road, and fragments had entered his lung. Even so, he stayed most of the night on the enemy side of the dike, firing periodically to either flank. In the predawn of the morning, two Germans crept up and leaped into Tex's hole with knives. He succeeded in killing both of them. Just before dawn, Tex returned to the

south side of the dike, bringing his light machine gun along. The surviving Germans on the dike fell back to the brick factory before daylight, and the dike belonged to the 501st.

A later count of German dead on the reverse slope and in the field nearby revealed 26 German bodies, many killed by Tex McMorries. Once again, Tex was written up for a DSC, but would never receive the medal.

The Diary

For the next several days, long-range engages ensued, with both sides taking potshots at each other across the pasture. Tex and Baldwin each got several chances at a German officer as he moved among enemy positions near the river. "Just when you thought you had him, he would do the unexpected," Tex later said. "His timing was unbelievable, and he had no doubt fought in many battles."

Finally, observers reported that there was no activity in and near the brick factory. The last of the enemy had evidently crossed to the north bank of the Neder Rhine.

That night, a patrol worked its way down to the factory and found it deserted, except for German bodies. Near one body was a diary, with daily entries dating back to the 17 September airborne operation. Tex recovered this book and turned it in to S-2 for translation.

Shortly after WWII ended, Tex returned to Texas with the dead man's diary. It had belonged to a lieutenant from Jena, Thuringia, named Kurt Martin. Martin was assigned to *"Regiment von Rautenfeld,"* which was apparently an *ad hoc,* non-divisional unit named for its *Waffen-SS* commanding officer. Inside the cover of the diary was the home address of Martin's wife in Jena. Tex wrote a letter to that address, presumably to Martin's widow. He was amazed to receive in return a letter in English from Martin himself. He had not been killed, and his diary had evidently dropped from his pocket near another man in the brick factory before Martin escaped across the river.

The abridged text of the letter appears below:

3 May 1947

Dear Mr. Melton:

When I came home to my family after some time, my wife gave me your letter. I was very surprised but at the same time very glad…I shall write to you today, as I am interested to know how my address came to your knowledge. After all you write in your letter, I am no doubt the man of whom you speak. I was in September and October in the bridgehead near Arnhem and have commanded same as last German officer. On October 10, I was gravely wounded. In the evening of the same day I was brought across the Rhine in the military hospital of Appeldoorn, for the hospital of Arnhem was already overcrowded. The next day I had to undergo an operation. For five days I was between life and death. Finally, however, I got away with life. In February 1945, I had to return to the front and was taken prisoner by the Americans in Germany in May. After my release, I returned to my family in September '46.

So I have been away from home for 7½ years. My children had grown up in the meantime. You are right, the war was hard for all of us, but I have only done my duty as has every decent soldier for his country. We are glad that the war is over and that we can work in peace … we hope to receive soon a long-lasting peace because only in that way can the people march into a better future. We have had to suffer very much as a consequence of the war, and it will take a long time until we can live better. But in spite of all this, we will not lose our courage but we will work and help to get a good agreement between all the nations…

I am sending you best regards as comrades, and I should be glad to hear from you soon. Please tell me if you want to know further details from me then.

Sincerely yours,

MARTIN

Thus began one of the most remarkable pen-pal relationships to develop between former enemies of WWII. The warriors exchanged photos of their children and informed each other of the situation at the dike battle, each from their own perspective.

Among other things, Tex learned that Martin had been the elusive target he had missed with his machine gun. He also learned that after the big battle in which the Germans were driven from the dike, *Leutnant* Martin had sent English-speaking patrols up to the dike each night in darkness. They had listened to the 501st troopers talking and had learned the name "McMorries" was responsible for the death of so many of their comrades. Martin informed Tex that he had offered a high decoration as a reward for the killing or capture of McMorries.

Holding Period

With the Germans driven across the Neder Rhine in the Heteren area, a long period of holding began. Snipers fired across the river from ranges near 700 yards. Artillery and mortar fire were exchanged on a regular basis. The 101st would spend nearly two full months – the bulk of October and November – on the Island. A total of 73 days was spent on the front lines in Holland, and the Germans were unable to dislodge the tip of the *Market-Garden* salient.

The flanks of the dike position offered little concealment for a possible buildup to destroy the US bridgehead, and the only other alternative would have been an amphibious crossing of the Neder Rhine. Although this was a remote possibility, numerous patrols crossed the river at night to find out if the Germans were indeed massing for such a push and to find out

Guarding the Dike
A classic photo of a dike position near Randwijk. The troopers are from 2nd/506th. *Krochka*

Rhodes and Sharp, F/501st

Emerson Rhodes and Taylor Sharp, members of 3rd Platoon, F/501st, man an M-1919A4 light machine gun on the dike near the windmill west of Heteren in October 1944. A small road ran perpendicular to the dike here. Rhodes recalls that his large mesh helmet net was then out of style in the 501st. *Krochka*

what units were opposing the division across the river. Although some of these patrols got into shoot-outs on the enemy shore, they returned with little information.

Another Kind of Heroism

Since the Germans had vacated the brick factory east of Heteren, a squad of American troopers manned the building at all times. One night, a squad from H/501st occupied the building. A small fire was built inside the factory to heat water for coffee and to generate some warmth. It was difficult to get the fire going well, so J. C. Mann, a Normandy veteran, tossed some gasoline onto the fire. But the handle of the canteen cup bearing the flammable liquid caught on his sleeve and gas spilled all over the front of his field jacket. Mann burst into flames and another trooper received lesser burns.

Mann was badly burned over much of his body. This had happened near dawn, and the men in the outpost found that injecting Mann with morphine was doing nothing to ease his agony, because of the nature of his injuries.

By daylight, the situation was intolerable, but the men realized that they were supposed to remain in the position until relieved. They also realized that moving across the 300-yard pasture between the factory and dike in daylight was almost suicidal. Leonard Morris called on the radio and reached Staff Sergeant John McMullen at the CP, explaining the situation. McMullen conferred with the company commander, Captain Lytle Hilton, who relayed orders not to attempt to evacuate the burned soldier until nightfall, as the movement would attract artillery fire from across the river.

Ignoring orders, Morris said over the radio, "We're coming in. Tell the old man to have an ambulance ready when we get there."

Morris placed Mann in a fireman's carry and began the journey back across the pasture, fully exposed to enemy observation from across the river. He had to pause to rest numerous times, but the Germans never fired. Perhaps they felt admiration for this courageous act, maybe even compassion for the wounded man.

Sergeant McMullen told Morris "The old man wants to see you," shortly after Mann was turned over to the medics.

Morris entered Captain Hilton's office and received a blistering chewing out, but no further action was taken against him. Men sometimes do what they feel they have to do.

Long-Range Warfare

The long-range warfare alluded to earlier was characterized by hide and seek and sniping activities. The cunning Germans had anticipated this and had prepared for it.

In one tall house behind the dike, an upstairs window was visible from across the river. The Germans had hung a white bed sheet on the wall across from the open window before they retreated across the river. A trooper standing in the room later, thinking he was safe because of the great distance to enemy lines, was silhouetted against the sheet.

Glen A. Derber had been an NRA rifle champion before the war. For some reason, the Army placed him in the 2nd/501's Light Machine Gun Platoon. Glen didn't like the machine gun. The precise, well-aimed rifle shot was what he understood and the skill at which he excelled, so Glen was allowed to carry

"I Got My Teeth Into It"

Trooper E. O. Parmeley, an original member of F/502nd, is among those who jumped in Normandy in June 1994 to observe the fiftieth anniversary of D-day. He recalled the inspection depicted in the photo, in the Chappie Hall newsletter #11 (19 March, 1969):

After we had been in Holland for about a month, our second battalion was assembled for an inspection by General Taylor. Morale was low, we were all tired, each company looked like a platoon. I would say we were a sad looking lot. Well, General Taylor, on previous occasions had remarked that what we wanted was to get our teeth into this war and in our Bn., some of the men were always yelling, "You got to get your teeth into it!" General Taylor arrived in a green jacket, no webbing of any kind on, but in his hip pocket he had a .45 with just the butt sticking out. I think he was there to boost our morale for as he came down the ranks he spoke to most of the men or asked such questions as, "Know how to use that rifle?" or to the bazooka man, "Have you hit any tanks with that, soldier?" There was a man in D Company, I believe, who had no teeth. His false ones were in his pocket. When General Taylor asked him how he was, he said "Well, General, Sir, I got my teeth into it!" and then proceeded to give him his best Colgate smile. There were a lot of laughs and this story spread around. It was a terrific morale builder.

General Maxwell Taylor, Commanding General of the 101st Airborne, inspected 2nd/502nd in Holland, October 1944. Here, Taylor *(center)* is questioning a member of the 81mm mortar platoon. On the left *(with vertical strap on helmet)* is Captain James Roy Martin, Headquarters Company CO. *At the extreme right* is Major Thomas Sutliffe, the 2nd/502nd's Executive Officer.

an M-1903A3 Springfield bolt-action rifle. Up on the dike near Heteren, he was able to excel at long-distance sniping by using that weapon.

Glen's diary excerpts from that period give a fascinating insight into some of his activities on the dike:

I borrowed a pair of field glasses and started some sniping activities with my '03. I saw a Kraut about 600 yards or so away, lying outside his hole in the warm sun, so I tried a shot. He didn't move. I guessed the bullet couldn't have gotten to him, so I set my sights up to 700 yards and tried again. He scrambled to his feet and ducked into his foxhole, then looked around, wondering who was shooting at him. The next time I fired, he ducked into his hole again. When he came up to look again, he had his rifle. I tried another shot and he went down again. I checked

Two Buddies on the IslAnd, October 1944
The man at left wears a resurrected M-42 jumpsuit. The trooper at right wears the then-current M-43 combat suit. Krochka's caption indicates both men died a week later on a patrol. *Krochka*

"The Rumor Mill," a field latrine on the Island. *Krochka*

with the field glasses after each shot, and when I looked after my last shot, he was aiming at me!

I got ready to fire again, and a bullet cracked above my head. It seemed pretty wide to me and I was all for this game. This was something I could enjoy, for I had great confidence in my rifle and my ability to use it. The next shot I fired must have hit him in the head for he bounded out of his hole as if by reflex action and went tumbling head over heels down the side of the dike. Some other Kraut came over to take a look at him, and I scared him off with a shot.

I had a lot of fun that afternoon, wounding two more and two probables…The following day, I got in some more sniping, with no definite results.

There was the usual exchange or mortar and artillery barrages. The nights were getting cool now, and dense ground fog would move in on us…

I was sent back to the CP to get some rest. Didn't like the boredom back there, so I would go up on the dike when I got a chance and do a little sniping. I just loved to fire my rifle.

Well, it seems the Germans had caught on to this sniping, too, and they had a well-concealed sniper at work on a certain section of our lines. Two men had been hit in the head when they stuck their heads up over the dike to look around. I was itching for a rifle fight this day, so I thought I'd try to find him and have a little duel. I tried all the tricks I knew. I'd push my helmet up at one place and then sneak up near a place where I had background against which I couldn't be easily seen. Then I'd poke the glasses through some grass and look around the landscape, trying to locate that sniper. He must have had a powerful telescope or something because he would never shoot at just a helmet stuck up in view. And I can thank my lucky stars that he wasn't too good a shot,

Quick Shave

One of the typical barnlike garages behind the dike was photographed near Heteren by John Primerano of HQ/501st. A trooper named "Keith" is trimming the whiskers of Walter Craley. Craley was among the victims of the truck-mine explosion outside the Bastogne seminary in January 1945. *Primerano*

Holing up on the Island

Lieutenant Emzy Gaydon, A/502nd, in a log-roofed bunker on the Island, in October 1944. *Locasto*

A paratrooper of the 501st bicycles past the clock tower in Heteren. It was from this tower (which was battered by numerous German bullets and shells) that David Smith of the HQ/501st's S-2 section observed German movements across the dike. He was awarded a Bronze Star for his efforts. *Krochka*

The large windmill behind the dike between Randwijk-Heteren was easily identified by the large shell hole in one side. Above, Walter Craley, 501st Demolitions, sits with his back to the dike. *Primerano*

181

because here I was looking through the glasses, when all of a sudden a bullet hit the sod directly across the road from me. Six inches higher would have put it right through my head.

Colonel Johnson's Death

On 8 October, Colonel Johnson of the 501st was behind the main dike west of Heteren, inspecting the front-line of D/501st. With him were a number of officers, including Captains Pelham and Snodgrass. Intermittent artillery shells came in from across the river, but the colonel was loath to take cover in front of his troops. When a very close 88mm round came in, the other officers hit the deck, but Jumpy remained upright as the shell exploded near him.

The colonel went down with numerous wounds and was rushed by jeep to the aid station, then moved by ambulance to a field hospital, still alive and conscious.

Major Francis E. Carrel, the 501st's regimental surgeon, examined the colonel on an operating table. He first examined a wound on the front of Johnson's right shoulder. As Carrel cleaned that wound, Johnson said, "Doc, it's my back that hurts." Rolling the colonel part ways over, Carrel could see a gaping entry hole above the right hip, near his lower back. The shell splinter had gone through sideways and not quite exited near the lower left abdominal area. Carrel was able to remove a piece of jagged steel one inch wide and about five inches long. There was massive damage to the colonel's spleen and bowels. Johnson died on the operating table. Johnson's death sent a shock wave through his entire regiment. He had been a link with home and was closely identified with as the image and identity of the entire unit. Most of his men were surprised that their larger-than-life leader could actually be killed. As Critchell wrote, "To outlive him seemed strange." Lieutenant Colonel Ewell assumed command of the regiment.

Colonel Johnson's Funeral

Colonel Johnson was undoubtedly one of the immortal leaders of the 101st Airborne and will live on in the annals of the division as long as its history is preserved. The colorful colonel was one-of-a-kind.

Half a dozen members of G/501st went to Nijmegen for the colonel's funeral service. (Johnson's body

The same windmill up close, with Gillis, Newton, Wilson, and Turer of 3rd Platoon, F/501st walking past the shell hole. Gillis recalled staging this photo for Krochka's camera. *Krochka*

A small funeral service near Nijmegen for Colonel H. R. Johnson. *Duggins*

was later returned to the States and now rests in Arlington National Cemetery.)

One of the men on the honor guard told me that they fired tracers from their rifles in the 21-gun salute, as "Jumpy would have liked it."

Colonel Johnson's burial is best described in the haunting poem written by Melton "Tex" McMorries of G/501:

Geronimo Is Dead

This is the beautiful land he played a leading role in liberating.

The once quiet, peaceful land of Holland.

Its orchards are scarred and injured. Most of its neat little homes lie as only crumpled brick.

The smooth farmland over which his little Geronimos moved on toward Arnhem

Lies flooded.

His body lies far below the heights he lived on:

For Geronimo was king of the paratroopers;

None hit the silk as he.

This was not his first invasion, but it was his last.

He could have stayed in some other place, but it's more peaceful where he now lies.

One hundred and thirty odd times he'd felt the cold chill of the prop –

Never again for him.

Colonel Johnson's parachute days are through.

Lean, tough paratroopers of his Geronimo band stand at attention amid the cold grey crosses.

Death to them was no stranger –

Yet burial was.

So that's what they do with the ones that fall; we thought they just lay where they fell.

Farther in the field grey soldiers of another army stand as ghosts to mock the dead.

They are the PWs, the grave diggers,

Who must love their job.

He shouldn't be lonesome here.

He has so much company, acres and acres, beneath the damp cold earth.

They should understand his faint whispers, men of the 101st and 82nd Airborne.

Yet somehow he looks lonesome.

The Chaplain has said his word, the volley is fired, the generals file past his grave.

Now the other ranks file off slowly.

They pass among the rows, careful not to disturb the sleeping.

Case, Baldwin, Serawatka, Kane, Parrish, McMorries;

Each pauses at his grave, gazes in at the camouflaged parachute the king sleeps in.

It looks cold down there; wonder if he'll keep warm.

Slowly the moving picture camera clicks away, recording the procedure;

But never could it record the feelings of the tough men who pass the grave.

No pity, no tears.

They had lived too long for that, saw death too often.

Three of the men who pass that way, their guns have killed over thirty in one day.

Somehow it's wrong.

Maybe a year ago it would have been easy to figure.

Geronimo is dead
This classic portrait of the CO of the 501st, Colonel Howard R. Johnson, was made during the regiment's training in the States. Johnson's death sent shock waves through the 501st. *Amburgey*

But now it's too late; you only know that as soon as the last man of the honor guard files past you will go back to the line and the only life you do understand, war.

No, he is not going back.

Propellor blasts have died away.

His parachute days are through.

Yes, there will be a telegram;

Oh! but if she only knew.

The sun is getting lower, the words they speak are few.

Yet each trooper's thought lingers on Geronimo,

King of the parachute crew.

Mission of Mercy

On the night of 22/23 October, the larger of two rescue operations was launched across the Neder Rhine, to evacuate the last British "paras" who had survived the Arnhem slaughter. With help from Dutch civilians who hid the men in houses and barns for over a month, with little food, the British troopers had hidden in the vicinity of Renkum/Doorwerth. Most of the rescue detail was recruited from E/506th, but G/501st men and members of several other companies were also involved.

The rescuers followed white engineer tapes to the shore and were ferried across the river by Canadian engineers. Bofors guns fired tracers as a diversion, and a Morse "V" was flashed from the far shore with a red flashlight.

Firing on the enemy shore was forbidden. The rescuers moved forward with knives at the ready.

Tex McMorries of G/501st was involved in one of the crossings, and in the larger operation, about 130 British paras and a few Allied fliers were rescued. Tex wrote:

The survivors were starved and exhausted to the point that only a thread separated them from insanity and for some, the thread broke. But still, they had the pride of being a trooper, and I think this carried them the extra hour and day that salvaged them from destruction and insanity.

The Incredible Patrol

Near the end of October, the S-2, 501st dispatched a patrol that crossed the Neder Rhine below Renkum in darkness to capture a prisoner. Lieutenant Hugo S. Sims had conceived the patrol, which in fact returned with 31 prisoners. Sims had been disappointed in the efforts of various companies to cross and return with a prisoner, so he requested that he be allowed to lead this patrol himself, "as a stimulus to the battalions." Colonel Ewell initialed his approval on the written request, and Sims selected six of his best men to make the patrol.

Sergeant Peter Frank, a French- and German-speaking soldier who came from Belgium, would accompany Sergeant Bill Canfield, Robert O. Nicolai, Roland J. Wilbur, and Frederick J. "Ted" Becker.

The patrol members blackened their faces, wore wool caps, and carried Tommy guns and .45-caliber pistols, except Wilbur, who was known to shoot for the head with his M-1.

Using aerial photos, Sims had selected landmarks in advance with the patrol reaching each one at a pre-planned time. Occupying a house on the Utrecht-Arnhem highway, the patrol stayed there for most of the following day, capturing numerous German soldiers who entered the dwelling unaware that it was occupied by Americans.

Later, a truck containing 13 *Waffen-SS* artillerymen was captured with all aboard, and the troopers prepared to drive back to the river with their growing bag of captives. A *Waffen-SS* captain arrived in a *Schwimmwagen* (amphibious jeep) to look for his missing truckload of men. He was added to the collection. The group drove toward the river until the truck broke down. Then the group marched briskly, passing other Germans who thought the Americans were prisoners.

The German prisoners complained about the brisk marching speed, and the *SS* captain bolted away into the woods but was apprehended and returned to the group by Nicolai, who administered a few swift kicks to the captain's posterior. Passing in a marching formation right through the town of Renkum, the group cleaned out a few German outposts on the riverbank, then blinked their signal for pickup to the friendly shore. Rowboats came across, manned by men who had volunteered because they were strong swimmers.

Ed Hallo of A/501st was among them and recalled that two troopers manned each boat. On the return trip, two prisoners rode in the center of each boat, rowing, while the Americans fore and aft guarded them. Eventually, all 31 prisoners and the patrol members arrived safely on the south shore.

Only two (warning) shots had been fired on the entire patrol. The prisoners were taken south to the "Slob Farm" along a canal northeast of Zetten for interrogation. Lieutenant Werner Meier had his work cut out for him in questioning this big batch, and Lieutenant Joseph Pangerl, the 502nd IPW officer, drove up from Dodewaard to view the catch.

This patrol received widespread publicity throughout the ETO and earned Sims a DSC, followed shortly by promotion to captain. The other patrol members received the Silver Star.

Life at Dodewaard

Southeast of Opheusden, elements of the 502nd held the southwest flank of the division line near Dodewaard. Action in the area was mostly limited to patrolling, and many men were killed or wounded by the thousands of German land mines planted in the area.

A press photographer visited this sector during October and told Schuyler Jackson that he wanted to get

The Slob Farm
The Slob Farm on the canal near Zetten, Holland, as it looked in 1944. This was used as POW interrogation site. The building has since been torn down.

Return of the Incredible Patrol

A view inside the Slob Farm (a POW interrogation site) soon after the return of the 501st's Incredible Patrol, showing Lieutenant Werner Meier (right) with some of the captives. Waffen-SS Captain Walter Gartner, CO of *1st Battalion, SS Artillery Regiment 502* (part of *II SS-Panzer Corps*), is visible with M-43 cap and fur collar at left. Joe Pangerl, the 502nd PIR's IPW officer motored up to see the large group of prisoners. Pangerl was stationed at Dodewaard at the time he took this photo. *Pangerl*

a great action photo. At a loss for what to do, the men decided to "stage" a picture. They planted some C-2 explosive rigged with a remote detonator in a nice pile of mud and positioned one trooper to the rear of it. The trooper struck a pose with his weapon at the ready and at a given signal, the charge was detonated. The photographer snapped a still photo of the explosion and the photo was later published in many books, newspapers, and magazines. The caption said the picture showed an American paratrooper near Arnhem, advancing under 88mm fire. It was hailed as one of the great action shots of WWII.

Gone without a trace

In 1989, the de Hartogs showed the author the former site of the Slob Farm. It used to be on the bank of this canal.

A Tragic Accident

On 22 October at Dodewaard, Sergeant George Sheppard of the 502nd regimental demolitions platoon was unwinding wire from a German "Riegel" antitank mine. Nearby was a large pile of the mines that had been recently recovered from the surrounding terrain. The mine in his hand exploded; this touched off the entire pile. Lieutenant Richard Daly and all present, except two, were killed immediately. Oresti "Rusty" Quirici had a metal-covered bible in his chest pocket that stopped a piece of shrapnel, but Rusty was blown into the nearby canal. One of his buddies, Corporal Robert Brigham, lived until the following day, then died. Quirici, the sole survivor of the blast, visited Holland in September 1994, with

his metal-covered Bible. Also killed in the blast were Ed Ambrose, Joe St. Clair, Joseph Hill, and Warren Grunert. Staff Sergeant Oswald Schlensker was killed later the same afternoon while lifting a mine one-fourth mile away from the location of the earlier accident.

A Little Humor

Lieutenant Ed Wierzbowski of H/502nd had survived the nightmarish fight near the canal with Joe Mann outside of Best. In the late 1960s, Lieutenant "Whizbow," as he was nicknamed, sent a humorous story to the *Chapie Hall Newsletter* (the 502nd veterans' newsletter), recalling an incident at Dodewaard:

… the Power that be decided that the boys were out of condition, having spent so much time on the front lines. The order came down that H Company would have a period of exercise. Naturally, the assignment was mine. At any rate, as I called the company to attention, out of the corner of my eye, I saw a couple of my boys walking across the farmyard with two Dutch girls. (I won't mention their names, but they are well remembered, I can assure you.) Coming from the barn where they had spent the night teaching the girls my name (that's what they told me) … so there we are, the company at attention and me waiting for these characters to join the ranks. When suddenly the girls began to shout (bowing and grinning all the time) "*Gut Morgen* Lieutenant Chickashit, *Gut Morgen* Lieutenant Chickashit." They were grinning so much that it broke everyone up as well as the P.T. session.

IPW Teams

Captain Joe Pangerl *(left)*, IPW Team #1, was an excellent prisoner interrogator for Lieutenant Colonel Steve Chappuis's 502nd. The IPW teams were a part of each regiment in the ETO and performed a vital function in obtaining unit identifications; troop dispositions and strengths; order of battle; and other facts from German prisoners. Many of the interrogators were first or second-generation immigrants from Europe, and many were Jewish. The team usually consisted of one or two officers (a captain and a lieutenant) and four enlisted men (usually a master sergeant, a staff sergeant, and two technicians). During the first week of the Holland invasion, all of the regiments had an ample supply of prisoners and myriad German units were identified from the disintegrating German *Fifteenth Army. Pangerl*

Deadeye

Glen A. Derber of the Light Machine Gun Platoon, HQ/2nd/501st, is shown sighting down an M-1919A4 light machine gun. Glen engaged in long-range dueling using a Springfield M-1903A3 rifle on the Island in October 1944. *Derber*

3rd/502nd Company Commanders At Dodewaard

Sitting: Champ Baker, Company I (with first-aid kit on his helmet); Ralph Watson, Company G. *Standing:* Robert Jones, Company H; Frank Lillyman, HQ Co/3rd, in Elst, Holland. *Author's Photo*

The Death of Ben Shaub

Another prime example of the lives lost resulting from the numerous land mines sown near Dodewaard is to be found in the screening patrol launched toward the canal below Opheusden by F/502nd.

The patrol reached a Dutch house near the canal embankment and stayed in position for several hours, calling in reports on a radio. Near the house was a minefield that had been swept by the 326th AEB; red flags marked the numerous mines that were located but not yet removed.

Looking into the basement of the house through an open door revealed a three-step stairwell leading to a wooden table. Stuck into the top of the table was a beautiful Nazi dagger of some sort.

"Don't even go down there," Joe Pistone cautioned his men. It was almost certain that the stairs or the dagger itself were booby-trapped to explode.

Chow Time

The 1st/502nd chow line at Dodewaard, Holland, October 1944. *Molsberry*

Thanks for a Job Well Done
Lieutenant General Sir Miles Dempsey, commander of the British Second Army in Holland, addressed a contingent of troopers from subunits throughout the division, thanking them for a job well done. *Krochka*

Ignoring the warning, Ben Shaub, who had earned the Silver Star in Normandy for his heroic decimation of a German artillery battery, walked onto the front lawn of the house. There was a loud explosion, and the men looked out to see Shaub lying on the lawn with one foot blown off below the ankle. Leaves were fluttering down from the trees from the concussion of the blast.

Without hesitation for his own safety, Private Andrew Hemrock walked out onto the lawn and grabbed Shaub under both arms. He began dragging him back.

Another explosion rocked the area, and Hemrock fell wounded with an identical wound. The second blast had also inflicted a critical wound to Shaub's head and upper body.

A medic named Knapp, who had replaced Baker after Normandy, braved the mined lawn, walking out and giving both of the wounded men shots of morphine.

The medic received help from four or five men who dragged the wounded troopers back to a clearing where there were no mines. A half hour later, more troopers arrived with stretchers and carried the wounded men out. As Hemrock was leaving, he lay on the stretcher, smiling and twirling a Dutch derby hat on a bayonet blade. Hemrock's indomitable spirit was an inspiration to his buddies, but Ben Shaub, the hero of Normandy, was dying.

"Hank Gogola's Night Vigil"

While on guard duty in the basement of a house southwest of Coffin Corner, Henry Gogola, B/506th, had a memorable experience on the night of 12

November:

This night is still vivid in my memory – though I'm reluctant to talk about it, I'll never forget it. We were on forward outpost duty in a farmhouse from which we could see the blown-out railroad bridge at Coffin Corner.

It was the platoon C.P. and was also used as an artillery observation post for the 321st GFAB. We had foxholes which were manned at night, I guess, as listening posts to our front between us and the River-Lower Rhine.

There were rumors of the British paratrooper survivors attempting to get back through our lines, from across the river. At that time, I had inherited the position of phone and wire man. We had phones installed in the foxholes for the night so they could keep in touch with the C.P., what with artillery and mortar shells, which were occasionally thrown our way. They had the uncanny knack of blowing some of the phone lines. I would have to go out and feel around for the wires and splice them together again. Talk about Blind Man's Bluff [*sic*]! On your hands and knees, feeling around for wires, dark as a cat's ass, every little noise making your stomach quiver, and wanting to jump out of your shoes. Not exactly what I would call a picnic, but it had to be done. As a result of this, I had very little, if any, sleep in 72 hours, which I know was not uncommon. Several nights in a row, crawling around like that can make you a little hyper, and you tend to have a little difficulty sleeping anyway. Well, that particular night, groggy but not sleepy, I had just finished checking the outposts, and with the new relief in place and the others sacked out in the basement, we were in. It was a two-room affair, with a wall between them, and a doorway leading to either room. I was in the room away from the stairway, the others were sacked out in the room where the stairs leading up were. Lieutenant Long was at the Company C.P. at the time. John Garrigan was on guard duty at the barn door overlooking the yard, when I heard footsteps coming from upstairs. I thought it was the lieutenant coming back; instead, it was Johnny coming down to tell me that a Kraut patrol was in the yard, milling about. We started to try stirring up the others, but it was too late. A tall, shadowy figure had already come down carrying a hand generated flashlight, which he kept pumping to keep it lit.

I had put out the candles we had lit before he came down, so it was pitch black in the basement. John had come into the room I was in and I guess the Krauts only saw the men sacked out. "Hands up," he shouted, still pumping away at the flashlight. John, meanwhile, kept moving back and forth between me and the doorway. I had a P38 pistol in my hand, and stood in the doorway, but a little bit back from it. John moved in front of me as the Kraut shouted "Hands up" again. I shoved John away from me, and I recall saying "Hands up, your ASS," at the same time he turned toward me, felt my hand jerk three times, without realizing that I had shot at him. I couldn't miss, as he was no more than three feet in front of me. He fell like a poled ox at my feet, and I knelt down, feeling for the pistol in his hand. I grabbed it and shouted out to the others, who were awake by now, to hold their fire and to cover the stairway. The other Krauts had scattered, as the shots were fired, and were still around in the yard. The man I shot was an SS sergeant, but the rest of the patrol must have been inexperienced. They were in front of the building by now, and seemed to be arguing about what to do. Suddenly, one of them fired his machine pistol, when I felt a hot sting across my right temple; I fell to the floor. Talk about seeing a new galaxy of stars, it still remains unnamed to this day! I finally got up and went to the phone to call the company C.P., to tell them that we were under attack, and to send a medic. I guess that by this time, the others, as they awoke, took over and caused the Krauts to scatter back to their lines. Things were a little hazy for me, as I was nursing a king-sized headache by now. I know that I was taken to the medics to have my head wound taken care of, and I was questioned as to what had happened. After that, I rested awhile and was anxious to get back to see how the others made out. I returned at daylight and as I was walking through the yard, I saw the body of the man I had killed. There was a giant of an old sow pig nibbling at it; what a disgusting sight. The rest of the platoon were glad to see me back, and filled me in on what had happened after I left. Still without any sleep to speak of, Lieutenant Long left orders that I be relieved and ordered me to sack out for as long as I needed to. I must have slept on and off, for about 18 hours. Thanks, I needed that! I still can't figure out how that Kraut patrol got through our outposts. To this day, whenever we get together at reunions, those involved in that incident won't let me forget it, and I wish they would stop it already. It was no big deal, and no one, to my knowledge, got hurt except me. I was just a crabby, overtired dogface, who lashed out at the first thing that stood in my way.

Withdrawal and the First Shower in 72 Days

The 501st had just left its dike positions when the Germans placed an aerial bomb in the dike at the curve east of Coffin Corner. They blew open the dike and the current of the Neder Rhine sent water rushing under the railroad viaduct and flooding the land behind the dike as far west as Opheusden. Much of the area was under water for over six months, until Canadian engineers repaired the dike with bulldozers in 1945.

It was late November, and the 101st Airborne Division was being withdrawn to go into reserve at the new location of the First Allied Airborne Army at Reims, France. Assorted divisions and airborne battalions from throughout the ETO were being consolidated there.

The area east of Opheusden was already flooding when Don Burgett's buddies were finally evacuated. They had been issued empty five-gallon gas cans to use as emergency flotation devices, and were perched on rooftops "like chickens on a roost," when Canadian engineers picked them up in boats. Don and friends were taken to a monastery equipped with a field shower and had their first shower in 72 days before leaving the Island for good.

MARKET-GARDEN in Retrospect –
One Trooper's Summary

Leonard Swartz and Georgie Dietz
Leonard Swartz, regimental mail clerk of the 502nd, with Georgie Dietz, a nine-year-old from Andelst, Holland, in early October. Georgie was later killed by a German bomb while playing in the street. *Musura*

General Taylor visits the Currahee Regiment

General Taylor chats with a 2nd/506th medic during Holland inspection. The tall officer with hands clasped behind his back is Colonel Sink. Dick Winters is to the immediate left of Sink. *Photo courtesy Winters*

After leaving Holland, Dick Ladd, 502nd S-2 section, wrote:

Market-Garden, indeed an imaginative strategy … an abortive end run around the Siegfried Line, could have worked. We, the Airborne, were the "magic carpet" over which the British Second Army was to roll. Unfortunately, a combination of poor geographical planning (operation predicated on one sole corridor highway), and poor British tactics…Regarding the latter, the British Army had no dash nor vigor in moving with alacrity, or smashing and bypassing resistance. When a lead tank or armored car was hit or "brewed up," their armored units seldom seemed to react or maneuver the way American armor or German panzer elements responded. So much for learning much in the desert from Rommel. British Infantry – excellent fighters, tough to dislodge if they didn't want to go. However, I suspect that many priggish officers and class-conscious ways mitigated against effective relationships with their men. Consequence was the British Second Army languishing in a dead-end corridor until early February 1945. A lot of troops, gas, and material expended at the expense of a breakthrough to the Rhine by George Patton's Third Army… but Monty had his way with Ike.

Flooded Foxholes

Sergeant Ed Benecke, A/377th, in his dugout near Elst, Holland, in November 1944. The Germans had blown the dike near Coffin Corner, and water was starting to seep into the foxholes, causing the men to build up higher with crates and discarded materials to get above the new water table. *Benecke*

The new location of the First Allied Airborne Army's US troops was in the vicinity of Reims, France. The 101st Airborne Division, along with the 82nd Airborne, was garrisoned outside of Reims to recuperate and refit after being withdrawn from Holland. Replacements were to be absorbed into the existing units, and weapons were to be replaced along with other worn-out equipment.

The 101st was situated in stone French Army barracks, which had more recently housed German armored troops. Large murals of nude women had been painted on the walls of the mess hall by the former German tenants. One of the regimental chaplains deemed that the murals were morally unfit for the troops to gaze upon while eating and ordered them painted over. The stone billets of the 101st were in the town of Mourmelon le Grand. On the other side of Reims, the 82nd was stationed at Camp Suippes. Numerous other small, independent airborne units were also assembled near Reims.

The barracks at Mourmelon had a toilet and sewage system of sorts, but this proved inadequate when an outbreak of dysentery suddenly afflicted dozens of troopers. The epidemic was caused by tainted food – some leftover turkey brought out of Holland and other mystery meat served at the new base camp. While a big football game was scheduled and awaited between the 502nd and the 506th (The "Champagne Bowl"), some troops were sent on three-day passes to Paris. Other troops invaded the city of Reims, and the inevitable mayhem erupted when the Screaming Eagles clashed with 82nd All-Americans after consuming copious amounts of wine, cognac, and other assorted spirits. Shots were fired, entire bars were temporarily commandeered by US paratroopers, fights broke out, troopers swung from crystal chandeliers or made demonstration jumps from third-floor balconies, MPs were attacked and disarmed, and a strict schedule was established to ensure that soldiers of the 82nd and 101st went to town on different, alternating nights.

In his book, *Those Devils in Baggy Pants,* Ross Carter of the 82nd Airborne's 504th PIR wrote:

When eventually we did get passes to Reims, the troopers took the town by storm. We left a shameful record for which I apologize to all Frenchmen, but I think part of the blame should be farmed out to the top brass. After all, old fighting men should not be treated like recruits. But maybe it would have happened anyway. I'm afraid that the people of Reims will henceforth judge the American way of life by our conduct. They would be wrong of course, but after all, most people form opinions on what they see and hear, and the citizens of Reims saw plenty. It is unfortunate that most of them didn't understand what they heard.

The two-buckle combat boots had been forced upon the jumpers before they went to Holland. This became an extra sore spot in late 1944, when the troopers came out of combat in Holland to discover rear echelon, non-jumping personnel walking around wearing jump boots. Most straight-leg officers were also wearing jump boots.

Don Burgett recalled:

We couldn't get jump boots, and we were the paratroopers. A guy in my company [Slick Hoenscheidt]

saw a major in Reims wearing jump boots. This hit him at the wrong time, and he proceeded to just beat the hell out of this major. He said, "You non-jumping, rear-echelon son of a bitch! It's 'cause of people like you that we can't get jump boots."

After he beat the major up, Slick took a knife and cut the boots off the major's feet. MPs were called, and they arrested Slick. Lieutenant Borelli came to the stockade, vouched for Slick, and got him released, telling him to go straight back to camp. But Slick stopped off in a bar to have a quick drink *en route* back. Coming out the door, he came face to face with the same major, whose eyes were black and face all puffed-up. The major started screaming for MPs, but Slick took off running and escaped. That major later circulated wanted posters around the ETO, trying to locate Slick so he could bring charges against him.

Division CP, Mourmelon le Grand

This brick building was the 101st's HQ for almost three weeks. Ed Hallo, A/501st, had the detail to lower the flag on the roof each evening. *Benecke*

Rest And Recuperation

These 101st Airborne IPW officers had a brief recuperation period at Camp Mourmelon, France, late in 1944 *(left to right):* Loeffler, Al Gion, Vidor, Werner "Mike" Meier, Kipnis, Schwisow, and Pangerl. Werner Meier detected a sense of antagonism from his CO, Colonel Johnson, along with a lack of appreciation of the importance of the job the IPW teams had to do. Meier felt that Johnson's ruthless attitude toward the enemy, which was transferred to many of his troops, contributed to more deaths – on both sides. After Johnson's tragic death in October 1944, Meier worked with Lieutenant Colonel Ewell, the new CO, in a better spirit of cooperation. Meier recalls asking the troopers to take more prisoners so he would have more material to work with to gain information. "Don't forget," Meier later said, "many of our troopers were 'mean machines.' A little bit of pressure on the trigger meant the difference between a live prisoner and a corpse." Other factors, however, contributed to the dearth of prisoners: Joe Pistone, F/502nd, recalls capturing a badly-wounded German officer who refused a blood transfusion because it wasn't pure Aryan blood. As a result, the German bled to death. *Pangerl*

The Unforeseen Counteroffensive

Ever since the humiliating defeat of his *Seventh Army* near Chambois, Hitler had contemplated a massive counteroffensive to turn the tide of the fighting in Europe. A massive attack hurled against a thinly-held sector could drive to Antwerp, capture a coastal port, and perhaps inflict catastrophic casualties that would compel the Allies to sue for peace. Hitler also believed that the partnership between the US and the UK was tenuous and could be torn asunder by a massive German onslaught.

To this end, Hitler had overseen the rebuilding of many elite units that had been decimated in Normandy, including the *2nd* and *116th Panzer Divisions, the Panzer Lehr Division,* and the *1st, 2nd,* and *12th SS-Panzer Divisions.* By late fall 1944, Hitler had quietly moved these rebuilt divisions and massive numbers of tanks and other armored vehicles toward the weakest sector in the American front lines.

Operation *Watch on Rhine* (*Wacht am Rhein*) would launch this powerful counterthrust through the traditional German attack route of the Ardennes Forest in Belgium.

Rest Camps at Mourmelon.

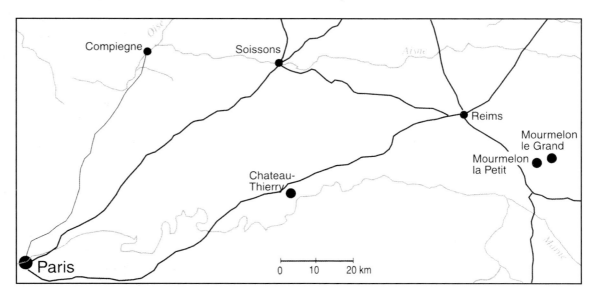

Mourmelon, before the Bulge

Donald Zahn (*left*, with BAR) and Lou Vecchi (with M1 carbine), members of H/506th, with an A-4 light machine gun in the rear, in December 1944.

Steve Chappuis makes Bird Colonel

At Camp Mourmelon in late 1944, General Taylor pinned a bird on the collar of Chappuis before the general left to attend a conference back in Washington, D.C. Chappuis assumed command of the 502nd after Colonel Mike Michaelis was wounded twice and evacuated from Holland. *Chappuis*

Two green American infantry divisions held the north-south line from Monschau to the Schnee Eifel area – the 99th and 106th Infantry Divisions. Below them were two veteran divisions, battle weary from the drive across western Europe and the recent fighting around Aachen and the Hürtgen Forest, the 28th and 4th Infantry Divisions. Elements of the green 9th Armored Division, 14th Cavalry Group, and other small units were also on the line in the Ardennes front area.

By early December 1944, Hitler's target area was most definitely narrowed down to the Ardennes front, scene of the most successful part of the German offensive in 1940. Other factors – surprise, fog, and the worst weather of any western European winter since 1900 – would all be of help to Hitler's offensive. The quiet sector just west of the German frontier was about to explode.

The Battle of the Bulge Begins

Just before dawn on 16 December 1944, massive German artillery barrages heralded the opening of Hitler's Operation *Watch on the Rhine*. Hitler's *Sixth Panzer Army*—mainly consisting of the *I* and *II SS-Panzer Corps*—followed the thundering barrage on the northern sector, with tanks and infantry swarming along the roads south of Monschau. The 99th Infantry Division, although inexperienced, held firmly at the northern shoulder, soon joined by the 2nd

Infantry Division and then the 1st Infantry Division. They stopped the drive of the *12th SS* in front of the Elsenborn Ridge and massed artillery to kill hundreds of *SS* troopers at Dom Butgenbach. Just south of there, however, *Waffen-SS* Lieutenant Colonel Jochen Peiper's combat group of the *1st SS Panzer Division* was driving madly westward, through Lanzerath, Honsfeld, Bullingen, then skirting south of the city of Malmédy. At the Baugnez crossroads, members of the *1st SS* opened fire on a group of over 100 unarmed American POWs in a snowy field; some 86 were killed and a few others feigned death, later managing to escape to tell the tale. Word of this massacre spread quickly throughout the Ardennes, which only ensured Allied retaliation and bolstered US resolve to achieve vengeance through victory.

More German armored spearheads broke through the lines in the Schnee Eifel, destroying two regiments of the 106th Infantry Division. To the south, elements of the *Fifth Panzer Army* were pushing the stubborn 28th Infantry Division westward and driving toward Bastogne. After desperate fighting to delay the Germans at St. Vith, the 7th Armored Division eventually withdrew. The Allies had definitely been caught by surprise, and the largest pitched battle of the ETO had begun.

At 0400 on 18 December 1944, the 101st Airborne's troopers were nestled snugly in their beds at Camp Mourmelon, when unit leaders walked in and yelled, "Wake up and start getting ready; we're moving out!"

Don Burgett, A/506th, heard a noncom yell, "Pack your seaborne rolls!" This meant only one thing – a return to combat.

In F/501's area, Sergeant McKenney was shouting, "Pack three rolls; we're moving out!"

Lieutenant Sefton at D/501st was sound asleep when Captain Snodgrass shook him and said, "Get up! We're committed; we're going in." Sefton recalled:

I thought it was a lousy joke and suggested a couple of things he could do, but he finally convinced me that we were alerted, and we were going somewhere. Information at the company level was hazy, but we thought we were going in to exploit a breakthrough, which in view of the history of the war up to that point, seemed a very logical explanation of all the haste and urgency.

Leo Gillis, who had recently been transferred into Staff Sergeant Joe Kenney's home for wayward souls (2nd Platoon, E/501st), recalled the chaos and shortage of equipment:

We heard all kinds of rumors, that the Germans had run over an entire American Army and they couldn't be stopped…It was a real gaffed-up affair as far as equipment was concerned. Everything had been turned in after Holland. If you got a rifle you were lucky, if you got an entrenching tool, you were fabulously lucky. Clothing, boots, overcoats were all at a minimum.

Many recently-arrived replacements had not yet completed their unit training and been assimilated into their companies; the coming fight would quickly make veterans of all of them. Some men, like members of the 501st's band, had been kept out of combat in the previous missions. They viewed this as possibly their last opportunity to fight in WWII. They asked Father Sampson for permission to join the combat troops, but he refused to give them permission. On the other hand, he didn't deny them permission. They quietly made their way to their former companies and went to battle. Bob Robertson, a drummer with C/501st, would be seriously wounded by artillery in the *Bois Jacques*. Julius Schrader returned to Company I from the band and survived the battle of

Wardin. Unlike many others, he was not captured.

Late-war fatalism had set in with some individuals. Sergeant Fletcher "Doc" Gainey, a buddy of Gillis's in F/501st, had a certain feeling that he would be killed or maimed in the coming battle. A. J. Sokol of A/327th was enjoying his last few seconds in a warm bunk when his friend, Sergeant Bennie Castleman, said, "You know, Andy, I don't think I'm gonna make it." (A direct hit by a mortar shell on 10 January 1945 would blow off Gainey's leg at the hip. Castleman was killed by artillery fire on Christmas morning.)

Major General Maxwell Taylor, was not present when the division moved out. He had returned for a conference in Washington D.C. following operations in Holland. In Taylor's absence, Brigadier General Anthony C. "Tony" McAuliffe, the division artillery commander, would serve as acting division CG.

Scores of 101st troopers were visiting Paris when the alert was called, and Major Cecil L. Simmons was assigned to round them up and put them on a train back to Mourmelon.

Starting at midday and continuing into the evening of 18 December, units of the 101st loaded onto large, open-backed semi trucks and departed Mourmelon for Belgium, a trip of over 200 miles. General McAuliffe and an advance party rode up ahead of the division. The 82nd Airborne had also been alerted to move against the German forces in the Ardennes. They departed first, passing through the Belgian city of Bastogne and continuing northward to Werbomont. There they would dismount and head east to join the fighting at Cheneux and points south along the Ambleve River.

General Troy Middleton's VIII Corps headquarters had been in Bastogne, a town where seven roads and two railroad lines converge. The town had been liberated by the US Army back in September, but was now threatened by advancing units of the *Fifth Panzer Army*. Being a road and rail center in the path of the German breakthrough, it was logically an important place to establish a defense. Thus, with the 82nd Airborne already gone to the north, arriving trucks bearing the 101st Airborne were diverted to fields west of Bastogne, near Mande Saint-Etienne and neighboring villages. The troops would jump off their trucks, crawl under the pine trees, and get a few hours of chilly sleep before moving out.

Gillis recalled the truck ride from Mourmelon:

Bastogne Bound

Lieutenant Corey Shepard, I/502nd; Lieutenant Ralph Watson, G/502nd; and Sergeant Graham Armstrong, S-2, 502nd (Armstrong later received a battlefield appointment to second lieutenant) leaving Mourmelon, France, on 18 December 1944. *Pangerl*

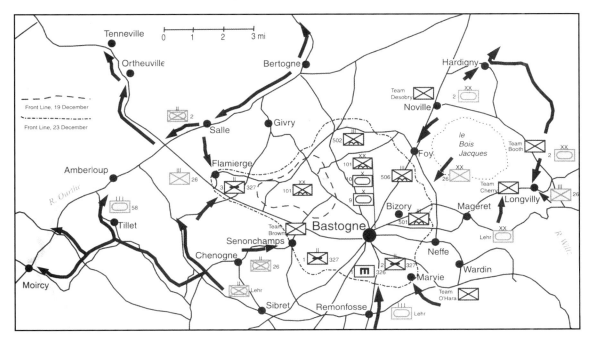

Siege of Bastogne.

We loaded onto these great big semis, and they were brand-new trucks. Brand new. I remember Ed Turer – we had said goodbye to him in the hospital. We were in the trucks, we were moving, going down the road, and here comes Turer, running along behind us, with his hospital pajamas on, wearing boots, not laced up. We pulled him aboard the truck. Even though he was real sick when we saw him in the hospital, he decided that he wasn't as sick as he thought he was.

The troops were forced to stand up during the 12-hour drive; after darkness, the convoy hurtled on with headlights ablaze in violation of usual blackout procedures.

The 101st Airborne and *Fifth Panzer Army* weren't the only military units converging on Bastogne at that moment. Elements of the 9th and 10th Armored Divisions, VIII Corps Artillery, and two engineer battalions also took part in the defense of Bastogne.

Stragglers from miscellaneous units who chose to stay and fight at Bastogne were organized into Team SNAFU. By 21 December, German forces completely encircled Bastogne. The defending garrison would successfully hold out against elements of seven German divisions until 26 December, when relief forces of the Third Army would break through from the south.

The 101st Airborne provided some 11,000 of the town's defenders, but an approximately equal number were provided by all the miscellaneous units also trapped there.

That night, near Margaret, east of Bastogne, Team Cherry of the US 10th Armored Division had played a crucial role in delaying the *Panzer Lehr* Division from entering Bastogne from the east. The resultant delays gave the 501st time to move east from Bastogne and meet *Panzer Lehr* head on in the mor-ning, some miles east of Bastogne. There, the intrepid paratroopers, aided by 105mm howitzers of the 907th and men and vehicles of Team Cherry, were able to stop the *Panzer Lehr.*

As paratroopers moved out near dawn, they were sent to various towns surrounding Bastogne, small villages where the actual defensive fighting would take place. A ring of defenses was formed all around Bastogne, with the last arriving units, the 502nd and the 327th, positioned near the debarking area, west of Bastogne. Colonel Cooper's 463rd PFAB with 75mm howitzers had recently joined the 101st at Camp Mourmelon. The 463rd was equipped with special howitzer loads with which they had successfully knocked out German tanks and halftracks in Italy and France. Their new colleagues were skep-

tical of these tales but would soon see proof that the 463rd could KO armor with their little pack howitzers.

The 506th went north, with 2nd and 3rd Battalions digging in between the railroad line east of Foy, and the woods south of Recogne. The 1st/506th continued north to Noville. The 501st went east, directly in the path of the German approach. The 327th took the entire southern edge of the perimeter from southeast to southwest, with the 326th AEB in support. The 502nd held the western and northwestern portions of the perimeter, and most of the artillery units were positioned west of Bastogne.

As paratroopers, many without weapons, moved forward to meet the enemy, they passed hundreds of retreating infantrymen and scores of vehicles from tanks and halftracks, to jeeps. Some men tried to borrow a weapon from the retreating troops, without success. One paratrooper was carrying a large tree branch. He shook it aggressively in the direction of the enemy for the benefit of those going the opposite way. "By this evening I'm gonna have me a Mauser rifle," he said.

Tommy Thomas of F/501st was armed only with a nightstick he had "liberated" from an MP in Reims. He was twirling it in contempt of the oncoming German might as his unit marched toward Bizory.

Emerson Rhodes saw retreating troops race past, clinging to a westbound jeep. "You'll be sooorrrrryyyy" they called.

A major in a retreating vehicle called out "You'll never stop 'em boys!"

"We're going to have a try at it, sir," replied Lyle Snyder of F/501st.

Moving toward Bizory, Sergeant Joe Bass of the 501st encountered a retreating halftrack, driven by a lieutenant. Bass stopped the vehicle, pointed his M-1 at the officer and said "You can go, lieutenant, but you're leaving that vehicle here!"

Thus, Bass commandeered a halftrack which later came in handy for hauling heavy weapons and ammunition. His men would later drive it as far as Alsace.

By morning of 19 December 1944, the stage had been set for the Battle of Bastogne, one of the most dramatic battles of American military history.

Some of the troopers passed the road signs and asked, "What's a 'Bas-TOG-neee?' "

Jim "Pee-Wee" Martin of G/506th had a premonition, however. "Take a good look at the name on that sign," he told his friends, "because we're gonna make history here."

The village of Noville, Belgium, lies some five to six miles north of Bastogne, and on 19 December, it was being held by troops of the 10th Armored Division, soldiers under the command of Major William Desobry. Elements of the *2nd Panzer Division* were bypassing Noville to the north in their westward drive, but by holding the village, the road coming into Bastogne from the north was blocked. Desobry was already asking for permission to withdraw his forces from Noville. He was told to hold it as long as possible, however, and that a battalion of paratroopers would be sent north to reinforce him. This was the 1st/506th. While in Noville, the 1st/506th CO would be killed by an artillery hit on his CP. Major Bob Harwick would replace LaPrade as battalion CO.

Company A led 1st/506th's northward march from Bastogne to Noville, and passed the smaller village of Foy *en route*. At the side of the road, a jeep trailer had been parked, filled with bandoliers of ammunition, some grenades, and boxes of loose .45-cal. ball ammo. The ammunition was handed to troopers as they walked past. Many were still without a weapon. Don Burgett was handed several handfuls of loose .45-cal. ammo, which he stuffed into his pockets for his pistol. His former platoon sergeant, Staff Sergeant Ted Vetland had just rejoined the regiment after being wounded in Holland. Vetland was among those entering Noville without a weapon, but

he would later borrow Charlie Syers's bazooka and venture out in the thick fog, firing three rockets at as many German tanks. Vetland was awarded the Silver Star for crippling one of them and knocking out another.

Thick fog, formerly an asset to the Germans in their surprise offensive, had grounded Allied planes. At Noville, however, it would enable the outnumbered American forces to survive in the face of massive German manpower and tanks. The lightly-armed paratroopers would find themselves in the midst of this mighty force, always outnumbered and outgunned, but their invisibility in the pea soup mists protected them.

To Don Burgett, "The fog was like looking into a glass of milk." To Hank DiCarlo, who fought nearby at Foy, "The fog went up and down like a theater curtain."

The German tanks often emitted little engine noise, even when driving past, and sometimes the fog would lift to reveal an enemy tank only 15 to 20 feet away from an occupied American foxhole.

As the battalion marched up toward Noville, Colonel Sink spotted Staff Sergeant Charles A. Mitchell leading the 3rd Platoon of B/506th. Sink took him aside and already knew that Mitch was soon to receive a battlefield appointment to second lieutenant. Sink told him, "Sergeant Mitchell, before morning, you're gonna see more Kraut tanks than you've ever seen before. You're going to want to leave, but you're going to remember that I told you not to..."

With this grim forecast, Mitchell and the rest of his battalion moved up to carry out a seemingly suicidal assignment: hold Noville until authorized to withdraw, regardless of the odds.

After arriving in town, Companies A and C of the 506th went east to occupy a ridge of high ground outside the village. After crossing a wide field, they climbed the ridge to see many German tanks facing them right on the opposite slope. Company C troopers ran down the hill to the east edge of Noville, followed by direct fire from the tanks on the ridge. The enemy artillery continued to pound them as they dug in there.

During that long, long night spent at Noville, most of the troopers continued their struggle to stay alive, whether in the cellar of a Belgian farmhouse or in a frigid foxhole.

Don Straith lay in a cemetery on the north edge of town, sweating out incoming mortar shells until he was wounded and evacuated. His ambulance was ambushed while driving south and was the last one to get out of Bastogne before the town was completely encircled. Straith's helmet was nicked by a bullet that penetrated the ambulance.

Throughout the night, German armor passed through US positions and skirted the town. The thick fog continued to hide the Americans.

Don Burgett
Private Donald R. Burgett of A/506th survived Noville and fought in the woods between Luzery and the railroad track. *Burgett*

Withdrawing from Noville

When General McAuliffe finally authorized 1st/506th to pull out of Noville, they had made an epic 27-hour stand, denying the Germans entry on the northern approach to Bastogne. At 1315 on 20 December, the withdrawal began, with the numerous wounded loaded onto halftracks and any available vehicles. The men of C/506th had just led off when Lieutenant Joe Reed suddenly spotted a German position as the fog lifted momentarily. He shot the Germans point-blank with his Tommy gun. The fog once again proved an ally to the Americans, shielding the column until it was 500 yards short of Foy.

Kangaroo Headquarters

Divisional CP for the 101st Airborne during the Bastogne siege was in this complex of Belgian Army barracks just north of town. *Macri*

When the lead vehicle stopped suddenly, a multiple rear-end collision of armored vehicles took place, and German troops opened fire from ditches on both sides of the single, tree-lined road. The turret was blown off a tank, blocking the road, and the column skirted to the west of Foy. Some vehicles were manned by paratroopers who drove them or fired both the main guns and the machine guns toward the enemy in Foy. Sergeant Eugene Esquible of C/506th was outstanding in firing a .50-cal. machine gun mounted atop one of the tanks. Company A

Historic Figures

Several historic figures in the Bastogne drama hold aloft one of the more pristine signs for an official photo. *Left to right:* Major Paul Danahy (G-2), General Anthony McAuliffe, and Lieutenant Colonel Harry Kinnard (G-3). *US Army*

Temporary Graves
Temporary burial of American dead in the civilian cemetery in Bastogne; they would later be reinterred at Henri Chapelle or the US Cemetery in Luxembourg. *Krochka*

Among them was Father Delvaux, the village priest, who was the first man shot.

Luzery

Survivors of the Noville battle had barely arrived in the Luzery area north of Bastogne for some rest, when they were alerted to move out again. A weak battalion (about 250 men) from a *Volks-Grenadier* unit had worked in along the railroad line in the *Bois Jacques* forest and were now located in a patch of woods in the 506th sector. The 1st/506th was the only unit in reserve and was therefore available to root these Germans out. Marching north once again, the battalion reached a wooded area, turned right, and moved in to locate and destroy the enemy force. The battalion was seriously understrength: A/506th totaled 58 men still standing from the Noville fight, and C/506th was also drastically understrength.

Don Burgett describes some of the action:

We took turns on point acting as scouts, and Siber Speer and Alvarado led off. Speer could spot anything first with his keen eyesight, but he had a bad habit of shouting, "There they are! There they are!" We had tried to tell him just to open fire and hit the ground when he spotted Germans. He did the same thing this time. We were in a line of skirmishers with C/506th on our left. Lieutenant Borelli had his platoon to the left of 2nd Platoon.

Suddenly, Speer said, "There they are!" He pointed, but beyond another German who he didn't see – they were well-camouflaged in white. This man was just 20 feet in front of Speer and he shot him in the mouth. Speer was dead before he hit the ground. As the German worked his bolt, Alvarado shot him with a carbine. I never had much faith in the carbine. The German drove the bolt home and shot Alvarado. The impact of the bullet knocked the carbine from Alvarado's hands. As he was going down, Alvarado yanked

***Bois Jacques*, near Foy**
This foxhole scene was shot by Forrest Guth of E/506th. *Via Winters*

Clear Skies at Last

On 23 December, one day after the German surrender ultimatum was delivered, the fog lifted enabling troop-carrier planes to make a massive resupply drop. This view across the rooftops of Bastogne was recorded by Al Krochka. *Krochka*

his knife out of the sheath on his leg and he jumped forward the two or three steps, whatever it took, and he finished killing the German with the knife. Since Speer and Alvarado were between us and the Germans, we couldn't fire, but when the Germans were both killed, we went forward with the attack.

This was kind of a vicious attack. There were 58 of us and a platoon-size group from C/506th. Jack Bram and Jerry Janes were firing machine guns from the hip. Bram seemed to have a big anger that he hadn't displayed earlier in the war, and he was shouting, "I'm a Jew! Come on you Nazi bastards. I'll kill every one of you! I'm a Jew!"

Bielski also had a .30-caliber tripod-mounted machine gun. He would fire, lift the weapon, move it forward, flop down, and fire again. We would leapfrog past each other as we moved forward. The attack slowed down, and I rolled down into a shallow spot with Liddel. He said, "Well, Donnie Boy, we're in it now! We're amongst 'em."

At that moment, a tracer bullet which was just about spent, stuck in the tree between us. It was spewing these little sparks out. "Well, it's time to leave this place," said Liddel as he took off. As he did, I thought

he had kicked me. Later that night I discovered I had a bullet stuck in my hip bone. It wasn't all the way in, I was able to take it out. It was just about as spent as the tracer that had hit the tree.

The attack regained momentum. I saw one trooper rolling on the ground in hand-to-hand combat with a German. I couldn't get a clear shot at the German with my .45, but the trooper killed him. I went around to my right, came upon a young German, so close I didn't think I could miss. I fired point-blank at him, and it turned out that I did miss. He fired at me with his rifle and cut my helmet's chinstrap with the bullet. The buckle flipped up and hit me in the eye with such an impact that I was knocked down. I thought the bullet had passed through my head. He raised up out of the hole and worked the bolt. I was lying face down, and I knew he was going to give me another shot. Some of Borelli's men were coming around our left flank. The German swung around, aimed at one of them and fired. I brought my M-1 up while he was cranking the bolt, and I shot him through the left cheek. It came out the right side and took his whole ear off. He dropped straight down in the hole; I ran the two or three steps to him. I grabbed him,

How was the states, General?

This cutting question as well as his absence in the glory days of the Bastogne siege would haunt General Taylor to the end. Many who survived those days could not forget the general's presence in Washington, D.C., when the German breakthrough happened. *Musura*

199

Meeting in Noville, 15 January 1945. General Maxwell Taylor met with staff officers in Noville. *Musura*

threw him down on the edge of the hole, and laid my rifle across him, used him as a sandbag as I shot at two more Germans.

About that time, Dobrich to my left fired at the German running from our right to left, and the German burst into flames and fell to the ground. "Did you see that? Did you see that?" Dobrich asked. Evidently, the German had been carrying a Molotov cocktail to use on tanks.

Around then, Bielski had fired the last bullet from his first belt of machine-gun ammo. He did something that he knew better … he raised up to his knees, opened the top of the machine gun and started to put a new belt in. I was to the right rear of him and a bullet struck him between the eyes. I saw the vapor come out the back of his head, through his helmet. He stayed on his knees with a real surprised look on his face for about the count of three, then all of a sudden he collapsed over the gun. He was a very, very good friend of mine. About the time I collected myself and started to jump for the gun, another trooper slid in from the left and said "I'll take it!" He rolled Bielski's body off it and finished loading it. I saw some Germans up ahead behind a log or an embankment and fired at them. I saw a couple of them go down; I knew one of them had probably shot Bielski.

When we reached the railroad embankment, some of the Germans had run across to the other side. We could hear the 501st shooting at them.

A bazookaman saw a German running away down the road and instinctively fired his bazooka at him. The rocket hit behind him and after the dust and dirt and debris disappeared, he was gone. That bazooka was the biggest weapon used in this battle. Everything else was small arms, knives, pistols, rifles, and machine guns—no mortars or artillery fire.

We assembled back in a group after we realized all the Germans were dead or wounded. I was getting out of it mentally. Everything just closed in on me. After all the attacks and battles I'd been in, I'd always been able to stand there with a few other guys and

look around. I began to wonder, "Why me?" Why was I always one of the few survivors?

The smell—you never forget the smell … the burnt powder, raw iron, warm human blood, splintered bone where the leg used to be, the communications wire and limbs were down…I suddenly took aim at this badly wounded German in a hole; I was going to kill him. Just then, Phillips walked up. I looked at him and said, "Are you still alive?"

He says, "Yeah, I was gonna ask you the same thing."

I said, "One of us should be dead by now." We both survived the war.

He says, "What are you doing?"

"I'm just gonna kill this Kraut."

He says "Naw, he's too badly shot up. Leave him alone," and he pushed the barrel of my rifle away. Then an older German who had been shot in the leg came up from the left and surrendered to me. A paratrooper walked up from behind me and said, "Has he got a Luger?"

I said "No," so Ka-Blam! He shot the German. The German thought I shot him, so he started swearing at me, before he died. So there was just a lot of death in that one area, a lot of carnage, a lot of unnecessary killing. It seemed like everything just finally came in on both sides. The Germans were really vicious at this time, and we were, too.

After this fight, 1st/506th made a 180-degree turn, heading back to the highway. Two more firefights erupted along the way, and Private Charles D. Horn was killed. Mercifully, most of the worst fighting for 1st/506th at Bastogne had ended.

Foy

The hamlet of Foy, Belgium, was situated between the American front line and German forces to the north, closer to Noville. For several weeks, it was in no-man's land, being occupied alternately by each side. Some men estimate that the small town changed hands at least seven times. A number of sizable German groups were ambushed and decimated in the fields nearby, mostly by 2nd/506th troopers. Art DiMarzio of D/506th heard the ratio of nine German bodies for every dead American in the area.

The tiny village was the scene of some armored battles and was hit by P-47 fighter-bomber attacks several times. In all, eight houses in Foy were completely destroyed although only one villager was killed.

The distance between the railroad line and Recogne is considerable. Members of 2nd/506th and H/506th were spread quite thinly along this front. Lieutenant Alex Andros, H/506th, felt that a German regiment could have marched undetected through one of the gaps in the line.

The Apathetic SS Sentry

As reported elsewhere, the shelling, horrible weather conditions, and little prospect of relief had worn down the morale of both sides. Periodically, bad news from home like a "Dear John" letter would arrive, causing some individuals to cease caring or to lose their will to survive. Conditions at the front were such that this kind of apathy was soon met with disaster. One foggy afternoon near the railroad line in Jack's Woods, Hank DiCarlo saw a sergeant from the 3rd/506th Light Machine Gun Platoon yelling at a lone sentry who stood near the woods across the tracks, wearing a long overcoat. The sentry stood as still as a statue, with his back to the tracks.

"Hey, is that G Company?" the sergeant yelled.

The sentry didn't answer or move.

"Hey! Is that G Company?" the sergeant repeated, growing angry, as the sentry was ignoring him.

Finally, DiCarlo saw the agitated sergeant walk briskly across the tracks and grab the sentry by the arm.

"Dammit! Answer me when I ask you a question!"

Suddenly, the American sergeant pivoted and walked back across the tracks, past DiCarlo.

DiCarlo later learned that when the sergeant grabbed the sentry by the arm, the sentry had half-turned to face him, and he was wearing SS lightning runes on his collar. The sergeant recoiled in shock and walked away. The German continued standing in his watch position. The exact reason for the indifference of this SS man to whatever happened around him will remain a matter of speculation.

Perhaps he was fed up with the futility of Hitler's Ardennes offensive?

Jack's Woods

The section of dense pine forest that runs from west to east between Foy and Bizory was known as the *Bois Jacques,* and the troopers Americanized it as "Jack's Woods." The railroad line that cuts through these woods on a 45-degree angle was the boundary line between the 501st and the 506th.

A large supply of burlap sacks had been discovered back in Bastogne, and a quantity of them reached 2nd/506th. They were worn wrapped around boots to help prevent frozen feet. A large warehouse of flour had also been found in town. Cooks made pancakes with it, and jeeps carried these out to men in front-line positions. Some troopers had brought bottles of cognac from Mourmelon and used the liquor as pancake syrup.

Searching out foxholes in the dim light before dawn, the cooks would flip an ice-cold pancake into each hole with the announcement "Breakfast is served!"

Both sides did a lot of patrolling in the woods above Foy, and the Germans attempted to infiltrate during darkness on a number of occasions.

Ross Goethe from Nebraska was a member of B/506th and obviously of German descent, but he was among the most livid of German haters in his company. His buddies could not understand why Goethe was so hard on the enemy, but his buddy, Bob Reeves, was aware that Goethe never seemed to get any mail from home.

One night in suspenseful darkness, B/506th men were on line in the pine woods and could barely hear German scouts creeping quietly toward them along the forest floor.

One German, groping in the pitch blackness, felt the leading edge of Goethe's foxhole. Reaching forward with his bayonet in hand, the German swept the edged weapon from side to side. Goethe was laying back out of range of the bayonet, but he suddenly grabbed the German's wrist and yanked him into the foxhole, stabbed him several times with his own bayonet, then flung him back out, in the direction from which he had come. The troopers didn't want to fire their weapons in the dark as it would give their positions away. Bob Reeves, who was in the next foxhole remarked, "I don't think I would've had the guts to pull the German in the hole and knife him. I think I would've had to shoot him." The wounded German lay groaning outside Goethe's hole until almost dawn, when he finally died.

Goethe and Reeves
Troopers of B/506th, Ross Goethe and Bob Reeves. Goethe pulled a German into his foxhole and knifed him, throwing him back out again. *Reeves*

The story of the 101st at Bizory is mostly the story of 2nd/501st, with Company A also involved. The first phase started on 19 December when 2nd/501st first moved east from Bastogne and met advanced elements of a German division near Bizory. A line was established near the village, with Companies E and F on line in a perfect defensive position. There was as yet no snow on the ground, and when a battalion of Germans attacked on the early morning of 20 December, most of the American riflemen and machine gunners had a field of fire. All the available artillery in Bastogne was also massed on the German attack. The German tanks held back, and one was left behind, disabled. All the prior experience in combat had made the 501st a deadly killing organization and the Germans blundered into a veritable meat grinder.

The next day, snow blanketed the area, but no more major thrusts came from the same direction. During the rest of the siege, long-range sniping was done by both sides, with the usual exchange of mortar and artillery rounds.

On Christmas Eve, the Germans shelled the area with captured WP mortar shells and played music over loudspeakers, including Big Crosby's "White Christmas" and some Count Basie tunes. There were also propaganda leaflets shot over in a futile attempt to get the paratroopers to surrender. The 2nd/501st S-2 section was stationed in the cellar of the Goose family chateau on the north edge of the village. This sizable home was surrounded by a stone wall that enclosed the cobblestone courtyard. Louis Frey recalled that the German troops in the area formed a makeshift choir and serenaded the Americans with "Silent Night" and other classic carols like "Good King Wenceslas." The Germans were quite close at hand when singing. Then, around 0300 hours, came their Christmas present—a counterattack in which the Germans set fire to the Goose chateau.

Frey and his friends escaped out the back, but in the garish light of the flames, he saw his friend, Allen Hurd dash into the courtyard, among the attacking Germans, firing his M-1 rifle from the hip. Hurd must have seemed a demonic apparition to the Germans as they fell to his rifle fire. He had stuffed a long Nazi flag into his rear pants pocket, and it was dragging on the ground behind him like a crimson cape as he ran around the courtyard. The entire scene lent an air of unreality to the night.

The 501st's Attack of 3 January

The 1st and 3rd Battalions of the 501st braved the enemy mortars and artillery; crossed the railroad tracks; and moved in a sweep of the forest north of the railroad.

Company G, supported by the Light Machine Gun Platoon, met heavy resistance as soon as they entered the trees on the north side. George "Scotty" Sciortino was killed there, and his buddy, Lee Parish, was

Tank Destroyer
An M-18 "Hellcat" tank destroyer behind a house in Bizory. The M-18s were new when the Bulge started, and a few were trapped inside Bastogne during the siege. This specimen supported 2nd/501st. The 2nd/501st CO, Lieutenant Colonel Sammie N. Homan, recalls chatting with a TD vehicle commander whose head and upper body were protruding from the Hellcat's open turret. Suddenly, a flat-trajectory artillery shell hit the vehicle commander, pulverizing his upper body into a red spray that covered Homan's face. "Talk about waking up with screaming nightmares," Homan later recalled. *via Leone*

knocked down by a bullet that glanced off his helmet. A German was popping up and down in his hole, firing a WWI-vintage MG08/15 water-cooled machine gun like a jack-in-the-box. The next time he jumped up, Joyce Chesney fired his M-1 from the hip and drilled the German gunner between the eyes.

The other companies of 2nd and 3rd Battalions met only sporadic small arms fire from deeper in the woods and fired at muzzle flashes, or guesstimated where the Germans were. The Germans in their path faded back several hundred yards. The troops dug in on a new line, held for several hours, then were ordered to fall back to the previous line.

Company E was the reserve company of 2nd/501st that day and were on the south fringe of the *Bois Jacques* expecting no action when the attack of the *12th SS-Panzer Division's SS-Panzer-Grenadier Regiment 26* hit their positions. Actually, the grenadiers, accompanied by tanks and captured American half-tracks, were passing the woods on an angle, intent on driving toward Bastogne itself. They overran two or three listening posts (LPs) positioned on the snowy open ground in front of the woods, but were forced to pivot toward the woods when a torrent of American bullets pelted them from the right flank.

The Germans drove their tanks and halftracks into one of the forest-surrounded alcoves south of the railroad and began pouring fire into the foxholes dug under the pine trees. Vehicles mounting 20mm flak guns jockeyed back and forth, spraying the exploding rounds at the American positions. Deadly marksmen of the 501st picked off all Germans in sight. It was a bloodbath for both sides.

Lieutenant Joe MacGregor, who had miraculously returned from the hospital after being shot in the head outside Veghel, took a bazooka and a couple of assistants and knocked out several German armored vehicles. Sergeant McClure was awarded a Silver Star for manning the machine gun on a knocked-out German half-track to use it against other German troops. He was wounded in the action and later received his Silver Star in the mail after returning home.

Among the HQ/2nd/501st men killed that day was Harry Artinger. He was walking back to the woods from an overrun LP when an MG42 sprayed him and Pelham Noyes. Artinger was killed, but Noyes feigned death to survive his sixth and seventh bullet wounds of the war.

A platoon of infantrymen had been hit on the open ground by a mortar barrage that killed most of the men in the hole. German armor had then overrun the position. Artinger and Noyes had escaped from that position only to be gunned down just before reaching the woods. Later in the afternoon, Charlie Eckman and Henry Schwabe ran across the open ground to the wiped-out position. During the 200-yard run, Eckman was grazed on the hip by a bullet and other rounds shattered the stock of his Tommy gun. He jumped into the pit containing about 14 American bodies with "glazed eyes." Sorting through the bodies, Eckman and Schwabe found Harry Coffey of their company buried under a number of dead men. He was babbling and incoherent. After dusk, Eckman and Schwabe dragged the disoriented Coffey back to the woods.

When the German attack was at its zenith, Leo Gillis crawled out to one of the overrun outposts on the open ground and manned a bazooka with another trooper. They fired without result at some retreating German armor. Before returning to the woods, Gillis noticed an abandoned M-1919A6 machine gun that the Germans had overrun, shoving the muzzle down into the muddy, snowy ground. As he was about to return to the woods, Gillis looked across the open

Milky Fog
Troopers of E/501st strain to see toward the advancing Germans through thick fog in the *Bois Jacques*. Leone

area to a hay pile where a number of troopers had gotten hay to line their foxholes with the previous night.

He recalled:

I looked back over at that hay pile, and man there's all kinds of Germans standing around that hay pile. So I took that machine gun that was stuck down in the mud, faced it around, threw out the belt, and I fired 250 rounds without a miss! Man, I cut that haystack in half. You could hear the Germans yelling and everything else. I killed about a dozen guys there.

Evidently, these Germans had stopped to take a break, thinking they were out of view of the American line. They actually were, but Gillis's trip to the LP had put him in a different vantage point. Carl Beck with H/501st relates more of the action:

We crossed the railroad track and went through the woods on the north side. The ground sloped gradually uphill for several hundred yards. This turned into an all-day affair. We went down trails into these real thick woods, looking for some American tanks that had gotten mouse-trapped.

A tanker with the "battle rattles" came walking up this trail. Someone asked him, "Where are you going?" He had on one of those long head protectors with the visor in the rear. He said, "I gotta go get a new tank!" and continued back.

Our platoon leader was Staff Sergeant Harry Plisevich. We were pretty much at full strength. He got us

Foxholes in the Snow

These foxholes are occupied by members of the 501st. Visible in the background are sections of the *Bois Jacques.* The 501st's new regimental photographer, Joe "Gopher" Sloan, snapped this nice photo. *via Wilbur*

on line, we went down through these thick woods, firing as we went, then made a turning movement. The woods were so thick, it was hard to contact each other. I set the A-6 machine gun up on a tree that had been blown over and was able to get it up a little higher. This put us on the flank of a *Volks-Grenadier* outfit that was moving up to relieve the *SS* troops in the area. They had a little tank and a big tank. The little tank was zigzagging in front of the big tank, with the infantry following.

The infantry had their communications people unreeling wire as they moved along. The big tank shot and killed John O. Bay, and our medic Goolsby got the Silver Star for waving his red cross brassard and going out to get his body. I had the A-6 over the roots of this tree, with Duffy down beside me as second gunner.

Apparently, they were going to try to flank us because they sent a squad with an MG42 around and they were walking right toward us.

In the meantime, all these Germans are walking past saying, "Cease fire. Cease fire." Their voices sounded like crickets, you know, under a lot of strain.

Plisevich said, "O.K., let 'em have it!" and we wasted the machine-gun crew.

I could see the shadow of faint light coming off the helmet of the first man coming toward me with the MG42. I saw my tracer go through him, and I shot the whole squad behind him.

We had a replacement named Gussie Hill, known as "Cussless Gus" because he didn't swear. He would say, "Oh, phooey!" or "Gosh darn it!" He sat on the edge of a foxhole and shot about 21 Krauts before he was hit. He shot a German major that was stan-

ding up on a mound of earth, shouting orders to his troops.

Medic Goolsby came to treat Cussless Gus and was patching up wounds to his front, when he turned Gus over and found much worse wounds on his back. Gussie died there. We lost a lot of people, but we wiped out the German unit.

A general withdrawal of 2nd and 3rd Battalion troops was ordered late in the afternoon, and the Americans moved south, re-crossing the railroad track to their line of departure. The 2nd/501st troops could hear Germans digging in across the embankment; they had followed the US troops right back to the tracks.

Sergeant Plisevich stayed on the north side of the track to help organize the withdrawal and to make sure nobody got left behind. In a large bomb crater, he found a number of wounded troopers, including an I/501st man whose diaphragm seemed to have collapsed from the concussion of a near explosion. As Harry was moving through the woods, he made a wrong turn and came face to face with a German tank. He was captured and taken to the rear for interrogation in a Belgian farmhouse. While there, he saw Lieutenant Joseph Forney of G/501st, who had also been captured that day.

Harry was to spend the duration as a POW. He weighed only 75 pounds when liberated. He was not a cooperative prisoner.

A Buddy's Act of Devotion

That night after darkness fell, Harry Plisevich's best buddy, Leonard Morris, was wondering why Harry hadn't returned. Was he dead, wounded, or cap-

The Ordeal of Charlie Eckman

As a member of 2nd/501st's Light Machine Gun Platoon, Charlie Eckman had been with the regiment since Camp Toccoa. At 5 feet, 4 inches and less than 120 pounds, the 17-year-old trooper had been through Normandy and Holland and had gained a reputation as both the youngest and most-often-wounded trooper in the 501st.

Around 4 January, Charlie received his seventeenth combat wound, a 9mm slug in the ankle, which drove a boot eyelet into his leg. As he lay on the ground in the Bois Jacques, awaiting treatment, a medic pulled off his boots and saw blackened flesh.

"My God, boy, your legs are gonna be cut off! You've got frozen limbs!"

Charlie hadn't removed his boots since coming to Bastogne as he knew his feet would swell up, preventing him from getting the boots back on. He had done toe-ups and prayed his feet wouldn't freeze, but now it appeared that it was too late to save his feet.

A surgeon with the rank of major came up to examine Charlie's wound. Lying beside him on the ground was another paratrooper with a leg wound, and "his legs didn't hardly look dark yet," remembered Charlie.

The major turned to Charlie. "What's wrong with you, boy?"

"Well, I'm wounded in the foot, sir," said Charlie, showing the major his blackened leg.

"Wounded in the foot? Hell! You ain't gonna have legs! You're next! Soon as I cut this boy's legs off. ..."

As Charlie recalled, the surgeon prepared to cut that troopers legs off, "right there on the damn ground. Honest to God, he had his medical supplies and saw. ... It just seemed so brutal to me."

The other wounded man said, "Well Doc, I've walked around on 'em for 24 years, but if I have to have 'em off. ..." "Hold that kid there," the major said to Charlie. "You're next!" "Major, you're not cuttin' my legs off."

"Don't you tell me what to do. I'm a major! What rank do you have?"

"Hey, I'm respectin' you as a doctor, but that's not a field rank. To me, your rank ain't as much as mine. At least I'm a BullyBully Private."

"Get him the hell outta here! He's gonna die anyhow!" said the major.

Medics carried Charlie back to a tent hospital, where he was placed in a sheeted-off section and examined. In addition to his blackened legs, his throat was swollen with diptheria. Charlie was stripped naked, allowed to bathe in a tub of hot water, then placed in a bed with his feet suspended up in the air in loops.

"This is crazy! I can't get no circulation!"

A doctor entered and said "I'm sorry son, but your legs are going to have to come off. The gangrene is starting to set in."

"No, no. Give me a chance to warm up."

"No, boy, you don't understand," said the doctor. He took needles and ran them into Charlie's feet.

"See? Nothing." "Well, ... no. Give me a chance." "Well, what do you want to do, die?" "Well, I believe so. I don't want my legs cut off." As soon as the doctors left to have a meeting, Charlie got

out of bed and "started to do push-ups and squats, and I rubbed and rubbed my legs. I heard 'em coming and I plunged back in that bed."

"Gosh darn, it looks like the color's a lot better than it was just 20 minutes ago," the doctor said. "But, boy, there's still no circulation."

"Well you just give me a couple of days, then I'll decide whether I want to die or have 'em cut off."

"Well I can guarantee you that in a couple of days you're gonna die."

Charlie kept squatting and exercising all night long.

He had to disconnect the intravenous tubes from his arms and "caught hell for this each time. ... I lied and told them the tubes were painful."

Each time the nurse came to check his thermometer, Charlie would plunge back into bed. "I didn't want 'em to see what I was doing or know what I was doing."

The next day, the doctor returned to examine him. "A miracle happened," the doctor said. "We were going to cut your left leg off above the knee and the right one below, but now we can cut off the left one clean below the knee, and the right one at the ankle."

"No, no. ..."

The next day the doctor said, "Jesus, boy, a miracle has indeed happened. It's because you're so damned young! Some of the feeling has come back and we're getting some blood out of your legs. We're gonna cut four toes off the left foot and three off the right. How's that, boy?"

"No, no. I want one more day."

Thus did Charlie Eckman retain both legs and all his toes. He would remain in the hospital a few months, missing only the Alsace campaign.

Eckman and Madden

Denver Madden (*left*; KIA in Holland) spars with Charlie Eckman (*right*). Both were in the Light Machine Gun Platoon HQ/2nd/501st. Eckman was wounded 17 times in WWII and nearly had both legs amputated at Bastogne because of gangrene.

tured? Leonard couldn't stand the mystery, so he crept across the railroad embankment alone, moving quietly through the German line to prowl around for hours in the dark, enemy-held woods in search of his friend. Anyone who has visited the area can realize what an incredible act of bravery and devotion this was. Before daylight, Morris realized his search would be fruitless, and he re-crossed the railroad to American lines.

It is very easy to get lost in the *Bois Jacques*, and Frank Whiting of A/501st spent three lonely days wandering in these woods after Company A's first battle, dodging enemy patrols until he found other Americans.

By beating back the *SS* attack, 2nd/501st ended one of the most-remembered engagements they fought in WWII.

Because of the see-saw tactics of the *Bois Jacques* fighting, 2nd/501st was forced to attack sideways through the same area again on 10 January. Support on the right flank was from the 6th Armored Division. Encountering a complex of German dugouts, the F/501st men used leapfrog tactics to blast and grenade the Germans out of their holes.

The area above Bizory in the *Bois Jacques* figured prominently in the fighting for the next week as the 327th and the 502nd pushed along the railroad line though the woods in their approach to Bourcy. *(See Chapter 48.)*

Team O'Hara

Armored troops, probably from Combat Command B, 10th Armored Division (Team O'Hara), near Bizory, with Hayden Faulk and Silver Star recipient Walter Lengieza (in snowsuit), of F/501st. *Newton*

Gloom in the *Bois Jacques*

The gloomy atmosphere of these bitter woods northeast of Bastogne was captured in this photo of Maurice Sandquist, HQ/2nd/501st, by Louis Frey. *Frey*

The towns of Mont and Neffe lie very close to each other directly east of the city of Bastogne. A squad of engineers delayed an attack by German armor on the morning of 19 December. Then on 21 December, Private John Mishler of B/501st stifled another attack by knocking out the leading German tank with his bazooka, effectively blocking the road west for a critical amount of time. Mishler was seriously wounded during this act, but survived to wear his Silver Star.

The 1st and 3rd/501st, supported by the 907th GFAB, dug in facing east near Mont. To their right were glider troops. Despite the first contact being made at Neffe, 2nd/501st would repulse the first major German attempt to enter Bastogne from the east at Bizory. (See Chapter 43.)

One company of 3rd/501st did not settle in at Mont on 19 December. Company I had entered the fray with Lieutenant Claude Wallace at the helm. All the senior noncommissioned officers in the company had been transferred during the stay in Mourmelon due to a scandal started by a French camp follower.

Debacle at Wardin

Carl Sargis from B/501st replaced the erstwhile first sergeant, and Staff Sergeant Erminio Calderan, formerly of D/501st, had also arrived recently. These were good men, as were some of the new replacement officers, but they didn't know the individuals in I/501st nor their capabilities. The company was about to be subjected to the severest of tests, a desperate fight for survival against overwhelming German panzer forces and King Tiger tanks. Colonel Ewell, in retrospect, regretted the shifting of leaders in the company, but that was with hindsight. The entire Bastogne battle happened with no advance notice, and the debacle at Wardin could not have been foreseen.

The approach march to Wardin, which is over five miles southeast of Bastogne, took several hours. The company took a difficult route decided on by the new leaders, passing through numerous wooded areas. There was not yet snow on the ground, and many troopers shed their overcoats and other winter accessories on the sweaty, difficult approach march. They entered Wardin without resistance after turning left at a small bridge that crosses a stream on the edge of the village.

A company CP was established in a farmhouse on the western side of the street. Bill McMahon led his machine-gun section up a small rise facing south at the southern edge of town. Radioman Frank Guzy had a radio, but was unable to make contact with 3rd/501st or a group of friendly tanks that sat back to the southwest on higher ground.

Guzy later realized he was under German observation as he sought higher ground just outside Wardin on which to set up his radio. When German tanks opened fire, they started toward the church from the south. The opening 88mm round went through the CP into the attached barn, killing First Sergeant Carl Sargis. McMahon's group swept a line of German panzer-grenadiers coming over the ridge, then saw the tanks.

Being a survivor of Normandy and Holland, McMahon made a snap decision to get out of town as quickly as possible. He told his squad to take off, heading west. They re-crossed the main road in town, leaving the light machine gun behind with much other equipment. Given cover by smoke from the exploding tanks shells, the retreating troopers splashed right through the stream on the far edge of town and made their way uphill to the nearest patch of woods. From there, they watched the town burn.

Marvin Wolfe witnessed a crucial action by Wilbrod Gauthier of his company, who was normally a machine gunner. After firing a light machine gun for a while, Gauthier left the gun and ran onto the road with a bazooka. He fired a rocket into the lead tank, disabling it and causing a critical delay for the Germans. This enabled many of his comrades to escape from the town. Gauthier was killed by machine-gun fire from another tank in the process. He remains one of the many heroes who was never decorated for his heroism.

Of the 140 men who went into Wardin on 19 December, only 83 escaped to reorganize the following day. The survivors made their way back piecemeal, surviving any way they could.

Kia in Wardin?

Captain Claude Wallace, CO of I/501st, was KIA on 19 December 1944, the day the company entered Wardin, Belgium. According to most accounts, Wallace died near Lieutenant Shoemaker in Wardin, but some survivors of the company claim he actually died several days later. *Hamilton*

Work detail

Prisoners on work detail, clearing rubble and debris from roads inside Bastogne. Their guard is identified as a member of HQ/326th AEB by his helmet stencil. *Tocco*

Erminio Calderan and Robert Vaughn joined a group of Belgian civilians who were walking west, pushing their possessions along in carts. The troopers obtained a woman's coat and dress and donned them, then walked west in the group, pushing a baby carriage. The Germans in the distance spotted their boots and opened fire. The duo hit the ditch and managed to make their escape.

Richard Hahlbohm survived Wardin, but was captured. Hahlbohm wrote of his experience:

Wardin is a small town, about six or seven houses, and was of no value to us or the enemy. We were just to find out where the enemy were. Believe me – we did.

There was a long wood pile, neatly stacked to my side, so I crouched behind it. I was waiting for the Krauts to come through the hedgerow, but they must have backed off. I then heard a tank coming up the road. He stopped in plain sight of me, to my left. I noticed right away it was a new Tiger Royal. He was firing down into the open field.

I gathered that my company, or a part of it, was making a run for it as we only had bazookas to fire at them. The tank's machine gunner was firing, but he didn't see me. I looked over my shoulder and saw my buddy, Julius J. Schrader, behind a tree to my left. I was in the only position to fire at the tank. I noticed behind the corner of the house was a bazookaman. I yelled, "Tank!" and pointed. When I took another look, the bazooka was there, but the gunner wasn't.

Meanwhile, I had knocked off the machine gunner in the tank turret and drew attention. The 88 swung in my direction. I knew he couldn't penetrate the whole wood pile with his first shot, so I got up on my haunches to make a dash behind the house after he let the first one fly. But he realized this also, so he backed his gun up to make a ricochet shot from the house so it would get me and whoever was in back of the house.

I figured now was the time to make tracks, as a new turret gunner was peppering the area. I started my 10– 12-foot leap, and he let loose and the bullets imbedded in the house. The 88 concussion caught me halfways there. It made me like a rag doll flying through the air. As I hit the ground, I heard the machine gun open up at the same time. Someone pulled me behind the house. My overcoat was ripped in a few places by shrapnel, but luckily, I wasn't hit.

We took refuge in the house. My ears were ringing like two dozen phones. We were trapped in the house. As we were preparing to fight from the house, it caught on fire. As I looked out the window, I saw wall-to-wall Krauts. It looked like a whole regiment. After a few minutes of debate, I told the other seven men with me to break down their weapons and scatter them all over and in the walls as I had heard the Krauts shot you with your own weapons. Surrender was a bitter pill to swallow, but we had to survive. I was wondering how Captain Wallace, my CO, was making out and hoped he saw the odds against him.

They took us out and put us up against a hedgerow and brought up a GI halftrack with a .50-cal. on top. The gunner cranked in a round and leveled the gun on us. I figured we had had it for sure. A machine gunner who had been wounded earlier was shot through the ass, in and out. His bandage was falling off. I forgot about being a prisoner and leaned over to push the bandage back on. I almost got shot for my trouble. So I quickly said in German, "My comrade has been wounded."

The Germans took one look at his wound and all started to laugh. The interrogation officer came out and took us away. They put us against the hedgerow two more times and again we were saved by the officer. He then took us to the rear.

The survivors of I/501st regrouped at the regimental CP in the Bastogne seminary or at the farmhouse CP of 3rd/501st at Mont. They were used to fill in on the lines.

Around 2000 on the night of 20 December, the Germans began a concerted effort to break through the 501st's lines in the Neffe-Mont area. Enemy troops moved along the highway toward 1st/501st, supported by several tanks. Another concentration of Germans stormed 3rd/501st along a slope between Neffe and Mont. This group also had tank support, but in both sectors, the German armor held back, never becoming a serious threat. A series of barbed-wire fences and cattle pens covered the area in front of 3rd/501st, and the advancing enemy had to pause to climb each fence. Cross-firing US machine guns tore them to ribbons.

Team O'Hara

Farther south, Lieutenant Bill Russo with his platoon from C/501st was dug in next to Lieutenant John Sallin with his B/501st platoon. The brunt of the attack in that sector was taken by 10th Armored tanks from Team O'Hara. Asked Russo:

Have you ever heard of Team O'Hara? Well, they should get more credit because they really took the brunt of that attack. We could hear tank guns firing, and we didn't have any. They really got a whacking, buddy.

Battered Bastards

Ballard's Battered Bastards of the Battling Bastion of Bastogne, Belgium. These HQ/501st survivors proudly display a bul letriddled sign. *Standing, left to right:* Waldo Brown, Jim Ganter, Belgian civilian, R. J. Wilbur, Dave Smith, Chief Sayers, Joe Sloan (photographer), and Budd. *Front, left to right:* Eugene Amburgey, W. C. Dunn, Ted Becker, Bill Canfield (holding sign), and Duane Henson. *Sloan*

One thing I used to do, and Sallin on my right knew about it: take a German machine gun with white tracers, and fire it at them when they attack. You want to cause some confusion … all the way back to Berchtesgaden? They'll back off every time! They have to! Because who is it firing at them? When you're moving around like that things happen. Sometimes your own troops fire at you.

Whatever the Germans do, they'll do twice. You know, your men are kind of slack after a little shootout? I used to tell all of my gunners, "Reload and loosen all your belts because they're gonna be back."

Mayor of Bastogne

During the battle, Mr. Leon Jacquemin was mayor of Bastogne (center); he is shown here behind an American ambulance, with other city officials. *Musura*

An Odd Christmas Eve Encounter

On 24 December, First Sergeant Donald Deam of Service/ 501st went to a Christmas party at HQ/101st and obtained an armload of champagne and cognac to carry out to his men on the line near Mont. Returning just before dusk, Deam followed the railroad track eastward, then cut through the underpass. While under the railroad culvert, Deam came face to face with a German sergeant, who entered from the opposite side. Both men made a frantic grab for their weapons, slipping and sliding on the icy ground. Their eyes met, and Deam smiled and winked at

the German. "Got a cigarette, Yank?" the German said in English. Both men relaxed, sat down, and began to talk. They

produced photos of their relatives from wallets, exchanged names and addresses, and shared a bottle of cognac. Deam learned that the German was a Frankfurt college graduate.

After that brief interlude from the war, the two enemies parted from opposite sides of the cutvert. Each man raised his weapon – an MP40 and a Tommy gun – and fired a burst straight up in the air.

Many years after the war, Deam was contacted by the daughter of this German soldier (she was an interpreter working at the UN in New York). He learned her father had survived the war, but died in 1975.

And Goddammit, they were, within ten minutes. They'll do it twice. I don't know if it was a matter that they couldn't go back and say they failed, I don't know. But it was ridiculous. I couldn't understand the Germans making their troops walk over their dead to get to us. That's not too damn encouraging, you know, their dead still laying there?

They were so desperate. That army was shot, I'm telling you.

Among the machine-gun crews of 3rd/501st that night was Carl Beck with assistant Dick Duffy and their light machine gun. Beck has described his part in the repulse of the enemy attack:

We occupied a position along a sunken road where this M-18 tank destroyer [TD] was in turret defilade. A machine-gun section from HQ/3rd got knocked out near the haystack. The Germans were attacking at night, and it was so foggy that when a flare went up, all you would see was a glow; you couldn't distinguish anything except movement. The haystack had been set afire by tracers, and Captain Hilton asked me to go out up this cut bank next to that TD and shove my machine gun through that fence line and set up final protective fires.

We were able to do that, although we were taking intense small arms fire. We started firing and fired for 15–20 minutes out there.

The TD near me could swing his turret around and fire the .50-cal. machine gun from the turret. As I was moving up, they fired the 76mm main battery, which knocked me down. A .31-cal. bullet [German 7.92mm] went bouncing off the bipod, which further complicated matters. The TD guy kept on firing the .50-cal. We continued firing until the enemy was on the run; of course, we couldn't see them, but their firing slowed.

They left me a little souvenir with a potato masher grenade, which exploded right off the end of the machine gun and threw a bunch of shrapnel in my head and face. It was dark and all I could feel was a lot of blood. Duffy remarked, "He's bleeding like a stuck hog."

They carried me down the bank past this M-18, and a medic took me down the road to an aid station set up in this house, where I was treated and patched up. There were no evacuation procedures because there was no place to go. The Krauts had overrun our hospital.

While we were in this aid station, another M-18 came around the corner and fired his main battery, I don't know at what. This huge piece of furniture came over and landed on all of us that were lying rolled up on stretchers. That helped relieve the tension a little bit. Well somebody set this furniture back up and got it off of us.

A few minutes later, here came that gunner who had been firing that .50-cal. off the turret of that M-18, and he had a .31-cal. bullet lodged up in his nose. He come shakin' in there sayin', "Hey! You know I saw those damn things comin', but I couldn't duck in time!" What had happened was somebody fired a machine gun at him, and one of the rounds hit the ring mount, ricocheted down, and hit him in the nose. But he was all right; he was still cussin' the next morning.

Anyways, the people I knew had nowhere to go, so we just went back to the outfit. We were so low on ammunition that another attack might've finished us off. By the way, there was 72 dead out there the next morning when we got back on the line. Apparently, that took a lot of starch out of 'em because we weren't hit again on that part of the line, except by some artillery.

New Year's Eve at Neffe

It was New Year's Eve, and 1st Platoon of F/501st had been moved down to the Neffe sector. They had ringside seats to observe an attack by the 6th Armored Division to take the town.

Tanks approached through the cover of the woods, crossed the railroad track, and started across an open field toward the small town. Neffe erupted with small arms and panzerfaust fire. The attack of the tanks stalled and numerous armored infantrymen lay bleeding in the snow.

Sergeant Joe Bass of F/501st was observing, got frustrated, and said, "They're gonna die out there!"

When he could stand it no longer, Bass recruited a team of troopers, and the 12-man group swung through the woods as the tanks had done. A "Mexican Standoff" had developed. The Germans had retreated to the cellars with their panzerfausts and were afraid to come out. The tankers were unwilling to go in and get them.

Bass led his group past the tanks, saw the infantry lying in the snow, and in Sergeant Charlie Palmer's words, "Made a beeline straight into Neffe." Bass entered the first house with two of his men, burst into the cellar and shouted *"Hände Hoch! Komm' Sie 'raus! Schnell!"*

A small group of Germans came out to surrender.

Gradually, the remaining Germans peeked out, saw that their comrades were not being shot, and a general surrender began. "It was just a case of being brave enough to go in and get them," said Palmer.

The armor officer in charge asked, "Where do you get these men?" The armor then drove the rest of the way through town to consolidate the newly-gained territory.

Sergeant Tom Enright had the opportunity to observe a 10-man group of German prisoners taken in Neffe that afternoon. The prisoners stood shoulder to shoulder and, remembered Enright:

I suppose most of them were in their early twenties, and good-looking soldiers: well-dressed, neat, their hair was cut. You kinda had to admire them as being soldiers. But they're all standing there at *Heil* Hitler attention, and one of 'em on the end could speak English. But he was telling us that they were going

to go to Antwerp, then sail to Canada and invade the United States. I'm sure that they believed this…He'd say this and the rest would answer *"Ja-Ja, Ja-Ja."* I'm sure they understood what he was saying, because they knew when to say *"Ja-Ja."*… My God, it was like a puppet show or something. Not really, but whatever this guy on the end said, the others chimed in.

"Just what would you bastards say if I told you I'm gonna shoot the whole lot of you right now?" asked Sergeant Bass.

"We aren't afraid of that," said the guy on the end, "because our comrades would find our bodies and then they will kill all of you!"

"Ja-Ja, Ja-Ja," said the chorus.

Tragedy at the Seminary

Although the seminary in Bastogne wasn't actually in any of the towns mentioned in this chapter, it was not far from Mont on the east edge of the city. On 5 January, a tragedy occurred in the courtyard of the seminary. The building had served as a field hospital and regimental HQ for the 501st.

On 5 January, a detail of men from the 501st's Demolitions Platoon was loading a truck with land mines. Leo Runge was in the vicinity and noticed that some of the safety pins were missing from the mines. He pointed this out to the men on the loading detail, but they didn't seem too concerned.

When a considerable number of mines had been loaded, the truck was driven into the courtyard of the seminary by Robert L. Rutherford of the regimental Service Company. Lieutenant Roy F. Waring exited the truck and entered the seminary to talk with other officers in the CP. While he was in there, all the mines aboard the truck suddenly exploded. The exact cause of this will never be known. Perhaps a random German mortar or artillery shell scored a direct hit? Or the weight of the stacked mines may have reached critical mass, due to partial thawing. A tremendous explosion rocked the seminary, and the 13 men aboard the truck were blown to pieces: Private Robert

Wounded Monument

A WWI statue in Bastogne. The WWI monument was situated near the center of town until a direct hit by a German bomb or artillery shell blew it to pieces. *Krochka*

In 1989, the author located the same (repaired) monument in front of the church across from the site of the 501st CP. Damage is still evident, despite repairs, and half the wounded man's head lies on the base of the monument now.

A tragic accident
A view of the truck that exploded in the seminary courtyard near the 501st's CP in Bastogne on 5 January 1945. Along with the truck, 13 paratroopers of the 501st were vaporized in the terrific blast. Through the efforts of former 501st band members Len Cinquanta and Julius Schrader, a permanent marker was placed at the seminary courtyard in 1999. Both Len and Julius died less than a year after the marker was put in place. *Duggins*

L. Rutherford, Service/501st (the rest are from the regimental Demolitions Platoon), Private Walter Craley, Staff Sergeant Leon W. "Pappy" Brown, Private Frank Baer, Private Michael Balducci, Private Harold Brisco, Corporal Bonnie Caroon, Private Latcher Coney, Private Wallace Diefenbach, Private James A. Keel, Private First Class Sam A. Lappin, Corporal William B. Maue, and Private Earl S. Smith.

A crude, small marker was erected there immediately after WWII, but medic Richard E. O'Brien visited the spot over 40 years later and discovered the sign was missing. Through his tireless efforts, a new marker has recently been placed at the spot, in tribute to the men who died there.

A number of artillery shells hit the roof of the seminary during the siege, and the stained glass rained down on the wounded men inside. Another unforgettable incident happened when a 500-pound bomb came through the roof during a German air raid, went through the floor into the basement and failed to explode.

Marvie

45

A small village on the southeast corner of the Bastogne perimeter, Marvie became a focal point of several German attacks as it was situated near a road that enters the city of Bastogne. Lieutenant Colonel Inman's 2nd/ 327th were joined there in the defense by C/326th AEB, a platoon each from B/326th and A/501st, several halftracks and tanks of 10th Armored Division's Team O'Hara, and were anchored on the flank by elements of 1st/501st. (See Chapter 44.)

On 20 December, the first German attack came in, a brisk charge by four German tanks and six halftracks, accompanied by infantry. Two of the German tanks were knocked out by side shots from American tanks, another was hit by bazooka fire, and the last one retreated. A self-propelled gun was hit and burned as infantry infiltrated houses in the village, where fighting continued.

At 1840 on 23 December, the Germans launched another attack, surrounding a platoon of G/327th on Hill 500, south of Marvie. Also on that hill were members of C/326th AEB. Some of these troops managed to retreat to Marvie, but others were killed or taken prisoner.

An American halftrack met the German attack head-on and retreated north into Marvie at top speed. This vehicle was mistakenly knocked out by friendly fire, but later served as an effective roadblock in preventing the German armor that followed from passing through Marvie. Two German tanks were halted there, and a self-propelled gun was hit by an American tank and burst into flames in the fading light. Tanks and infantry of Team O'Hara pulled back 100 yards to the west.

Returning to the night fighting in Marvie, the German infantrymen were silhouetted by flames from burning houses in the village, which aided the troopers in shooting them. Yet another German tank found the narrow road blocked by the knocked out halftrack and was blown up while turning to go back.

A failed daytime attack in the nearby F/327th sector was repulsed by men of Lieutenant Smith's platoon and acting platoon leader Staff Sergeant Oswald Butler. A truce was called, allowing the Germans to pick up their wounded.

Demand for Surrender

To the right of Marvie as the perimeter faced south, is the highway running from Bastogne to Remoi-Fosse. Company F, 327th GIR had a defense line dug in perpendicular to the road, with E/327th on their left. Two significant night attacks had hit this section of the perimeter, with one of them overrunning part of E/327th.

It was along this road that a group of German "parliamentaries" came on the afternoon of 22 December. Leo Palma, a BAR gunner, and his assistant gunner were in a foxhole in the ditch beside the road. But Staff Sergeant Carl Dickinson went forward to meet the German group.

Dickinson recalled three enlisted men walking in front, the center man waving a large white flag, the men on either side waving smaller ones. Following closely behind them were two German officers with shiny

Carl Dickinson

Sergeant Carl Dickinson of F/327th met the German ultimatum party on the Arlon road on 22 December. Carl missed out on much of the subsequent publicity, as he was wounded and evacuated in January 1945. *Dickinson*

jackboots and leather overcoats. The infantry major could only speak German. The medical captain spoke fluent English.

The captain announced himself to Dickinson, stating, "According to the Hague and Geneva Conferences, we have the right to parley."

Word spread quickly along the line that there was a cease-fire, and the troops got up to stretch, shave, and write letters home. They assumed that the Germans were trying to surrender to them, but it was quite the opposite. The Germans came bearing a written ultimatum, presumably authored by *General der Panzertruppen* Heinrich *Freiherr* von Lüttwitz, Commanding General of the *XLVII Panzer Corps* which encircled Bastogne. The document threatened total annihilation of Bastogne and its defenders if the American forces didn't surrender within two hours.

Leo Premetz, an F/327th medic who could speak German, was summoned from the platoon CP in a nearby house, but with the English-speaking German captain, translations weren't necessary. The three German enlisted men were left at Palma's foxhole. The two officers were blindfolded and led to

Herding Pows
Surrendering Germans being herded toward Bastogne. *Mihok*

Safe snow
Sergeant Howard J. Sloan gets safe snow for coffee on 10 January 1945. *Signal Corps*.)

On the move

Left to right: Private First Class M. L. Dickman, Private Sunny Sundquist, and Sergeant Francis McCann. Dickman and McCann were mem bers of F/327th. How Sundquist, H/506th, wound up with them in this photo on 30 December 1944 is a mystery that Sunny's H/506th buddies are still pondering. *US Army*

the company CP, where they were held while their written surrender demand was carried back to HQ/101st in Bastogne.

General McAuliffe was handed the message, but was preoccupied with other matters. He crumpled the letter and said, "Nuts." Upon learning that the Germans were awaiting a formal written response, he was at a loss as to what he should write. Harry Kinnard told him, "Your first remark would be hard to beat."

"What did I say?" McAuliffe asked.

"You said 'Nuts'," Kinnard reminded him.

A formal note was typed:

To the German Commander:

NUTS

The American Commander

Colonel Harper, commanding the 327th, was delighted with the response, and elected to deliver it personally to the German emissaries. He traveled back to the F/327th area by jeep. The German officers were led back to the foxhole line, still blindfolded.

Captain von Peters, the German medical officer, from Ramzelten, Austria, said, "I'd rather be walking in the park with my wife."

The Germans were unblindfolded and handed the note with General McAuliffe's reply.

They were puzzled about the meaning of "Nuts."

"It means go take a flying shit at yourself," Harper explained.

The Germans were still confused.

Harper lost his temper and said, "Nuts is strictly negative; it means the same thing as 'Go to Hell!' If you

continue this foolish attack, we will kill every goddamn German who tries to break into Bastogne!"

The Germans stood stiffly to attention.

"We will kill many Americans; this is war."

"On your way, bud, and good luck to you," said Harper, later regretting he had wished them luck.

The exact text of the surrender ultimatum was reproduced in McAuliffe's famous Christmas message to the troops.

Word of the surrender ultimatum soon reached all parts of the defense perimeter, and the troops braced themselves for an anticipated avalanche of 210mm artillery shells. Curiously, the sector where the ultimatum had been delivered was not hit until two days later, but some parts of the perimeter did get an unspectacular barrage that afternoon. The later barrage hit F/327th GIR heavily and succeeded in killing two forward observers from an artillery outfit.

As of 1800 on 24 December, Colonel Harper's 327th was given responsibility for the perimeter from Marvie to northwest of Hemroulle—over half the total defenses around Bastogne. Due to heavy forestation to the south of the city, that area was considered less suitable for passage by German tanks.

On 26 December in the same sector, the first tanks of Lieutenant Colonel Creighton Abrams's 37th Tank Battalion of the Third Army's 4th Armored Division made contact with Lieutenant Duane J. Webster of the 326th AEB, and the encirclement of Bastogne was officially ended.

Far from being the end of the ordeal of the 101st in the Battle of the Bulge, it was just the beginning.

46

The Western Perimeter
Hemroulle, Savy, Champs, Rolle

On 19 December, the 463rd PFAB arrived near the gently rolling hills at Hemroulle. On arrival, Hank Rodenbach yelled, "Hey, Colonel, we can't dig in here…There's no trees for the officers to hide behind!"

The 463rd set up their positions there, facing west, and not far away, the 377th PFAB and the 321st GFAB set up their 75mm howitzer positions near the village of Savy.

Although the west side of Bastogne was skirted by both the *2nd* and *116th Panzer Divisions,* their concern was mainly to bypass Bastogne and continue westward toward their objective – the Meuse River.

When the first concerted attacks came from the west after 23 December, the artillery units played a significant role in repulsing them.

The area west, and especially far west, of Bastogne was initially considered to be in the rear and thus safe from German attack, so the 326th Medical Company and hospital were set up near the *Bois de Chabry,* at crossroads "X," so named because the road running southwest from Bertogne forms a perfect "X" with the road running west out of Bastogne.

On the night of 19/20 December, the hospital was overrun, and most of its staff and patients were captured or killed by a German armored unit. This was long believed to be group from the *2nd Panzer Division,* but extensive research by Belgian historian Andre Meurisse indicates it was more likely an element of the *116th Panzer Division.*

While attempting to retrieve medical supplies from the captured hospital, Father Francis Sampson, Catholic chaplain of the 501st, was captured and spent the duration as a POW.

Elsewhere on the western perimeter, Captain Swanson's A/502nd was initially deployed to the right flank near Monaville, but would be rotated to the west. They were in position near Champs on Christmas Eve to repulse a concerted German attack from the west.

Chateau Rolle

A medieval chateau owned by the Rolle family and still inhabited by Madame Rolle and her infant son became the CP of Colonel Steve Chappuis's regiment. In the barns and surrounding buildings, members of HQ/502nd and service companies made improvised billets. A number of S-2 patrols were

Opposite: **Legendary leader**
Captain Wally Swanson was the legendary leader of A/502nd whose men repulsed the German attack on Champs on Christmas morning. Wally is shown in partial snow camouflage.

Below: Captain Frank Lillyman, of Normandy Pathfinders fame, served in HQ/3rd/502nd at Bastogne. *White*

launched from here to determine enemy strength and intentions to the north and west. Lieutenant David White had recently joined the 502nd and now led the S-2 section. He personally accompanied most of the S-2 patrols, one of which went as far as a wooded ridge overlooking Gives.

From concealment on the ridge, patrol members could see numerous American vehicles moving in the distance. It was believed, but not confirmed, that these were captured vehicles, currently being driven by German troops. Many rumors had circulated of German troops speaking English wearing captured American uniforms and infiltrating the lines. Everyone was paranoid about this, and the S-2 patrol had encountered a "questionable" M-8 armored car while moving toward Gives. The commander had blond hair and a large handlebar mustache. The S-2 scouts were about to blast him, but decided not to when he shouted, "Christ! Don't shoot!"

Coming back toward Ruette, the S-2 men hitched a ride with a column from the 705th Tank Destroyer Battalion's recon outfit. The column consisted of three M-8 armored cars and two or three jeeps. Dick Ladd rode facing backward on the last M-8. Behind the M-8 was a jeep with a .30-cal. light machine gun mounted on it. When Ladd's M-8 took a turn behind a building, a Volkswagen loaded with four or five Germans fell in behind the M-8. Ladd realized the safety of his Tommy gun was "on." In the seconds it took to release the safety, a German in the VW cut loose with a machine pistol. The slugs ripped into both of Ladd's hands, splintering the wood stock of the Tommy gun, spraying pieces of wood in his face.

Meanwhile, the following American jeep rounded the corner, opened up on the VW with the .30-cal. light machine gun, and caused it to crash at the side of the road. Several Germans leaped out of the vehicle and ran. Ladd wound up in an aid station west of Bastogne.

As elsewhere in the perimeter, the icy winds whipped across the area, making conditions almost unbearable for the combatants, especially those confined to foxholes. John Schwartz of the 502nd was wearing no less than four pairs of trousers and was still cold.

Action at Flamierge

One of the first concerted German efforts to break into Bastogne from the west fell against the lines of the 1st/401st. Robert D. Lott of C/401st described his role in repulsing this powerful enemy thrust:

On the 23rd of December 1944 at an outpost of the roadblock set up near Flamierge, Belgium, I awoke that morning to find it was so cold that my M-1 Garand rifle had frozen shut since I last pulled my turn at guard during the night. The ejector was frozen shut, so I urinated on the metal parts, which was a sure way of thawing the rifle so it would be ready to use when needed.

Later that morning, I left my foxhole to go into a farmhouse that was situated right behind our hole. There I stripped my rifle down, including the trigger group; cleaned and oiled all the parts; and reassembled the weapon. I cocked it to make sure I had assembled the gun properly. Then all hell broke loose.

I jumped up and ran out to my foxhole and noticed a group of tanks across the open field. I thought General Patton had broken through, then I noticed the type of tanks and knew we were in trouble. The tank crews and infantry following the tanks didn't seem to spot our outpost. With me at the outpost was Sergeant Robert Bowen with a Thompson subma-

The Bed Sheets of Hemroulle

The most famous story from the battle at Hemroulle involved Lieutenant Colonel "Long John" Hanlon, CO of 1st/502nd. He visited the mayor of Hemroulle and directed that the church bell be rung to summon the civilian inhabitants, most of whom were hiding in their cellars.

The civilians were reluctant to come out, but a message was relayed to them that the Americans lacked white snow camouflage, a situation that gave the German attackers an advantage. The villagers were asked to donate all their white bed sheets, tablecloths, and – for helmet covers – pillow cases, which they did. Hanlon promised to replace these items at some later date.

Shortly after the war, Hanlon was able to publicize this incident in the media and received hundreds of bed sheets from donors throughout the United States. He returned to Hemroulle a few years later, and the mayor again tolled the church bell. This time, the populace assembled at the church and received repayment in the form of new linens, as Hanlon had promised.

Bedsheets of Hemroulle
Promising they would eventually be replaced, Lieutenant Colonel "Long John" Hanlon asked the villagers of Hem roulle to donate their bedsheets and pillowcases for use by his 1st/502nd troopers as makeshift snow camouflage. After the war ended, Hanlon made good on his promise, returning to Belgium with enough new linen for the whole village. *Benecke*

chine gun; our BAR man, Horkay; and Jack Gresh and myself equipped with M-1 rifles. Automatic weapons were not desirable for this situation, so our M-1s would work out best against the white-clad Jerry infantry. We could now see 12 tanks and never did estimate the number on foot. For awhile, Jack and I used our M-1s to the best of our ability and tried to put as many of their troops out of commission as possible, without giving away our position and also conserving our ammunition.

For this one battle, I was given a citation for killing 22 of the enemy. I don't know who did the counting, but Jack Gresh should have credit for his share.

As we were picking off the enemy, I spotted near my hole an abandoned bazooka and one shell that was half buried in the ground. I dug the shell out, straightened the fins, and wired it up to the bazooka, taking a guess at the range. I set the sights at 350 yards, hoping to hit in the general area of the tanks, if the shell ever left the tube of the bazooka. I knew the

Mexican Pete

A Hispanic member of the 502nd, noted on the back of the photo only as "Mexican Pete," mans a light machine gun on the northwest section of the perimeter. *Krochka*

This crossroads near Champs, Belgium, was photographed by Lieutenant David White of regimental S-2 of the 502nd.

bazooka would draw fire from the tanks and give away our position, but I knew the tanks didn't like to cope with bazooka fire. It was possible this shot could delay their attack and allow us to get back to our company or get some help.

When I fired the bazooka, the shell lobbed through the air and looked like a sure miss, but to our surprise, the shell hit a Mark IV tank in its rear bogey wheel, crippled the tank, and wounded or killed a soldier walking behind it.

The tank tried to get out of the way, but would only go into a circle. All hell broke loose again! They spotted where the bazooka shell came from, and they fired everything they had. The four of us kept down, and it felt like the end of the world had come. It would take a few minutes for the smoke to clear up, so I said, "Let's get out of here." But Sergeant Bowen thought we would get help now.

When the smoke cleared, we could see the disabled tank's personnel trying to leave their tank into another tank that came up alongside it. Then the tanks withdrew over the ridge with what I assumed was the tank commander sitting up on the tank turret, waving his arms as though he was directing the other

Lonely outpost

This position was situated in front of the castle housing HQ/502nd at Rolle. The .50-caliber machine gun is manned by a member of "the Deuce," the regiment's colloquial moniker. *Krochka*

A Panther tank knocked out in the northwest sector. *Krochka*

tanks. I shot my M-1 at the possible tank commander and missed him with six shots.

I thought, My God! I had been shooting like a beginner, wasting valuable ammo and not giving the tank a lead. Then, I aimed my seventh shot with a lead on the moving tank, and when I squeezed the trigger, I saw him reel over backwards. I then thought, that was worth seven shots.

In a short time, our planes came out for the first time since we had been in Bastogne defense. They flew over the battle area and never spotted the large force in the open field as the enemy. We had hoped they would finish the battle for us.

We held there until dark without much opposition. Finally, Sergeant Bowen said he would go back to get us some help and ammunition. In a couple of minutes, he came running back and said we were cut off from our troops. The Germans had circled around in back of us and were out in front of the farmhouse. We jumped up, leaving behind a can of homemade chicken soup that I had received in an early Xmas package from my aunt in Messhopen, Pennsylvania. We ran out along the farmhouse, right across the road, right through their ranks, taking them by surprise. This enabled us to get 50 yards away in the dark before they started shooting at us as we ran along the ditch to battalion HQ. We found our outfit heading back toward Bastogne and were happy to be with them.

At that time, I learned that we four had achieved a real accomplishment—that our battalion was able to withdraw when the tanks had moved back.

Captain Towns, our company commander (who was killed on 26 December), came over and congratulated me on knocking out the tank, then reminded me that he had promised a pass to Paris to any soldier in his outfit if they knocked out a tank.

On 26 December, my best buddy, Jack Gresh, was killed. On the 28th, Sergeant Bowen was put out of commission with a loss of hearing and later captured. On the same day, Horkay lost a thumb, and that evening I was shot in the face, which ended my part in the Battle of the Bulge.

A check of decorations in the back of the 101st's official history indicates that despite his heroic actions,

Lott received only the "citation" mentioned in his narrative. No medal for valor was awarded, yet most readers will probably agree that his action deserved at least the Silver Star.

Christmas Morning on the West Perimeter

Elements of the *15th Panzer-Grenadier Division* had massed for an all-out attempt to break into Bastogne from the west on Christmas Eve – actually 0300 hours on Christmas morning. A concerted infantry attack actually broke into the A/502nd lines at Champs and fighting from house to house went on through most of the night.

Sergeant Willis Fowler of that company had, for some unknown reason, completely stripped and cleaned his light machine gun the day before. On the night of the attack he found himself on the flank of the German infantry thrust, firing belt after belt from a position near a potato storage shack. The Germans were not aware of his location, and he took a heavy toll of them. Some actual hand-to-hand fighting was reported in the houses in Champs, and other 1st/502nd companies were shifted to meet the threat.

During that bleak night before Christmas, a German officer of the attack element found himself in the Champs schoolhouse. While there, he quickly scribbled a poignant message on the chalkboard, which was discovered when the schoolmaster returned later. The message was as follows:

Let the world never see such a Christmas night again. To die far from one's children, one's wife and mother, under fire of guns, there is no greater cruelty.

To take away from his mother a son, a husband from his wife, a father from his children, is it worthy of a human being? Life can only be for love and respect.

At the sight of ruins, of blood and death, universal fraternity will rise.

A German Officer

By 0600, the 502nd had launched a counterattack to drive the Germans from the houses they held for only three hours. By 0800, the town was cleared and

Christmas morning hero
Sergeant Willis Fowler of A/502nd *(center)* was the Christmas morning hero at Champs, Belgium. He earned the Silver Star and went to Paris for a "Combat Diary" radio interview. *Glenn Johnson*

Below: Bringing in German prisoners on the western perimeter. *Swartz*

the locals counted some 99 German bodies and many more wounded in the area. Whether the author of the above sentiment survived is unknown.

Sergeant Fowler had fired six to ten 250-round belts of ammo through his machine gun. Because of his crucial role in devastating the enemy attackers, Fowler was awarded the Silver Star. When a request was made for an infantryman to represent the 101st Airborne Division on a Paris radio program called "Combat Diary," Fowler's name was submitted by his first sergeant, and he departed on 26 December for Paris. Also going to record the show for broadcast to the states were General McAuliffe, a medic, and an artilleryman.

To the south of Champs, a large German task force spearheaded by 17 tanks (mostly *Mark IV*s with at least one Panther in the group), broke through the lines of the 1st/401st and A/327th. Some of the tanks were hit by 75mm howitzer shells, bazooka rounds, and small arms fire. They menaced the CP of Lieutenant Colonel Ray Allen, CO of the 1st/401st, and he fled on foot, making his escape and nearly being gunned down by men of the 502nd as he approached their lines on foot.

Tank destroyers helped whittle down the German tank force, as did Colonel Cooper's 75mm howitzers of the 463rd PFAB. The German infantry, in at least battalion strength, had fallen behind the rampaging tanks and were mowed down in a terrific crossfire from machine guns of the 1st/401st. A number of .50-cal. machine guns had been retrieved by the glidermen, still in cosmoline, near Crossroad X a few days earlier. These were cross-fired in such a devastating manner that the Germans fell atop each other in heaps. After breaking through, the surviving German armor spread out, one tank driving up into Champs and others menacing the 502nd CP at Rolle. Cooks, clerks, and radiomen of the 377th PFAB and other units fell out in the snow with rifles to stop the holiday breakthrough.

At the Chateau Rolle approach road, 502nd demolitions sergeant Schuyler Jackson armed himself with a bazooka and waited behind the second tree to knock out the approaching enemy tanks. Twenty-five years later, Schuyler returned to the spot and told a reporter from the *Army Digest*:

This is really a strange feeling to be standing here now. Five tanks had broken through. Four had already been hit when the fifth was coming by me. I was behind this tree. Right after it passed, I stepped out and let him have it with my bazooka. It went a few more yards, then went off the road up there where you see that bale of hay. The Germans came tearing out of that tank; let me tell you, they were ready to fight. We shot them down.

Sky Jackson earned the Silver Star for this action, and Sergeant Gordon Little was down the road where another tank had gone off the road into a ditch. It, too, was hit by a bazooka rocket, which "buzzed around inside." The German commander was killed when he climbed out of the turret.

None of the 17 German tanks that had broken through that day made it back to enemy lines. The tank that entered Champs was destroyed by bazooka fire from Johnny Ballard (later KIA on 4 January 1945), of A/502nd. This lone tank's crew had hidden with their vehicle for several hours within the American perimeter, after the first bazooka round fired by Sky Jackson bounced off it near Rolle. Later in the afternoon of Christmas Day, this "maverick tank" made a mad dash to regain German lines, but was hit in the engine compartment by Ballard's rocket, after passing about 15 yards from his position. Sergeant Charles Asay and Staff Sergeant Willis Zweibel also

Hitching a ride
Members of the 502nd catch a jeep ride in the snow, near Rolle, Belgium. *via Swartz*

Above: **Aerial lifeline**

Another perspective on the glorious day of aerial resupply on 23 December. This photo was made near Savy, Belgium, where guns of the 377th PFAB were emplaced. *Benecke*

Below: **Lead Scout**

Corporal Newman Tuttle (*left*, S-2 patrol lead scout) with Sergeant Gordon Little and Sergeant Graham Armstrong on the road to Bastogne on 30 December 1944. *White*

captured 25 Germans, who they discovered hiding behind a woodpile in the town of Champs. By Christmas afternoon, the western perimeter was decorated with numerous knocked-out tanks and some half-tracks, plus numerous German corpses. Some of the German dead had fallen beside their tanks, and Len Swartz of the 502nd said, "I'll never forget the sight of the red blood on that white snow."

Another detail remembered by Swartz was that one of the knocked-out German tanks was staffed by two female Panzer women, who were crying as they climbed out into captivity. Swartz saw them taken away for interrogation.

After Patton's Third Army had broken the circle around Bastogne, Patton himself came to visit the western perimeter and reportedly derived great enjoyment from viewing the numerous tanks and infantry stopped in the 502nd sector. He arrived personally at the Chateau Rolle CP to decorate Lieutenant Colonel Steve Chappuis, who had just gone to sleep after being awake for several days and nights. The sleepy Chappuis stood to attention as his DSC was pinned on, and after some words of congratulations, Patton left. Although the 502nd had played a key role on Christmas Day, the majority of tanks were knocked out by other outfits. It is ironic that they were not able to share in much of the credit.

More Christmas Action

One of the engagements fought by the 502nd on the western perimeter was described in the US Army document *Combat Lessons No. 6.* The company described is C/502nd:

Leadership Is Aggressive

The value of aggressive action even against superior enemy forces is again illustrated by this story of a small group of men from the 502nd Parachute Infantry Regiment, as recounted by Private First Class William Reubendael:

"At daylight, Christmas morning, one group of 20 men encountered a German company of about 150 men supported by 4 *Mark IV* tanks. The Americans had 4 light machine guns, 2 bazookas, and their rifles and carbines.

The Germans were already digging in when discovered. Their tanks soon opened fire on the farmhouse around which the Americans had taken positions and forced our men back about 200 yards to the edge of a patch of woods. At that point, the hard-pressed platoon leader decided that his best defense was bold attack. He borrowed several riflemen from a nearby company and then had his machine guns keep the enemy infantry down and their tanks buttoned up while the two bazooka teams and the riflemen moved around to the German company's flank. This small but aggressive maneuvering force inflicted heavy casualties upon the enemy infantry, knocked out three tanks, and forced the other tank to withdraw to a point where it was totally destroyed by another American unit. Not content with this accomplishment, the paratroopers moved on to attack a nearby enemy-held farmhouse. The German occupants surrendered, turning over their weapons to some American prisoners they had been holding in the same building."

A Tragic Accident

Members of the 502nd's regimental demolitions platoon had devised and rigged up a fiendish booby trap in the woods near a stream, some distance from their CP. This consisted of a clump of C-2 plastic explosive embedded with horseshoes, nails, and assorted scrap metal – all planted against the base of a tree with a tripwire ignition system.

Although the location was known, it was not precisely marked, which would lead to a tragedy.

On 28 December, a recon patrol was sent in the vicinity of the boobytrap. Because headquarters was aware of the booby trap's presence in the vicinity, a guide was sent along with the S-2 men to make sure

Digging their own Graves?
Len Swartz recorded this photo of POWs digging a straddle trench. He said, "The Italian guards told the Krauts that they were Jewish. The Germans probably thought they were digging their own graves." *Swartz*

they avoided it. This guide was a new replacement, who had only recently joined the 502nd.

When the patrol reached the vicinity of the trap, the guide appeared uncertain of precisely where it was located. Then, seeing the stream, he remarked, "Now I know, it's over there."

"Let's move out," said Bob Paczulla, who was leading the patrol.

Just then, a member of the patrol must have kicked the tripwire. There was a horrible blast, and Private Louis P. Migliarese, a close friend of Paczulla's, dropped with a mortal wound. Another trooper received multiple fragments in his legs, but survived. Paczulla was also hit.

Battalion Cos Pow-Wow
Conference of battalion COs of the 502nd at Bastogne, circa January 1945: Lieutenant Colonel Thomas Sutliffe (2nd/502nd), Lieutenant Colonel John Stopka (3rd/502nd), and Lieutenant Colonel "Long John" Hanlon (1st/502nd). Stopka was killed by mistake in an attack by P-47 fighters on 14 January 1945. *Musura*

Panzer-Grenadier POWs from the *Panzer-Grenadier Regiment 115* are inventoried by an officer of HQ/502nd at Rolle, Belgium on Christmas afternoon, 1944. These were survivors of the abortive morning attack. *Hugh Roberts*

Devastated by the death of his friend in this tragic accident, Paczulla carried Mig's personal effects back to the Chateau Rolle, found his way into the chapel, and prayed for his dead friend.

A demotions lieutenant apologized to Bob for the mistake, "But it didn't bring Migliarese back," said Paczulla.

Teamwork

In many ETO battles, the TD had proven less successful than anticipated in its role of knocking out enemy armor. The vulnerability of these vehicles to counterfire was demonstrated again and again during the battles at Bastogne. The M-10 TD was the most common.

Among the TDs caught in the Bastogne encirclement were M-18 "Hellcat" tank destroyers – low, exceptionally fast (but lightly-armored) vehicles mounting 76mm main guns. Many of these belonged to the separate 705th TD Battalion. Some M7B1 self-propelled 105mm howitzers were also pressed into service as tank destroyers.

The original concept of deploying TDs was to send them out in search of enemy armor. But experience had proven they did better lying in wait in a defensive role.

The TDs fared somewhat better in this role, but despite success in taking out enemy tanks as at Marvie or on the western perimeter, they always seemed to lose some of their own vehicles to retaliatory enemy fire. Teamwork and improvisation was called for in each situation.

Combat Lessons No. 6 contained the following example of such improvised use of teamwork, although the specific units and locations are not given:

In the Savy, Belgium area on the west perimeter of Bastogne in December 1944, several members of D/377th PFAB are shown during a break in the action. An unknown lieutenant stands at left, his jeep driver is at center, smiling. 1st Sergeant Johnston can also be seen with 377th PFAB markings on his helmet (cannonball with tic at 6 o'clock). *Hettrick*

Locating Enemy Tanks at Night

Suggested by the Assistant G-2, 101st Airborne Division, "At night, we placed a machine gun on both sides of a TD. When hostile tanks were heard approaching, the machine guns fired tracers until ricochets indicated that a tank was being hit. Both guns would then fire at the tank and the TD would fire at the 'V' formed by the converging machine-gun tracers."

Company B, 502nd had repulsed one major German attack and shifted to a ridge overlooking open ground on the right of A/502nd. Some distance behind them was Champs; Longchamps was situated to their right rear.

Sergeant Forest Jay Nichols had established his squad on this crest and had a .50-cal. machine gun on the left of his squad. The weapon had been salvaged from another unit and had a bent top plate. The troopers had repaired it and used it in their defensive position. More unusual was the British Bren gun they had set up on the right edge of their squad. Jay Nichols had found the gun at Elst, Holland, on The Island, had brought it back to Mourmelon with a good supply of British .303-cal. ammo. These weapons proved to be a superb supplement to their rifles and Tommy guns.

On New Year's Eve, after dark, Jay went back to Champs to get some K-rations for his men. He went from foxhole to foxhole, handing the food down to the occupants. As he was kneeling above one hole, a terrific German artillery barrage began. A shell exploded near Nichols, and he fell with multiple wounds atop the man in the hole. Doc Archie treated Nichols and found wounds on his face, left arm, left hand, and left side. The war was over for Nichols, but he would survive. Corporal Milton S. Lowry, his assistant squad leader, was killed by the same barrage.

Later in January, as troops of the 17th Airborne and 35th and 87th Infantry Divisions moved up, the 101st Airborne units on the western perimeter would move north and east, toward Bourcy and Houffalize.

Above: On 27 December 1944, this C-47, named "*Dust," of the 92nd Troop Carrier Squadron, 439th TCG, was shot down while towing a resupply glider into the Bastogne perimeter. Lieutenant Don Hettrick of D/377th PFAB photographed the C-47 making an emergency landing between Savy and Luzery, Belgium. *Hettrick*

Below: Christmas Day 1944, this Mark IV tank—possibly from the 15th Panzer-Grenadier Division— was KO'd at Champs, Belgium, by the 502nd PIR. The name on the side of the main battery gun is *"Lustmolch,"* meaning "The Happy Salamander." This is believed to stem from the notion that a salamander thrown into a fire will not burn. Note the helmet stencils. *Hettrick*

On the top: An unusual rear view of "*Dust" taken from the rear, with no landing gear down. *Hettrick*

Above: A nice side view of "*Dust" showing the left engine shot away. The pilot was seriously wounded and was rushed to Bastogne by jeep to recieve medical attention. The nose art name and J8 marking for the 92nd TCS are nicely depicted here. The trooper at left foreground in profile is a member of the 321st GFAB, according to his helmet stencil, a cannonball with tic at 3 o'clock. *Hettrick*

Opposite: Members of an artillery unit search a German corpse, west of Bastogne. *Krochka*

The word Longchamps means "Long Fields" in French, and members of 2nd/502nd will never forget the area north of the town where they formed their defensive perimeter. The town itself lies near the northwest corner of the circular Bastogne defense line, and the area north of the town is characterized by a huge valley. A single road runs from the town northbound, into the valley and continues northward up the far side and beyond.

The 2nd/502nd dug in on the higher ground on the south edge of the valley, facing north. F/502nd was on the left (west) side of the road, with the remaining companies strung out to the east toward the next village (Monaville). From Monaville east was the 3rd/502nd, whose line extended as far as Recogne, where it tied in with G/506th.

"I Don't Need Any Company. I'm from Chicago!"

Germans trying to find a way into Bastogne didn't get around to trying the Longchamps area until late December. The first sizable contact may have been with a two-man F/502nd LP late one night near Christmas.

Frank Tiedeman and Howard Matthews took a light machine gun across the big valley and set up a LP in the woods near the road. In the darkness, they became aware that a lone trooper from another company was dug-in on the other side of the road.

"Hey, why don't you come over here and join us?" Frank called to him.

"I don't need any company. I'm from Chicago!" the lone trooper replied, staying put in his position.

Around 0400, the Americans heard the sound of hobnailed boots marching toward them. An entire company of Germans was marching toward them in neat columns, unaware of their presence. Holding fire until the head of the column was abreast of their position, Tiedeman and Matthews opened up with the light machine gun, taking the large enemy force totally by surprise. The lone trooper across the road also fired his rifle as fast as possible. The stunned German survivors withdrew, seeking a different approach to Longchamps.

In the light of dawn, the Americans found several dozen German bodies lying on the road. They withdrew to the main line of resistance.

The Attack of 3 January

A number of patrols and skirmishes took place in this area before the main German effort hit on 3 January when a coordinated and concerted drive to break into Bastogne from the northeast and northwest simultaneously was planned by the Germans. The attack on Longchamps would be launched by the *SS-Panzer-Grenadier Regiment 19* of the *9th SS-Panzer Division.* This unit had opposed the 101st at the dike positions across from Renkum in Holland.

On the night of 2 January, a German runner mistakenly walked up to a foxhole of 2nd/502nd in the darkness and asked a question in German. He was punched in the face by Lincoln Bethel of the 502nd and was captured by Bethel and Reg Davies. They took the prisoner back to the 502nd CP for questioning and Rene Schmidt, the interpreter, informed them that this was perhaps the most valuable prisoner taken by the 101st in WWII. This runner had maps and details of the attack plan of his regiment, scheduled for the following day. Armed with this information, the Americans called artillery concentrations into the staging areas of the *9th SS* and were able to disrupt and weaken the coming attack.

This was most fortunate because, even in a diminished state, the *19th SS* launched a devastating attack against 2nd/502nd on 3 January.

Lawrence Silva, manning a radio, first reported German tanks moving up. During his last transmission, a German tank was parked directly over his hole. His body was found later. He had no marks on him and had presumably died as a result of carbon monoxide poisoning from the exhaust of the tank.

When the tanks and panzer-grenadiers did come in, they hit D/502nd on the right side of the highway first, threatening to break the line near Monaville. German tanks stopped and pivoted over individual foxholes, crushing the paratroopers inside with their tracks. Part of F/502nd was sent across the road to help Company D.

Silver Star
Franklin "Ray" Blasingame *(left)* earned a Silver Star on 3 January 1945 at Longchamps for knocking out two tanks with his bazooka. At right is his pal, Willard Davis. *Sapinski*

Monaville
German prisoners being brought into town east of Longchamps on 17 January 1945. *White*

Here, Franklin "Ray" Blasingame of F/502nd was able to hit a half dozen German tanks at point-blank range with his bazooka, although most of the rockets deflected or failed to explode.

Bert Ellard served as loader for Blasingame, and the pair did succeed in knocking out two of the tanks. For this, Blasingame was awarded the Silver Star. Ellard also lived to tell about it. He recalled that some of these "tanks" were actually turretless self-propelled guns, thus they couldn't aim their main guns without turning the entire chassis of the vehicle. This may have helped Ellard and Blasingame to avoid large-caliber counterfire.

Over on the west side of the highway, crack shots were devastating the Germans as they came forward in masses on foot. The panzer troops had more men than tanks, so they used some of their panzer crewmen as infantry, advancing across the snowy white valley in their stark black tunics.

They ran forward with zeal in the belief that they were breaking through, but the Americans mowed them down. Numerous analogies have been drawn between the defense of the Alamo and the siege of Bastogne. Here on this ground above Longchamps, the comparison was perhaps a good one. When the shooting stopped, the valley floor was dotted with black-uniformed panzer troops and the nearest one to Joe Pistone's hole lay only three feet away!

East of the road, it was chaos. The battle was not going well for the 502nd; Hans Sannes, D/502nd – among those who lay wounded, with German tanks passing close to his position – expected to die, but like many others, found himself still among the living when the German troops withdrew. Guns of the 321st GFAB and 81st AAAB helped stop *SS-Panzer-Grenadier Regiment 19*.

Over 40 members of F/502nd were wounded and captured by the *SS* troopers, no doubt the largest number of 101st men ever captured right off a frontline in any battle of WWII. Frank Tiedeman and Howie Matthews had left to get ammo in a jeep. They drove back into the line just in time to be captured. As the Germans lined them up, American artillery fire came in, wounding a number of friendly troops, including Tiedeman, who was sprayed in the face, arms, and body with shrapnel. Earl Hendricks, the company commander, was shot in the arm and also captured. Blasingame, Ellard, and First Sergeant Les Harder managed to escape along with about a third of the company.

The hamlet of Recogne, Belgium, lies several miles north of Bastogne. Company G/506th dug in in the woods facing Recogne from the south. There, in snowy foxholes, they would suffer the effects of the weather, perhaps more so than the other units, as there were no farmhouses in or behind their line into which they could rotate for occasional warmth. The men did build a huge bonfire on Christmas Eve and miraculously received no German fire despite the glow, which was no doubt visible for hundreds of yards.

The Overcoat with 22 Bullet Holes

In the area west of Recogne, H/502nd had established an LP in an isolated clump of pine trees in front of their front line. In this post were three troopers manning an light machine gun. One night, German tanks were heard in the area, so at dawn First Sergeant Harry Bush walked to the forward post with a bazooka and two rookie replacements to provide more firepower to the LP.

Unknown to the three Americans as they walked forward, the men in the LP had fallen asleep and had just been captured by a German patrol. The three German intruders had them face down on the ground when Bush's group approached.

Bush gave a low whistle at the clump of pines and said "Sergeant Bush coming in."

He was greeted by a fusillade of 9mm bullets coming from the trees. Bush unslung his Tommy gun and returned fire. Machine-pistol slugs nipped his overcoat and dropped the two men beside him. Bush sprayed the trees with one magazine, loaded another,

and continued spraying. Return fire had diminished by the time he was firing the third magazine. Bush noticed that the hot bore of his Thompson barrel had expanded and the slugs had no velocity in coming out the muzzle. He could see them dropping before they even reached the trees. Slinging the submachine gun on his shoulder, he produced his .45 pistol and emptied that into the trees also. Finally, First Sergeant Bush walked forward, aware that his right arm was bleeding. One slug had hit him between the elbow and shoulder.

It was quiet as he parted the branches and saw three Germans down. Two were dead, the third was badly wounded and on his knees. Bush grabbed the Thompson with both hands behind the front sight and swung it downward like a club, smashing the wooden stock over the helmet of the wounded German.

The captured outpost men were still alive. They took Bush to a field hospital where his overcoat was removed. In the skirt and arms of the coat, the medics counted 22 9mm bullet holes; 11 slugs had passed through making two holes each. Only one slug had hit Bush.

"Mein Kopf!"

After one of the evening attacks against G/506th, German bodies were strewn across the open ground in front of Recogne. One of the Germans kept screaming *"Mein Kopf! Mein Kopf!"* ("My head" in German) Ed Slizewski heard one of his buddies comment, "That fanatical Kraut bastard – he's dying and he's yelling, *'Mein Kampf'.*" Finally, Pee Wee Martin saw

Peaceful Pines

A classic view of snow-laden pines near Bastogne. *Krochka*

Heroic Medic
Combat Medic Irving "Blackie" Baldinger, H/506th. Admired by all in his company, Blackie showed great courage in carrying wounded buddies from bullet-swept open fields near Recogne. *Andros*

Killed at Recogne
Private First Class Charles Merritts, F/501st, was the best friend of Leo Gillis. Merritts was killed in Company F's tragic attack on Recogne. *Gillis*

one of the men walk out with a .45, saying, "I'm tired of listening to him; he's not going to make it anyways."

A pistol shot ended the yelling.

Other Attacks

One of the worst barrages came in when a few TDs pulled in behind the company front line.

"We hated to see them because they always attracted the German artillery," said Pee Wee Martin.

As shells came flying in, the men got low in their holes, and one of Pee Wee's friends, Sergeant Dean Christensen, got behind and under a TD, thinking it was the safest place to be. A mortar shell landed right behind the TD, though, and shrapnel killed Christensen.

The heaviest German attack saw a battalion-sized infantry unit with tank support drive against the G/506th line. In the face of this, most of the men left their positions and fell back, to be stopped by an officer 200 yards to the rear. One machine gunner, Stan Clever, who had been captured in Normandy but escaped, never received the word to withdraw. He wasn't aware of being alone, but he also didn't consider being captured again an option. Clever single-handedly mowed down many Germans and held the line until his buddies returned to their positions. He was reportedly a bit angry that he had been left alone on the firing line. This intrepid act was recognized only with a Bronze Star.

Sometime in January, Pee Wee Martin observed a patrol from H/506th make an assault across a snowy field near Recogne. The snow was knee deep, but an icy crust had formed on the surface. It was pos-

sible to walk some distance, breaking through the surface only occasionally.

The lead scouts of the group were cut down by machine-gun fire, and a dark-haired medic nearby began stripping off his musette bag and webbing.

"What are you doing?" Pee Wee asked him.

"I'm the medic; it's my job to go out and get them."

"Well, hell, you'll be killed … you're not going to help anyone that way."

The medic took off running across the open area and dragged and carried two wounded men back, one at a time, across the cruel, icy, exposed field.

The medic, "Blackie" Baldinger, survived. Blackie was another unsung hero who was not recognized with a medal for his heroic acts. He passed away in the early 1990s. His son served in combat with the 101st Airborne in the Vietnam War.

The hamlet of Recogne had changed hands several times by 9 January, but on that day, it was being held by the Germans. A plan was laid to bring F/501st around to assault and retake the town from the south entrance.

The night before F/501's attack, a wire-laying team had walked right into the town in the dark, then realizing their predicament, dropped the wire spool on the road and ran back. Thus, during the following day's attack, the German commander could have hooked onto the wire and conferred with the American commander had he been so inclined.

During daylight, F/501st left the treeline that had been home so long for G/506th, came down the hill, and approached Recogne. Third Platoon came right up along the road from the south. First Platoon had almost reached the first buildings when the Germans opened up and pinned them down.

Sergeant Bass, caught in the open, was screaming, "Get 'em offa my back!" He ran to the shelter of a chicken coop, but Art Lufkin was caught on the open ground, wounded. Nine slugs eventually tore into his jaw, neck, back, and legs, but he survived. While he lay wounded, a hog trotted over and began to nibble at his wounds. Art's buddies shot the pig, which fell between him and the Germans, offering some concealment at last.

During the attack, Gillis's best friend, Charles Merritts, was fatally wounded.

Under command of acting CO Clair Hess, F/501st rampaged into the town. A single sniper on the approach had killed a number of men and O'Neill thinks the sniper was among those killed in the first house, but this will never be known for certain. Company E came up to assist F/501st in clearing the houses, but Lieutenant Joe McGregor was shot in the head a second time while crossing the road. This time, the wound was fatal.

In all, 25 men and three officers were lost by Companies E and F in the taking of Recogne. Colonel Julian Ewell, commander of the 501st, was seriously wounded on 10 January and had to be replaced by Robert A. Ballard. Ballard commanded the 501st until its deactivation after V-E Day.

Around 10 January, the entire 501st had been moved to the area north of Bastogne. The woods in the Foy-Bizory-Fazone areas were still being cleared of German troops. Bill Russo of C/501st recalled an episode from that period:

We had a lieutenant in C/501st named Grimaldi – Alfonso Grimaldi. He was with the coast artillery in New York City, then he joined the parachute troops. He joined us as a first lieutenant replacement.

Over to the left of us was a very thin woods, sticking out like a peninsula. Three sides were exposed to German fire… and they told Grimaldi to go clear that woods. That was murder, what happened to him. He led a patrol in there, they were ambushed, and Grimaldi was killed. Lt. Defelice and a few others escaped with wounds.

Later in January, the 502nd pushed northeast along the railroad line through Jack's Woods, toward the town of Bourcy. The 327th was nearby, and 3rd/501st was still in position south of the railroad line. P-47 fighter-bombers gave close-in support, but with the

confusion caused by the heavy forest close to both sides of the track, the inevitable happened. The 3rd/502nd was crossing a small snowy clearing when some P-47's swooped down and dropped bombs on a group. Major John P. Stopka, who had earned the DSC in Colonel Cole's bayonet charge at Carentan, was among the men killed.

Lieutenant Felix Stanley looked into the field from G/501st positions and saw a number of badly-wounded troopers bouncing on the field in their death throes. A brief truce was called, and medics of both sides

Smiling Mortarman
An 81mm mortarman of the 501st at Foy, Belgium, 1945. *Signal Corps*

Attack on Bourcy, 16 December
Lieutenant David White of the HQ/502nd's S-2 section recorded this scene of the attack. Germans vacated the town just before American troops entered. *White*

You Found A home in the Army, Chum!

Looking like a scene from the movie Battleground, this is an actual view of troopers sheltering during an artillery barrage. *Krochka*

Company G of the 506th was situated in a woodline about .3 mile south of Recogne. They suffered badly from the severe weather, as there were no houses or buildings nearby to enter for warmth. This photo was taken there, with G/506th men displaying an unusual arsenal, ranging from an American M-1919A6 light machine gun and an M-1928A1 Thompson, to a British Sten Gun and a German MP44 assault rifle. *Captain Joe Doughty*

appeared to collect the wounded and dead. Also in that area, Leo Pichler, an original member of the 502nd and a member of the boxing team, was killed right on the railroad line while putting out aerial recognition panels. Total losses that day numbered 12 dead and 25 wounded.

When the town of Bourcy was finally assaulted, the Germans pulled out, leaving the town to the US Army.

Since just before midnight on 31 January 1944, and continuing throughout January 1945, another German offensive had been launched against General Alexander Patch's US Seventh Army to the southeast of the Ardennes. Commencing in eastern Lorraine and in the Low Vosges Mountains of northwestern Alsace, the offensive, dubbed Operation *Nordwind* and conducted by *Oberstgeneral* Johannes Blaskowitz's *Army Group G,* had failed to gain its initial objective, the Saverne Pass. As a result, Blaskowitz shifted his main effort at the end of the operation's first week to the Rhine Plain in northern Alsace. Throughout history, Alsace had changed hands numerous times in wars between Germany, France, and even Austria. Much of the populace spoke Alsatian, a dialect of German with heavy French influence, as well as French and German. The people themselves mostly have ethnically German family names, and the architecture, food, and other cultural aspects display heavy German influence. Also, since Hitler had declared both Alsace and Lorraine to be provinces of Germany, thousands of Alsatians had been conscripted into the German armed forces and were serving in the *Wehrmacht.* The loyal-ties of the civilian population were sometimes questionable.

By 21 January, the defensive sector along the Moder River near Hagenau was being held by elements of the 36th, 42nd, 79th, and 103rd Infantry Divisions. The 101st was trucked directly from Bastogne to this sector.

Lieutenant Sefton of 2nd/501st described the trip:

We boarded the Air Corps vans with no roofs on them, and that ride of some 200 miles was probably the most miserable experience of the entire Battle of the Bulge for us. We were in those things, stamping our feet on the steel beds, trying to keep from freezing. The trucks were so thoroughly uncomfortable, and the pace was so great, that everybody on that trip suffered terribly. Our morale was already pretty low. I had gone into Bastogne with 40 men in the platoon, and there were only 14 of us left, counting the mortar squad – and that was not an abnormally shrunken unit.

We had lost a lot of people, and those who were left were feeling pretty much that the war was a lousy business and that we had been ill-used, and we were hardly cheering about the fact of going down and trying to pull chestnuts out of the fire in another area.

Upon arrival in the sector on 26 January 1945, the 327th and 501st relieved the 42nd Infantry Division's 222nd Infantry Regiment, which had taken heavy casualties when German troops attacked across the river. They left many of their dead lying in the snow, until a plea was made to their commander to come and remove them. The 42nd Infantry Division men used to paint little signs with a facsimile of their rainbow patch and the words "The Rainbow Division was here." Members of the 501st obtained some paint and wrote next to their graffiti: "Where the hell are you now?"

Divarty to Alsace

This truck, bearing markings of the 377th PFAB, actually contains members of the 101st's Division Artillery headquarters as they were moved to Alsace Lorraine from the Bulge. Left to right: Landrum, J. Miller, Necikowski, Powell, Cahill, O'Shaughnessy, Dilloway, Town, R. Miller, Clarence Theaker. *Theaker*

Above: **Strolling Through the Alsace**

This photo of a typical scene in an Alsatian town was made by Al Krochka. *Krochka*

Below: **Happy Warrior**

Waldo Brown, a member of HQ/501st's S-2 section. His portrait was made in Alsace by Gopher Sloan. *via Wilbur*

The initial 101st line faced north across the Moder River from Hagenau to Neuborg, a front of about four miles. On right (eastern) flank was the 79th Infantry Division and on the other the 103rd Infantry Division, recently taken over by General McAuliffe of "Nuts" fame.

Operation *Oscar*

Company A/501st had recently lost two commanders. Captain Stach had been sent back to the states as last surviving male in his family. Lieutenant Charlie Seale had been accidentally shot to death in the woods north of Bastogne. Lieutenant Hugo Sims, of Incredible Patrol fame, was sent to A/501st as its new commander. The company was given the honor of leading the only significant incursion across the Moder River in Operation *Oscar*, a raid conducted the night of 31 January to 1 February. Also participating was B/501st and E/327th. Engineers of B/326th installed two footbridges cross the Moder near Neuborg to facilitate the operation.

Ed Hallo, operations sergeant for A/501st gives a brief account of his company's role in the raid:

We walked right across this frozen river – it was wintertime. Company B crossed in another area. We went over about 1,000–1,500 yards behind the lines. I had to run up to Sims. I said, "Captain, slow down! You're losing your men back here!" He didn't know the men in the company, and he had given orders that if anybody got wounded, they're to make it back on their own – don't stop to help anybody out. So we went up there, we got along a road, and these Germans came up in platoon formation, "links-links-links …" When they got in the middle of us, we let loose and we slaughtered them.

In the meantime, Ed Gulick of the third platoon got shot. "We'll pick him up on the way back," Sims said.

"Let's go." And he took off. When we all went back, I told the guys to pick up Gulick. We picked him up, put his body in a raincoat, and carried him back... didn't find out until after we got him back that he was dead.

I walked right into battalion HQ with Lieutenant Sims and they pinned the Silver Star on him.

He turned to me and said "Hallo, this won't get you the Silver Star, but I don't know what I would've done without you."

I didn't say anything, and you could've heard a pin drop. This guy, every time you turned around, he got a medal.

Later, when we got to tent city at Mourmelon le Petit, some of the replacements got a furlough and went to Paris. I was an original member of the company and hadn't had a furlough yet. Sims took off for Paris and left word with the executive officer, "Don't let Hallo go on furlough."

I complained to the ExO that some of the men were going on their second round of furloughs. He said, "I can't help it, Hallo. Sims says not to let you go, and I've got to follow orders."

The net results of Operation OSCAR for the 501st were five killed, eight wounded, and three missing. Company B's first sergeant, Joe Henderson, was among those killed. One German officer and 20 enlisted prisoners were brought back.

The 327th lost one man killed, 13 wounded, and one missing. They captured one German officer and 13 enlisted men.

Numerous lesser-known patrols went across the Moder River during this period, the patrols always careful not to cross twice at the same spot. Troopers like Tex McMorries of G/501st prowled the German rear and became like hunters. Don Burgett returned from one patrol by wading across the Moder River. He found it was only waist deep in that spot.

New replacement Ken Parker of C/506th observed the survivors of the Bastogne fighting. He recalled, "None of them talked much; they all looked extremely exhausted, and they were all absolutely filthy dirty – every inch of their uniforms. Apparently, in Bastogne, they'd never had a chance to change or wash or do much of anything except eat and survive."

Fearless or Crazy?
A Dinner at Neubourg

Some of the troopers in rifle companies were fortunate to have the shelter of homes in the Moder River area. By scrounging and using 10-in-1 rations, the combat troops could sometimes concoct a sizable meal.

The following incident as related by Tex McMorries of G/501st gives an insight into the death-defying humor which was characteristic of some of the more fearless troopers:

A bunch of guys prepared a feast. We had the food on a table in Neubourg [Alsace], when suddenly German artillery started coming in. One round tore a corner out of the house. All the levelheaded guys went to the cellar – also two or three officers with them...

I don't know whose idea it was, but Frank Serawatka and I decided what a joke it would be to go ahead and eat. So with everyone else deep in the cellar (where we should have been), Serawatka and myself sat down at the table. With artillery raking the town and a couple more rounds tearing into the house, plaster falling in our food, dust filling the room, we sat at the table, enjoying the food, the joke, and watching the bricks jump and dust fly as the rounds pounded Neuborg – just like a ringside seat.

Mess Line
Mess line in Hagenau or Neuborg area was recorded by Jim Duggins of HQ/501st. *Duggins*

Chow Cart
Using a farm cart as dining room table, members of A/377th PFAB dine in Alsace. *Benecke*

235

Above on left: Letter of Death

Oscar T. Sanders of HQ/2nd/501st's 81mm mortar platoon sends another letter of death to Herman the German from a sandbagged dugout in Alsace. *via Tuel*

Above on right: Seasoned Warrior

Ken Casler, who had fought in assorted 1st/501st companies from Hell's Corners to Bastogne, sits in his hole in Alsace. *Sloan*

Below: **Off to the Front**

A member of 1st Platoon, F/501st, going to the front line in Alsace. *Korvas*

Opposite: **The Club Mobile**

A Red Cross wagon dispenses coffee and donuts in Alsace, February 1945. *Duggins*

Also, we enjoyed kidding about the German gunners: Should we go make a deal for them to fire every day at mealtime? Or should there be blood on the moon tonight (a common expression we used), and should we revoke their licenses to fire those big guns because of their bad manners firing at mealtime? Of course, you know what the permit revoking means.

Mean as a Rattlesnake

Sergeant Jimmy Edgar, an original member of I/501st, who was mean as a rattlesnake, got wounded while in Alsace. His company commander, Lieutenant Bill Morgan came to say goodbye as Edgar was being loaded onto a stretcher.

"Sergeant Edgar," Morgan said, "why don't you take advantage of this wound and go back to the States. You've done more than your share."

Edgar's eyes narrowed and he replied, "Lieutenant, I've kicked sand in three dying company commanders' asses, and I'll be back to kick sand in yours!"

"Want a Light?"

A team of 101st pathfinders jumped at Prum, Germany, to signal a resupply drop of gasoline for the 4th Armored Division. For a few of them, like Lieutenant Schrable Williams, it was their fourth combat jump in WWII.

George "Frenchy" Blain had helped mark the DZ, then moved to the edge of the field designated as the DZ for the resupply. Near the edge of the field, he saw a Jeep parked with two field-grade armored officers standing up in it, watching the approach of the C-47 resupply planes.

Blain approached and saluted them.

"Major, it might be a good idea for you to back that Jeep away from the DZ. Some of the loads have been known to break loose and come down like a bomb."

The armored major removed the field glasses from his eyes and "looked at me like I was dog shit," said Blain.

"OK," said Blain. "Suit yourselves." The arrogant officers never said a word but continued to observe the resupply mission.

As the parachuted bundles of jerry cans were kicked out of the planes, one can broke loose, came down at full speed and hit the front end of the Jeep. The can burst open, splashing gasoline all over the occupants and the vehicle.

Frenchy walked over to them, produced his Zippo lighter, and asked, "Want a light?"

Tough Hombre

"Ridgerunner" Jimmy Edgar, I/501st, inflicts pain on a comrade at Camp Toccoa. After being wounded in battle and then told to go home after recovery by his CO, Bill Morgan, he replied, "Lieutenant, I've kicked sand in three dyin' company commanders' asses. I'll be back to kick sand in yours." And he did return. *Edgar*

Ungrateful Dead

"The dead always looked so damned uncomfortable, you wanted to readjust their bodies," said Don Burgett. He was speaking of men like this *Luftwaffe* soldier killed in Alsace, who lies twisted in death. *Benecke*

Hagenau, 31 January 1945

Privates Arno Whitbread and Martin Chisholm (behind gun) of HQ/327th with a scrounged .50-caliber MG, commanding an approach to Hagenau. The MG's muzzle is covered until ready to fire to keep snow out of the barrel. *Signal Corps*

Survivors

Survivors of Wardin from 1st/ 501st were captured on film in Alsace by the camera of Billy Ogle. *Left to right:* Johnson, Ogle, Welch, Turner, and Higgins. *Ogle*.)

In late February, the 101st Airborne Division was pulled out of Alsace and loaded onto WWI-vintage French railroad boxcars known as "40 & 8s" because they were the right size to hold 40 men or eight horses. A lengthy train ride carried them south to the Reims area once again, to the smaller of the two Mourmelon towns. An advance guard had departed ahead of the rest of the division to set up a huge tent city using German POWs for labor. The troopers would once again reside in M34 pyramidal tents like those used in many parts of England before D-day.

Allen Hurd, a member of 2nd/501st's S-2 section, described the train trip in a letter to his parents:

We came back to France to base camp on freight cars. We rode first class. First class in France means "40 & 8" boxcars with hay on the floors. Plenty of fresh air and good opportunity to give the countryside the once-over when you ride these broken-down relics. We passed bridge after bridge demolished by our air force. Railroad cars and tank cars litter the side of the track. I know now what it means when they say, "Our air force bombed the Marshalling yards at such and such a place." Believe me, they do a devastating job of it. In the fields of France, you can read the history of the war. Foxholes, thousands of them, forests split and torn by artillery shells, burned-out vehicles of all descriptions, bomb craters, ration cans, ammunition boxes – all this and so much more shout their gruesome history at you as you pass by.

After arriving at Mourmelon, some men received furloughs and passes to Paris or other French tourist attractions, but the majority of men were sweating out the climactic final combat jump of the war, possibly into Berlin as part of the planned Operation *Eclipse*. For those who had been fighting since Bastogne without a break, the delays in going to Paris were intolerable. Hurd also wrote of this situation:

Hurd, a lousy Pfc, protests to the world on the pass and furlough policy of the 101st Division. In other words, why aren't I in Paris, instead of sitting in the woods of France. (The division was recently returned to same camp we were at when we were so rudely interrupted that fateful December morn.) Maxwell Davenport Taylor, our commander, who at the time of the breakthrough was sojourning in Washington, said at the time, quote, "Well done!" as they placed the Christmas turkey before him. McAuliffe, our acting commander said at that time, while residing in the deepest cellar in Bastogne, said, "NUTS!" Now, while we watch C-47s practice their formation daily overhead, we "The Battered Bastards of Bastogne," without any furlough in sight want to say, "Nuts."

Above: **Airborne Railroad**

Boxcars like this transported the 101st Airborne from Alsace to Mourmelon le Petit. *From top down:* Ken Collier, Bill Canfield, Smoky Ladman, Frank Sayers, Frank Castiglione, Roland J. Wilbur, Joe Sloan, and an unknown trooper. *Sloan*

Opposite: **"40 & 8" Boxcars**

Sergeant Ted Vetland and Luke Easley of A/506th haul hay to line the floor of the railroad car that will carry them from Alsace to Mourmelon le Petit. Note the bandages on their left shoulders, which conceal the eagle patches for security reasons. *Kennedy*

Line 'Em Up

The 2nd Platoon, F/501st at tent city, Mourmelon le Petit. Left to right: O'Neill, Bones Reed, Imhauser, Guthrie, Jumbo Moore, Toner, and others. *Hughes*

We are back off the stage, waiting and "sweating out" our appearance in the climactic final act. If you don't hear from me for a long time, you'll know I'm in combat and a review of the papers will tell you where.

Distinguished Unit Citation

On a more optimistic note, on 15 March 1945, the entire 101st Airborne Division was assembled on a field near Reims to receive a Distinguished Unit Citation for the defense of Bastogne. It was the first time an entire division was so recognized. General Eisenhower made the speech and presentation, and it was a happy day for all.

Ike stated it was a "great personal honor" for him to present the award, which was the beginning of a new tradition in the US Army. Ike realized that some of the 101st soldiers who had fought in Normandy and Holland did not rate Bastogne as their toughest fight, but it was appropriate that the division should be cited for that battle. Being rushed in to hold that position was of utmost importance, and all the elements of battle drama were there. Ike attached the Distinguished Unit Streamer to the division's flag, and the thousands of assembled troops marched past in review.

Training Continues

While at Mourmelon, a number of men from A/501st, E/501st, and G/502nd were killed in live-fire training. Johnny Altick, one of the youngest men in E/501 –

Mourmelon-le-Petit, Spring 1945

Left to right: Major R. J. Allen, Colonel Robert Ballard (CO of the 501st), unknown, Lieutenant Colonel Sammie Homan, Brereton, Major Ray Bottomly, and Major Doug Davidson. *Duggins*

who had survived Normandy, Holland, and Bastogne – was hit by a burst of machine-gun fire at the end of a training problem and died. Lieutenant Jesus Cortez of G/502nd was among those killed when some mortar rounds fell short on another training exercise.

To the Ruhr

On 24 March, the 101st watched C-47s take off carrying men of the 17th Airborne Division toward Wesel, Germany, where they would conduct a combat jump across the Rhine. This along with two other crossings of that German water barrier would set the stage for the commitment of the 101st to the Ruhr, the most important industrial area in Germany. In early April, the entire division, except for the 501st, boarded trucks and headed north to hold the west edge of the so-called Ruhr Pocket near Dusseldorf, Germany.

The 501st would remain behind at Mourmelon where it was divided into teams to drop onto a number of German *Stalags* and *Oflags* to rescue Allied POWs from possible massacre by the dying Nazi regime. This mission, named Operation *Jubliant*, was never executed, although smaller teams from the Special Allied Airborne Reconnaissance Force (SAARF) were dropped near some camps to monitor the treatment of POWs from a distance.

"A Great Personal Honor"
Stating that it was a "great personal honor" for him, General Dwight Eisenhower presented the 101st Airborne with the Distinguished Unit Streamer on 15 March 1945. It was very rare for an entire American division to receive the Distinguished Unit Citation (which is symbolized by the streamer), as it was awarded for "extraordinary heroism in action," and is the equivalent to the award of a DSC for an individual. *Krochka*

Germany's industrial Ruhr region was manned by almost a third of a million German troops in early April 1945. They held in place as part of Hitler's no-retreat policy, which was particularly enforced in this critical manufacturing region. The Rhine, however, had been breached by the Allies in several places. Tanks of the 2nd and 3rd Armored Divisions had met at Lippstadt, and the area behind them was now a pocket about half the size of New Jersey, containing the bulk of Field Marshal Model's *Army Group B.* Isolated in the pocket were the great industrial towns of Essen, Dortmund, and Düsseldorf, Germany.

Raid on Himmelgeist

On several successive nights, each company of 1st/506th sent patrols across the Rhine River. The patrols of Companies B and C were small in numbers of men involved, but the Company A crossing on the night of 11 April was in company strength, supported by the 1st/506th's 81mm mortar platoon, the 321st GFAB's 75mm howitzers, and some 155mm howitzers.

Don Straith, who joined the 506th before Bastogne and was wounded and evacuated at Noville, had

Divisional HQ
"Kangaroo" sign outside HQ/101st in 1945, alluding to othe Division radio callsign. *Macri*

rejoined the regiment. Part of his account of the company's raid follows:

After dinner on the 11th of April, we went back to our quarters, and with much laughing and horsing around, blackened our faces for the raid. In the midst of this, someone bumped Santillan's mandolin from the windowsill, and it smashed on the pavement below. Although it could have been an omen of things to come, no one took it as such. We gathered our equipment and made our way to the company HQ at the edge of town.

We were briefed on our mission: cross the Rhine in small assault boats, proceed along a road and through a village [Himmelgeist], take what prisoners we could, and return in boats that the engineers would have waiting at the edge of the village. It now being dark, we hiked to the river road, turned upstream, and followed a curve to where our boats were waiting on the bank. As we assembled on the opposite shore a few minutes later, I became concerned about the amount of noise we were making and felt that a lot of men weren't taking this raid very seriously. When Syer said in a loud voice, "Where the hell is Straith?" I angrily hissed back, "Right behind you! Keep your damn voice down!"

When the last boats had landed a couple of minutes later, the company, with my squad as point, moved out on a road paralleling the river. The night was almost pitch-black, and men were bumping into each other with muttered oaths. This was soon followed by crashing sounds as we began tripping over and falling into small trees that the Germans had cut so as to land crosswise on the road. "So much for secrecy," I thought to myself. "If there are German troops here, they certainly know by now that we are coming."

The road turned north, and we had passed the last of the fallen trees, when from far out in a field to our left, a flare shot up and burst overhead. We froze – no time to hit the ground – and as we waited for the flare to burn itself out, I wondered if we were presenting a perfect silhouette to waiting enemy forces. Starting forward again, we had moved only a short distance when the order, "Halt!" rang out a few yards to our right. Instantly, almost every weapon in the point, except Syer's bazooka, fired in the direction of the voice. Before I could set down my two bags of rockets, the firing had ended and we could hear moaning out in the field. A couple of scouts moved out toward the sound, but the moans stopped. In the darkness, the unlucky sentry couldn't be found, so the column moved forward once more.

When we finally reached the edge of the village, we halted momentarily.

As we stood there, someone claimed to have detected a movement or light in the upstairs window of the first house, so we were ordered to put a rocket through it. Unfortunately, after loading the bazooka and trying several times unsuccessfully to fire it, we came to the conclusion that it was defective.

By this time, the other men in the company were moving around and through the village, so our squad and another one were told to set up a roadblock right where we were to protect our company's rear. From the road, a lane angled back toward a field, and we

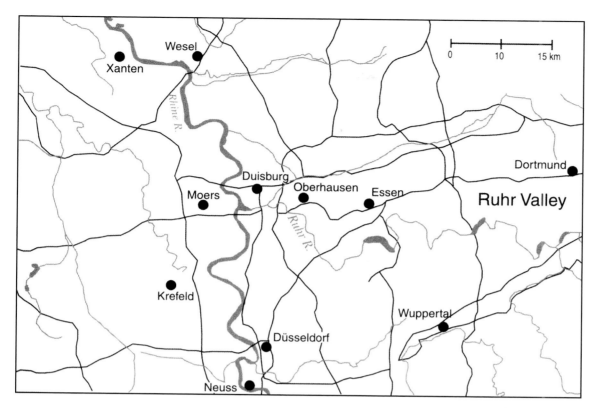

took up positions around where the two met. Syer, with that useless bazooka on his shoulder pointing down the lane, sat crosslegged behind a tree in the apex of the angle. The machine gun was set up on the right side of the tree, and Roy Runyan lay on the left with his rifle covering the way we had come. I lay behind Charlie, my head even with the feet of the men on either side. In a ditch to the rear, Santillan and Roberts waited with the BAR. The others took cover in and around the ditch where it passed under the lane. It's hard to say how long we waited there in the dark, the only sounds being distant shouts and an occasional shot from the rest of the company, as they swept through the town.

Suddenly, with only a fraction of a second warning, a salvo of shells bracketed our position, landing in the fields on either side and showering us with dirt. Ordered to hold our positions, we stayed where we were. The Germans must have really zeroed in on us

because a couple of minutes later, there were explosions all around us as another salvo landed in our midst. I was frantically trying to stretch my steel helmet to cover all of me, when one shell burst a few feet to my left rear, and a chunk of compressed clay and stone from the roadbed hit my head. Through all the noise and shouting, I heard Syer call out, "Jerry, I'm hit bad!" and he fell over on his side and lay there groaning.

Elkins yelled, "Quick, Straith, put a tourniquet on my leg and get this damned machine gun off me." The concussion had blown his 42-pound weapon, tripod and all, on top of him. To our surprise, Red and I were untouched, having been so close to where the shell landed that its fragments had arched just over us, one hitting Elkins and a bunch more tearing open Charlie Syer's back.

The shelling stopped and as I moved the machine gun, one of our medics ran up. After taking Syer's

243

Rowing Across the Rhine
Members of A/506th went back to the Himmelgeist area to search for the bodies of men lost on the raid of 11 April. *Kennedy*

pulse and listening to him groan (Syer had also begun to gasp for air), the medic decided to take care of the other casualty instead.

Syer's groans were becoming weaker and then stopped altogether. I could see the luminous dial of his watch, so I reached for his wrist and felt his pulse, but after only a few beats it stopped also.

When I reported this to the medic, he reached to check it himself and then confirmed that Charlie was dead. When the medic finished working on Elkins, we moved over to the ditch and found that the other medic, Alex

Abercrombie, was also a casualty. Although up and about, he was bleeding from a temple wound, where a shell fragment had pierced the side of his helmet. After being bandaged, he was sent on ahead to where we were to meet the boats. A short time later, in view of our precarious position, the command was given for the rest of us to head through town to the boats, so we loaded Elkins on a stretcher, and started out.

As we moved along the road, I noticed the glow of a cigarette in the ditch and in a whisper asked the others who it was and why he was still there. Someone in the darkness replied that it was Roberts, that he was dying, and that the cigarette was all that could be done for him. His partner, Santillan I was told, had been hit in the middle of the back by one of the shells and blown in half. Leaving the two of them behind, we moved on toward the center of the village.

Glidermen of B/327th
A squad of glidermen from B/327th posed in the Dusseldorf area in April 1945. *Meeker*

It was still pitch-black, and only a faint outline of the rooftops showed as a silhouette against the night sky. From the darkness ahead of us we heard a shout, crash, and much swearing as one of the men fell into a tank trap the Germans had dug across the road. If not for the noise he made, the four of us carrying the stretcher would have fallen in with our load, but we felt our way around the end of the hole, and a short way farther on, were directed down a lane on our left to the shore.

The boats were waiting as we were told, and we loaded the wounded man into one of them. Then we four knelt in the bottom of another, shoved off, and began paddling like mad. It was so dark that we couldn't see a thing, and we had no idea how far we had come or had to go when an explosion and a big orange fireball a few feet above the water lit up the river to our left. Whether it was from a tank or a field piece we didn't know, but the Germans had apparently rushed in some kind of artillery. This was presumably an 88, which was firing point-blank with shells timed to burst over our heads. Luckily, the current had carried our boat to one side of their line of fire, so we just crouched low and paddled faster. After half a dozen rounds, the firing stopped. Moments later, our boat ground to a sudden stop, and I had visions of us being stranded on a sandbar like sitting ducks. To our surprise and relief, we found we had safely reached the western shore again.

Dawn was breaking as we straggled back into Nievenheim. I was one of the first to reach our house and told Cofone about Syer, Santillan, and Roberts before going directly to bed. Later in the day we learned the results of the raid: three men dead, eleven others missing (including Abercrombie), and three prisoners. No one had seen Alex after he had been sent on ahead to the boats. The other missing men were presumed to have drowned when their boats capsized.

The prisoners were all old men who could provide little, if any, information, and certainly weren't worth the men we had lost.

There wasn't much time to rest. That same day, the company packed up again and moved about a mile north to the small village of Norf. Nothing eventful happened during our four days there except for the announcement of the death of President Roosevelt.

About a week after our ill-fated combat patrol, we got word that white surrender flags could be seen across the Rhine at Himmelgeist. When I heard that our company was to send a small party across to recover its three dead, I asked to go along, but was turned down. When the group returned later that day, they brought back four – not three – bodies from the common grave in which they had been buried by some Polish workers (all the German troops had pulled out of the area). Abercrombie, while on his way to the boats, had apparently passed out, bled to death, and was buried with the others. This closed the books on our Ruhr Pocket mission. Within a day or two, we packed up once again and were taken by truck to a nearby railroad, where a long train of "40 & 8s" was waiting for us.

Platoon briefing in Germany, spring 1945. Members of 2nd Platoon of A/506th, including Don Burgett. *Kennedy via Borelli*

Here Sleeps four American Soldiers
The bodies of four A/506th men killed on the April patrol near Himmelgeist, Germany, were found and buried by the Germans. A patrol returned to the area to recover the bodies. The German inscription on the cross reads "Here sleep four American soldiers." *Kennedy*

Landsberg Concentration Camp

The inhumanity of the Nazi regime was exemplified by the wretched victims found in concentration camps. This camp, east of Landsberg, was liberated by the 506th. In addition to the emaciated starvation and typhus victims, the burned bodies were men who ran from a barracks set aflame by the SS and were mowed down by a machine gun. *US Army via Hood*

Landsberg Concentration Camp

As Allied forces swept into Germany in the final weeks of WWII, they began to liberate concentration camps and saw first-hand, brutal evidence of what the Nazis had done to enemies of the *Reich*. Most 101st troops were not directly involved in capturing any camps, although some troopers toured Dachau and other camps after they were freed by other units.

An exception was 1st/506th, as they discovered the camp at Landsberg. They had interrupted their dash toward Berchtesgaden in amphibious DUKW trucks (called "Ducks") and disembarked after passing (and ignoring) long columns of surrendering German troops. Landsberg, Germany, was a town of approximately 30,000 people, situated about 45 miles west of Munich. Hitler had been imprisoned there after his famous failed *Putsch* in 1923; while there, he had written *Mein Kampf*.

Members of C/506th dismounted along the edge of a pine plantation, all the trees planted in neat rows with firebreaks between the sections and the trees all of a uniform height. A lengthy approach march followed, ending at the concentration camp, which was situated just outside the town.

Kenneth Parker, C/506th, described what transpired next:

We were told to deploy into the woods in a single column as deep as possible with approximately 20 ft between us, then sweep forward, staying in contact with one another and searching for any personnel that could be hiding in the woods. My first shock

occurred when I walked across the first opening. At the edge of the woods, there was a bush, perhaps four feet high. Behind this bush was a skeleton in a crouching position. The skeleton wore the tattered striped purple garment of a Jewish concentration camp member. I conjectured that he had either hidden here in order to escape, or in all modesty had gone behind the bush to go to the bathroom and had been too weak to return and died.

I went forward quite deep into the woods and could no longer see the road or the edge of the woods. As I progressed in my search, I began to feel very eerie; my senses were very acute in anticipation that something or someone would pop up in front of me at any minute. But something else was bothering me. As a young man (10-14 years old), growing up in upstate New York, I had a trap line that I tended each day. This necessitated daily trips through deep woods, and I was used to the sound of squirrels chattering, birds singing, ground animals scurrying away, wind blowing in the trees, and movement. I suddenly realized why I had the eerie feeling. There was no noise. There was no animal or bird life in the forest, and because of the needles on the forest floor, I could barely hear my own feet scuffling along, much less those of even the two troopers closest to me. I wondered if the Jewish concentration camp prisoners had worked in the forest and had killed and eaten every living animal and bird in order to stay alive.

After what seemed an hour or two of walking through the forest without incident, we came out on an open field with a slight mound across the road from what turned out to be a Jewish concentration camp. We swept the fields and headed for the open gates of the camp. Across from the gates, on this mound in the field, lay a dead German officer; from his epaulets I assumed he was an *SS* officer. He was stretched out on the ground face up, with the back of his head caved in. His boots and cap were missing when I went by. He was laying alongside a partially-dug grave. It looked as though he was having a Jew dig his own grave in front of the other prisoners across the street, when something distracted the German officer, and the Jew digging the grave hit him in the back of the head with the shovel, grabbed the German hat and boots, and headed home.

In crossing Germany, we had seen many displaced persons (Poles, Czechs, etc.) that had one pair of boots or shoes on and another pair over their shoulder and they were walking home (hundreds of miles).

Most of the inmates had left, but passing the barracks we could see some of the weaker and sicker inmates still stretched out on their bunks. Our platoon was sent to a rather remote area of the camp to search for German soldiers. We followed a narrow-gauge railroad track, similar to the tracks miners use to push ore in a hopper to the outside. At the end of the track, there were approximately three holes, about 25 feet long, maybe 20 feet across. The holes appeared to have sloping sides that were cemented. Whether the bottoms of the holes were cemented, I don't know. Each of these holes, to whatever depth they were, were filled with bodies. None of the bodies had clothes on, and they all appeared to be in about the same state of deterioration. It was apparent that they were all Jews that had died. How many were in these three holes, I don't know. Later, I discovered that these were just surplus pits for the bodies until they could go into the huge furnaces that were farther down the track. I could see the smokestacks, but I never got into that area. The huge furnaces were incapable of taking the bodies of all the dead Jews. They were loaded in the hoppers and dumped into the pits. This served as a waiting area, until the furnaces could take them, then the hoppers were reloaded with more bodies and pushed back down to the furnaces.

All of us, as we looked on the sight of all these bodies laying there in these three different pits, were quite shook up. We couldn't really fathom the enormity of it. Soon after seeing this, we were taken back outside the camp and went 6-8 miles to the town of Landsberg.

We were told that General Taylor, in view of what he had seen at the Jewish concentration camp, was pretty disturbed and had declared martial law in the entire area.

Robert Nelson and I were sent to Regimental HQ, where we received a detail to guard a crossroads.

Around 1030 hours, we heard a huge noise; there were swarms of people coming out of the town in rows. It looked like 6,000–8,000 people heading toward the concentration camp, carrying rakes, brooms, shovels, whatever implements they could pick up. Some of the 101st guys were walking with them, keeping them in line and moving along. They said General Taylor had declared martial law, and issued an order that all people from age 14 to age 80 were to be rounded up out of Landsberg and marched through the concentration camp. They were to haul the bodies (what was left of them) out of the furnaces, haul the bodies out of all the holes, rake up the remains, and bury them all. Dig holes and bury them all.

That evening, about 1800 hr, we saw the same crew of civilians coming back down the road from the concentration camp. Some of them were still puking; their hair was down. They were dirty. They did not look confident like they did when they went out. They looked totally distraught. I believe this process went on for several days while we were there.

General Taylor was so angry that he wanted these people never to forget what had been going on outside the town. Of course, they all pretended they didn't know what was going on. And I think probably they closed their eyes to a lot of it. The one thing I am sure of: the people in Landsberg, Germany, never forgot that experience.

A few days later, we loaded back up on our "Ducks" and headed off down the road to Berchtesgaden. But nothing ever impressed in my mind a thought worse than what I had seen in Landsberg.

Race to Berchtesgaden
Members of 2nd Platoon of A/506th aboard an amphibious "Duck" (DUKW) pause during the race to Berchtesgaden near Ludwigshofen, Germany. Justo Correa and Don Burgett are among those visible in the group. *Kennedy*

The Bavarian town of Berchtesgaden nestles amidst mountains and a landscape of breathtaking scenery in the southeast corner of Germany. Not far away are the Austrian and Swiss borders and the Brenner Pass to northern Italy.

Allied leaders still feared that Hitler might retreat to his Bavarian headquarters to command a last stand in the "Alpine Redoubt." This fear proved unfounded, although many thousands of German troops had converged in the area, either in retreat from the Western Front or in flight from the Russians on the Eastern Front.

Hitler, Bormann, Göring, and others had luxurious homes in the Berchtesgaden area. Below the Berghof, Hitler's mountain house, was a massive tunnel leading to subterranean chambers filled with liquor, silver services, fine crystalware, and untold other loot. Hitler's library and numerous films and written records were also stored in his home away from Berlin.

Racing the French to Berchtesgaden

The entire area held a mystique and promise of discovery that drove the invading armies on in a relentless race to get there first. The 506th in their "Ducks" were at the vanguard of the 101st forces. Detouring around a blown bridge, flying down the autobahn past negligible resistance, they raced with the French 2nd Armored Division to reach the prize.

The French columns were bypassed, only to overtake the American column a few hours later. Thousands of fully-armed German soldiers were on the median of the autobahn, marching westward to surrender. The 506th met a delay when they had to obtain permission to cross a bridge held by elements of the 3rd Infantry Division. The 3rd/506th lost several men to 88mm fire as they approached Berchtesgaden from the northern route.

A platoon of C/506th reconned Berchtesgaden, but found that the French had already arrived on the slopes of the Obersalzberg. Papers from the pillaged Berghof were already blowing across the mountainside. Such was the panorama when the first American troops arrived. Along with the 506th paratroopers came the 321st artillerymen and the 327th glider troops. Both the 501st and the 502nd would arrive some weeks later.

The complex was large enough that the French had only searched a part of it when the 506th joined the hunt with a vengeance. A huge wine cellar was discovered, and troops carried away armfuls of champagne and cognac. David Webster of E/506th later wrote that he was disappointed at the relatively

In the Eagle's Nest

The *Adlerhorst*, or Eagle's Nest, Hitler's hideout atop Kehlstein Mountain at Berchtesgaden. Note how small the men standing in the window look; this gives some perspective on the actual size of the building. *Nye*

Above: **Hitler hasn't been here lately**

Two new occupants relax in the Eagle's Nest. *Krochka*

Opposite: **Soaking up the sun**

Soaking up some Bavarian sunshine in one of the lounge chairs used by Hitler's staff and visitors at the Eagle's Nest is Pat Macri, Division Signal Company. Macri is enjoying the feeling of victory after a hard war. *Macri*

Below: **Still Smokin'**

The *Berghof*, Hitler's luxurious mountain house, was still smoking from bombing raids when the 101st arrived. A massive underground tunnel complex lay beneath the house and yielded many secrets and treasures to the conquering troops. *Musura*

Liberated SS Insignia

This intricately embroidered collar patch is for the rank of a major general in the *Waffen SS.* Bob Reeves of B/506th "liberated" this, along with a silver cap skull and embroidered officers' sleeve eagle, from an unknown SS general who was captured in the vicinity of the Berghof at the *Obersalzberg* complex. *Bob Reeves*

Above: May 45, while moving to Munich, an SS armored artillery captain of XIII *SS Corps* arranges surrender of his troops with Major Hank Plitt (101st Division G-2) *at left,* and IPW Team #9 leader Captain Joe Pangerl, *back to camera at right. Pangerl*

Opposite: **Jim Cox**

Lieutenant Jim Cox of C/326th in Normandy, 1944. Cox, formerly a first sergeant, was commissioned on the battlefield. *Crilley*

Below: **Medieval Masterpiece**

Shown here is one of the scores of rare paintings stolen by Hermann Goering from various European museums. Troopers of the 101st discovered the cache of artwork hidden in the Berchtesgaden area and put the paintings on display for visiting troops while trying to inventory the works and return them to their former owners. *Meeker*

Tankers of the French 2nd Armored Division talking with a member of HQ/101st in Berchtesgaden. *Macri*

cheap, recent-vintage liquors that were found there. Perhaps Hitler kept that supply only to entertain the nickel Nazis who visited there while hiding the better stuff elsewhere? In any case, Hitler himself was a teetotaler. Another trooper remarked that it was "the ambition of every American paratrooper to drink Hitler's champagne." This being the case, troopers swarmed through the Berghof and its underground chambers in quest of the good stuff. In quest of booze, cupboards were pried open with silver table knives bearing Hitler's Eagle, swastika, and initials.

Another room down the hall was filled with silver cream pitchers, sugar bowls, serving trays, and the like, all emblazoned with Hitler's unique national emblem and the initials "A.H." Bob Reeves of B/506th brought an empty barracks bag into this room and

filled it with silver items, then found it was too heavy to lift. He continued along, dragging the bag on the floor behind him. Later, while riding in a truck to Austria, Bob tossed pieces over each bridge as the truck crossed rivers and streams, to lighten the load. At this writing, he had given the last of the pieces away.

The Golden Age

The ensuing weeks became known as the "Golden Age" of the division, a reward for the hellish fighting of the previous year. Booze flowed, the soldiers managed occasional, unofficial fraternization with the local girls, luxury Nazi automobiles were liberated from their high-ranking owners, and horses were commandeered from the *SS* horse farm at Bruck, Austria, and galloped cowboy style.

In nearby fields, dozens of abandoned German armored vehicles and fighter planes were disco-

An old German *Jager*, or hunter, led Joe Pistone (left) and Lindfield to an SS hideout in the mountains where more diehards were captured. *Pistone*

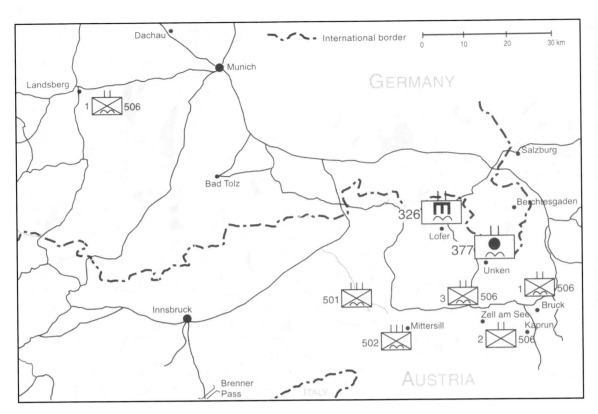

The 101st and the Occupation of Germany.

vered, along with artillery, machine guns, and other assorted ordnance. There were the inevitable plane crashes, accidental shootings, and car crashes.

Some troopers had managed to take off in German planes, but were killed while attempting to land them. A directive was issued banning attempts to fly these captured aircraft.

Himmler's Castle

Although the erstwhile home of Heinrich Himmler, *Reichsführer-SS,* was miles from Berchtesgaden at Zell am See, Austria, his castle at Bruck was the more intriguing feature of the area. This medieval, impressive Fischorn Castle, which was later used as Colonel

Hitler's Car?

The Mercedes depicted here toured the States on a Victory Bond tour, with Lieutenant Jim Cox of the 326th AEB (behind the wheel) and other ETO survi vors. Although the vehicle was presented as "Hitler's Personal Car," it had actually belonged to *Luftwaffe* chief Hermann Goring. Cox

Home of the 506th
Signs like this proliferated in Austria after VE-day. *Moulliet*

Chase's CP, had served as a repository for Himmler's records and loot.

About a week before Allied troops arrived, Himmler's personal secretary Erika Lorenz had showed up at the castle with some trucks and a group of *SS* men. Acting under secret orders from Himmler himself, she had overseen the burning of numerous files and typewritten directives, some of which may have been

A vehicle tunnel on the Road to the Eagle's Nest
One of the tunnels on the winding road going up Kehlstein Mountain toward the Eagle's Nest. *George Aprile*

General Tolsdorf the Mad
Tolsdorf, a reknowned German Panzer commander *(second from right)*, surrenders his troops to Colonel Bob Sink of the 506th *(center)*. *Mihok*

written orders pertaining to the Final Solution policy toward Europe's Jewish population.

Fischorn Castle had also reportedly housed the valuables looted from concentration camp victims: large quantities of jewelry; paper money and coins of numerous countries and all denominations; gold teeth; and so on. This stolen treasure was allegedly divided into three parts. One third, in a Bavarian cave, was discovered within weeks by Seventh Army intelligence personnel who tracked it down through relentless interrogations and searches. They turned in an unknown percentage, which was eventually used to finance certain covert operations in the looming Cold War. Another third of the treasure is reportedly still secreted in the bottom of a lake nearby; numerous attempts to recover it in postwar years have produced negative results. Some divers have met mysterious "accidental" deaths while exploring the area.

The last third of the money and valuables was reportedly stashed in a location known only to a few high-ranking *SS* officers, including *Standartenführer* Otto Skorzeny. He could access the money when it was needed to aid ex-Nazis, especially to pay legal expenses to defend accused war criminals.

Soon after the 506th arrived at Berchtesgaden, Sergeant Bill Knight of C/506th was told to accompany a major of Seventh Army Counter-Intelligence Corps to the Fischorn Castle. Together they made one of the first searches of the castle. They forced their way into locked rooms and found, among other things, a trunk containing centuries-old looted paintings. In the rear of the castle were a number of newly-built, garage-type structures in two rows, each one containing hoarded loot. One was filled with motorcycles. Another was full of small bins containing all varieties of German political and military insignia, too much of it for a company of souvenir hunters to carry away. Knight grabbed a few hand-embroidered *SS* officer sleeve eagles as a curiosity and left the rest.

Much like the loot in the Berghof, all the loot in the various garages would eventually disappear in thousands of different directions.

Surrendering Elite Guard

This Waffen SS enlisted man belonged to the *XIII SS Corps*. Here, in May 1945 at Kossin, Austria, he surrendered to the 502nd. He wears a black panzer wrap-around tunic with shoulder straps from the officer cadet school at Bad Tolz. Note the non-SS belt buckle. *White*

Cecil Simmons's S-2 Patch

The green sleeve patch designed by Lieutenant Colonel Cecil Simmons for wear by his S-2 personnel is shown here. Dick Ladd *(cap on sideways)* points to the patch, which was laid on the sleeve of Gordon "Bill" Little's Ike jacket for the photo. He didn't sew it on because it wasn't approved. There is only one known instance of the patch being sewn onto a wartime uniform. Also pictured *(left to right):* Jack Ott, Gordon Little, Lawrence Weber, and Roger Flurscheim. *Ladd*

The Day the War Ended

On the afternoon of 8 May, the day the war officially ended in Europe, Bill Knight was sent on another mission with two jeeploads of personnel from the 506th.

They had received word that an entire *Wehrmacht* division plus stragglers from assorted units was waiting in fields near Bad Gastein for instructions to demobilize and surrender. The 506ers located the German division and conferred with its commanders, who were living in a large mobile house trailer. The paratroopers spent the night in the trailer, and in the morning had the German commander instruct his troops to "disarm, go to Salzberg, and then go home." Knight and his buddies stood at the edge of the road as thousands of fully-armed German soldiers walked up out of the field, dropped their weapons in a ditch at the side of the road, then turned down the road, walking toward Austria. There would be no out-processing nor imprisonment for these troops.

An *SS* officer walked up to Sergeant Knight, handed him a ceremonial dagger with a chain hanger depicting skulls and lightning bolts and said, "A souvenir. ..." He then turned and joined the horde of marching, defeated troops.

Back at Berchtesgaden

Back at the Berghof complex at Berchtesgaden, an *SS* guard barracks that stood near Hitler's house had been placed off limits. The windows were boarded up, the electricity inside was turned off, and the floor was flooded with a foot of water. A few enterprising troopers from the 501st pried a board loose and went inside to explore. They had no flashlight and resorted to striking matches in the darkness. They found lockers full of uniforms, photos and papers, also numerous insignia. The rifle racks were still full of Mauser rifles. The troopers took as much as they could carry, but later lamented that they didn't have more illumination to aid in their search. The contents of that building also evaporated in the coming weeks.

Hitler's house and some of the adjoining buildings had been damaged by Allied bombers before the

Spoils of War

A massive pile of helmets, rifles, and sundry equipment from the surrendering *XIIISS Corps* in Kosin, Austria. One wonders what happened to it all. *White*

101st arrived, but some distance away was a complex of modern Alpine barracks also used by *SS* troops. These became the new home of the 501st when they rejoined the division following the cancellation of Operation *Jubilant*.

Hitler's conference building, known as the *Adlerhorst* ("Eagle's Nest"), up at the top of neighboring Kehlstein Mountain, was referred to by many troopers as the "Crow's Nest." This impressive building stood at the peak of the mountain and was partly accessible by a large elevator, which carried visitors up the last few hundred feet. Vehicles were left at a parking lot on a plateau near the entrance to the pedestrian tunnel, which led to the elevator. Ted Goldman of A/502nd recalled some details of the period that followed the surrender of the *XIII SS Corps* (excerpted from the *Chappie Hall Newsletter* #12, 28 August 1969):

In May 1945, A/502nd was stationed at Reit im Winkel, Bavaria, with the rest of 1st/502nd. For three weeks following VE-day, one of our chores was standing guard with and on 5,000 German remnants of the *SS*. Outposts were usually in the country or on the edge of a village. The Germans had bolt-action rifles and wore white armbands. They were supposed to control German traffic. We were on nearby outposts, usually 100 yards away. Our job was to keep the German outposts honest.

During May, the Bavarian nights are cold. For a week or so, the Germans moved to the American outpost after dark. We sent them to the sawmill regularly for firewood and practiced our "tradin' German" after dark. One evening, Lieutenant Colonel Hanlon had a battalion meeting in which he was rather definite about there being no further fraternization, particularly at the sawmill. At 0600 the next morning, Charles "Greek" Sakalakos and I arrived at the sawmill outpost for our 4-hr turn. A short while later... the longest touring car still operating in Europe drove up. I stopped it. It contained three Germans: the driver, a

At one of the track and field events soon after V-E day, General George C. Marshall, General George S. Patton, and General Maxwell D. Taylor are visible in the upper center of the photo. The personnel in the front row have been identified as (left to right): Lieutenant Jim Patton, 501st Demolitions Platoon; Staff Sergeant Dean Baxter, Service/506th; Major R. J. Allen, S-3, 501st; and Captain Hugo S. Sims Jr., A/501st. *via Meeker*

master sergeant, and two officers. The officers were a colonel who spoke excellent and polite English and an exceedingly fat lieutenant general, complete with lap robe, baton, and red lapels.

In response to my request for passes, the driver and the colonel produced valid I.D. documents properly signed by Colonel Ned Moore, 101st Chief of Staff. The general refused to answer and did not turn or indicate in any way that he heard me. A second request brought only the colonel's response that his pass was good for the general, too. We were already in trouble with Long John for fraternization, so I wasn't about to let anyone by without seeing his pass.

GIs have a dislike for generals, which comes naturally, and in May 1945, two GIs had theirs concentrated on the general at hand. I was standing in the middle of the road, and the Greek was on the other side, near the general. I told the general to produce a pass or dismount. He did neither. I told Sakalakos to fix his bayonet and nudge the general into obedience. By the time he had his bayonet in place, the door between the general and Sakalakos was open. The smallest nip showed the general that we meant business. The general dismounted, the colonel turned purple, the sergeant about choked, either with suspense or mirth, I wasn't sure.

The general produced his pass, at the same time stating in perfect English that he had never been so insulted and that General Taylor would immediately hear about this. I pointed out politely that a prompt and polite response to a legal request would have saved him a lot of trouble. The general turned to remount. The sight of that massive bottom was too much for the Greek. Although short, Greek was strong and

An assembly center at Namur, Belgium, had a large movie screen set up to entertain troops awaiting shipment back to the States. The photo was made by Charlie Placidi, 907th GFAB. *Placidi*

quick. He used the flat of his boot to the greatest advantage and landed a resounding smack across the backside of that mound of Nazi blubber. The general came hurtling across the width of the back seat, where he hit the inside of the door face first and collapsed in a heap on the floor. Since I was standing facing that door, I shall never forget the look of shocked amazement on the flying walrus' face. The colonel turned even darker purple, leaped into the car to pick up the general, and yelled at the driver to go, all in one motion. I collapsed in the middle of the road in gales of laughter, completely out of action. Whatever happened now would be anticlimactic. All Sakalakos could say was, "Fat German bastard."

Within 20 minutes, the phone started ringing. The officer at the CP asked, "What the hell have you guys been up to?"

I replied, "Nothing, why?"

"The Captain is on his way after having had calls from Division, Regiment, and Battalion."

In 5 minutes, Captain Swanson and his driver showed up. Swannie reamed us out good, but without his usual gusto. He was even smiling when he left. No one ever mentioned the general. Makes you wonder....

Although the non-fraternization policy was difficult to enforce, some troopers were officially punished for having German girlfriends, but this did not deter some troopers. Sergeant Jimmy Edgar of I/501st had returned from his Alsace wounding as he had vowed to do and now had two "shack rats" in the Berchtesgaden area: Ischi and Uscha, who had been Heinrich Himmler's teletype operators.

Patrols went into the neighboring mountains, and several Nazi war criminals were rounded up, including Karl von Oberg, former *Gestapo* chief of Paris, Labor Minister Robert Ley, and the infamous Jew-baiter Julius Streicher.

It seemed fitting that the weary survivors of the 101st spent the end of the war lounging in Hitler's furniture and grabbing their share of the plunder that was abundant in the Berchtesgaden area.

On 26 June 1945, the 501st was inactivated, and the high-point men were sent back to the States. The others were shipped to the 327th, the 502nd, and the 506th and integrated into companies in those units. To help add points toward discharge, a Bronze Star was awarded to all men who had made the three major missions of the 101st: Normandy, Holland, and Bastogne. Assignments followed, sending the 101st to Auxerre, France, where a "pay jump" was made in September (every paratrooper had to jump at least once per quarter to maintain eligibility for jump pay), and to Sens and Joigny, France. Many troopers visited Paris and the Riviera. It was a period of marking time before the happy return to the States and discharge from the Army.

Bill Russo in Paris

Lieutenant Bill Russo got into Paris after V-E day, with a replacement officer named Koenig. Russo recalled:

Koenig and I were sitting in one of those sidewalk cafes, and about 100 yards away is the Arc de Triomphe. Well, we didn't have too much faith in the French Army. The way they line up for battle, they have a jeep, two trucks full of chickens, broads, one tank destroyer . . . you think I'm joking, don't you, huh? Well I've got news for you. There's no joke. This is their attack plan, OK?

Well, Koenig and I were discussing various things and someone must have mentioned those French, you know, because they were never there. Never. We were pretty juiced up. Koenig gets up, walks over to the Arc de Triomphe, and pisses on it. Broad daylight! There was a riot! I never saw Koenig again. Boy, he was tough; God, he was a tough man. He was one of the few people I would really be hesitant about meeting. That guy was something else.

Pulling into New York Harbor after passing the Statue of Liberty was an unforgettable sight for millions of returning Americans in September 1945. *Probst*

In memory of Helen Briggs-Ramsey, known as Briggsy, Red Cross girl for the 506th. Helen was tragically beaten to death in her Capitol Hill, Washington, D.C. apartment days before the fiftieth anniversary of D-day in June 1994. She was loved by many and is mourned by all who knew her. *Yates*

Homecoming

Although the Screaming Eagles – who had covered themselves in glory in Normandy, Holland, and Bastogne – had looked forward to a triumphant homecoming and a victory parade down New York's Fifth Avenue or perhaps Washington's Pennsylvania Avenue, this was not to be. The 101st was inactivated on 30 November 1945 in Auxerre, France. The veterans who had served the 101st Airborne so well in combat returned to the States piecemeal, in various other units. A relative handful came back with the 82nd Airborne and got the honor of marching down Fifth Avenue in their victory parade.

The 101st would remain on the inactive rolls until 1949, when it was reactivated as a basic training unit at Camp Breckenridge, Kentucky. It continued in that non-jumping, training-unit status during the Korean War. The division was not reactivated in all its glory as a tactically organized and equipped airborne division until 1956. It has served at Fort Campbell, Kentucky, ever since, with considerable combat time in Vietnam and the Gulf wars.

Lieutenant Corey Shepard of I/502nd wrote a few thoughts about postwar readjustment:

The veteran returns from battle, and wondrous sights of courage of which no knight of old, no cowboy, no serial hero ever dreamed. Fighting wounds that heal slowly, school, interest rates, the thousand trials of feeding those mouths everyday – all require a different skill and a painstaking patience harder than patrol in enemy country because it's dull and you can't kill your enemies, only cope with them. These were men. Where others feared to go, they leapt. When others saw them, secret envyings ate at them. If there be nobility in such things as strength and bravery and self sacrifice, then these are princes of rare blood. If legends are made of this stuff, then these – for whom Alexander's, Caesar's, and Napoleon's legions could not be link-boys – these Battered Bastards can't fade away.

Captain George Lage was 2nd battalion surgeon for the 502nd PIR in Normandy and Holland. He took many photos in Normandy, some with Kodachrome color slide film. This photo was taken on 7 June, 1944, when Lage's medics were enroute to the 101st Divisional hospital at Hiesville, from their initial first aid station in Holdy. Prominent on the front of the jeep is medic Harvey Brotman. Also visible are Ernest Labadie, James Milne, and behind the steering wheel, S/Sgt John P. Durka, who was killed in action on *Bloody Sunday*, 11 June, 1944, while picking-up wounded near Bridge #4 on the Carentan Causeway. The jeep had been salvaged from a crashed glider and it was later returned to its original owners, in the 82nd Airborne Division.

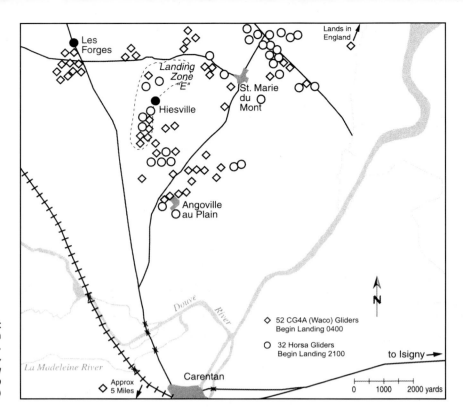

Landing Pattern 101st Airborne Division Gliders.

(Original Map Courtesy of Ivan Worrell and 101st ABD Association.)

◇ 52 CG4A (Waco) Gliders Begin Landing 0400

○ 32 Horsa Gliders Begin Landing 2100

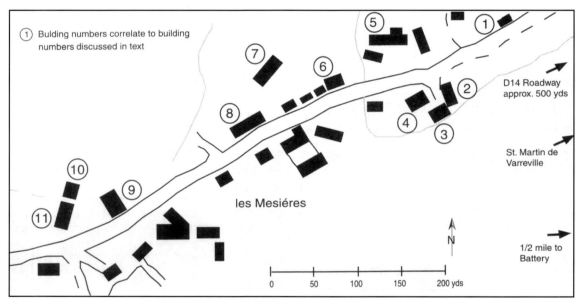

Staff Sergeant Summers at Objective XYZ, les Mesières

① Bulding numbers correlate to building numbers discussed in text

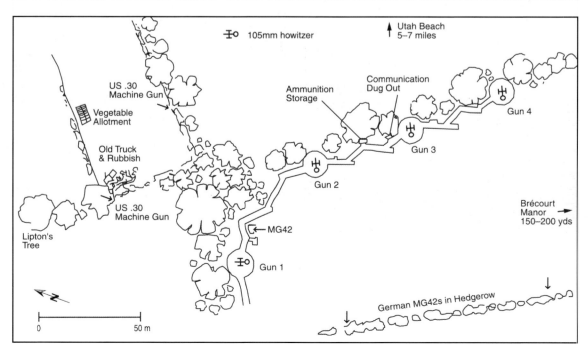

E/506th versus German Artillery Battery, in the vicinity of Brécourt Manor
(see p. 53 and 54).

Appendix A
Airborne Uniforms and Equipment

Unlike German paratroopers who were part of the *Luftwaffe*, American paratroopers were part of the US Army and, as such, largely wore and used uniforms and equipment that were similar to the rest of the Army. Some items, however, were adapted especially for use by the parachute troops, whose means of arrival on the battlefield necessitated special modifications. Beyond this, certain items became signatures of the elite forces that paratroopers undeniably were – in every armed force that had them – the world over. This section spotlights some of the most important pieces.

Uniforms

M-38 Field Jacket

The M-38 'Kitty Parsons' Jacket of Captain Cecil L. Simmons, H/502nd. This blanket-lined field jacket differed from the later M-41 jacket only in the pocket flaps on the side slash pockets. This specimen is adorned with a name tape, Type 6 American-made 101st Airborne Division shoulder sleeve insignia, and rank bars made of small pieces of parachute suspension line, ironed-flat and machine-sewn onto the epaulets by the riggers. This was done frequently for officers in the 502nd. The "bat wings and skull" regimental patch, later known as the "Widow Maker" insignia, is on the left breast of the jacket. The shoulder sleeve insignia originally had a white tongue, but the tongue was colored red with a pen. Simmons said this was common practice among his men, who didn't like the white-tongued patches. These patches had no significance, but were merely a manufacturer's variation, possibly during a factory shortage of red thread. One British patch manufacturer, thinking there was some significance to the white tongued patches, did imitate them in a cotton-on-wool variant. Simmons's M-42 jumpsuit, however, does have an unaltered white tongued patch on the shoulder. *Author's Collection*

M-41 Jump Jacket

This early M-41 "Coat, Parachute Jumpers," was issued to Sergeant Ed Hughes, F/501st, at Camp Toccoa in late 1942. Not realizing it was an earlier version of the M-42 jump jacket, Ed thought it was a factory defect and saved it for special occasions. He liked being different and appreciated its uniqueness, wearing it only at formations and on special occasions. Note the narrow, single-snap pocket flaps. As in early M-42 jackets, the snaps and zipper are made of brass. The pockets, chest, and back lack the expandable bellows quality of the later M-42 jacket. Most of the belt is sewn flat against the waist and a snap on the belt supplements the metal buckle. After V-E Day, Ed instructed at The Parachute School at Fort Benning, and added the concentric white, red, and blue airborne oval of the 1st Parachute Training Regiment behind his wings. *Author's Collection*

M-42 Jumpsuit

M-42 Jumpsuit

The classic American paratrooper uniform of WWII was the M-42 jumpsuit. Designed by then-Lieutenant Colonel (later Lieutenant General) William P. Yarborough, they featured characteristic slanted-bellows pockets and flaps secured by two snaps on each flap. Wear began in 1942 and ended some time in 1944.

The 101st's M-42 suits were turned in after Normandy, and were replaced by green M-43 combat suits for the duration of the war. The First Airborne Task Force used them in Operation draGoon in August 1944, and the 504th PIR (82nd Airborne) jumped into Holland wearing them in September 1944. That was probably the last organizational wear of M-42's in combat. Some troopers hid a set in the bottom of their barracks bag when the recall was done. Such suits began to reappear on a spotty basis later in the war. *Author's Collection*

M-42 Reinforced Jump Jacket

Details of an M-42 jacket. The quartermaster/manufacturer's label is intact and quite legible in the lower-right pocket and indicates that it is a size 36 Regular. It was made by the "Manistee Garment Co." on a contract let on 9 August 1943. *Author's Collection*

M-42 Jump Jacket

M-42 reinforced jump jacket belonging to Sergeant Jim Colucci, H/502nd. The belt has been deliberately removed, as it so often was, to avoid interference with the web waist belt. An American made Type 3 101st Airborne Division shoulder sleeve insignia is affixed to the left shoulder.

Before it came into Colucci's possession, the uniform belonged to Private First Class Charles DeLong, who died in the Netherlands on 15 November 1944. DeLong, a medic attached to the 3d/502nd, was with another medic, a Staff Sergeant Bryant, in Dodewaard when they both accepted a gift of wine from a Dutch civilian. Both became ill and died several days later, presumably of poisoning. *Author's Collection*

M-43 Combat Set

M-43 Field Jacket

In mid-1944 (after the 101st returned from Normandy), the entire US Army was undergoing a reform to eliminate all "non-standard" uniforms. The M-42 jumpsuits and paratrooper boots were recalled. Paratroopers were issued standard green M43 combat uniforms and combat boots. The latter had brown rawhide bodies and a flap secured around the ankle with two straps. Much protest was raised over these affronts, and the jump boots were eventually restored. M-42 suits, however, became a thing of the past.

To make the best of the situation, parachute riggers began converting the plain M-43 combat trousers to jump trousers, by adding a large canvas cargo pocket to each leg as well as tie-down straps, to secure the load in each pocket.

This particular suit was retained by Lieutenant Jim Loftus of F/501st because of its souvenir value. During the battle of Bastogne, near Neffe, Belgium, Loftus was running under mortar fire when a spinning fragment tore into his right chest pocket at an angle. It spun into the pocket, ripped up a pack of cigarettes, came through the inner lining, and dropped out before it could do any damage to Lofty. Jim jumped into a foxhole and didn't realize what had happened until he reached into his chest pocket for a cigarette. At that time, he found only torn paper and loose tobacco, and discovered a jagged hole on the edge of his pocket. The jacket has a Type 1 Americanmade 101st Airborne Division shoulder sleeve insignia and first lieutenant bars executed in white thread, in individual stitches by Lofty, on each shoulder. *Author's Collection*

M-43 Combat Trousers

Two pairs of M-43 combat trousers modified for wear by 101st troopers show some interesting modifications and differences. These green trousers were introduced before September 1944. They were worn in Holland, at Bastogne, and for the duration of WWII, replacing the earlier M-42s.

A special canvas, chemically-treated to be water-resistant (the same type used to reinforce pockets, knees, and elbows on M-42 suits), was made into cargo pockets by the riggers and sewn onto each pant leg of the M-43 combat trousers. Various government contractors manufactured the

trousers themselves. Of the pair here, the pair at right was issued to a 501st medic.

The tie-down straps, also added by riggers, are 3/4" tan web tape, the same as used on M-42 reinforced trousers. The same web tape was probably used on the earliest modified M-43s before the riggers switched to using long strips of folded and sewn canvas as tie-downs. These are of the same material as the pockets.

The pair below, from a 326th AEB officer, are of interest because although the cargo pockets have faded almost to white, the trousers themselves are still a rich green color. The green dye used on the treated canvas always faded at a faster rate than the M-43 trousers themselves, but these trousers are greener than the other pair, despite the fact that they have been washed more times, judging from the amount of fading to the pockets. The right pair had canvas tie-downs, which, as often happened, were cut off by the original owner. Some troopers considered the tie-downs an unnecessary hindrance. The right pair also features small pale brown plastic buttons, similar to those seen on many M-42 trousers.

A limited number of M-43 trousers were rigger-modified and of those which survived WWII, many were worn out by veterans on postwar hunting and fishing trips. Today, surviving examples are about as rare as reinforced M-42 trousers.

Regarding the green canvas material used to manufacture the pockets, Brooks Bush says, "I think it is the same material as the M-42 reinforcement. I found that canvas once – it was an aircraft canopy cover. The snaps, stitching, and thread were the same as the pockets. I think it was a canvas supplied to the Air Corps and then to the airborne riggers, although they did use other canvas similar to shelter half." *Author's Collection*

A2 Flight Jacket

Captain George Buker, regimental intelligence officer of the 502nd PIR, shown wearing his leather A-2 flight jacket on a field problem in England. On the chest is a leather name-tag and a 502nd regimental insignia, which is a decal applied to a circular leather disc which was then sewn to the jacket. *S.C. photo c/o N. Wierzbowski*

Class A Uniforms

Enlisted Man's Olive Drab Blouse

Private First Class John Mishler, B/501st, owned this Class A 4-pocket blouse, which was the standard issue US Army enlisted man's dress uniform until early 1945. Mishler jumped into Normandy with the Pathfinder stick led by Lieutenant Albert Watson, to provide security. Although not a trained radar signaller, Mishler was thus qualified to wear the Pathfinder insignia on his left sleeve. On 21 December 1944, near Mont, Belgium (east of Bastogne) Mishler knocked out a German tank with a bazooka. He was awarded the Silver Star, the ribbon for which is arrayed on the top row of ribbons on this uniform. *Author's Collection*

"Eisenhower" Jacket (right)

Four 101st troopers at Rainbow Corners in Paris on V-J day, 1945. All four wear the "Eisenhower" uniform, which was originally intended as a field ensemble. Beginning in early 1944, this was the uniform issued for dress wear by the US Army, and it was one of the most popular ever issued to American troops.

Garrison Caps

American soldiers assigned to airborne units did not wear the visored "service cap" with their Class A or B uniforms. Instead, they wore specially-modified garrison ("overseas") caps. Like all US Army enlisted men's garrison caps, airborne troopers' were piped in the branch color of the wearer, that is, light blue for infantry, scarlet for field artillery, and so on. Officers below the rank of general wore black and gold piping. Unlike any other American soldiers in WWII, however, airborne soldiers wore a patch on their garrison caps which signified their service with an airborne unit. From 1942–44, men assigned to parachute units were authorized to wear a round patch featuring a parachute and suspension lines. Irrespective of rank, the background color for soldiers assigned to a parachute infantry unit wore light blue, while field artillerymen of all ranks wore white parachutes on a scarlet background. Carl Beck, H/501st *(above)*, wears his white-on-light blue infantryman's parachute patch at Camp Toccoa, before his regiment deployed to Europe.

During the period that paratroopers were authorized parachute patches, soldiers assigned to glider units were authorized a similar cap patch. Lieutenant Harlan Rugg, 81st AAAB *(above on the right)*, wears a glider patch on his officer's garrison cap. Officers wore their glider or parachute patches on the right side of their caps because their rank insignia were displayed on the left side. Unlike later versions of the paraglide patch *(photo at opposite)*, which featured the glider pointing to the right for officers and to the left for enlisted men (so the aircraft would be appear to be flying forward, whether worn by an officer or enlisted man, respectively), the glider patch was designed with the aircraft facing left. Thus, it faced backwards when worn on an officer's garrison cap. Lieutenant Rugg was killed in action in Normandy.

In the studio portrait *(above)*, Len Morris (H/501st) wears the "paraglide" patch which replaced both the parachute and glider patches in late 1944. This red, white, and blue patch remained unique to paratroopers for decades after the war. While US Army parachute units adopted the maroon beret unofficially from 1974–79, and officially from 1980 to the present, even after the 101st became officially an "air-mobile" division in 1968 (and an "air assault" division in 1974), its soldiers continued to officially wear the garrison cap with paraglide patch until required to don the Army's new black beret in 2001.

Combat Boots vs. Jump Boots

Jump boots, long made by the Corcoran Company of Brockton, Massachusetts (and today made by the Cove Boot Company of Martinsburg, Pennsylvania), were a tremendous source of pride for paratroopers during World War II. When the rest of the Army was wearing shoes and canvas leggings into combat, paratroopers wore brown allleather jump boots that provided better support to the ankles and lower legs during the stress of parachute landing falls. Uniquely, jump boots were also authorized for wear with the Class A uniforms worn by soldiers on jump status. Much to the horror of most paratroopers, jump boots were withdrawn in late 1944, and the same two-buckle brown combat boot that was being issued for field wear to the rest of the Army became standard issue in airborne units as well. Adding insult to injury, during the Occupation, because of a shortage of low-quarter shoes, in many non-airborne units, combat boots were authorized for wear with the Class A uniform. This only made airborne soldiers more determined than ever to regain the right to wear jump boots; the airborne community breathed a collective sigh later in 1945, when jump boots were restored as the authorized footwear for all paratroopers.

A glider-riding member of Headquarters, 101st Airborne Division waits to board his CG-4A WACO glider, September 1944. He is wearing the two-buckle wrap around combat boots "asissued," with rough side out, unstained leather bodies, and smooth side out, unstained leather ankle flaps secured by 2-buckle straps on each leg. It is rare to see these boots before the ravages of mud and moisture changed their appearance, or before they were carefully "shaved" smooth and polished for dress wear during the Occupation. *S.C. photo*

Two members of Service Company, 502nd wearing their jump boots with their Eisenhower uniforms near Mittersil, Austria, 1945. *Musura*

Equipment

Parachutist's Steel Helmet

Parachutist's Steel Helmet with Camouflage Net

This belonged to Private Dominic Speranza, 3rd/501st LMG platoon, who had it from Toccoa to Holland. He brought is out when evacuated through the hospitals and ZI'd to the states. This is a 'D' bale helmet, with the original small-mesh, British-made net as worn in Market-Garden. The liner has no unit stencils on it, indicating that at least some liner stencils were added at some time after the Holland campaign. The relatively small diamond stencils on the sides of the steel pot indicate the 501st, with a tic at nine o'clock to indicate 3rd battalion. Dom wrote his name on one of the 'v' straps of the jump liner with a fountain pen, and also wrote his name on a piece of white adhesive tape, which is still stuck under the front rim of the liner. In the 501st, other examples of using white tape to identify equipment with the owner's name have also been observed, on such items as binoculars and compass pouches. *Author's Collection*

Parachutist's Steel Helmet 3⁄4-Rear View

View of the back of the helmet worn by 1st Lieutenant Donald Hettrick, a Forward Observer for Battery D of the 377th PFAB. Don wore this helmet while calling in support for the various com panies of 1st Battalion, 502nd PIR, the regiment supported by the 377th. This is a "D" bale helmet bearing the cannonball with tic at 6 o'clock, denoting the assembly symbol of the 377th. Also note the vertical bar at the rear, indicating the presence of an officer to those who were following.

The steel pot shows shrapnel damage sustained during a prolonged artillery barrage near St. Oedenrode Holland in September, 1944. The shrapnel barely penetrated the steel, inflicting only minor scratching to the inner liner and leaving Lieutenant Hettrick unscathed. *Author's Collection*

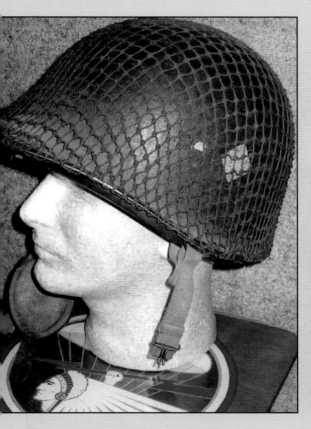

First Aid Kit

The kit consists of a brown cloth bag with two tie strings, which were used to fasten the kits to belts, ankles, arms, suspender harnesses, knife scabbards, and later, helmet nets. The contents included a Carlisle bandage in a cardboard box, a cloth torniquet, sulfanilimide powder in an envelope, and a one-shot disposable morphine syrette. Because of the morphine contents, some efforts were made to inventory and recall unused kits after each mission. *Author's Collection*

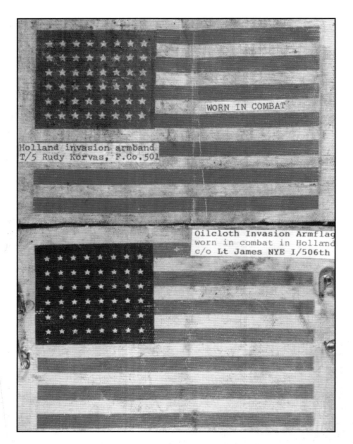

WORN IN COMBAT

Holland invasion armband
T/5 Rudy Korvas, F.Co.501

Oilcloth Invasion Armflag
worn in combat in Holland
c/o Lt James NYE I/506th

American Flag Brassards

The citizens of countries being liberated by American soldiers usually had no way of being familiar with the uniforms of their liberators. Flag brassards such as these identified the nationality of the wearer to the local inhabitants. These oilcloth armbands had been around for a year or two before the 101st used them: US amphibious forces had already worn similar arm brassards in 1942 during Operation torch in North Africa. Earlier examples usually have the top and bottom edge folded over and sewn. Eventually, it was discovered that this was an unnecessary and time-consuming frill, so that feature was eliminated by 1944.

Although brassards like those shown at right were worn by everyone in the 101st Airborne during the *Market-Garden* operation, photographic evidence indicates that they were not generally worn in Normandy by the 101st. Some esoteric subunits, such as the 501st Pathfinders, departing from North Witham airfield, may have worn them, but such instances in Normandy were few. The 82nd Airborne did wear flag brassards in Normandy, some of a narrower oil-cloth version, or a small, flimsy gauze version.

The two types shown were both issued with a pair of carbon steel safety pins. The flag brassard was much longer than shown, but was generally folded and pinned to the upper-right sleeve. The upper version, worn by Rudy Korvas of F/501st, is the more common type, with larger stars on a lighter blue field. This type was also more prone to color fading. The lower example from Lieutenant Jim Nye, who variously served with I, F, and Regimental HQ Companies of the 506th, has a dark blue field behind small stars. Actual size of each flag when folded as shown is 37/8" by 57/8". *Author's Collection*

ESCAPE KIT COMPASS
Capt.Robt. SPEER
HQ/2-502 PIR

Escape kit hacksaw blade
c/o C.Carlsen 501 PARA Maint.

AIRBORNE

CARENTAN

FRENCH
ASE BOOK

Normandy "Gadgets"

Displayed on a portion of a cloth escape kit map depicting the Cotentin Peninsula, are, from top to bottom: a steel hacksaw blade from an escape and evasion (E&E) kit; an M-2 switchblade jump knife; a compass, also from an E&E kit; a "cricket"; and a dogtag belonging to Captain Cecil L. Simmons, CO, H/502nd. *Author's Collection*

T-5 Parachutes

Troopers of I/502nd aboard a C-47, waiting to stand up and hook up before exiting the aircraft over the Fort Bragg military reservation in 1943. They are wearing the Type T-5 parachutes—the spring loaded clip fasteners of the main (back pack) chute harness are visible across the upper chests of the jumpers. These often tightened up because of the opening shock and descent, and many complaints were lodged by Normandy survivors that the buckles were too difficult and time-consuming to unfasten under combat conditions. Type T-5 chutes were used until mid-1944, when riggers began converting them by adding a harness equipped with a quick-release box (QRB). These were forerunners of the T-7 chutes on which QRBs were standard equipment. The jumpers shown are also holding the static line hook in their left hand—this was attached to a steel anchor cable which ran the length of the cabin just below the ceiling. When the jumper exited the door, the static line played out, ripping the cover off the back parachute. "Prop blast" from the propellers helped the canopy deploy. Thus the jumper only had to exit with the proper body position and his chute would open automatically in about four seconds. The red ripcord handle of the chest reserve chute was only pulled in the event of a malfunction of the main chute.

Data Plate for T-5 Parachute

Plates like this were sewn to the side of the main backpack of the T-5 parachute and this one indicates that the canopy inside is (multi-shade green) camouflage. Wartime records indicate that prior to D-day, parachute manufacturers were shipping parachutes with both white and camouflage canopies to England in equal numbers. Despite attempts to equip all D-day jumpers with camouflage ones, only about half of the chutes used on D-day had such canopies. The rest had glorious white ones, which made splendid targets for enemy machine gunners while the troopers descended through the Normandy night skies. *Author's Collection*

M-1 Rifle

Benny Niesner, D/506th displays his M-1 rifle, the standard weapon of American airborne and non-airborne infantry soldier alike during WWII. Firing semi-automatically from a disposable eight-round clip, the M-1 had an effective range of 500 yards. The semiautomatic action gave the American rifleman a distinct advantage over the average German soldier armed with a boltaction Mauser KAR 98. The range provided another advantage over enemy troops armed with 9mm caliber machine pistols (submachine guns) or, later in 1944–45, the MP43 or MP44 assault rifle. *Truax*

Thompson Submachine Gun

The Thompson Submachine Gun, shown below in the hands of Edwin H. Miller, A/377th PFAB, was a highly reliable weapon, providing devastating firepower at close ranges. Although heavy (11 pounds), it fired massive (230 grains) .45-cal. bullets from 20 or 30-round magazines to an effective range of 50 yards. Under early tables of organization and equipment, all infantry squad leaders and platoon sergeants were armed with submachine guns, and although later tables diminished the authorized numbers, there is strong evidence that many parachute units found ways to maintain their quantities. Extremely well made, the Thompson's complexity made it expensive; its close engineering tolerances meant it had to be carefully maintained under protracted tactical conditions. As a result, the US Army began replacing it with the ungainly, all-metal M-3/M-3A1 submachine gun in 1944. The trooper on the left, William R. Kowger, also of A/377th PFAB, wields his M-3 trench knife.

M-1 Carbine

The M1 carbine was commonly carried by junior officers and certain crew-served weapons crewmen. A version with a folding stock, the M-1A1, was especially developed for parachute units. Like its more common sibling, the M-1A1 fired .30-cal. carbine rounds – which were smaller, lighter, and considerably less powerful than the .30-cal. rounds fired by the M-1 and M-1919A4 and A6 machine guns – from 15-round magazines to a maximum effective range of 300 yards. Very late in the war, a curved 30-round magazine was introduced. Rudy Korvas, F/501st, is shown here with his carbine. *Korvas*

M-1919A6 Light Machine Gun

The M-1919A6 light machine gun provided the base of fire that enabled the maneuver of rifle squads in the 101st. Its firing characteristics were similar to its tripod-mounted A4 sibling except that without a traversing and elevating mechanism, its effective range was only 800 yards. The A6 weighed 32½ lbs., and was a much less cumbersome weapon in offensive operations than the A4. With one of these in each of its nine rifle squads, a parachute rifle company had significantly more firepower than its equivalent in a line infantry battalion; in the latter, there were only two M-1919A4s in the entire company and the squad automatic weapons were Browning Automatic Rifles (BARs). BARs were lighter than A6s, but being fed from a 20-round magazine and having a much lighter barrel kept them from being able to deliver anything like the firepower of an A6. Other than the very heavily-armed armored infantry found in American armored divisions, airborne infantry companies were the only ones which could slug toe-to-toe with German infantry companies, which were equipped with one MG34 or MG42 per squad. *Wilson*

M-1919A4 Light Machine Gun

Above: An unknown member of Item Co 506th firing an A-4 LMG. This was the weapon that equipped the battalion light machine gun platoons throughout the 101st Airborne Division during WWII. Mounted on a tripod with a traversing and elevation mechanism, this belt-fed weapon could fire its .30-cal. ammunition to an effective range of 1,200 yards at a cyclic rate of 550 rounds per minute. Although it fired the same ammunition at the same rate as the M-1917A1 heavy machine gun used in line infantry units, its sustained rate of fire was only 60 rounds per minute because of its air-cooled, rather than watercooled, system. The additional weight of the heavy machine gun (94 pounds with coolant), however, was deemed impractical for airborne units, so the much lighter (44½ pounds) M-1919A4 was standard issue in the 101st and other US Army airborne divisions. *Below:* Jim Alley of the famous Easy Company 506th PIR, holding an A-4 LMG. *Boback*

2.36-inch Rocket Launcher

The most serious shortcoming of airborne units – down to the present day – is their inability to deal effectively with enemy armor. In WWII, the rifle grenade issued as a round of ammunition to infantry units was only accurate at close ranges (75 yards or less) and did not pack the punch to penetrate many of the more recent German tank designs. Other than these and some British "Gammon" grenades – which were almost as dangerous to the thrower as the intended target – and some field expedient weapons like the "Molotov Cocktail," the 2.36-inch (60mm) rocket launcher, or "bazooka," was the only antitank weapon available to airborne units below the regimental level. It fired a 3½-lb. rocket accurately to about 300 yards, and was very effective against lightly armored vehicles and wood-and-earth field fortifications. It was also quite useful in built-up areas such as towns, but could not be safely used from inside a building, due to the backblast from the rocket as it left the tube. The early M-1A1 2.36 rocket launcher was about five feet long, which made it awkward to jump with, but the later M-9 could be broken down into two pieces, enhancing its convenience of carrying and jumping. Both versions weighed about 16 pounds, unloaded. *Frey*

M-3 Trench Knife

The M3 trench knife was issued to paratroopers – as well as soldiers from nonairborne units whose weapons did not take a bayonet – for use as a fighting knife. Over a dozen different companies made them on government contracts and some were maker marked on the blade, while later specimens are marked on the crossguard. Paratroopers usually carried these strapped to the ankle with web straps cut from musette bags, and a leather lace at the bottom to secure to the boot. Shown here is an M6 leather scabbard, and later knives were carried in an M8 fiber scabbard. *Author's Collection*

271

Normandy

17th SS-Panzer-Grenadier Division "Göz von Berlichingen"

Gotz von Berlichingen (1480–1562) was a late-medieval nobleman who was a sort of Germanic Robin Hood. A fiery Swabian warrior, he lost his right hand at the siege of Landshut in 1504, and had it replaced with a prosthetic fist made of iron. The men of the hard-driving Waffen-SS formation named for him took especially great pride in his most famous quotation, a defiant retort to a surrender demand in one of his many campaigns which can best be translated as, "Kiss my ass!"

On 3 October 1943, Adolf Hitler ordered the creation of the 17th SS-Panzer-Grenadier-Division, and decreed that it be named after this legendary figure of Germanic lore. It was raised in France with an officer and NCO cadre from experienced Waffen-SS divisions, and soldiers from all over Germany as well as Volksdeutschen ("racial Germans") from central and southern European countries; there were also a minority of Volksdeutschen from Belgium, Luxembourg, Alsace, and Lorraine. Many of the initial complement of Volksdeutschen were conscripts, and as the division received replacements for its casualties in 1944-45, draftees became the norm.

From the beginning, the 17th was especially trained in night operations, to compensate for the conditions its leaders anticipated for the battlefields of the Western Front, where the 17th was specifically expected to fight. Its leadership insisted that at least 25 percent of all tactical training being conducted under these conditions.

At the time of the Normandy landings, the training of the division was officially incomplete, although by this time of the war, the 17th had to be counted among the better-trained German divisions: roughly 33 percent of the enlisted men had completed 22 weeks of training, and the remainder about 25 weeks. Although the division was short about 1,800 officers and NCOs (a 40 percent short age!), it had an excess of about 750 junior enlisted soldiers, so overall, the division was fewer than 1,000 men understrength at 17,321 assigned.

The major maneuver elements of the 17th Panzer- Grenadier Division were SS-Panzer-Grenadier Regiments 37 and 38; SS-Panzer Battalion 17, which was equipped with 42 Sturmgeschutz 75mm assault guns; SS-Panzerjäger Battalion 17, which, at the time of the Normandy landings had not yet received its authorized 31 Jagdpanzer IV tank destroyers; but was instead equipped with 12 Marders armed with 75mm or captured Soviet 76mm antitank guns; and SS-Reconnaissance Battalion 17.

The Gotz von Berlichingen Division began moving toward the invasion beaches on 7 June. SS-Reconnaissance Battalion 17 was the first into action, arriving to support the 352nd Infantry Division on 10 June. Despite serious shortages of trucks for transporting men and materiel, other major units began arriving near Carentan by 11 June. SS-Panzer-Grenadier Regiment 37, supported by SS-Panzer Battalion 17, went into action on 13 June, attacking elements of the 101st Airborne Division south west of Carentan; all but the flak and engineer battalions were in position there by 14 June. The division fought extensively in the Normandy campaign, and suffered heavy losses of men and materiel there and during the subsequent withdrawal across France to Lorraine. During its protracted combat, it absorbed the SS-Panzer- Grenadier Brigades 49 and 51, and later fought against US Third Army elements near Verdun and Metz in the late summer and autumn of 1944.

In December 1944, the Gotz von Berlichingen Division was brought up to full strength again, and conducted the main attack of XIII SS Corps in eastern Lorraine during Operation Nordwind, the last German offensive in the West. Within the panzer-grenadier regiments, its ranks were filled largely with ex-Soviet prisoners, and the performance of the division in its attack against elements of the US 44th and 100th Infantry Divisions, was a deep disappointment to the German high command. On 3 January, many of its principal staff officers were relieved for cause, and six days later, the division commander, Standartenfuhrer Hans Lingner, was captured by a patrol from Company A of the 44th Infantry Division's 114th Infantry Regiment. Although Lingner was the first Waffen-SS division commander to be captured on the Western Front, his departure was only the most recent in Prussian Guard regiment in the Great War, his previous wartime commands included a panzer-grenadier regiment of the 4th Panzer Division, the 208th Infantry Division, and the 18th Panzer Division. He assumed command of the 709th in December 1943.

The 709th Infantry Division was actually overstrength on 6 June, and in addition to full strength infantry regiments (Grenadier Regiments 729, 739, and 919) also counted three battalions of former Soviet soldiers – Ost Battalions 561 and 649, and Georgian Infantry Battalion 795 – among its ranks. The division's artillery regiment only had three battalions instead of the authorized four, but two of them possessed an extra firing battery, so the actual strength of the division artillery was only short one battery of light howitzers by table of organization. The artillery regiment's 1st Battalion was equipped with Czech 105mm howitzers and captured French 105mm guns; 2nd Battalion had French 105mm guns and 155mm howitzers; and 3rd Battalion was equipped with captured Soviet 76mm gun/howitzers. The Panzerjager battalion employed nine self-propelled 75mm antitank guns and 12 towed ones.

According to German reports, the average age of the soldiers under Schlieben's command was 36, which obviously affected its ability for sustained combat and offensive operations. The communications and cohesion among the Ost battalions was also suspect, as many of the soldiers did not speak German, and had joined to fight Stalin, not the western Allies.

After defensive operations on the coast, the division withdrew to Cherbourg starting on about 16 June. Generalleutnant von Schieben was named as Commandant of Fortress Cherbourg, but surrendered his command to the 4th Infantry Division a few days later, on 26 June. With the surrender of all remaining German forces in Cherbourg on the next day, the 709th Infantry Division ceased to exist.

Parachute Infantry Regiment 6

Parachute Infantry Regiment 6 was originally an element of the 2nd Parachute Division, formed in January 1943. It was formed around a cadre of Africa Corps veterans, and was commanded by Major Friedrich August Freiherr (Baron) von der Heydte throughout most of its existence. The division served in Italy in the summer-fall of 1943, but was transferred to the Soviet Union in November 1943. Throughout the late autumn and winter of 1943– 44, the 2nd Parachute Division fought in the Ukraine, as a sort of "fire brigade," reinforcing units being pressed hard by growing Soviet attacks throughout the region. The division sustained severe casualties in the Ukraine, and in early 1944, was sent to Brittany for rehabilitation.

In early May, Parachute Infantry Regiment 6 was detached from the 2nd Parachute Division and attached to the 91st Air Landing Division in Normandy. At the time of the Normandy landings, the regiment was actually over strength, possessing about 3,500 men, but only autho rized about 3,200. Approximately 33 percent of the officer corps were combat experienced, as were 20 percent of the NCOs. The average age of the junior enlisted men was 17.5 years.

As the summer of 1944 wore on, with the destruction of Air Landing Division 91 in August, Parachute Infantry Regiment 6 became something of an independent unit. Additional personnel were added to man the regiment's flak company, transportation, logistical, and training units. These brought the regiment up to about 4,500 soldiers.

In late July, the regiment was attached to the 2nd SS-Panzer Division, and fought in the vicinity of La Baleine and Villedieu. In early August, the regiment was attached briefly to the 353rd Infantry Division before being ordered to Nancy, thence to Germany to refit. At this point, the regiment could count only a little more than 1,000 men left on its rolls; it had lost about 75 per cent of its personnel in fighting the Americans.

In early September, Parachute Infantry Regiment 6 was dispatched to Belgium, where it fought the British Guards Armoured Division in the vicinity of Beeringen. During Operation Market-Garden, the regiment fought against Allied airborne forces in the Netherlands, including elements of the 101st Airborne Division in the vicinity of Veghel.

In late September and the first half of October, Parachute Infantry Regiment 6 fought the Canadian 2nd Infantry Division near Woensdrecht, Holland, on the narrow neck of land that leads to Walcheren Island. They withdrew on 16 October after sustaining heavy losses. In mid-December, as part of Combat Group von der Heydte, the remaining elements of Parachute Regiment 6 participated in the last major German parachute assault of the war. As part of the German Ardennes Offensive, Combat Group von der Heydte's mission was to interdict American reinforcements for the sector being attacked by Sixth Panzer Army. Unfortunately for them, the night drop scattered the roughly 1,300 participating *Fallschirmjäger* over 600 square miles of Belgian and German country side; by daylight on the first morning of the operation, only 125 men had gathered with their commander to pursue the mission. Baron von der Heydte surrendered to American forces on Christmas Eve as most of his men were desperately attempting to evade death or capture, and simply make it back to their own lines.

Although this operation did not accomplish its mission, the dispersion of the drop resulted in gross misper ceptions of its scope among Allied intelligence officers and troops on the ground. Accordingly, a great deal of apprehension grew among the defenders, who feared a massive German airborne presence in their rear areas.

a long line of commanders to leave that post since Normandy. No fewer than six different officers had commanded the division since 6 June, and this sort of turbulence could only detract from the division's combat effectiveness.

After its failure in *Nordwind*, the *17th* conducted defensive and retrograde operations in Lorraine; the Saar and Palatinate; Baden; and Wurttemberg. The last scat tered remnants of the division surrendered in early May in Bavaria, near the Tegernsee and Achensee, near Kreuth, and along the Inn River near Jenbach.

91st Air Landing Division

The *91st* was formed in January 1944 at Baumholder, Germany, as a uniquely air-portable (not parachute or glider) infantry division. To this end, its major organic combat elements included only two infantry regiments, *Grenadier Regiments 1057* and *1058*, and an artillery regiment of four battalions. Two of the latter were equipped with 105mm mountain howitzers, however, and since these fired different ammunition than the standard 105mm *leFH 18*, there was a significant ammo shortage for several days after the American landings began.

During the Normandy landings, the 91st defended inland areas on the Cotentin Peninsula, including St. Mere Eglise, Marcouf, and other areas south of Cherbourg. The division suffered heavy losses: out of a total initial strength of no more than 8,000 on 6 June, by 12 June, the division reported losses of 2,212 men killed, wounded, and missing. By 24 June, the division reported losses of 85 percent of its infantry strength. To make matters worse, the Commanding General, *Generalleutnant* Wilhelm Falley, was killed in action on D-day.

While withdrawing through Lessy and Coutances, the division was essentially destroyed. Remnants were incor porated into the *344th Infantry Division*. The *91st Air Landing Division* was officially disbanded in August 1944.

243rd Infantry Division

This division was formed in Dollersheim, Austria *(Wehrkreis XVII)* in the late summer of 1943, and was transferred to Brittany in October of the same year. In April 1944, the division was transferred to Normandy, with its headquarters at Coutances.

At the time of the Normandy invasion, the 243rd was commanded by *Generalleutnant* (Major General) Heinz Hellmich. Hellmich had commanded the *23rd Infantry Division* during Operation BarBarossa, the German offensive against the Soviet Union in 1941. While still in Soviet-occupied Poland, soldiers of the division's famous *Infantry Regiment 9* encountered Soviets who abused a white flag, pretending to surrender, then killed six members of the regiment. Hellmich ordered that from that point forward, no Soviet white flags would be respected. Interestingly, Hellmich was later appointed the first "Inspector of Eastern Troops" in late 1942, and was charged with the training and organization of Cossack and other units made up of citizens of the Soviet Union who opted to fight for the Germans. Hellmich assumed command of the *243rd Infantry Division* in January 1944.

On the eve of the Normandy landings, the infantry battalions of the *243rd (Grenadier Regiments 920, 921,* and *922)* were at full strength, although *Grenadier Regiment 920* possessed only two of its three authorized battalions. The artillery regiment had three of its four authorized battalions, but all were at full strength: two were equipped with vehicledrawn captured Soviet 76mm gun/howitzers, and one with two batteries of vehicle drawn 122mm howitzers and one of 122mm guns. Regimental antitank companies were equipped with 75mm antitank guns, and the *Panzerjäger battalion* had 14 Marder self-propelled 75mm or 76mm antitank guns and ten *Sturmgeschutz III* 75mm assault guns. Although the engineer battalion was understrength and *Grenadier Regiment 920* was missing a battalion, overall, the division possessed about 11,500 soldiers of the 12,300 that were authorized.

The *243rd* took a fearsome beating in Normandy. *Generalleutnant* Hellmich was killed in action on 17 June, and by 11 July, the division had suffered losses amounting to over 8,000 men; it could count only 700 men in its line companies. By the end of July, its combat power had been reduced to four seriously understrength infantry battalions (of the original eight, *Grenadier Regiment 920* had only two battalions on 6 June), a total of eight captured Soviet 76mm antitank guns, three assault guns, and nine artillery batteries. Hellmich was awarded the Knight's Cross posthumously

and for the remainder of its existence, the division was commanded by Oberst (later *Generalmajor*) Bernard Klosterkemper, a Knight's Cross recipient and former commander of *Grenadier Regiment 920*, who, coincidentally, later commanded the *180th Infantry Division* in the Netherlands during the Market-Garden operation.

The division was disbanded in September 1944.

709th Infantry Division

The *709th Infantry Division* was activated near Kassel, in Hessen, in April 1941. It was transferred to Saint-Malo, France, on the Brittany coast in May 1941, and performed security and coastal defense duties there and in Normandy, where the division was located at the time of the Allied landings.

The commanding general, *Generalleutnant* (Major General) Karl-Wilhem von Schlieben, was a Knight's Cross recipient with extensive combat experience. In addition to distinguished service as a junior officer in a near Saint-Lô only in July. After extensive, protracted operations against the Americans, it was withdrawn from Normandy in August with very little equipment and only a handful of combat troops still on their feet. Their division commander, Generalleutnant Gerhard Graf (Count) von Schwerin, was relieved of command during the Normandy fighting for supposed lethargy and accusations of defeatism. He was reinstated a short time later. Upon reaching the German border near Aachen in early September, where the division was to be reconstituted and committed to defensive operations against the pursuing Americans, Schwerin declared that he intended to dissolve the division and send the troops back to their homes. This and his evacuation of a part of the city of Aachen led not only to his relief, but to a furious reaction on the part of Heinrich Himmler, who was astounded that Schwerin was willing to give up the ancient capital of Charlemagne and first major German city to be attacked on the ground by the Allies.

Heavily protected by his troops, Schwerin survived and was cleared of wrongdoing by a board of inquiry. He was reassigned to command the *90th Panzer-Grenadier Division* in Italy. *Oberst*, later *Generalmajor*, Siegfried von Waldenburg assumed command and helped guide the troubled division through the rest of the war.

After meager reconstitution and heavy combat near Aachen, the *116th* was transferred to the Netherlands, where it participated in operations against the Allied airborne forces and elements of British XXX Corps that were executing Operation *Market-Garden*. From there, it was redeployed to the vicinity of Aachen, and was more fully reconstituted. Immediately afterwards, however, the Greyhound Division participated in heavy defensive action in the Hurtgen Forest. Once again, the division's combat strength was seriously depleted, and in late November and early December, the *116th* was essentially reconstituted once again in preparation for the Ardennes Offensive.

In the first part of December, the personnel strength of the division was brought up to something resembling full strength, and the Division Personnel Officer, Major Fritz Vogelsang, opined that after training by the Division's Field Replacement Battalion, the replacements were "really well prepared." Still, there was a dire shortage of NCOs in the panzergrenadier regiments, and that would retard flexibility and initiative in the upcoming combat in the Ardennes. Also, although the artillery regiment was at nearly full strength, the armored maneuver elements of the division remained severely underequipped. The *2nd Battalion of Panzer Regiment 16* possessed only 26 Mark IV tanks at the outset of the Ardennes offensive, while the *1st Battalion* had only 43 battleworthy Panthers.

Nevertheless, on 16 December 1944, the *116th* attacked positions held by elements of the US 112th Infantry Regiment (one of three regiments of the 28th Infantry Division) near Berg and Lutzkampen, and had what Heinz Gunther Guderian, the Division's 1st General Staff Officer, called a "sobering" experience. On that day alone, the division lost two full panzergrenadier companies and 17 Mark IV tanks. Over the next two weeks, the *116th Panzer Division* fought in a variety of locales throughout the *Fifth Panzer Army* zone, including Bastogne, and made its deepest penetration of American lines near the villages of Hotton, Verdenne, Menil, Soy, and Wy, where it was stopped by elements of the US 84th Infantry Division. By Christmas, however, the division had lost its offensive capability; as Guderian put it, the situation "was most unpleasant." Vogelsang was a little more specific: according to him, the "Division suffered losses that were so high that the *Panzer-Grenadier* regiments, the *Reconnaissance Battalion, and the Panzer Regiment* … have to be considered as nearly destroyed." The *116th Panzer Division* spent the rest of its time in the Ardennes, all the way through the end of January 1945, in desperate defensive operations, while slowly rebuilding its strength as best it could.

From February through the early March, the *116th* fought British forces in the *Reichswald*, before being shifted to contest the British crossing of the Rhine River south of Wesel. In April, the *116th Panzer Division* fought against US Ninth Army units that were in the process of closing the Ruhr Pocket. By 16 April, all but a few small elements of the division surrendered there, while the rest surrendered in the Harz Mountains by 21 April.

59th Infantry Division

Although a low-numbered unit, the *59th Infantry Division* was only created in late June 1944, at Gross Born, Germany. A conventionally-organized infantry division, its major maneuver elements consisted of *Grenadier Regiments 1034, 1035, 1036,* and *Fusilier Battalion 59* (a bicycle-mobile light infantry unit for missions such as reconnaissance, raids, and so on).

Immediately after it was raised, the division was moved to the vicinity of Dunkirk, where it performed coastal defense missions in anticipation of a second Allied landing in the Pas de Calais. When this failed to materialize, the division was transferred to conduct defensive operations in the Bethune and Armentieres sectors. From there, the *59th* withdrew through Belgium, ironically, through the historic medieval battlefield at Courtrai and Oudenarde, site of one of the great battles of the War of the Spanish Succession, toward Ghent. From there, the *59th* was withdrawn to the Netherlands, where it defended against the *Market-Garden* landings in the vicinity of Best, Son, Oedenrode, and Veghel.

After its action there, in October, the *59th* pulled back across the Maas (Meuse) at S'Hertogenbosch and fought near Heusden. After refitting in Germany, at Wahn near Still, this was no substitute for the establishment of the blocking positions so important to isolating Dietrich's Sixth Panzer Army zone … and the casualties sustained in the operation effectively ended the regiment's existence. Remnants fought on until finally captured in the Ruhr Pocket in April 1945, but the Ardennes marks the final operation for Parachute Regiment 6 as a coherent unit.

The Netherlands

10th SS-Panzer-Division "Frundsberg"

The *10th SS-Panzer-Division* was named for Georg von Frundsberg, a chivalrous and valorous commander in the service of the Habsburg Holy Roman Emperors Maximillian I and Charles V. In addition to impressive battlefield exploits, Frundsberg's important contributions to warfare include the organization of a band of Imperial mercenary infantry called *Landsknechte*. These professional foot soldiers were the first of their type in Imperial service, and were far superior to the temporarily levied peasants that usually comprised the infantry of the day. Frundsberg's soldiers are considered by many to be the lineal ancestors of the German infantry of the nineteenth and twentieth centuries. Ironically, the division named for him was neither an infantry unit, nor was it comprised of professionals; most of the troops were members of the German Labor Service *(RAD)* who were conscripted into the *Waffen-SS*.

Organized and trained in France from early 1943 through early 1944, the division's major maneuver units included *SS-Panzer Regiment 10 "Langemarck,"* with a battalion of Mark IVs and *Sturmgeschutz* assault guns and one of Panthers; *SS-Panzer-Grenadier Regiments 21* and *22*; *SS-Reconnaissance Battalion 10*; and *SS-Panzerjager Battalion 10*. The division first saw action at Tarnopol, Galicia, in April 1944. It took part in rescuing German units from the Kamenets-Podolsk pocket. On 27 April, 38-year-old *Oberfuhrer* Heinz Harmel assumed command of *SS-Frundsberg*; he was destined to be one of the most respected and popular division commanders of the war, as well as one of the most long-lived. Harmel, a Lorrainer born in Metz when Alsace and Lorraine were part of Germany between 1871 and 1918, passed away in 2000.

The division was transferred to France in June 1944, and entered combat in Normandy by the end of the month. It was heavily engaged against elements of the British VIII Corps in the vicinity of Caen and Villers Bocage in late June and July, and against elements of the US XV Corps near Domfront in August. By the end of the third week of August, only remnants of the division escaped the Falaise Pocket; *SS-Frundsberg* lost about 10,000 men in Normandy, and by August, when it was sent to the Netherlands in the vicinity of Arnhem for reconstitution, only about 3,500 soldiers remained.

Although reconstitution was far from complete, during Operation Market-Garden, elements of the division fought both the British 1st Airborne Division near Arnhem, and American airborne units further south. Reinforced by King Tigers from the German Army's *Heavy Tank Battalion 506,* elements of Frundsberg continued the fight against Allied forces in the Eindhoven Nijmegen-Arnhem corridor well into October. The division was then withdrawn for further reconstitution near Geilenkirchen, Germany.

In January 1945, brought up to a personnel strength of about 15,000, *SS-Frundsberg* was committed to offensive action in Alsace, where the Germans were attempting to salvage the failing Operation *Nordwind,* their last offensive in the West. Elements of the division engaged and inflicted very heavy casualties on the US 12th Armored Division near Herrlisheim, but overall, the addition of SS-Frundsberg to the fighting in Alsace only delayed the ultimate failure of the German effort to split the French and American forces there. It also weakened the division on the eve of its final mission.

In March, the division was transferred to the Eastern Front, and conducted delaying and defensive operations in Pomerania and in the vicinity of Berlin. Nearly encircled and destroyed around Spremberg, the division

broke out to the west and survived, albeit without its vehicles. This prompted Himmler to relieve Harmel, who was then sent to command the remnants of the *24th SS-Mountain Division* in its (largely successful) attempts to keep Alpine passes open for German units and refugees fleeing from Tito's partisans. Under the command of *Obersturmbannfuhrer* Erwin Franz Roestel, *SS-Frundsberg* surrendered to Soviet forces near Schonau in early May 1945. Three days before the division's capitulation, Roestel was awarded one of the last Knight's Crosses, on 3 May.

116th Panzer Division

The *"Windhund"* ("Greyhound") Division was formed from the remnants of the *16th Panzer-Grenadier Division*—which had been mauled in the Ukraine—and personnel from the *179th Reserve Division* in France in the spring of 1944. Its major maneuver elements consisted of *Panzer Regiment 16*; *Panzer-Grenadier Regiments 60* and *156*; *Armored Reconnaissance Battalion 116*; and *Panzerjager* (Tank Destroyer) *Battalion 228*.

As part of the reserve held back initially from the Normandy fighting in anticipation of a second Allied landing in the Pas de Calais, the *116th* was committed October, practically all of its panzergrenadiers. In early November, the Brigade was withdrawn to Germany to form the core for a newly-constituted *25th Panzer-Grenadier Division*.

Landstorm Nederland

Formed in October 1943 from the *Landwacht Nederland,* a regimental-strength, part-time unit comprised of Dutch Nazis, Dutch Waffen-SS veterans of fighting on the Eastern Front, and German police. The *Landwacht* was originally created by the German occupation government to combat Dutch resistance fighters and Allied intelligence agents, but by October 1943, it was reorganized as an infantry regiment, titled *SS-Grenadier Regiment Landstorm Nederland*. The 3,000(+) strong unit was mobilized in mid-May 1944, in anticipation of the impending Allied invasion of France or Belgium.

During the fighting in Belgium and the Netherlands, including Operation *Market-Garden,* battalions of the *Landstorm* were attached to various German divisions. The *1st Battalion* fought with the *85th Infantry Division,* while the *2nd Battalion* was attached to the *719th Infantry Division*. The *3rd Battalion* was committed against Allied airborne forces near Arnhem. It was probably the *2nd Battalion* that was encountered by elements of the 101st.

The *Landstorm* was upgraded to a brigade in early November 1944, with the addition of an organic artillery unit. Called *SS-Volunteer Grenadier Brigade "Landstorm Nederland,"* it incorporated several miscellaneous *Waffen-SS* units, conscripted Dutch Nazis, various police organizations, and, importantly, Dutch former concentration camp guards. In February 1945, it was upgraded again, and became known as the *34th SS-Volunteer Grenadier Division "Landstorm Nederland,"* although it only had two infantry regiments of two battalions each, and understrength supporting units. By this stage, morale was apparently less than high, mainly due to the discomfort induced by including draftees and especially unsavory characters like the concentration camp guards. The fact that many of the original volunteers had enlisted to fight the Bolsheviks, but were now fighting the Western Allies, also contributed to morale problems.

Despite flagging cohesion and esprit, the Landstorm fought hard during its last few months. Officered primarily by German *Waffen-SS* officers, perhaps the Dutch rank and file realized that they had little choice, and that their post-war fate was sealed if the Allies attained their seemingly likely victory. In any event, after some successes in the winter of 1945, the *Landstorm* was overwhelmed near Arnhem during the final Anglo-Canadian offensive in early April, and it was broken up shortly thereafter.

Parachute Infantry Regiment 6

(See page 273.)

Bastogne

2nd Panzer Division

The *2nd Panzer Division* was one of the first of three such combined arms formations built by the German Army in 1935 as part of the open abrogation of the Versailles limitations on armaments and size and composition of the German armed forces. Commanded by Heinz Wilhelm Guderian, the father of German armored mobility tactics and *Panzer* units, it was used to test and prove the efficacy of highly mobile, combined arms formations in the crucial years before the war.

The *2nd Panzer* participated in the annexation of Austria in 1938, and although the armored might of the division was, indeed, impressive to the average Austrian who watched its battalions sweep through his country, the operation also proved the sad state of the panzers' reliability during protracted marches: Austrian highways were littered with broken-down tanks by the time the Anschluss was complete. Nevertheless, the point had been made and German armor was just beginning to be respected and feared.

275

Over the next year, the Division was stationed in and around Vienna, and assimilated thousands of Austrian soldiers. In 1939, the Division participated in the invasion of Poland, attacking the Polish Carpathian Army through the Dukla Pass and pushing it back to Lvov. The *2nd Panzer* suffered serious losses in the process, but was brought to strength in time for the conquest of France the next year.

In the spring of 1940, as part of Guderian's *XIX Corps,* the *2nd Panzer Division* was part of the famous thrust through the Ardennes that crossed the Meuse at Sedan and drove to the Channel Coast. The Division reached the Channel at Abbeville and thus spearheaded the isolation of Allied forces in Belgium and northern France. The *2nd Panzer Division* participated in the attacks on the Dunkirk Pocket.

From the end of the conquest of western Europe until the spring of 1941, the Division trained and also provided cadres for new armored formations. In April, it took part in the Balkan campaign, including the invasion of Greece.

During Operation BarBarossa, the Division conducted offensive operations as part *of Army Group Center,* and took part in the great encirclement near Vyasma in the autumn of 1941. By December, its reconnaissance units could see Moscow, but the Division retreated in the face Koln (Cologne), the *59th* was committed to defensive operations near Julich. It was destroyed in the Ruhr Pocket in April 1945.

347th Infantry Division

The *347th Infantry Division* was organized in late September 1942 in Hannover, Germany. Equipped as a static ("*bodenstandige*") division designed for coastal defense, at the time of the Market-Garden landings, its major maneuver units consisted of *Grenadier Regiments 860, 861,* and *880,* as well as *Fusilier Battalion 347.* Assigned to coastal duties near Alkmaar, the Netherlands, in early 1943, the division was transferred from Belgium in August 1944. It suffered heavy casualties during defensive fighting against elements of British Second Army and US First Army in late summer. In September, it was reorganized as a "mobile" division, to the extent that it received an antitank battalion and some trucks to move its heaviest equipment, although its four-battalion artillery regiment remained horsedrawn.

In November and December, the *347th Infantry Division* was committed in the Saar, and fought delaying and defensive actions against Third Army until the Ardennes Offensive. When the Seventh Army relieved elements of the Third Army in the Saar in late December, the *347th* faced the US 70th Infantry Division around Forbach and Oeting during its drive to the Saar River. The *347th* was destroyed in March 1945 during the American offensive through the Saar, although remnants fought on as combat groups throughout April.

Somewhat unusually for a German division at this stage of the war, the *347th* was commanded throughout its combat service by one officer, Generalmajor Wolf Trierenberg. A fifty-four-year-old Bavarian infantryman who commanded the *167th Infantry Division* in the invasion of the Soviet Union and for almost two years afterward, Trierenberg commanded the *347th* from December 1943 until the division's destruction.

363rd Volks-Grenadier Division

The *363rd Infantry Division* was raised in late December 1943 in Poland, from the staff and remnants of the *339th Infantry Division,* which had been destroyed in the Ukraine during the previous month. It was a conventionally organized infantry division, the major maneuver elements of which consisted of *Grenadier Regiments 957, 958,* and *959,* as well as the bicycle-borne *Fusilier Battalion 363.*

In early 1944, the division was transferred to occupation duties in Denmark where, due to the low threat environment, it continued its collective training. In May, it was redeployed to the Pas de Calais sector, near Dunkirk, and by July, the division was committed to defensive operations in Normandy. Much of the *363rd* was destroyed in the Falaise Pocket in August 1944, and it was reformed in Germany as a volks-grenadier division in September. Very shortly after its reconstitution, it was rushed into combat in the Netherlands, and withdrew toward Aachen afterward.

719th Infantry Division

The *719th Infantry Division* was raised in May 1941 in Brandenburg, Germany, as an occupation division for duty in the Netherlands. Its major maneuver units consisted initially of *Grenadier Regiments 723* and *743,* and by 1944, *Grenadier Regiment 766* had been added; the division also possessed *Fusilier Battalion 719.*

Apparently, the soldiers assigned to the *719th* were not of the highest caliber; one German officer described them as "elderly gentlemen who hitherto had been guarding the north coast of Holland and had never heard a shot fired in anger."

In September 1944, the division was committed in relief of the *347th Infantry Division* near Antwerp, and subsequently withdrew into the Netherlands. Badly mauled during the fighting in the Low Countries, includ ing combat against Allied airborne forces during Operation *Market-Garden,* the division was withdrawn for brief refitting in late November and trans-

ferred to defensive operations in the Saar in December.

The *719th* fought in the Saar throughout the winter of 1944-45, particularly near Saarlautern, but was destroyed by elements of Third Army when they began their final offensive into Germany in March 1945.

Panzer Brigade 107

This unit had a very brief existence. Formed in early August 1944 at the training center in Mlawa, Poland, *Panzer Brigade 107* was formed around a core of soldiers who had been members of the *25th Panzer-Grenadier Division* on the Eastern Front who had survived that unit's destruction near Minsk. Its maneuver units consisted of *Panzer Battalion 2107,* equipped with Panthers, and *Panzer-Grenadier Battalion 2107.* With barely six weeks of training and other organizational activities to integrate the preponderance of troops who came from training centers in *Wehrkreis V* (Wurttemberg), the Brigade was transported to the Netherlands by rail commencing 15 September. Its lead elements arrived near Son on 19 September, and went into action against British and American airborne forces almost immediately. For the remainder of September and all of October, the Brigade was engaged in constant combat against British and American airborne, infantry, and armored forces in Holland. The Brigade sustained very high casualties, losing both battalion commanders and, at one point in mid-France and Belgium.

As German elements withdrew into Belgium, *SS-Hohenstaufen* fought rear guard actions to cover their movement and in early September, was eventually withdrawn itself to the Netherlands for reconstitution. By the time it reached the vicinity of Arnhem, the Division counted only about 6,000 men in its ranks – down from a strength of about 16,000 when it had entered combat near Caen earlier in the summer.

Along with the *10th SS-Panzer Division,* its habitual partner unit in *II SS-Panzer Corps,* which was also amidst its reconstitution, *SS-Hohenstaufen* conducted operations against Allied airborne units during Operation *Market-Garden.* Elements of the Division operated mainly west of Arnhem against elements of the British 1st Airborne Division and the 1st Polish Independent Parachute Brigade, and were especially successful against the isolated, cut-off paras.

Following its success against British Airborne, *SS-Hohenstaufen* was moved to Germany to continue its rehabilitation. In mid-December, it was moved to the Eifel for participation in the Ardennes Offensive. Committed as part of *Sixth Panzer Army,* the Division attacked on the northern shoulder of the Ardennes salient, and participated in the ultimately successful attack on elements of the US 7th Armored Division and remnants of the 106th Infantry Division at St. Vith. Attempts to push further toward the Meuse, at Vielsalm and Recht, were also successful, but the Division was halted by elements of the 82nd Airborne Division and 7th Armored Division in the vicinity of Manhay, near Bra and Vaux-Chavanne.

As the attack on the northern flank of the *Sixth Panzer Army's* zone became mired down, by New Year's Eve, *SS-Hohenstaufen* was transferred south to reinforce the attack on the encircled American forces at Bastogne. The Division continued its attempts to break into the American perimeter throughout the first week of January, but they were fruitless and the Division was forced over to the defensive.

In early March, the *9th SS-Panzer Division* was transferred to Hungary and took part in the *Fruhlingser-Wachen* ("Spring Awakening") Offensive against Soviet forces near Lake Balaton. The Division sustained such heavy losses in the failed operation that its remnants operated as two separate combat groups until their final capitulation to the Americans in Austria in May.

12th SS-Panzer Division "Hitlerjugend"

The "Hitler Youth" Division was formed between the winter and summer of 1943 from a cadre from the *1st SS-Panzer Division "Leibstandarte Adolf Hitler,"* some Army NCOs, and junior soldiers born in 1926. Its major maneuver elements consisted of SS-Panzer Regiment 12 with one battalion of Mark IVs and one of Panthers; *SS-Panzer-Grenadier Regiments 25* and *26;* *SS-Armored Reconnaissance Battalion 12;* and *SS-Panzerjäger Battalion 12.* After extensive training in Germany and Belgium, by April 1944, the Division was transferred to France for the conduct of additional training and to serve as part of *the Supreme Command–West* armored reserve.

SS-Panzer-Grenadier Regiment 25 was one of the first elements of the armored reserve to counterattack against the Allied forces in Normandy, making contact with Canadian forces near Caen on 7 June. The Division's record in Normandy is mixed; its soldiers' ferocity was well established, but allegations of atrocities, both performed by its men and sustained at the hands of Canadian forces, are also part of the record of *SS-Hitlerjugend.* Throughout the Normandy campaign, the Division fought mostly against British and Canadian forces, and was caught in the Falaise Pocket by August. Losing practically all of its remaining armored fighting vehicles there, the Division also lost about 9,000 of its original approximately 17,000 soldiers in Normandy, and arrived in Germany in early September in dire need of reconstitution.

Throughout the autumn of 1944, that reconstitution was only partly accomplished to the extent that *SS-Panzer Regiment 12* consolidated its two panzer battalions into a single one with two Panther companies and two of Mark IVs, and the artillery regiment's field pieces were all towed, rather than including three batteries of self-propelled 105mm and 150mm howitzers. Additionally, besides *Waffen-SS* replacements, about 2,000 men from the *Luftwaffe* and *Kriegsmarine* were assimilated into the Division's personnel strength; many of these were used in non-infantry units, and the *Waffen-SS* soldiers formerly assigned to these billets were transferred into the panzergrenadier regiments.

During the Ardennes Offensive, as part of *Sixth Panzer Army's I SS-Panzer Corps*, *SS-Hitlerjugend* attacked toward the Elsenborn Ridge and the twin villages of Krinkelt and Rocherath on 17 December. Its combat groups sustained fearsome losses at the hands of elements of the US 2nd and 99th Infantry Divisions over two days of the fiercest fighting any of either side's soldiers experienced during World War II. After the withdrawal of American units, the *12th SS-Panzer Division* pressed their attack toward Butgenbach, only to be completely stymied by elements of the US 1st Infantry Division's 26th Infantry Regiment. Following several days of costly failure there, *SS-Hitlerjugend* was withdrawn on 23 December to prepare for another mission to the southwest.

From 27–30 December, the *SS-Panzer-Grenadier Regi- ment 25* and a battalion of *SS-Panzer-Grenadier Regiment 26* attacked elements of the US 75th Infantry Division, 3rd Armored Division, and 509th Parachute Infantry of the massive Soviet counteroffensive in the winter of 1941/42.

Throughout 1942 and 1943, the *2nd Panzer Division* fought in many of the most famous – and costly – battles on the Eastern Front. Its soldiers fought in the fierce battles around Rzhev from early 1942 through early 1943, and around Smolensk in the summer of 1943. In July 1943, the Division attacked the northern side of the Kursk Salient during Operation *Zitadelle*, and sustained heavy losses. After extensive defensive operations along the Dnieper River, the Division was withdrawn to France in January 1944 and reconstituted. By this time, the major maneuver units of the *2nd Panzer Division* consisted of *Panzer Regiment 3*, equipped with one battalion of Mark IVs and one of Panthers; *Panzer-Grenadier Regiments 2* and *304; Armored Reconnaissance Battalion 3*; and *Panzerjager Battalion 38*. The Division was deployed in the vicinity of Amiens, over 100 miles from Normandy, as part of the Supreme Command–West armored reserve when Operation overlord began.

The *2nd Panzer Division* arrived in the vicinity of Caen by 10 June, and spent several weeks fighting both British and American forces in an effort to contain the growing Allied beachhead. At the end of July, the *2nd Panzer Division* engaged the US 2nd Armored Division in the first of two vicious battles it would ultimately have with the "Hell on Wheels" Division during WWII. In early August, the *2nd Panzer Division* spearheaded the German counterattack in and around Mortain. Although it made better progress than some of the other attacking divisions, it failed and suffered heavy casualties in the process. Later in the month, the *2nd Panzer* lost almost all of its armored vehicles in the Falaise Pocket, and the remnants of its personnel were withdrawn to Germany for reconstitution.

During the Ardennes Offensive, the now nearly full strength *2nd Panzer Division* attacked toward the Meuse as part of *Fifth Panzer Army's XLVII Panzer Corps*. After overcoming stiff resistance from elements of the US 28th Infantry Division around Clervaux, the *2nd Panzer* attacked toward the Meuse. Held up temporarily at Bastogne by the 101st Airborne Division and elements of the 9th and 10th Armored Divisions, the *2nd Panzer Division* helped encircle them, then bypassed the American defenders and drove on toward Namur. After a sharp engagement with elements of the US 84th Infantry Division at Rochefort, the Division reached Celles, a few miles east of Dinant, by Christmas. It was there stopped by a combination of fuel shortages and the US 2nd Armored Division … with some assistance from the British 29th Armoured Brigade. Although the *2nd Panzer* achieved the deepest penetration made by any major German unit, it still fell well short of the objective at Antwerp, and didn't even reach the barrier of the Meuse River. Worse, it sustained very heavy losses during its encounter with its old adversary from Normandy, the 2nd Armored, and never recovered from the beating it sustained in the last week of the war.

As a unit of barely battalion strength, the *2nd Panzer* conducted defensive and delaying operations across Germany, from Prum to Bitburg to Worms, Fulda, and Bamberg. Final remnants of the Division surrendered near Karlsbad in Czechoslovakia at the end of the war.

9th SS-Panzer Division "Hohenstaufen"

Named for the medieval dynasty of German kings and emperors of the Holy Roman Empire of the German Nation, the *9th SS-Panzer Division* was organized in December 1942 as a panzer-grenadier division with volunteer and conscripted personnel from the RAD. Its major maneuver units consisted of *SS-Panzer Regiment 9*, with a battalion of Mark IVs (later converted to a mixed battalion of *Mark IVs* and *Sturmgeschutz* assault guns) and a battalion of *Panthers*; *SS-Panzer-Grenadier Regiments 19* and *20*; *SS-Armored Reconnaissance Battalion 9*; and *SS-Panzerjäger Battalion 9*. After training at Mailly-le-Camp in France, the Division performed various security and occupation duties at widely dispersed loca-

tions in Belgium (Ypres, Ghent) and France (Amiens, Forges-Eaux) before being committed to combat on the Eastern Front in April 1944 in Galicia. There, in concert with the *10th SS-Panzer Division* as part of *II SS-Panzer Corps*, *SS-Hohenstaufen* (minus its Panther and *Panzerjager* battalions) participated in operations supporting the breakout of the *First Panzer Army*, the 300,000-man "moving pocket" *under General der Panzer-truppen* Hans Hube.

The Division was then immediately committed to another breakout attempt, this time to assist German forces near Tarnopol. The attempt failed, and after a period in *Army Group North Ukraine* reserve, *SS-Hohenstaufen* was redeployed to the Western Front commencing 12 June. There, after linking up with its Panther battalion (but minus *Panzerjager Battalion 9*, which was still in training), the Division saw its first combat against the Allies in late June, when it was committed to action against British forces near Caen. After sustaining over 1,200 casualties by the first week of July, the Division was withdrawn and briefly held in reserve. Throughout most of July and August, *SS-Hohenstaufen* participated in the seesaw battles in Normandy, and sustained casualties so high that both panzer-grenadier regiments were consolidated into one, temporarily entitled *SS-Panzer-Grenadier Regiment "Hohenstaufen."* Despite its serious losses, in August, the Division played an important role in keeping open the escape route from the Falaise Pocket, which enabled considerable numbers of German personnel, if not armored fighting vehicles, to withdraw to eastern ticipation in the Ardennes Offensive.

Still well under full strength in its panzer regiment (with only 78 tanks), *Panzer Lehr* attacked in the Ardennes as part of *Fifth Panzer Army's XLVII Panzer Corps* on 16 December. After Clervaux and other strongpoints manned by elements of the 28th Infantry Division were eliminated—mostly by the *26th Volks-Grenadier Division* and the *2nd Panzer Division*, which led the initial attack— on 18 December *Panzer Lehr* crossed the Clerf River and drove forward toward Bastogne. However, a tenacious, *ad hoc* American force staying behind in the village of Consthum poured artillery fire on the combat groups of *Panzer Lehr* as they advanced and inflicted heavy casualties, particularly on the panzer-grenadiers mounted on the advancing tanks. After stopping to deal with these die-hard infantry, anti-aircraft, and field artillery units, *Panzer Lehr's* now badly-damaged lead elements finally arrived at Bastogne on the morning of 19 December. Over the next day and a half, *Panzer Lehr* participated in the encirclement of the key crossroads town, but then dispatched most of its elements to attack further to the west, toward the Meuse River. A combat group of *Panzer- Grenadier Lehr Regiment 901* remained behind, attached to the *26th Volks-Grenadier Division*, to continue the attacks on Bastogne.

The lead elements of *Panzer Lehr* were delayed significantly by US Army engineer and field artillery units near St. Hubert and Tillet, but the Division eventually reached Rochefort and attacked elements of the US 84th Infantry Division there on 23–24 December. Over the next few days, *Panzer Lehr* engaged in desperate battles with not only a regiment of the 84th, but also elements of the 2nd Armored Division and 4th Cavalry Group. The Division expended its last combat power in this fighting, and on Christmas night, the very small remnants of *Panzer Lehr* were withdrawn from the fighting around Humain. With this quiet night, relief by elements of the *9th Panzer Division*, the once mighty Division's offensive activities in the Ardennes were ended.

For the rest of the war, *Panzer Lehr* fought in various locations in western Germany as a combat group of roughly battalion strength, and ultimately surrendered to American forces in the Ruhr Pocket.

15th Panzer-Grenadier Division

Formed in Sicily in July 1943 from units intended for the reconstitution of the *15th Panzer Division*, which had surrendered in Tunisia a few months earlier. The major maneuver units consisted of *Panzer-Grenadier Regiments 104, 115*, and *129 (Regiment 115* was later disbanded, and *Regiment 104* redesignated as Regiment 115), *Reconnaissance Battalion 115*, and *Panzer Battalion 215* (later renumbered as *115*).

Almost immediately upon activation, the Division conducted defensive and delaying operations against American forces in Sicily, and was withdrawn to Caserta, Italy for rehabilitation in early August. In Italy, the Division fought from just north of Salerno in September 1943, to the Volturno River between Castel Volturno and Grazzanese, to multiple locations in the Gustav Line, including Cassino.

After the fall of Cassino in May, the Division fought a series of offensive, defensive and delaying actions from Cisterna to Tivoli and Florence. The Division was withdrawn to western Europe in August 1944.

Initially, the *15th Panzer-Grenadier* was committed to defensive operations in Lorraine, such as the defense of the Forest of Parroy, in which it engaged the US 79th Infantry Division during several weeks of costly operations. Later in the autumn, the *15th Panzer-Grenadier Division* was transferred to the Netherlands in the vicinity of Roermond and Venlo, where it conducted defensive operations against British forces. In late November, the Division was withdrawn and rehabilitated in preparation for participation in the Ardennes Offensive.

The *15th Panzer-Grenadier Division* was not committed to combat in the Ardennes until 22 December, when it went into the line in the vicinity of Bastogne. On Christmas Day, in concert with units of the *26th Volks-Grenadier Division*, elements of the *15th Panzer-Grenadier Division* (a task force built around *Panzer-Grenadier Regiment 115*) attacked the 101st Airborne Division's positions near Hemroulle and Champs, and continued their attacks into the next day. Although they made some progress and the combat was intense, the attacks failed, and by the end of the day, elements of the US 4th Armored Division were attacking the *15th Panzer-Grenadier Division* from the west, forcing them to face about from Bastogne and attempt a sort of contravallation. This costly effort, which reduced *Panzer-Grenadier Regiment 115* to about half strength, ultimately failed. The ring around Bastogne—which the *15th* had been sent in specifically to reinforce—had been pierced.

For the remainder of the months of December and January, elements of the *15th Panzer-Grenadier Division* were locked in a series of defensive, delaying, and counterattack operations in the Wiltz Corridor which steadily and markedly sapped its units' combat power. The Division was withdrawn in January and fought in the Netherlands, then Ems, Langstedt, and Hechthausen. In the last days of the war, the remnants of the *15th Panzer-Grenadier Division* surrendered to British forces.

5th Parachute Division

The *Luftwaffe's 5th Parachute Division* was formed in the vicinity of Reims, France, in March 1944. Its maneuver units consisted of *Parachute Infantry Regiments 13, 14*, and *15*. According to *Oberleutnant* von der Heydte, only Battalion in an attempt to seize the Hotton-Erezee Ridge. In vicious fighting, the infantry units of *SS-Hitlerjugend* were again repulsed, and by 30 December were withdrawn for transfer to yet another sector – Bastogne.

On the eve of their commitment to their new area of operations on the last New Year's Eve of the war, *SS-Hitlerjugend's* panzer-grenadier battalions were down to at least half strength, while its consolidated *Panzer Battalion* could muster only 30 combat-ready tanks. *SS-Panzerjager Battalion 12*, however, contributed 15 *Jagdpanzer IVs*, and the supporting *Army Heavy Tank Destroyer Battalion 560* counted 28 *Jagdpanzer IVs* and 13 *Jagdpanzer Vs* among its battle-ready resources.

On 3 January, *SS-Hitlerjugend* attacked elements of the 101st Airborne Division and 6th Armored Division in the *Bois Jacques* near Bastogne. For three days, battle raged in the snowy woods and along the narrow dirt tracks, and by 5 January, *SS-Hitlerjugend* was nearly completely burned out. One panzer-grenadier battalion was down to an aggregate strength of one NCO and 28 junior enlisted men in its three rifle companies, and the others were not much better off. The remaining armored units were also devastated: *SS-Panzer Regiment 12* lost 13 of its 30 operational *Mark IVs* and *Panthers*. *SS-Hitlerjugend* was ordered out of the line on 8 January, and returned to Germany for its final reconstitution shortly thereafter.

After completing a partial rehabilitation, the *12th SS-Panzer Division* was transferred to Hungary to take part in Operation *Fruhlingserwachen* near Lake Balaton. After the failure of this, the final German offensive of the war, *SS-Hitlerjugend* conducted delaying and defensive operations into Austria, where its remnants, still almost 10,000strong, surrendered to Americans near Enns, Austria, on 8 May.

116th Panzer Division (See pages 294–5 above)

Panzer Lehr Division

The *Panzer Lehr Division* was formed in January 1944 in France from a variety of German Army school and demonstration units. Its major maneuver units included *Panzer Lehr Regiment 130*, with an overstrength battalion of Mark IVs and a similarly overstrength battalion of Panthers; *Panzer-Grenadier Lehr Regiments 901* and *902*; *Armored Reconnaissance Battalion 130*, and *Panzerjager Battalion 130*. Not only were the tank battalions initially kept considerably overstrength in armored fighting vehicles, but all four panzergrenadier battalions were equipped with armored halftracks, instead of the usual proportion of one with armored vehicles and three with trucks. From the beginning, because it included so many highly skilled school troops—many of whom were veterans with outstanding records—*Panzer Lehr* was considered a highly elite unit.

In March, *Panzer Lehr* was briefly committed in Hungary as occupation troops, but by May had been redeployed to France. At the time of the Normandy landings, the Division was spread out between Le Mans and Chartres, but by 8 June, elements of *Panzer Lehr* were arriving in the vicinity of Caen. With its armored units at or above full strength, the Division possessed 196 tanks, 31 tank destroyers, and 10 assault guns. On the following day, the Division's first units attacked elements of the British 7th Armoured Division, and from then on, *Panzer Lehr* was essentially continuously engaged against Allied units in Normandy. In the month of June alone, the Division lost about 3,000 men, or roughly 18 percent of its personnel strength. By far, the greatest casualties were in *Panzer Lehr Regiments 901* and *902*.

July brought further tribulations for *Panzer Lehr*, including not only heavy combat against American forces around St. Lo, but the most devastating air attack ever launched against tactical targets. *Panzer Lehr* was directly in the path that American heavy bombers saturated with 4,000 tons of high explosives during Operation Cobra in late July. Although it lost few tanks or other armored fighting vehicles and probably sustained a total of about 1,000 casualties, the shock effect of such a bombing seriously disrupted the coherence of its defense, and the *Panzer Lehr Division* was overrun by rapidly advancing American units.

Throughout the first several weeks of August, elements of *Panzer Lehr* were, at different times and places, moved into reserve and refitted. Combat groups of the Division were continuously rotated into the line, either under the Division's command or attached to other German units trying to contain the ever-expanding Allied beachhead. When it was finally pulled out of action in the third week of August, *Panzer Lehr* could count a total of 20 tanks that were ready for combat; the division had sustained 7,411 casualties in ten weeks of combat.

During the German retreat through France and the Low Countries, *Panzer Lehr* fought important delaying actions against Allied forces. In September, it was withdrawn to Paderborn, Germany, where the Division was reconstituted, albeit to nothing like its previously overstrength glory. *Panzer Lehr Regiment 130*, for example, could muster only 77 *Mark IVs* and Panthers, 111 fewer than it had possessed before the Normandy campaign.

In the last week of November, the Division attacked southward from the Saar around Eywiller, Gungwiller, and Sarre-Union against elements of the US Army's XV Corps as they broke through the Saverne Gap enroute to the Rhine. After being rebuffed, the *Panzer Lehr* fought delaying actions against US Third Army units in the Saar around Diemeringen, Lorentzen, and Saarlautern, before being withdrawn in early December to prepare for par-before being committed in November to defensive operations in the *Westwall* and in Luxembourg. As part of *Fifth Panzer Army's XLVII Panzer Corps*, the 26th was charged with penetrating American defenses and establishing crossing sites over the Clerf River in the vicinity of Drauffelt and opening the way to Bastogne and beyond for the *2nd Panzer* and *Panzer Lehr Divisions*.

On 16 December 1944, the *26th Volks-Grenadier Division* drove forward from its assembly areas, crossed the Our River, and attacked elements of the US 28th Infantry Division's 110th Infantry Regiment. Encountering fierce resistance, the Division took two days to penetrate the American defenses and establish crossing sites over the Clerf River and reach the villages of Drauffelt, Wilwerwitz, and Alscheid. As the *2nd Panzer Division* then passed through to begin its attack, the *26th* moved forward, too, often crosscountry to avoid being caught in the massive traffic jams that evolved on the narrow, muddy forest roads.

As *Fusilier Regiment 39* screened the Division's right flank, *Grenadier Regiments 77* and *78* attacked toward Longvilly on 18 December. On 19 December, in concert with elements of the *Panzer Lehr Division*, these regiments seized Longvilly from units of the 9th and 10th Armored Divisions, then pushed west, closer to Bastogne. Over the next five days, the *26th Volks-Grenadier Division* repeatedly attacked through Mageret and Bizory toward Bastogne, engaging elements of the 101st Airborne and 10th Armored Divisions, all to no avail. Although the Division sustained fearsome losses, the attacks climaxed on Christmas Day, when it attacked in concert with elements of the *15th Panzer-Grenadier Division* and *Panzer Lehr Division* at multiple points around the Bastogne perimeter.

By the morning of 26 December, it was obvious that the attacks had failed, and the Division went over to primarily defensive operations. Its six infantry battalions could count only 80–300 men each fit for duty, and even this was only achieved by combing out the rear echelon units for every available soldier.

The *26th Volks-Grenadier Division* conducted defensive and delaying operations in the Ardennes east of Bastogne in late December and January, and conducted further operations near Duren and Andernach on the Rhine as the war drew to a close. The Division surrendered to elements of the US 8th Armored Division in the Ruhr Pocket in late April.

340th Volks-Grenadier Division

Formed in Thorn, West Prussia *(Wehrkreis XX)* in September 1944, this division took the traditions and subunit numbers of the *340th Infantry Division*, which had been destroyed in Galicia, near Brody, in late July.

Otherwise, it was a completely new unit, with personnel from a variety of non-infantry sources. Its maneuver elements consisted of *Grenadier Regiments 694, 695*, and *696*, *Fusilier Company* (not Battalion) *340*, and *Panzer-jager Battalion 340*; the infantry regiments all possessed two battalions, and the *Panzerjager* battalion was equipped the same way as its counterpart in the *26th Volks-Grenadier Division* (see above.)

After defensive operations in the vicinity of Julich in November, the Division was brought up to strength in preparation for participation in a follow-on phase of the Ardennes offensive. The *340th Volks-Grenadier Division* did not participate in the initial attacks in mid-December, but rather was committed in early January to strengthen German efforts against

American forces in the vicinity of Bastogne.

From its assembly areas near Bourcy, on 4 January, the Division attacked toward Mageret and broke through the American outpost line; by the next day, the *340th* hit the American main line of resistance around Bastogne itself. The Division took over the sector vacated by the *12th SS-Panzer Division*, from the Noville-Bastogne road to the Benonchamp-Bastogne rail line. At this point, due to both battle and non-battle casualties, the division's strength was estimated at four weak infantry battalions and two average ones; the *Fusilier Company* was already understrength as well. The Division continued to defend in sector.

American forces attacked the Division on 10 January and made immediate inroads. By the end of the day, the strengths of the Division's infantry regiments varied from a high of 422 present for duty *(Grenadier Regiment 695)* to a low of 120 *(Grenadier Regiment 696)*. Further American attacks over the next two days by elements of the 4th and 6th Armored Divisions drove the Division back to Oubourcy and Arloncourt; the American attack was only halted by a security line of obstacles built by the engineers of the *10th SS-Panzer Division*.

By 16 January, incessant American attacks literally destroyed the *340th Volks-Grenadier Division*. By that evening—according to the Commanding General in his post-war report—only 15 infantrymen remained on their feet, and the remaining artillery was completely immobile. The Division was withdrawn to Clervaux for refitting, but most of the 550 ex-*Luftwaffe* technicians who constituted the replacements were unfit for duty.

At the end of January, the "Division" (actually about the size of a small battalion) was overrun, and the remnants were ordered out of the line on 28 January. The remaining fragments of the Division were withdrawn to the vicinity of Spangdahlem and eventually surrendered near Altenburg in late March.

about 10 percent of the personnel were actually trained parachutists, and only about 20 percent of the officers had received infantry training. By the time of the Normandy landings, the Division was at about 74 percent strength in personnel overall (approximately 13,000 present for duty out of an authorized strength of about 17,500). It was missing, however, a great deal of equipment, including even basic armament such as rifles; literally, the Division possessed only about 20–25 percent of its heavy weapons, such as artillery pieces and antitank guns.

The *5th Parachute Division* was dispatched from Rennes, whence it had been transferred in May, to the Normandy battlefields in a piecemeal fashion, with infantry battalions arriving only after 25 June. Its subordinate infantry units were attached to various other divisions such as *Panzer Lehr* and the *17th SS-Panzer-Grenadier Division*, so the Division never really saw action in Normandy as a coherent unit. Its units suffered severe casualties in Normandy: by the time the Division's ele ments were withdrawn from Normandy to northern Holland, its strength was reported as roughly 4,000.

After reconstitution to nearly full strength in the Netherlands, mostly from non-parachute, non-infantry *Luftwaffe* personnel and *Kriegsmarine* sailors, the Division was committed in a purely ground role during the Ardennes Offensive. As part of the *Seventh Army*, it was assigned the mission of covering the Army's right (northern) flank, which was the boundary with the *Fifth Panzer Army*. With *Parachute Regiment 13* attached to the *352nd Volks-Grenadier Division*, this was a difficult mission to accomplish with only two foot-borne infantry regiments, even though a company of assault guns had been attached.

On 16 December, the Division attacked the US 28th Infantry Division's 109th Infantry Regiment around Walsdorf and Fuhren, Luxembourg, and drove forward in bitter fighting. By the morning of 18 December, the *5th Parachute Division* bypassed the strongpoints still held by the 109th Infantry and continued toward Wiltz. Although the *5th Parachute Division* was supposed to continue on toward Bastogne, against the orders of the Commanding General, *Generalmajor* Heilmann, elements of the Division attacked Wiltz from the south on the afternoon/ night of 19 December, while the *26th Volks-Grenadier Division* launched an assault from the north. This combined attack was successful, and by the morning of 19 December, Wiltz was in German hands; the road to Bastogne was open.

Beyond this success, however, the *5th Parachute Division* was destined to play an overwhelmingly defensive role. Its units were parceled out piecemeal in efforts to accomplish the mission of covering the *Seventh Army's* northern flank, and it was ultimately stretched out over a distance of 18 miles, from Neufchateau back to the Sauer River. While in this precarious tactical posture, it was pierced at several points by attacking elements of the US Third Army, advancing north to relieve the encircled American garrison in Bastogne. In particular, all three regiments *(Parachute Infantry Regiment 13* returned to the Division on 23 December) were attacked vigorously by the US 4th Armored Division on 23 and 24 December near the villages of Bigonville, Warnach, and Chaumont. Although elements of the 4th Armored broke through to Bastogne on the day after Christmas—after a furious fight with elements of the *5th Parachute* and *26th Volks- Grenadier Divisions* at Assenois—other elements, with infantry battalions of the 80th Infantry Division attached, continued to hammer at the *5th Parachute Regiment's* strongpoints for several days thereafter.

On 30 December, *Parachute Infantry Regiment 14* was subordinated to elements of the *1st SS-Panzer Division "Leibstandarte Adolf Hitler"* for an attack on the village of Lutrebois, which was defended by units of the US 35th Infantry Division. Apparently, the 14th did not perform as the SS expected, and several of the *Leibstandarte* officers attempted to have the commander of the 14th brought before a court-martial. In any event, other elements of the *5th Parachute Division* fought on in the snowy fields and forests east and southeast of Bastogne for the next several weeks. Ultimately, most of the Division surrendered to American forces near the village of Adenau on the Eifel in March 1945, but remnants survived until April, when they surrendered in the Ruhr Pocket.

26th Volks-Grenadier Division

The *26th Volks-Grenadier Division* was formed in September 1944 around a core of personnel of the *26th Infantry Division*, which had been destroyed in eastern Poland earlier the same month. Most of the Division's new soldiers, however, were former *Luftwaffe* ground personnel and *Kriegsmarine* sailors, although there were conscripts from *Wehrkreis VI* (the Rhineland, which was the original *26th Infantry Division's* home area) as well. Its principal maneuver units consisted of *Fusilier Regiment 39* and *Grenadier Regiments 77* and *78* (contrary to the assertions in some sources, all three were conventionally organized *Volks-Grenadier* infantry regiments, each with two infantry battalions. See the comments by the Division Commander, *Generalmajor* Heinz Kokott, in his postwar manuscript done for the US Army, B-040, The *26th Volks-Grenadier Division* in the Ardennes Offensive.); *Fusilier Battalion 26* (a light infantry battalion); and *Panzerjager Battalion 26*, equipped with a single company of assault guns, one of antitank guns, and one of antiaircraft guns.

The Division trained for about six weeks at the maneuver area in Warthelager, Posen (Occupied Poland)

560th Volks-Grenadier Division

This unusual unit was activated in Norway in July 1944, and was manned mostly by soldiers culled from units which had been performing occupation duty in Norway. Young, fit, but inexperienced, the Division was brought to full strength and trained for over three months – an unusual amount of training for a *Volks-Grenadier* division – before it was transferred to Denmark in November, and thence to Germany for participation in the Ardennes Offensive. Its maneuver units consisted of *Grenadier Regiments 1128, 1129,* and *1130,* as well as the Division *Fusilier Battalion*.

Initially part of *Fifth Panzer Army's LVIII Panzer Corps*, on 16 December, the Division attacked with two regiments abreast toward US 28th Infantry Division positions at Sevenig and Heinerscheid. (One of the grenadier regiments was still moving up, and was initially unavailable to take part in the attack.) The Division achieved quick success by bypassing Heinerscheid, crossing the Our River, and driving 3,000 meters further east. The other regiment, however, was held up by elements of the US 112th Infantry at Sevenig. The defenders of Sevenig continued to successfully defend the town until 19 December, when they were finally overrun. Great damage had been inflicted on *Grenadier Regiment 1130*, however, and even though the Division's third regiment finally caught up on the night of 17 December and immediately detached a battalion to it, the regimental strength did not exceed 600 men fit for duty by the time Sevenig fell.

The *560th Volks-Grenadier Division* drove on toward the villages of Weisswampach, Nadrin, Wibrin, and Haie de Bellain by 20 December, and by 23 December was locked in fierce, seesaw combat with elements of the 3rd Armored Division (reinforced by the 1st Battalion, 517th PIR and 509th PIB) near Dochamps, Lamormenil, and Freyneux. At this stage, all of the Division's infantry bat talions were committed to the fighting, and their strength was being worn away steadily. By Christmas, the *560th Volks-Grenadier Division's* infantry regiments varied from 250 to 400 men present for duty. Further fighting around Bastogne only wore down the Division's infantry strength even further, and by January, only *Grenadier Regiment 1130* remained as a coherent, identifiable unit.

The remnants of the *560th Volks-Grenadier Division* were withdrawn to Germany in January 1945, and they fought on as a combat group around Trier … only to be destroyed near Bruchsal in March.

Alsace

47th Volks-Grenadier Division

The *47th Volks-Grenadier Division* was formed September 1944 from the remnants of the *47th Infantry Division*, which had been destroyed by American forces in Belgium just a few weeks before. Built and trained for about five weeks in Denmark, the Division was committed to defensive operations in the Hurtgen Forest in late October, and fought there through November. A conventionally organized volksgrenadier division, its maneuver units consisted of *Grenadier Regiments 103, 104,* and *115,* as well as *Fusilier Company 147*. After again sustaining heavy casualties in fighting around Aachen and Duren, the 47th was withdrawn in early January and rehabilitated near Bergisch Gladbach.

After just a few days to take on and attempt to assimi late replacements, the Division began its move, by foot march and train, to Lower Alsace. On 9 January, one regiment of the *47th Volks-Grenadier Division* was attached to the *25th Panzer-Grenadier Division* for its attacks against elements of the US 79th Infantry Division and 14th Armored Division in the vicinity of Hatten. By 21 January, the regiment was back under the control of the *47th*, and the Division moved up to the Moder River over the next two days.

On the night of 23/24 January, the *47th Volks-Grenadier Division* stealthily crossed the Moder River, but withdrew on the same night. For the next several weeks, the Division fortified its positions on the north bank, and conducted patrols opposite the US 42nd Infantry Division along the Moder River Line. This activity continued well into midMarch, and it was in February that the Division encountered the 101st Airborne Division along the Moder.

In late February, the *47th Volks-Grenadier Division* was ordered to prepare a second line of defenses in the *West-wall* near Wissembourg, and it was in this split posture when the US Seventh Army's final offensive began in mid-March. The *47th* delayed the American advance for a few days, then was withdrawn to the vicinity of Speyer, where it was finally destroyed in March 1945.

Achevé d'imprimer sur les presses d'Arti Grafiche à Pomezia (Italie)
pour le compte des Editions Heimdal à Damigny/Normandie (France),
Georges Bernage, éditeur, en mai 2012.